Rock of Contention

Rock of Contention

Free French and Americans at War in
New Caledonia, 1940–1945

Kim Munholland

Berghahn Books
New York • Oxford

First published in 2005 by
Berghahn Books
www.berghahnbooks.com

©2005 Kim Munholland
First paperback edition published in 2006
Reprinted in paperback in 2007

All rights reserved. Except for the quotation of short passages
for the purposes of criticism and review, no part of this book
may be reproduced in any form or by any means, electronic or
mechanical, including photocopying, recording, or any information
storage and retrieval system now known or to be invented,
without written permission of the publisher.

Library of Congress Cataloging-in-Publication Data

Munholland, J. Kim.
  Rock of contention : Free French and Americans at war in New Caledonia, 1940-1945 / Kim Munholland.
   p. cm.
  Includes bibliographical references and index.
  ISBN 1-57181-682-8 (hbk.) -- ISBN 1-84545-300-X (pbk.)
  1. France combattante. 2. World War, 1939-1945--New Caledonia. 3. United States--Foreign relations--France. 4. France--Foreign relations--United States. 5. New Caledonia--History--20th century. I. Title.

D754.N43 M86 2005
940.53'9597--dc22

2005046941

British Library Cataloguing in Publication Data

A catalogue record for this book is available from the British Library

Printed in the United States on acid-free paper

ISBN-10: 1-57181-682-8   ISBN-13: 978-1-57181-682-5   hardback
ISBN-10: 1-84545-300-X   ISBN-13: 978-1-84545-300-8   paperback

DEDICATION

This book is dedicated to Anne, my wife, and to our children, Chris and Sophie

Contents

Acknowledgements	ix
List of Maps and Figures	xi
Introduction: The Franco-American *Mésentente*	1
1. The Free French and the Americans before Pearl Harbor	**7**
France under Siege	7
De Gaulle, the Formation of the Free French, and Colonial Resistance	12
Disaster at Dakar	15
The Empire Defense Council and the Allies in the Tropics	19
Free-French Representation in the United States	24
2. The New Caledonian Rally to the Free French	**33**
Disunity in Local Allegiances and Foreign Interests	36
The Political Showdown Begins	42
The New Caledonian Coup	48
Pro-Vichy Partisans	53
3. New Caledonia in Limbo: Preparing for War in the Pacific	**61**
Local and Foreign Anxieties over New Caledonia's Defense	61
De Gaulle's Desire for Centralized Control and the Brunot Mission	69
The d'Argenlieu Mission	73
4. Going to Pieces: The 1942 Riot	**84**
The Americans Arrive: January–March '42	86
New Caledonia in Political and Military Crisis: April '42	93
Things Go Awry: May '42	98
Calm is Restored but, Mésentente *Sets In: May–July '42*	107

5. **The Rooster and the Eagle: Governor Montchamp, Admiral Halsey, and the American Occupation**   118

   Admiral Halsey's Arrival   119
   Guadalcanal, the Solomons Campaign, and the Expansion of
      U.S. Military Presence: August '42–August '43   123
   The Governor's Graveyard: Montchamp, d'Argenlieu, and Vergès   134

6. **Governor Laigret and the American Economic and Cultural Challenge**   142

   Local Politics and the Arrival of Governor Laigret   142
   Grievances and Complaints against the Americans   148
   Laigret's Anti-Americanist Campaign and Increasing Mésentente   158
   American Ambitions for New Caledonia?   165

7. **Roosevelt and de Gaulle: Conflicting Visions of a Postwar World Order**   173

   Anticolonialism and Yankee Imperialism   173
   Anti-Americanism and the French Empire   178
   American Security and the Fate of the French Colonies in the Pacific   185
   Liberation, 1944   189

8. **From Combat Base to Rest and Rehabilitation Area: The American Departure**   198

   Governor Tallec   198
   Autonomist Sentiment and Social and Labor Unrest   204
   American Materialism, Entertainment and the Issue of Withdrawal   210
   Anti-Communism versus Anticolonialism   218

Conclusion: V-J Day and Postwar Assessments, Accounts and Balances   226

Bibliography   233

Index   239

ACKNOWLEDGEMENTS

This book, a voyage of discovery that took me from the United States to France and to the South Pacific, would not have been possible without the generous support of the many institutions and individuals who have assisted me. It is with great pleasure that I express my gratitude for the vital encouragement that I have received.

Throughout my career as historian, the Graduate School of the University of Minnesota has provided support in the form of research leaves that have relieved me of teaching obligations and administrative duties. Both the University of Minnesota's McMillan Travel Fund of the University of Minnesota and travel and research grants from the Department of History, made possible several research trips to France. Two grants from the 'Travel to Collections Program' of the National Endowment for the Humanities made possible trips to Australia, New Zealand and New Caledonia. Support from the Western European Studies Center at the University of Minnesota allowed me to consult archives in Washington, D.C. and the Public Record Office in London. This institutional support proved critical, enabling me to compare the differing versions of events in wartime New Caledonia that appear in these official sources.

In all of these locations, archivists and librarians provided professional assistance that greatly facilitated access to their resources. In France the staff at the archives section of the French Foreign Ministry opened access to the diplomatic correspondence between New Caledonia and the Free French headquarters in London that touched off my initial interest in the topic. At the Archives Nationales, the very competent staff obtained the necessary dispensations that allowed consultation of the Pleven and Cassin papers, and the d'Argenlieu family kindly granted permission to consult Admiral d'Argenlieu's papers (also housed at the AN). Madame Chantal Bonazzi proved an essential guide to the papers held in the Section Contemporaine of the Archives Nationales. Finally, the staff of the Section d'Outre-Mer of the Archives Nationales in Paris and then in Aix-en-Provence offered important assistance in finding the often scattered records of wartime correspondence with New Caledonia. To all of these individuals I offer my appreciation of their professionalism.

The same professionalism facilitated access to documents held in the Australian National Archives in Canberra and the New Zealand National Archives in Wellington. Ismet Kurtovitch, now archivist at the Territorial Archive of New Caledonia, provided a number of documents as well as enthusiastic support for the project. In the United Kingdom the archivists at the Public Record Office guided me into the well-organized documentation dealing with New Caledonia. In Washington Kathy Nicastro and Sally Marks offered their expertise in introducing me to the Diplomatic Branch of the National Archives. The staff of the Military Branch of the National Archives greatly facilitated access to the military intelligence reports that offered an American perspective on New Caledonia during the war.

Some of the material in this study has been published previously. I very much appreciate the permissions granted by Duke University Press, the French Colonial Historical Society and the Western Society for French History for authorization to use portions of articles that appeared in *French Historical Studies, Proceedings of the French Colonial Historical Society* and *Proceedings of the Western Society for French History*.

A number of individuals have played key roles in advancing my understanding of wartime New Caledonia. Prior to publication of his massive study of the Free French movement, M. Jean-Louis Crémieux-Brilhac offered his insights into the atmosphere at General de Gaulle's Free-French headquarters in London. M. Yves Tallec discussed the activities of his father, Jacques Tallec, governor of New Caledonia at the end of the war, providing an insight that could not be obtained from the written evidence. Robin Miller supplied letters and publications of her father, Lewis Feuer, during the time he was stationed in New Caledonia. To all of these individuals I offer my deepest appreciation.

Other individuals read and discussed the manuscript during the process of creation, giving essential advice on how to make a very lengthy original text manageable. The late William Cohen read the original version and made important suggestions on how to trim and focus a bulky manuscript. His moral support was enormous, and I am eternally grateful to a good friend to whom I pay posthumous tribute. My colleague Richard Kuisel also made valuable suggestions on how to strengthen the original manuscript, and Irwin Wall's critical reading enabled me to make important, further revisions of the manuscript. Ismet Kurtovitch, chief archivist for the Territorial Archives of New Caledonia, provided important documentation, contacts and encouragement. At Berghahn Press an excellent editor, Janine Treves-Haber, gave shape and form to the manuscript on its way to publication. Thanks to her efforts, the final product is much clearer, concise and structured. Mark Stanton of Berghahn Press has seen it through to publication. John Jenson prepared the index and Phil Voxland provided computer rescue services. I extend my gratitude for the support of these individuals. The mistakes that remain are my responsibility.

My deepest gratitude goes to those who have been personally involved in this project for many years, my family. Anne has given me hours of comfort and encouragement during the agonizing process and frustrations of research and writing. Chris and Sophie have patiently tolerated a father's sometimes-curious behavior. The love, understanding and support of my family truly have made this book possible.

List of Maps and Figures

Maps

1. New Caledonia.   34
2. Nouméa, New Caledonia in 1940.   49
3. U.S. Supply Routes to South Pacific, 1942.   85
4. The Solomon Islands.   124

Figures

2.1. Governor Sautot, Michel Vergès, Raymond Pognon and crowd sing the Marseillaise as they march from the dock to the Government House to rally New Caledonia to the Free French.   53

4.1. General Patch and Admiral d'Argenlieu reach agreement on defending New Caledonia.   90

4.2. "One might have said the Martians had landed," Gabriel Païta.   92

4.3. "It is the American takeover of New Caledonia," Admiral d'Argenlieu.   94

4.4. The Caledonian crowd hears General Patch's declaration of neutrality.   100

4.5. The crowd calls for Governor Sautot's return.   104

5.1. "This photograph 'entirely refutes the impression Admiral d'Argenlieu gave us'."   128

6.1. French Caledoniennes serving thirsty GIs on Bastille Day, 1942.   155

6.2. Kanak working for the Yankee dollar at Camp Joe Louis.   157

8.1. It is Donald Duck, agent of American Imperialism.   214

INTRODUCTION

THE FRANCO-AMERICAN *MÉSENTENTE*

"Louis, I think this is the beginning of a beautiful friendship." With these words the great film *Casablanca* comes to an end as Captain Louis Renault (Claude Rains) and Rick Blaine (Humphrey Bogart) walk off into the night away from Casablanca, heading, we believe, to the Free-French colonial town of Brazzaville in French Equatorial Africa.[1] Renault's decision to join Rick in his flight to Brazzaville comes just after his symbolic demonstration of an allegiance transfer from neutrality under Vichy to resistance when he drops a bottle of Vichy water into a trash basket and then kicks it over. The renowned art historian Erwin Panofsky "greatly admired" this metaphorical gesture.[2] Rick and Renault are going off to fight the good fight against the common enemy, inspired by the up-to-then unsentimental Rick giving up his love for Ilse Lund (Ingrid Bergman) so that she could continue to support her husband, Victor Laszlo (Paul Henreid), in his fight against the Nazis. A higher ideal prevails and Renault reveals the true Rick behind the tough-guy façade declaring, "Well, Rick, you're not only a sentimentalist, but you've become a patriot." And Renault finds his own patriotism in the France of resistance.

According to the director Peter Bogdanovich, "*Casablanca* is, for many Americans, the quintessential World War II romance … ."[3] However there were two romances. One was the personal romance between Rick and Ilse, sacrificed to the demands of the war, and the second was the political romance between the American, Rick, and his French soon-to-be comrade in arms, Captain Renault. *Casablanca* takes place as the Americans plunge into the war at the time of Pearl Harbor. They find a sympathetic ally in the France that was resisting the Germans, a political romance between two countries with a common cause and a common history of alliance and friendship.[4] Yet the unhappy, historically correct ending to this romance is that the relationship went sour, and it may have been sour from the beginning.

1

If there were two romances, there were two "Casablancas." One was the film with its heart-warming promise of French–American cooperation and eventual victory that caught the imaginations of those who saw the film when it was released in December 1942. The other "Casablanca" was that of 8 November 1942 when American troops under the command of General George Patton waded ashore on Moroccan beaches to be greeted by hostile fire from French troops loyal to the Vichy Government. Five hundred and forty-three Americans lost their lives before a desperate cease-fire was arranged that ended Vichy's resistance to the Anglo-American landings in North Africa.

But that was Vichy. What about the Free French? Renault was headed to Brazzaville, presumably to join the resistance of General de Gaulle and his colleagues, who were fighting the Germans with whatever weapons they could find. Surely this was where the political romance between Rick and Renault found its fulfillment. Unfortunately, historical reality did not live up to the promise of cinematic art. The political romance between the Free French and the Americans was stormy, not beautiful. The American president, Franklin Roosevelt, did not get along at all with the head of the Free French, General Charles de Gaulle, who had thrown his bottle of Vichy water into the trashcan right after the defeat in 1940.

This American/Free-French discord at the highest level has been extensively studied and has been described as a relationship not between friends but between "hostile allies."[5] A great deal of effort has gone into determining why the Americans and the Free French, both committed to the defeat of the Axis powers and the eventual liberation of France and the French Empire, should have experienced such a difficult and frequently acrimonious relationship during the Second World War.[6] Despite this critical literature, the image of Rick and Renault as friends and allies was difficult to abandon entirely. *Casablanca* had artfully crafted a beautiful hope. Surely traces of their friendship could be found somewhere. After all, France was liberated, and General de Gaulle and members of the resistance, followed a day later by the Americans, marched down the Champs-Elysées in triumph at the end of August 1944. It was a happy ending, so why was it so stormy along the road back to Paris?

Both American and French historians hold President Roosevelt responsible for the hostility that developed between the Americans and the Free French during the war. They blame FDR's unwillingness to recognize Charles de Gaulle as the representative of a true France, the France of resistance, for the antagonism. And there is much to criticize in Roosevelt's shortsighted dealing with de Gaulle and his cause. Yet it is hard to believe that the Americans were solely responsible for the antagonism with the Free French. There are usually two sides to a relationship.

Rather than revisit the high level contest between Roosevelt and de Gaulle, I decided to examine one place where the Americans and Free French were compelled to work together in the interest of defeating their common enemies.

The site chosen to explore wartime Free-French relations with the Americans was a French colony, the island of New Caledonia in the South Pacific that had rallied to the Free-French movement in 1940. In New Caledonia there was a continuous American/Free-French contact that lasted from shortly after the American entry into the war until V-J Day and the American departure.

During the war New Caledonia was home for thousands of Americans when it became the main staging area for the Solomon Islands campaign. An estimated one-to two-hundred thousand American soldiers, sailors and Marines were either stationed on the island or passed through on their way to the battle-grounds of the South Pacific.[7] Nouméa, the capital, became headquarters for the American Navy, the Army Air Force and for the Army's Americal Division that relieved the Marines on Guadalcanal. Nouméa also became a major American naval base, and New Caledonia provided airfields, training ground, storage facilities and hospitals for American forces. The interaction of the Americans with the fifty-seven thousand New Caledonian inhabitants, consisting of French settlers or "Caledonians" (*Caldoches*), Gaullist officials, native Kanak (Melanesians) and Asian laborers provides the multilayered human and social context in which the story of American relations with the Free-French movement in the South Pacific unfolded. While the Americans got along with the Caledonian, Kanak and Asian inhabitants, they found themselves in constant conflict with the Gaullist Free French sent out to defend French interests in the South Pacific.

My search for a beautiful friendship revealed at best a wary relationship that was marked by misunderstandings, mutual mistrust, suspicion and cultural differences. New Caledonia became a metaphor for the stormy and uneasy alliance that developed between the Americans and the Free French during the war at every point of contact. The French refer to New Caledonia as "Le Caillou", or "The Rock," a designation that suggests both the relationship and the rocky terrain of the island. A mountain spine runs the length of the 250-mile island, which extends in a northwest to southeast direction about 900 miles off the northeast coast of Australia. Along the eastern coast of the island, which is in the path of the trade winds, the vegetation is lush and tropical. The mountainous ridge that divides New Caledonia along its length is rocky but rich in minerals notably nickel and chrome. In the lee of this mountain chain, the plains along the western coast are dry and sparse, best suited for cattle ranching. Thus the "Caillou" takes on a double meaning as both a physical description and metaphor for a "rocky" relationship.

Although Roosevelt has received much of the blame, it turns out that the Americans were not solely responsible for the hostility and friction that developed with General de Gaulle and his Free-French colleagues. While warmly welcomed upon arrival in New Caledonia in March 1942 by the local French Caledonians, who had rallied to the Free-French cause some eighteen months earlier, things went awry when General de Gaulle's representatives became convinced that the Americans had come to New Caledonia to take it over. When a simmering quarrel between the local French Caledonians and General de Gaulle's Free-French representatives erupted shortly thereafter, the Gaullists blamed the Americans for their troubles with the local population. Out of this dispute they fashioned an abiding suspicion of American policies and attitudes toward the Free French and France itself. At the same time the Americans became convinced that General de Gaulle's pursuit of *grandeur* for France was more important to him than winning the war.

On several occasions in New Caledonia suspicion of the Americans became active and deliberate anti-Americanism on the part of the Gaullist Free French. Not only American actions and policies but an American physical presence came to be seen by them as a threat to French national and imperial identity. De Gaulle's resistance to the Americans became a counterbalance to American wartime power and presence, which was "anti-Americanism" in that it meant resistance based upon principle. The Americans were, and are, "just too big," as a French historian once commented in explaining the persistence of anti-Americanism in France. Although a pronounced strain of anti-Americanism existed in France before the war, a particular Gaullist, Free-French hostility and resentment toward the Americans during the Second World War emerges from this tale of contact in the South Pacific.[8] General de Gaulle and his colleagues were determined to defend French imperial interests and a French way of life against what they perceived to be American domineering behavior and imperial ambitions.

If the clash in New Caledonia confirmed General de Gaulle's suspicion of American intentions toward France and its empire, Free-French behavior in New Caledonia convinced President Roosevelt that General de Gaulle was more interested in his political objectives than in helping the Allies win the war. Although his administration promised both Vichy and the Free French of the United States's intention to restore France's place in the world after the war, President Roosevelt began to reconsider these promises in light of the stormy events in New Caledonia. A *mésentente* was born, complicated by underlying cultural differences and practices. Americans and French differed in matters of authority and hierarchy, formal versus informal social relations, sociability and privacy, and methods of problem-solving and decision-making.[9] Each side had a different image of the other, and the two negative images often were constructed from existing biases, assumptions and suspicions.

The *mésentente* that is at the heart of this uneasy wartime alliance and rivalry implies more than a "misunderstanding," or *malentendu*, that could be cleared up with a bit of good will and explanation. *Mésentente* has to do with disagreement, dissension, or dissidence at the heart of the relationship. It emerges from the language used in the memoirs, published letters, histories of the time, and in traces left in the archives as well as from the constructions, assumptions, biases and attitudes that the participants had of each other.

New Caledonia became "a rock of contention" between the Free French and the Americans during the war, and its history serves as metaphor for a generally difficult and often abrasive relationship that developed then and would continue into the postwar years. The Franco-American *mésentente* would be a persistent one among sometime friends and sometime hostile allies. New Caledonia anticipated an emerging Franco-American rivalry over empire, over decolonization, over global influence and status and over cultural values and preferences. After 1945 this rivalry would be found in Indochina, Africa, and in a number of transatlantic *mésententes* and disputes as successive French governments resisted American ambitions, interests, and influence that were in conflict and competition with their own.[10] New Caledonia revealed ways in which Americans and French differed in their manner of interpreting events and assessing each other's intentions, which also would emerge in the many disagreements and conflicts that would mark French-American relations in the postwar world.

Notes

1. The ending with Rick and Renault headed for Brazzaville was, like so much else in the making of *Casablanca*, an improvised, last minute decision. See Aljean Harmetz, *The Making of Casablanca: Bogart, Bergman, and World War II*, previously published as *Round up the Usual Suspects* (New York, [1992] 2002), 237–38.
2. Andrew Sarris, *"You Ain't Heard Nothin' Yet": The American Talking Film, History and Memory 1927–1949* (New York and Oxford, 1998), 129.
3. Cited on back cover, Howard Koch, *Casablanca, Script and Legend: The Original Screen Plan and 25 Classic Stills* (Woodstock NY, 1992).
4. Richard Corliss, "Casablanca: An Analysis of the Film," has provided a careful interpretation of the two theories, one political and the other repressed homosexual fantasy. The political reading is the one stressed here. Koch, *Casablanca*, 234–35.
5. Milton Viorst, *Hostile Allies: FDR and Charles de Gaulle* (New York, 1965).
6. In addition to Viorst, the following have discussions of the Roosevelt-de Gaulle relationship. André Béziat, *Franklin Roosevelt et la France (1939–1945): la diplomatie de l'entêtement* (Paris, 1997); Philip G. Cerny, *The Politics of Grandeur: Ideological Aspects of de Gaulle's Foreign Policy* (Cambridge and New York, 1980); Charles G. Cogan, *Oldest Allies, Guarded Friends: The United States and France since 1940* with foreword by Stanley Hoffmann (Westport, Conn., 1994); Charles G. Cogan, *Charles de Gaulle: A Brief Biography with Documents* (New York, 1996); Frank Costigliola, *France and the United States: The Cold Alliance since World War II* (New York, 1992); Jean-Louis Crémieux-Brilhac, *La France Libre: De l'appel du 18 juin à la Libération* (Paris, 1996); Robert Dallek, *Franklin D. Roosevelt and American Foreign Policy, 1932–1945* (New York, 1981 ed.); Arthur Layton Funk, *Charles de Gaulle: The Crucial Years, 1943–1944* (Norman, 1959); Nerin E. Gun, *Les secrets des archives américaines: Pétain, Laval, De Gaulle* (Paris, 1979); Julian Hurstfield, *America and the French Nation, 1939–1945* (Chapel Hill, 1986); André Kaspi, *Franklin D. Roosevelt* (Paris, 1988); Jean Lacouture, *De Gaulle*, vol. 1 *Le rebelle* (Paris, 1984); Robert O. Paxton and Nicholas Wahl, eds., *De Gaulle and the United States: A Centennial Reappraisal* (Oxford/Providence, 1994); Mario Rossi, *Roosevelt and the French* (Westport Conn., 1993). Eric Roussel, *Charles de Gaulle* (Paris, 2002); Irwin M. Wall, *The United States and the Making of Postwar France 1945–1954* (Cambridge, 1991), ch. 1.
7. The estimates of the number of Americans who were in New Caledonia range as high as an exaggerated one million in some French accounts. An accurate account is difficult since many troops came ashore for brief periods, and the records do not always catch these individuals. A French claim of one- to two-hundred thousand may be found in several sources and is probably

as good an estimate as any given the irregularities in record keeping and the number of Americans who may have gone ashore without any official notice. The U.S. official figure of 30,300 is given for army personnel in New Caledonia as of 31 January 1943, Adjutant General's Office, Machine Records Branch, Monthly Strength of the Army, cited in Ken Coates and W.R. Morrison, "The American Rampant: Reflections on the Impact of United States Troops in Allied Countries during World War II," *Journal of World History*, 2, 2 (1991): 206n. 12.

8. The literature on French anti-Americanism or apprehensions about America as a model for France is extensive. David Strauss, *Menace in the West: The Rise of French Anti-Americanism in Modern Times* (Westport Conn., 1978); Philippe Roger, *L'Ennemi Américain: Généologie de l'antiaméricanisme français* (Paris, 2002); Jean-François Revel, *L'obsession anti-américaine: Son fonctionnement et ses causes, ses inconséquences* (Paris, 2002); Denis Lacorne, Jacques Rupnick, Marie-France Toinet, eds., *Rise and Fall of Anti-Americanism: A Century of French Perception* (New York, 1990); Jacques Portes, *Une fascination réticent, les États-Unis dans l'opinion française, 1870–1914* (Lille, 1991); Charles W. Brooks, *America in France's Hopes and Fears, 1890–1920* (New York, 1987); Donald Ray Allen, *French Views of America in the 1930s* (New York, 1979); Jean-Philippe Mathy, *Extrême-Occident: French Intellectuals and America* (Chicago, 1993); Richard Kuisel, *Seducing the French: the Dilemma of Americanization* (Berkeley, 1993); Tony Judt, *Past Imperfect: French Intellectuals, 1944–1956* (Berkeley, 1992), esp. ch. 10 "America has Gone Mad: Anti-Americanism in Historical Perspective." Differences in perceptions and attitudes on both sides of the Atlantic have been explored by Irwin Wall, "From Anti-Americanism to Francophobia: The Saga of French and American Intellectuals," *French Historical Studies* 18, 4 (Fall 1994): 1083–100.

9. See, for example, Laurence W. Wylie, *Beaux gestes: A Guide to French Body Talk* (Cambridge, Mass., 1977); Laurence Wylie and Armand Bégué, *Les Français* (Englewood Cliffs, 1970). An example of the literature that tries to explain the French to the Americans and vice-versa (to a lesser extent) is Gilles Asselin and Ruth Mastron, *Au Contraire! Figuring out the French* (Yarmouth, Maine, 2001).

10. For the issue of American influence in postwar France, see Irwin Wall, *The United States and the Making of Postwar France 1945–1954* (Cambridge and New York, 1991).

Chapter 1

The Free French and the Americans before Pearl Harbor

The weather was sweltering in Washington on 14 June 1940. President Franklin D. Roosevelt sought relief by taking a cruise on the Potomac aboard the presidential yacht *Sequoia*. As he awaited tea, an aide brought him a cable from France reporting that the German Army had crossed the Seine River and was marching toward the Loire. There were few prospects for continued French resistance. The French Army had been beaten in less than six weeks. The president turned to René de Chambrun, his guest on board, and glumly declared, "René, the show is over." Roosevelt feared that Great Britain could not hold out if France surrendered.[1] The United States would have to get involved in the war in Europe if Britain were to resist Hitler and his seemingly invincible Wehrmacht. Involvement in a European war was something President Roosevelt hoped to avoid on the eve of his campaign for an unprecedented third term.

France under Siege

A few days before receiving the cable aboard *Sequoia*, the French Prime Minister Paul Reynaud had desperately appealed to President Roosevelt to increase all aid to the beleaguered Allies short of sending an expeditionary force. He concluded, "I beseech you to do this before it is too late."[2] Roosevelt had already declared his intention of providing material aid to the Allies in his address to the graduating class at the University of Virginia in Charlottesville on 10 June where he denounced the fascist dictatorships and offered Great Britain and France all possible assistance short of war, while at the same time stepping up America's own rearmament. Roosevelt's reply to Reynaud repeated this promise of material support, and he urged Reynaud to continue the fight from North Africa if necessary, as he had indicated that he was prepared to do.[3] In his exhortation to continue the fight, President Roosevelt stressed the importance of the French fleet as essential to the "mastery of the Atlantic and other oceans."[4]

Presidential promises and exhortations proved little more than encouraging words as the French military collapse continued. On 11 June Reynaud's government left Paris for Bordeaux with stops along the way at Briare and Tours in the Loire valley where the cabinet divided over the question of continuing resistance or seeking an armistice. Despite Churchill's efforts to keep France in the war, the chief of the general staff, General Maxime Weygand, insisted upon an armistice in the face of a catastrophic military defeat. The hero of Verdun, Marshal Philippe Pétain, agreed and these became the decisive voices within Reynaud's government.

In a last minute effort to avoid signing an armistice, Reynaud sent yet another appeal to Roosevelt on 14 June in which he asked for an American commitment to military intervention. He informed the president that the German Army had just entered Paris; the only way to save France was an American declaration that it would "come into the war within a very short time." The fate of France rested with his decision. Reynaud recognized that Roosevelt could not declare war without the consent of the American Congress, but his was a desperate, last minute appeal. While William Bullitt, the American ambassador to France, stayed in Paris, Anthony Biddle, ambassador to the Polish government in exile, accompanied the French Government in its flight to Bordeaux where he reported that Reynaud "was in a state of profound depression and anxiety." Only with an immediate American intervention could France consider continuing the war from North Africa. If there were not a favorable reply to Reynaud's appeal, France would be compelled to surrender.[5]

When the government reached Bordeaux on 15 June, Reynaud insisted that the final decision to seek an armistice or continue the struggle from North Africa should await Roosevelt's response. In the meantime, British Prime Minister Winston Churchill agreed that the French might ask for German armistice terms on the condition that the powerful French fleet would be sailed to British ports and kept out of German hands. Meanwhile, in an attempt to keep France in the war Churchill offered a political union between France and Great Britain, at least for the war's duration.[6] General Charles de Gaulle, who was under–secretary for war in Reynaud's Government, transmitted this offer from London to the Reynaud Government on the morning of the sixteenth.

This daring offer was not enough to keep France fighting. That evening, after receiving Roosevelt's negative response to his request for an immediate American intervention and little support from his cabinet regarding a Franco-British union, a fatigued and despondent Paul Reynaud resigned. The aged Marshal Pétain, who decided to seek an armistice without further consultation with France's British ally, replaced him. On the eve of his resignation Reynaud assured Ambassador Biddle that the French fleet "would never fall into German hands."[7]

In the armistice agreement the Germans promised that they would not take over the French fleet during the war, although they insisted that French naval units, other than those needed for colonial service, return to French ports. The French retained control over the fleet and the empire, but the potential threat of a German takeover remained, certainly in the minds of Franklin Roosevelt and Winston Churchill. The British Government, skeptical of the armistice terms concerning the fleet, took drastic action to insure that the French fleet would not be used against them. Two weeks after the armistice had been signed a British squadron attacked the portion of the French fleet stationed at Mers-el-Kebir, the French naval base near Oran in Algeria. Nearly 1,300 French sailors lost their lives in this attack, which intensified the anti-British feeling that now swelled within Marshal Pétain's Vichy Government and within the ranks of the traditionally Anglophobe French naval officer corps. After Mers-el-Kebir Marshal Pétain's Government broke diplomatic relations with Great Britain. In an effort to prevent Vichy from turning against its erstwhile ally or turning the fleet and empire over to the Germans, President Roosevelt embarked upon what has been termed the American "Vichy gamble"[8] to stiffen Marshal Pétain's resistance to German pressures.

Roosevelt's reaction to the French defeat and armistice has been extensively discussed in histories of the period. He believed that the French had given up the fight too soon, and he had little respect for those who quit in the face of adversity.[9] Rather than following his advice to continue resistance from the empire, the French Government had sought an armistice and opted out of the war, leaving Great Britain to face Hitler alone. In Roosevelt's opinion the defeat meant that France had fallen from the ranks as a major power and would require many years to recover. Although armistice terms left the fleet and empire under Vichy control, they provided no guarantee that the Germans would not gain access to the French Empire.

Roosevelt was concerned that the capital of French West Africa, Dakar, would be used as a port for raiding Atlantic commerce and would perhaps provide a bridgehead for Nazi penetration into Latin America. French possessions in the Caribbean were another danger if they fell under Axis control. The security of Latin America preoccupied Roosevelt in the summer of 1940. Later that year he sent a close advisor, Admiral William Leahy, to Vichy as ambassador with the assignment to persuade Marshal Pétain to keep the fleet immobilized and the empire free of German presence. From the beginning American relations with France, whether with Vichy or, later, with the Free French, were strongly influenced by Roosevelt's concern over the status of the French Empire and fleet.

While Marshal Pétain's Government was capitulating to the Germans, a voice of resistance could be heard, that of General Charles de Gaulle. In one of his dispatches to Roosevelt, Churchill had mentioned de Gaulle as a young general who was in favor of pursuing the fight.[10] Little was known in the United States about this officer, who had only recently been promoted to brigadier general and was a second-level minister in Reynaud's cabinet.[11] After his mission to London, where he was involved in drafting the agreement on an Anglo-French union, de Gaulle had returned briefly to Bordeaux. When he realized that Pétain sought armistice terms, he left Bordeaux for London. There on 18 June 1940 he made a now famous radio address on the British Broadcasting Corporation in which he called upon all French people to reject the armistice and continue resistance.

In his broadcast General de Gaulle invoked the empire and its traditions to support his contention that France's defeat was not total and resistance remained possible: "France is not alone! She is not alone! She has a great empire behind her. Together with the British Empire, she can form a bloc that controls the seas and continue the struggle. She may, like England, draw upon the limitless industrial resources of the United States."[12] Although few were listening at the time, this plea contained the essence of the military and political strategy that General de Gaulle would pursue throughout the war. By continuing the resistance, using the resources of the empire in alliance with Great Britain and calling upon the industrial strength of the United States, France would be present at the victory celebration and resume the country's rank as a major power. General de Gaulle expected that the French Empire would provide the basis for continued resistance.

During the confused days that surrounded the armistice signed on 22 June 1940, it was not clear at first that General de Gaulle would become the leader of a resistance from overseas. De Gaulle initially offered to work under any high-ranking military officer or colonial official who was prepared to take the lead. In his memoirs de Gaulle states that the broadcast of 18 June marked a decisive break in his life, a break with the traditions of order, discipline and the unity of the French Army to which he had devoted himself.[13] This version gives a sense of drama to the speech that was not apparent when it was made. In the days that followed his historic broadcast, de Gaulle searched for a way to serve France in resistance without entirely severing a connection with the authority of the French State or disobeying the principles of hierarchy that had been an integral part of his career. He hoped the government in Bordeaux would continue the war, if necessary from North Africa, and he offered his services to negotiate in Great Britain for the transfer of German prisoners of war to North Africa and for obtaining military supplies from the United States. The response was not that which he had hoped.

The Bordeaux Government, responding to de Gaulle's 18 June broadcast, ordered him to return to France the following day. In his reply to General Weygand, who had become minister of national defense in Marshal Philippe Pétain's Government, de Gaulle declared his intention to return to France within twenty-four hours but only if an armistice were not signed. Rather than accept a dishonorable settlement, he urged Weygand to leave France and assume leadership of French resistance from overseas. He again offered his services as liaison officer in England. The only reply to this appeal was a telegram, delivered by the *chargé d'affaires* from the French embassy in London, informing de Gaulle that he had been court-martialed for disobedience in the face of the enemy and for urging other soldiers to disobey orders.[14] His failure to appear at the military prison in Toulouse would mean condemnation in absentia.

De Gaulle also cabled General Noguès, high resident for Morocco and commander-in-chief of French Forces in North Africa, on 19 June to offer his services if Noguès should reject the armistice, an offer that he repeated on 24 June. He also sent messages to Gabriel Puaux, high commissioner in Syria and Lebanon, to General Eugène Mittelhauser, Weygand's successor as commander-in-chief of French Forces in the Levant, to Marcel Peyrouton, the French resident in Tunisia, and to General Georges Catroux, the governor general of Indochina. He urged them to form a committee for the defense of the empire, and, repeating his message to Weygand, he offered to serve this committee as liaison officer in London. Although they did not respond to de Gaulle, these individuals at first considered continued resistance,[15] notably General Noguès, who on 18 June informed Weygand that his troops were anxious to fight.[16] Noguès was sensitive to the shame and loss of prestige that the armistice would have among the native peoples of North Africa, particularly if it appeared that France had capitulated without fighting to the absolute limit of the empire's resources. Weygand refused all of Noguès's entreaties.[17] With the signing of the armistice Noguès decided to remain loyal to Marshal Pétain and to Vichy right up to the Allied landings in Morocco on 8 November 1942, when he ordered his troops to fire upon the Anglo-American invaders. With his choice of obedience and duty to the military hierarchy, Noguès lost an opportunity, with all of the attendant risks, of assuming leadership of a French resistance based upon the empire. Responsibility for that action fell upon the relatively young, recently promoted general, who had already broadcast his appeal for resistance over the BBC.

Dissidence meant rebellion against French authority embodied in Vichy. General de Gaulle promptly justified this position, announcing on 19 June that "all forms of authority [had] disappeared" in France. Since the government "has fallen under the bondage of the enemy and our institutions have ceased to function," he declared "in the name of France" that it was "the clear duty" of all Frenchmen under arms to continue the struggle. This argument became the basis of the Gaullist claim to legitimacy, namely that the armistice was illegal as well as dishonorable. By signing it the government had committed treason against the French people, and the only correct line of conduct was that of resistance. Among others he directed this message toward the soldiers of the French Empire, invoking the higher interests of France. He cited the examples of Generals Clauzel, Bugeaud and Lyautey, who had conquered North Africa, to remind General Noguès and others of a long colonial military tradition in which overseas commanders had seen themselves as both builders of empire and defenders of the true interests of the nation.[18]

De Gaulle, the Formation of the Free French, and Colonial Resistance

The General's appeal to a tradition of colonial resistance failed to persuade the most illustrious of the French colonial commanders to defy metropolitan authority in the name of higher French interests. There would be no proconsul to emerge from the French Empire in 1940. Noguès refused the call and virtually all others at least initially fell into line. The only high ranking colonial military leaders who responded favorably in the summer of 1940 were General Georges Catroux in Indochina and General Paul Legentilhomme, commander of the French Forces in Djibouti. While willing to risk disobedience to Vichy's authority, both of these officers left their posts without being able to rally their colonies or bring more than a brigade of troops with them.

The uncertain response to his appeal and the modesty of the military forces at his disposal did not prevent de Gaulle from moving toward establishing an organization that would represent France and assure a continued French presence in the war against Hitler's Germany. In his initial discussion with Churchill, de Gaulle raised the possibility of forming a French National Committee that might offer an alternative to the Vichy Government and provide a focal point for those who wished to continue the war effort. This proposal implied that de Gaulle's movement would acquire the status of a government-in-exile, but after a few days he abandoned the idea of setting up a French National Committee, at least for the time being. Instead, on 28 June Churchill's Government issued a statement that recognized de Gaulle as the head of all Frenchmen who might rally to the Allied cause.[19] This statement fell short of full recognition of a government-in-exile, but it represented an important support to give legitimacy to de Gaulle's efforts and to insure that he represented something more, as he put it, than a kind of "military band" operating from England.

Meanwhile London became headquarters for the Free French—a designation first used on 22 June—which was little more than an exile band during the first weeks after the 18 June appeal. For much of July, de Gaulle remained preoccupied with overseeing the formation of the nucleus for a Free-French fighting force, however disheartening that process might have been. Of the 20,000 French troops, airmen and sailors who had been in England at the time of the armistice, the total forces at the end of July represented barely one-third of this number. The majority returned to France. At the same time, the rudiments of a political structure, or at least an administration, for Free France began to emerge. With office equipment borrowed and cajoled from British agencies, the Free-French organization acquired offices, first in St. Stephens House, adjacent to the House of Commons along the Embankment, and eventually in Carlton Gardens, which became the headquarters for the movement during the next three years.

General de Gaulle gained a further measure of recognition on 7 August. He and Churchill signed an agreement that formally recognized de Gaulle's leadership of a volunteer force, including army, navy and air force units, that would be equipped by the British and financially supported for the duration of the conflict but would be a distinctive French and French-controlled operation. The sums advanced were to be repaid at the end of the war. In this agreement, de Gaulle insisted that the British Government agree to the restoration of the full independence and greatness of France, including the territory of metropolitan France and the French Empire. De Gaulle set great stock in this provision. Churchill replied that he would not be able to guarantee such frontiers but promised, as he had with other exiled governments, that the British Government would "do [its] best" to bring about such a restoration. De Gaulle accepted this qualification with the laconic observation that he hoped one day that the British Government would be able to consider this question "with less reserve."[20]

While this agreement further confirmed British support for the Free French, it also contained the basis of subsequent misunderstanding on the issue of restoration of French territory. De Gaulle, already convinced that British support rested upon British interests, suspected foreign designs upon French territory from the outset, and this suspicion extended to the United States as well. If de Gaulle remained passive, the Anglo-Saxon powers, as he liked to refer to them, would appropriate whatever French territory might prove useful in the war against Nazi Germany. De Gaulle's task was "as much as possible to deter England and perhaps one day America from the temptation to secure [French territory] for themselves for purposes of war and their own advantage."[21]

De Gaulle turned his eyes toward Africa and the possibility of rallying French territories there. By early August there were signs that a number of colonies in French Equatorial Africa, which were dependent economically upon trade with neighboring British possessions, did not wish to break these ties as the Vichy Government ordered them to do.[22] De Gaulle saw his African opportunity south of the Sahara, whence messages of support had been sent to him.[23] The former German colony of Cameroon, which had been placed under French mandate at the end of the First World War, seemed particularly anxious not to fall under Vichy control and risk a return of German administration. The governor-general of Cameroon, Richard Brunot, found himself caught between the apparent Free-French sympathies of the population and the demands of loyalty to Vichy rule.

More encouraging was the attitude of Félix Eboué, the governor of Chad, who had contacted de Gaulle shortly after his declaration of resistance. De Gaulle urged him to maintain contact with a hope of rallying the colony at an opportune moment. Recognizing that an isolated rally would leave Eboué in a precarious position, de Gaulle turned to other colonies in Black Africa where stirrings of resistance had been detected. The objective was to rally all of French Equatorial Africa, although chances of a successful rally in parts of Equatorial Africa seemed less certain than in Chad.[24]

After a brief flirtation with resistance the previous governor-general in the French Congo, Pierre Boisson, although a veteran from the First World War and unsympathetic to Germany, remained faithful to the Vichy call. The reward for Boisson's loyalty was an appointment as governor-general of French West Africa in Dakar. Boisson was a tough, no-nonsense colonial administrator who believed that any toying with the terms of the armistice would lead to German intervention in and control of the French Empire. When the governor of Upper Volta expressed his intention of joining the Free French, Boisson promptly had him jailed. Boisson's replacement at Brazzaville, General Louis Husson, described by de Gaulle as "an estimable soldier but prisoner to a mistaken notion of discipline," was also unwilling to break his bonds to Vichy.[25] De Gaulle realized that he needed to move quickly to exploit any support that existed in Central Africa. A rally in Chad might have a domino effect that would bring other French African colonies into the Free-French camp.

The British were anxious to promote Gaullist dissidence in the colonies, particularly in those regions of Africa where British colonies were close to French possessions. The British minister for colonies, Lord Lloyd, was sympathetic and ordered officials in Africa to cooperate fully with de Gaulle's representatives. British transportation was made available to send a Gaullist delegation to coordinate and promote the rallies of French possessions in Equatorial Africa. Yet this was to be a fully French-led operation to avoid appearance of a British attempt to gain control over the French Empire and feed Vichy's anti-British propaganda campaign. It was hoped that even a miniscule Free-French force, or presence, would be sufficient to sway the populations of Chad, Cameroon, the French Congo, Ubangi and, eventually, Gabon.

De Gaulle selected a handful of trusted Free-French recruits to bring these African possessions into his movement. One was René Pleven, a businessman who was formerly director of an American company and part of the French mission that had been sent to the United States in 1939 to arrange a sale of fighter aircraft to the French Government. Claude Hettier de Boislambert, a cavalry officer who had become de Gaulle's adjutant, accompanied him to Africa as did Commander André Parant, another officer who later became the Free-French governor of Gabon. A last minute addition to this delegation was Captain Philippe de Hauteclocque, a career officer who had been wounded in the fighting in Champagne and had just escaped from France across the Spanish frontier, joining de Gaulle in London on the eve of the Gaullist delegation's departure for Africa. Assuming the *nom de guerre* of Commander Leclerc to protect his family still in France, he was to become one of the most illustrious commanders of the Free-French military forces. In Africa they were joined by Colonel Edgar de Larminat, who had been General Mittelhauser's chief-of-staff in Syria in 1940.

The delegation gathered at Lagos, the capital of the then British controlled Nigeria, on 13 August to make their preparations. They decided first to rally Chad, followed immediately by Cameroon and then Brazzaville. On the twenty-sixth Governor Eboué, supported by the commander of the colonial military garrison, announced that Chad was rallying to the Free-French movement. The next day

Leclerc and Boislambert reached Duala in Cameroon where French colonists sympathetic to the Free French welcomed them. They proceeded upriver to Yaounde where a formal transfer of authority confirmed Leclerc as military commander and governor of the colony.

A similarly bloodless coup occurred at Brazzaville, capital of the French Congo, where de Larminat with full support of the Belgian governor at Leopoldville simply crossed the river to take charge of the colony in the name of the Free French. The way had been prepared by a local delegation headed by Médecin-Général Adolphe Sicé that had persuaded the protesting governor of French Equatorial Africa, General Husson, to yield. The administration and the military forces in the French Congo all rallied, with Husson requesting that he be repatriated. A few days later Ubangi also rallied. With the exception of Gabon, which would rally in November, the Gaullists had picked up a solid base of support in French Equatorial Africa by the beginning of September. The Free-French movement had a territorial basis for their claim to sovereignty. Halfway around the world reports from Tahiti announced that French Polynesia had voted overwhelmingly in favor of adherence to the Free-French cause.

The successful rallies of French colonies in Africa and the Pacific had piqued American official interest in the Free-French movement. From Leopoldville and Lagos, American diplomats provided details of the way in which Chad and the other territories of French Equatorial Africa joined the Free-French cause.[26] The consul in Leopoldville was positive in his reporting of these events, noting, "The change of Government and declaration for de Gaulle were greeted with great enthusiasm on both sides of the Congo River."[27] From the Pacific the American minister to Australia, C. E. Gauss, kept the State Department informed of the rally and referendum in Tahiti, and he provided accurate and detailed accounts of the dramatic events that brought New Caledonia into the Free French camp on 19 September.[28] In Africa and the Pacific the momentum of successful rallies gave a boost to the Free-French movement and drew the attention of the Americans.

While pleased that most of French Equatorial Africa had now joined his movement, de Gaulle understood that the key to sub-Saharan Africa was Dakar, the capital of French West Africa and the westernmost port and naval station on the African continent. If Dakar could be persuaded to join the Free-French movement, the Gaullists would be given an enormous boost and gain control over a vital strategic point in the mounting sea war in the Atlantic. On the other hand, Dakar in the hands of the Germans would pose a potential threat to the British and might serve as a bridgehead for Nazism into the Western Hemisphere. Dakar was of considerable interest to Churchill, Roosevelt and de Gaulle.

Disaster at Dakar

Given Dakar's strategic importance, Churchill was anxious to rally French West Africa to General de Gaulle and assure its control in friendly hands. At first prospects for a successful rally seemed promising. Reports indicated that local French patriots were prepared to seize control of the town and its port.[29] On 5 August Churchill sent a note to the war cabinet proposing to send de Gaulle immediately to Gibraltar, where he would sail with his staff for Dakar, and the prime minister asked that the chiefs of staff give immediate consideration to his proposal.

Although his military advisors were initially skeptical of the Dakar operation, Churchill remained enthusiastic. On the morning of 6 August Churchill summoned de Gaulle to 10 Downing Street where he produced an imaginative and dramatic vision of how the operation would take place. In a much cited passage from both de Gaulle's and Churchill's memoirs, we have an account of the prime minister pacing the cabinet room, describing how Dakar would awaken one fine morning to see a vast armada of one hundred warships and transports on the horizon. This display of force would enable de Gaulle to enter the port and negotiate terms of French West Africa's adherence to the Free-French cause—with perhaps a few shots fired "for honor's sake." The peaceful transfer would conclude with a banquet and toasts to the common victory.[30] De Gaulle went along with this colorful prediction, since he saw possible gains, despite the risks, for his movement if the attempt succeeded, and he feared that if he did not join the operation the British would at some point settle the Dakar situation "for their own account."

The grandiose plans for Dakar began to go awry from an early stage. Had the expedition been sent quickly, it might have succeeded, but the delay enabled the Vichy Government to strengthen its defenses at Dakar. Rather than the 1,400 Senegalese infantry, which British intelligence had initially reported, there were three battalions totalling 7,000 men in Dakar.[31] To strengthen its hand in West and Equatorial Africa, Vichy requested permission from the Armistice Commission in Wiesbaden to send a squadron, consisting of the heavy cruiser *Strasbourg*, two other 10,000 ton cruisers, one light cruiser and several destroyers to Dakar. The ultimate objective was to bring dissident African colonies back under Vichy's control.[32]

When the Allied force appeared off Dakar on the morning of the 23 September, they discovered that a thick fog had settled in, and the inhabitants had no way of seeing the Allied naval force that Churchill hoped would impress them. De Gaulle tried to negotiate a peaceful transfer of power. A motor launch, flying both a white flag and the tricolor, made its way into the harbor, bearing a Free-French delegation led by Captain Georges Thierry d'Argenlieu, a naval officer who had left the navy after the First World War to become a Carmelite monk. D'Argenlieu had gone back into naval service as a reserve commander at the beginning of the Second World War. After the armistice d'Argenlieu escaped from German captivity and made his way to London where he became an early and faithful supporter of General de Gaulle. It was hoped that d'Argenlieu's credentials as an officer and ardent Catholic would recommend him to his colleagues in the French Navy, and he carried with him letters to be delivered to Governor Boisson and the heads of the army and navy. Instead of being allowed to deliver his letters, he was told to leave or face arrest, and the launch quickly left under a hail of bullets, wounding d'Argenlieu. Both the shore batteries and the guns of *Richelieu* then began firing upon the Anglo/Free-French ships. At eleven the British began a somewhat ineffective bombardment, designed to discourage what was proving to be very accurate fire from the shore batteries and the fifteen inch guns of *Richelieu*, all of which bolstered the morale of the defenders.

In an effort to salvage the situation Admiral Cunningham issued an ultimatum to Governor Boisson in which he warned of severe action to prevent Dakar falling into enemy hands. Boisson curtly rejected the ultimatum and promised to defend the city "to the end." The next day British forces began an air and sea bombardment of Dakar, but again the Vichy side had the better of the exchange and morale among the French sailors in the port soared. Late that afternoon, a gloomy war council was held aboard Cunningham's flagship. The British were downcast and frustrated; they decided that the operation had failed and had to be ended. De Gaulle sought a face-saving device in announcing that the engagement had been broken off at his request to avoid spilling more French blood in a fratricidal combat. British accounts all express admiration for the dignity of de Gaulle in the face of a bitter disappointment. He concluded the war council with the brave statement: "In any event and whatever happens, Free France will continue."[33]

Although he showed stoic calm, de Gaulle faced a test of his determination in the aftermath of Dakar. Where and how the Free French were to continue after this setback was not immediately clear, nor was de Gaulle's course of action. British and American newspapers ridiculed the folly of the Dakar attempt and blamed de Gaulle for its conception and its failure. De Gaulle bitterly commented upon the "tempest of anger" in London and "a hurricane of sarcasms" in Washington. Vichy propaganda quickly exploited this failure and continued to portray de Gaulle as the renegade instrument of British ambitions. In his memoirs, de Gaulle stated that he felt as if he had gone through an earthquake with his house falling on his head. He briefly fell into despondency and apparently at one point thought of "blowing [his] brains out,"[34] but that mood did not last long.

In a letter to de Larminat, Leclerc and Eboué he was much more philosophical about the Dakar setback: at least the Free French had won the first set in Africa and the Pacific while the Germans using Vichy had won the second at Dakar.[35] In a letter to his wife he stated that those who were faithful to him were determined to go on, and he was hopeful for the future. He had been thrown into the forefront of the greatest drama in history with all of the inevitable, cruel blows inflicted upon those who were on stage, but he would recover because "no storm lasts indefinitely."[36]

He made his way with the British squadron to Freetown where he received the comforting news that the French Pacific colony of New Caledonia had joined the Free-French movement. He was encouraged by the determined attitude of his followers, who had been infuriated at the actions of Vichy officials at Dakar and were just as determined to continue the struggle, even at the risk of conflicts with other French. In the House of Commons Churchill gave a stirring defense of the Dakar attempt, somewhat silencing the critics. But the legacy of Dakar was to be a long one in wartime relations among the Allies. The Americans were now certain that the Free French could not be trusted if there should ever be an attempt to bring the French territories in West and North Africa back into the war. Roosevelt became convinced that de Gaulle was a bumbling military adventurer, supported by the British. He feared that the Dakar attempt might bring the Germans into French West Africa. The Dakar fiasco greatly increased Roosevelt's distrust of de Gaulle.

Anglo-American doubts about the Free French and de Gaulle in the aftermath of Dakar only strengthened de Gaulle's determination to continue, and he was further heartened by his reception in Equatorial Africa. Escorted by Admiral Cunningham's squadron, de Gaulle reached Duala on 8 October where he was greeted by a cheering crowd and a military parade organized by Leclerc from the 2,500 troops of the Foreign Legion that were present in the colony. He arrived in the colonial town to be overwhelmed by the sight, as he later put it, of French civil servants, colonists, Black African leaders, and officers and troops of the colonial forces, "swimming in a full tide of patriotic euphoria." This experience convinced de Gaulle that an indissoluble bond of unity henceforth held together all of those who had rallied to the cross of Lorraine. He also felt the adulation of the crowd that, he later confessed, placed him in a kind of bondage, a role that he could henceforth never escape. The reception at Duala strengthened his sense of pride and reinforced his determination to always speak and represent France by his actions and behavior. "The fact of embodying for my comrades the destiny of our cause, for the French masses the symbol of their hope, for foreigners the image of an indomitable France amidst its ordeals, was to dictate my bearing and impose upon my personality an attitude that I could never again change."[37]

This African experience strengthened de Gaulle's determination and established a pattern of behavior that would lead to friction with his Allies and enemies alike. His determination never to relax and to be constantly aware and vigilant toward the interests of France became a source of bewilderment, particularly for Americans, who had difficulty understanding how an individual could embody a nation.[38] The Americans were uneasy with de Gaulle's conception of a personal embodiment of France, which carried royalist overtones. In the American political tradition the fundamental source of nationhood was not an individual, but a document, the Constitution, and American presidents were sworn to uphold a legal instrument that had almost as much symbolic, even mystical, importance and resonance as the concept "France" did for de Gaulle.[39]

As the French historian François Furet would later remark, in America "the Constitution takes on the character of a Sacred Arch."[40]

For the next two months de Gaulle remained in Africa, consolidating the Free-French movement there, strengthening what he saw as the territorial as well as the moral foundation for his movement. Strategically Africa offered the most direct way in which Free France might contribute to the liberation of a partially occupied and subservient metropolitan homeland. For the moment the affairs of the much more distant Pacific colonies that had also rallied seemed remote, although de Gaulle would become concerned over these Free-French territories during the winter of 1940/41 when tensions with Japan developed over Indochina and New Caledonia.

The episode at Dakar was in many ways a turning point for the Free-French movement. Certainly Vichy exploited the events at Dakar, labeling de Gaulle an agent of the British and evidence of a British intention to lay hands on the French Empire by force if necessary. Vichy's resistance in Dakar was used in negotiations with the Germans as evidence that they were determined to defend the empire against the Anglo-Gaullists. Vichy representatives argued that the armistice commission should allow reinforcements to defend the French Empire. They also used Dakar as an argument to reach the increasingly elusive goal of a final peace settlement with Germany.[41] De Gaulle bitterly resented Vichy's attacks upon his movement and its claim that he was no more than a British agent, but he also recognized that he had to establish his clear independence of Great Britain, despite his need for British political and financial support. Dakar became a setback or momentary defeat on the path toward liberation, but it strengthened de Gaulle's determination that the Free-French movement offered the only alternative to national humiliation.

Much more heartening was the fact that de Gaulle still had important support and continuing loyalty from those territories that had rallied. In the aftermath of Dakar and while he was in Africa and on French colonial territory, de Gaulle decided to give his movement a more clearly distinct, political character when he created an Empire Defense Council on 27 October. This important initiative had far-reaching implications for his movement since it was a first step toward the formation of a provisional government and General de Gaulle's claim to legitimacy as the political as well as military leader of the French resistance.

The Empire Defense Council and the Allies in the Tropics

The formation of the Empire Defense Council reflected de Gaulle's reaction to events at Vichy, particularly Marshal Pétain's collaboration with Germany, offered to Hitler at their meeting in the French village of Montoire on 24 October. General de Gaulle was determined to create a structure that would enable him to deal with other authorities in all matters affecting French interests. Three weeks later he issued an "organic declaration" in which he demonstrated that the "pseudo-government of Vichy" was an unconstitutional and illegal regime and could not represent French interests.[42] As de Gaulle insisted, "'Free France,' that is to say, *La France*" was what he represented.[43] The Empire Defense Council became a de facto governing body for the Free-French movement, and it was composed of various leaders who were in London or serving as governors of territories that had rallied and were continuing the war.[44]

De Gaulle saw the council as an oversight body for the administrative structures that were now necessary to run what was the Free-French Empire. Negotiations on terms of trade and exchange, necessary for survival, had to be made through the offices of the Empire Defense Council. Without formal attributes, a Free-French government and administration had been created to handle the many problems of organizing a military force, supplying and feeding a scattered collection of rallied French possessions, and dealing with other governments, notably those of Great Britain and the United States. As General de Gaulle would later state to Churchill, his was no longer merely a movement but a territorial force.[45] Charles the landless now had a firm base for operations and a structure for administering the rallied colonies.

An irritation toward de Gaulle and a whiff of compromise were both in the air when de Gaulle returned to London from Africa on 18 November 1940. His return followed a rather peremptory summons from Churchill in which he insisted on the need for consultations in light of what Churchill described as a situation between France and Britain that "has changed remarkably since you left."[46] The atmosphere that de Gaulle discovered in London upon his return was an apparent determination to preserve the status quo as far as the French Empire was concerned. British support for any further rallies that might lead to a German intervention in North Africa or French possessions in the Middle East under Vichy control was to be avoided. British resources were stretched thin in the Mediterranean and elsewhere. This cautious approach to relations with Vichy upset the General, who feared that Churchill's acceptance of the status quo would neutralize the French Empire and block his efforts to bring the rest of the empire into the war against Nazi Germany. From de Gaulle's perspective any deal with Vichy compromised French interests, primarily the need to be among the victorious powers at the end of the war. Any "Vichy gamble," whether American or British, was a bad bet in de Gaulle's eyes.

The territorial base of the Free-French movement was General de Gaulle's best bargaining chip to gain recognition and acceptance by the Allies. For this reason he was determined to broaden the territorial base of his movement while defending French imperial interests. No less than Vichy, de Gaulle was alert to any effort to exploit French weakness for the benefit of the British Empire or for the benefit of American security interests. He believed that any appeasement of Vichy and neutralization of the French Empire played into Hitler's hands and prevented France from joining the resistance to the Nazis. The acquisition of a territorial base in Africa gave General de Gaulle a degree of independence in his relations with Great Britain. The territorial and imperial argument also offered a way to gain support from the United States. In his relations with the Americans he would use strategic French colonial territory to obtain some American support for his movement. He turned toward the Caribbean in an initial attempt to find this support.

American officials feared that French possessions in the Antilles would be a threat to American security if they were to be used by the Germans. At the end of June the nations of the Western Hemisphere had signed a series of declarations in Havana that opposed any transfer of European controlled territory in the Western Hemisphere from one nation to another. The Havana Declaration authorized the takeover of any territory so threatened. This was an obvious warning to the Vichy Government against any accommodation of German demands regarding the use of French colonial possessions in the Caribbean, notably Martinique and Guadeloupe, as submarine bases. If these territories rallied to General de Gaulle, however, that threat would be removed.

In the summer of 1940 news from Martinique and Guadeloupe suggested that the local populations might be prepared to join the Free French. The American consul in Martinique reported that while conditions were apparently calm, local opinion was divided over loyalty to Marshal Pétain.[47] On the other hand there was strong popular support for de Gaulle, particularly among the Black and Creole populations who feared a racist reaction under Vichy. On 4 October the American consul was asked to forward a letter to General de Gaulle claiming that an overwhelming majority of residents favored his movement. If a referendum were held on the islands, no more than 100 votes out of 300,000 residents would support Vichy, according to this source.[48] If a break with Vichy should occur, however, the island would become dependent upon imports from either British colonies or the United States, and the prospect of economic dependency upon the United States carried with it a possibility of an American takeover of French territories in the Caribbean.

De Gaulle proposed to administer the colonies if the Americans decided to intervene. On the eve of his announcing the formation of the Empire Defense Council in October, he contacted the American consul in Leopoldville, the capital of the then Belgian Congo, across the river from Free-French territory. De Gaulle claimed that he had messages of support from these colonies, and if the Americans supported a rally, he would negotiate agreements with the American Government for use of bases in these and other territories under Free-French control. The General warned the American Government that any unilateral takeover would be deeply resented by the French, but American cooperation with a Free-French administration would be welcomed.[49] The Americans made no response to this offer.

Instead the Americans negotiated with Vichy, much to General de Gaulle's deep anger. The Americans wished to neutralize the French colonies in the Western Hemisphere. They also wanted to regain possession of 112 American aircraft in Martinique that were awaiting transport to France at the time of the armistice. Washington asked Vichy to sell these planes back to the United States, but Vichy rejected this request. To make sure that these planes would remain in the Western Hemisphere and that the French Antilles would not be used against the United States, the American Government had sent Rear Admiral John Greenslade in July to negotiate an agreement with the high commissioner for the Antilles, Admiral Georges Robert. Admiral Robert gave no promises, and Greenslade came away empty-handed. Greenslade's approach to Admiral Robert alarmed the Free French. From New York the Free-French representative, Maurice Garreau-Dombasle, warned de Gaulle's London headquarters that the Americans were about to do something in the Antilles, and the solution might not be what the Free French would wish.[50] He feared the Americans would exploit French weakness to take control of French colonies in the Western Hemisphere.

Shortly after Marshal Pétain's meeting with Hitler at Montoire, which announced Vichy's collaboration with Germany, Admiral Greenslade returned to Martinique. This time he threatened to station an aircraft carrier off shore to observe French fleet movements with orders to sink any French ship that tried to come out.[51] Admiral Robert then reached a "gentleman's agreement" to provide the United States with four days' notice prior to any ship movements, allow a United States naval observer at Fort de France, and permit American naval ships to patrol within the territorial limits of Martinique and Guadeloupe. In exchange for these commitments, the Americans agreed to supply food to the extent that shipping allowed.

All of this activity aroused Free-French suspicions of American intentions toward Martinique. General de Gaulle resented an arrangement that neutralized the territory and left Admiral Robert free to suppress any movement on the island in favor of the Free French, which he did vigorously. The prospect of a rally of Martinique and Guadeloupe faded when Admiral Robert cracked down upon dissidents in the colony. His actions included dismissing the local governing council that was controlled by Creole and Black politicians, who were correctly suspected of Gaullist sympathies. From the Gaullist perspective American neutralization of these Vichy controlled colonies enabled Admiral Robert's repression and strengthened Vichy's hold on the colony.[52] De Gaulle considered the Robert-Greenslade agreement to be a deliberate strategy of dealing separately with local authorities, which would weaken France further and open French colonial territories to American exploitation. From this point Gaullist resentment and suspicion of an American policy of dealing separately with French local authorities whether Vichy or, later, Gaullist, became fixed.

While building a territorial and political foundation for his Free-French movement in Africa, General de Gaulle also kept his attention focused upon the Pacific where tensions were beginning to develop. At the time of the Dakar fiasco, he requested that a Free-French representative participate in discussions that Americans, British and Australians were holding on the defense of the Pacific. De Gaulle's rationale was that the rally of French Pacific territories should give the Free French a voice in Allied strategy. The British Government refused to forward de Gaulle's request, much to the General's annoyance, on the ground that the Free-French representative in the United States did not represent a sovereign state.[53] In British eyes, the Free-French movement still had a way to go to achieve that status, something that de Gaulle felt had been at least partially accomplished with the Empire Defense Council.

The General's vision for Free France became increasingly global as the contest for the Pacific and its resources intensified. The Pacific became, along with Africa and the Middle East, a focus for de Gaulle's concern in early 1941 on the eve of his departure for the Middle East. Here he would do battle with his British allies over the British Government's decision to rally Syria and Lebanon to the Free French without much consultation with General de Gaulle or his representative, General Catroux. In the Pacific de Gaulle was particularly alarmed at growing Japanese pressure upon Indochina, which became apparent during a border dispute between the Vichy controlled colony and Thailand at the end of 1940 and beginning of 1941. The government of Thailand hoped to use French vulnerability in Asia to press for a return of land that had been annexed to French Indochina in 1907, and the Thai Government had Japanese support in pressing their claim. This dispute led to a conflict between Thai and Vichy land and naval forces. The French got the better of the engagement at sea, but the Thai dealt a severe blow to French forces along the Mekong River. The Japanese became directly involved when they offered to mediate the dispute, and they favored the Thai claim. Japanese pressure forced the French administration to give up the territory that the Thai demanded.

The Japanese threat to French imperial possessions led Garreau-Dombasle to propose sending a Free-French military expedition to Singapore. General de Gaulle responded that the Free French did not have resources for such an undertaking. He also warned that a provocative action might bring a strong Japanese response against Indochina and against the French possessions in the Pacific that had rallied, notably Tahiti and New Caledonia. But he advised Garreau-Dombasle to be cautious in dealing with the Americans in their dispute with the Japanese since American policy "has been to push France and England to take a firm position toward Japan but never to engage themselves" in such action.[54] The Japanese menace to the French Empire, including those Pacific territories that had rallied to the Free French, had become serious.

Growing Japanese expansionist ambitions in French Indochina and the Southwest Pacific fueled the General's anxiety over the security of the mineral-rich colony of New Caledonia, which had rallied to the Free-French cause in September 1940. He feared that Japan might support Vichy efforts to regain control of New Caledonia.[55] A report that he received at the beginning of 1941 showed that Japan considered New Caledonia to be within a Japanese sphere of influence.[56] Although overshadowed by events in Africa and the Middle East, the

Pacific was very much on de Gaulle's mind, and he decided to strengthen the Free-French authority in the South Pacific, particularly in New Caledonia.

An American interest in the strategically located island was another reason for de Gaulle's decision to strengthen a Free-French presence in New Caledonia. At the end of 1940 the United States proposed the establishment of a consulate in Nouméa, a suggestion that the Caledonians welcomed.[57] At Carlton Gardens this American interest was considered an opportunity to establish some kind of relation with the United States. Free France could no longer be ignored in Washington. However, formal terms for acceptance of an American consul were arranged through Vichy, not through Carlton Gardens. In this way the State Department avoided recognition of the Free French. The American consul to New Caledonia, Karl de Giers MacVitty, obtained his visa from Vichy but was given permission to locate an office in Nouméa by the Free French. This arrangement revealed the complexities of American policy toward France.[58]

Free-French Representation in the United States

An opportunity to improve ties with the United States seemed to be at hand for the Free French. De Gaulle understood, as he had stated in his 18 June 1940 broadcast, that the material resources of the United States would be essential for the defeat of Germany and the liberation of France. He later wrote that it was "of extreme importance" to have the best possible representation in the United States.[59] The trouble was that Gaullist representation in the United States was badly fragmented and plagued by personal jealousies and rivalries.[60] Their conflicts produced what one Free-French observer called the "panier des crabes" among the French exile community in New York.[61] In the American official mind the image of Free France was unimpressive during these first months and provided the State Department with a rationale for dealing cautiously with General de Gaulle and his followers.

Captain Thierry d'Argenlieu, one of General de Gaulle's closest and most trusted supporters who was on his own mission in Canada at the time, warned that rivalries among these factions had created an unfavorable impression.[62] A number of exiles urged de Gaulle to resolve the conflicts, including a telegram from Eve Curie urgently asking that de Gaulle send a mission to the United States.[63] The foreign office noted that "General de Gaulle is badly represented in the U.S.A.," and they hoped that General de Gaulle would send a personal representative to the United States who would be authorized "to sack the present crowd of nincompoops who represent de Gaulle in the States."[64]

General de Gaulle decided to bring some order into the Free-French crab basket and establish better contacts with a skeptical State Department by sending one of his close associates, René Pleven, on special mission to the United States. In his instructions, de Gaulle wrote, "Given the nearly belligerent attitude of the United States, the more and more apparent collaboration of Vichy with Germany, finally the special economic conditions of the Free-French colonies in Africa and Oceania, the moment has arrived for us to organize our relations with America."[65] This was, as the General put it in another letter, "an exceptional opportunity to be seized" and his departure was an urgent matter. The British Foreign Office hoped that Pleven might overcome the American State Department's reservations about General de Gaulle and the Free-French movement. A memorandum argued, "It should be possible to persuade the State Department that it is now time to come out wholeheartedly for de Gaulle, and cut the painter with Vichy."[66]

De Gaulle remained concerned about possible American intervention in the French Empire for purposes of defense without taking the Free French into account. Free-French control of colonial territory was an alternative to Vichy. Pleven was told to impress upon the Americans that Vichy's promises that the fleet and empire would not be turned over to the Germans were without any value.[67] Free France, he insisted, ought to receive the full support of the United States Government.[68] To carry out this important task, Pleven was given full authority to speak for de Gaulle and the Empire Defense Council in his dealings with the American administration.[69]

Pleven seemed ideally suited for this demanding mission. He spoke English fluently, and he had been general director of the Automatic Telephone Company of Chicago in France before the war, which gave him connections in the American business community. In Washington he was on good terms with the assistant secretary for war, John J. McCloy, which gave him access into the administration. The Pleven mission also received enthusiastic support from a personal friend of President Roosevelt, Anthony Drexel Biddle, the former ambassador to Poland who became American ambassador to the European governments-in-exile after the fall of France. Biddle praised Pleven as "a serious, sincere, courageous and intelligent patriot" who sought "some gesture of sympathy and understanding" in Washington.[70] Among General de Gaulle's advisors René Pleven was the best connected in the United States.

Despite these connections, Pleven's mission was much more difficult than he expected. He lamented that the Free-French cause in the United States was little known due to Vichy propaganda. The exile community had produced discouragingly little support for the Free-French movement or made its aims and objectives known in America. Sumner Welles, the under-secretary of state, initially declined to meet him although Lord Halifax, the British ambassador, was able to give Welles a memo from Pleven.[71] Pleven requested Lend-lease aid, stressing the "moral and economic" value of this support as a way of boosting morale and demonstrating "solidarity between the democracies."[72] Progress was frustratingly slow, however, and Pleven admitted that he had few concrete results to show for his first month in the United States save for some slight improvement in the way that the Free French were viewed in Washington.[73]

The War Department did accept General de Gaulle's invitation to send a military delegation, headed by Colonel Harry Cunningham, to Free-French

Africa for the purpose of inspecting airfields and naval bases that had been offered to the United States for its use.[74] The government also authorized the Red Cross to send medical supplies and equipment to the Free French. A sticking point was American relations with Vichy and the continued but ultimately unsuccessful American attempts to persuade General Weygand to consider re-entering the war on the side of the Allies.

Pleven believed that America's Vichy policy might be modified. The State Department was upset over the Japanese move into Southern Indochina in July without Vichy offering any resistance. Even the courting of General Weygand in North Africa was under reconsideration. There were, Pleven reported, an increasing number within the State Department who thought it would be better to be a Gaullist than to be on the side of those who signed the armistice. A week later he confirmed the Cunningham mission, which would arrive in French Equatorial Africa on 5 September. Both American public and official opinion were moving toward aiding Free-French territories, and the State Department was disposed to discuss practical matters.[75]

Despite these hopeful signs Pleven still had not been able to obtain arms and military equipment for the Free French under Lend-lease. The Americans would provide only medicine, which greatly upset General de Gaulle by creating the impression that the United States was indifferent to Free-French military needs and potential contribution to the war effort. "We are not beggars," the outraged Free-French leader replied, the Free French "only want the means to fight."[76] American illusions about Vichy only served Hitler, de Gaulle argued. As for any Free-French participation in a three-way discussion with the British and the Americans, the Free French would do so as equals or not at all. General de Gaulle's sensitivity toward the Americans and resentment over their unwillingness to treat him as an equal and their indifference to his concerns about French sovereignty were becoming apparent. De Gaulle ordered Pleven to return home by the end of the month, clearly upset that the Free-French cause had made such little progress in Washington. Pleven replied that he understood General de Gaulle's impatience with the slow pace of events in Washington, but he was like a swimmer who was halfway across the river and now was asked to turn back. Furthermore, his return would not be seen favorably in Washington.[77] Pleven would remain in the United States for another two months.

Actually, the United States was willing to offer military assistance under Lend-lease, although the offer was indirect to avoid any recognition of the Free French as a government-in-exile. In June the Free-French high commissioner for Free-French Africa, General de Larminat, specifically requested aircraft, anti-aircraft and anti-tank guns that were urgently needed for the defense of Free-French territories in Africa. Two days later a similar appeal came from the governor-general of the Belgian Congo. In response to these requests, Sumner Welles pointed out that military supplies to the Free French and the Belgian Congo were handled through Lend-lease to Great Britain. The Free French were advised to direct their requests to the British, while the Belgians could make their requests in the United States through their accredited representatives.[78] In this way Sumner Welles avoided any implied recognition of the Free French as legitimately accredited to the United States.

A major success of Pleven's mission was to establish a Free-French delegation in Washington to counteract the effect of the Vichy embassy's anti-de Gaulle campaign and be able to engage in direct negotiations with the American Government. The State Department informed Pleven that it would welcome a Free-French delegation in Washington as long as its leader "was not too closely associated with the New-Yorkaise atmosphere" that had existed since the armistice.[79] This meant eliminating de Gaulle's St. Cyr classmate, Jacques de Sieyès, as head of the mission, which Pleven said was unavoidable for many reasons that he would explain to General de Gaulle upon his return to London.[80]

Pleven proposed two candidates to head the Free-French delegation in Washington. One was Etienne Boegner, a businessman who was the son of Pastor Marc Boegner, the head of Protestant Churches in France. The State Department as well as the British foreign office favored his candidacy, but the British realized that their endorsement would be fatal. As a foreign office memo put it, Boegner had "two demerits in the General's eyes": he was an Anglophile and had "spoken strongly and independently to de Gaulle."[81] Boegner became the acting head of the delegation and later quarreled bitterly with de Gaulle. Pleven acknowledged that Boegner was diplomatic and had good relations with officials in the State Department who favored his appointment, but the General turned to the other choice, Adrien Tixier.

Tixier's previous career identified him as a man of the Left, who enjoyed good relations with both the Communist dominated Confédération Générale du Travail and Catholic unions in France. De Gaulle chose Tixier not to please the Americans but to strengthen his own status with the labor movement in France. Pleven suggested to de Gaulle that resistors among the unions in France would welcome Tixier's appointment, and it would be a riposte "to those who accuse Free France of being a reactionary movement."[82] He had been a strong advocate for France at the International Labor Office in Geneva. In the traditions of French unionism he made no distinction between patriotism and the idea of social progress. These qualities greatly pleased General de Gaulle. In his reply to Pleven, de Gaulle called Tixier a "loyal and solid" man, noting that "the social question is the great issue for tomorrow."[83]

As it turned out Tixier's relations with American officials were difficult, due to his abrasive, secretive personality and a tendency toward intrigue. He developed a habit of reporting one thing to de Gaulle and something else to the Americans. Raoul Aglion, who served as secretary of the delegation, described Tixier as someone who would be frantically anti-American when among the French, and then he would turn around and be critical of de Gaulle when dealing with the Americans.[84] The British felt that he lacked "some of the diplomatic qualities …

for such a position" and wished that Boegner rather than Tixier headed the delegation.[85] The delegation was settled, though, and it occupied the vacant Italian embassy in Washington.

Having placed Gaullist representation in the United States on a better foundation, the General asked Pleven to return to London as soon as possible. Before leaving the United States Pleven at last had an interview with Sumner Welles. Pleven found Welles "always very cold" and distant. He considered Welles to be one of those Americans who believed that they understood France better than the British or the French themselves. Welles remained evasive about direct Lend-lease aid to the Free French since this action might imply recognition of Free France, but he reassured Pleven that the Free French could obtain Lend-lease assistance through Great Britain.

Much more encouraging was evidence of the State Department's disillusion with Vichy, particularly after the Japanese entry into southern Indochina. Crucial to Free-French concerns about American intentions toward the French Empire was Welles' initial statement that "the policy of the United States government was to restore the independence and integrity of France and the French Empire." This commitment to a restoration was important not only for sentimental reasons, Welles assured him; it reflected the American position of the need for France to continue to play an important role in world affairs. Welles added there was "an identity of aim between the U.S. government policy and the aims of Free France."[86]

On the eve of his departure from the United States, Pleven thanked Ray Atherton for arranging the interview with Sumner Welles. He again expressed his gratitude for the statement that the aim of the United States was the same as that of the Free French, notably the restoration of the independence and integrity of France and the French Empire.[87] Then on 11 November Roosevelt informed the French National Committee that Lend-lease equipment would be made directly available to Free-French forces without having to pass through British intermediaries. While still falling short of any kind of official recognition, direct Lend-lease aid represented a major improvement in United States/Free-French relations.

During Pleven's mission to the United States, the British government on behalf of American officials asked for Free-French cooperation in the creation of a series of airfields for heavy bombers on certain Pacific islands and wished to have New Caledonia and the New Hebrides included in this network.[88] De Gaulle replied that there already was a plan for the defense of these islands in cooperation with Australia, but the Free French were prepared to discuss a general plan for the Pacific in cooperation with Great Britain, Australia and New Zealand. He informed Pleven that the Free French supported plans for the creation of a heavy bomber landing base on New Caledonia, and the Americans would be allowed to establish air bases at Bora Bora in Free-French Oceania.[89] He insisted, though, that the rally of these colonies was evidence of the Free-French commitment to continue the war at the side of the Allies. This meant that in all negotiations concerning these territories, he exercised the attributes of a government in matters of administration and defense.[90] To assure that the French National Committee would have a significant role in the defense of French Pacific territories, de Gaulle insisted that all matters of policy be negotiated through London.

With evidence of Japanese ambitions in the Pacific, New Caledonia became a focal point for both the Free French and the Americans. American interest in New Caledonia began at the time of the rally in September 1940, but it grew with anxieties over Japanese interest in the mineral rich island. The presence of MacVitty as consul in Nouméa was an expression of this concern. New Caledonia's strategic location astride the sea-lane between the United States and Australia caught the attention of American military planners in Washington. The State Department asked that the American consul provide information on the strength of the island's defense and an estimate of the size of the Japanese population living in New Caledonia.[91] The Americans began to look into the strategic value of New Caledonia in the fall of 1941, but they neglected to inform de Gaulle of the extent of their interest.

Cooperation between the Americans and the Free French was at hand in the South Pacific, but it would not be easy. The circumstances of New Caledonia's rally to General de Gaulle's Free-French movement would be an important event in shaping the relationship between the Americans and the Free French at the time of the American arrival in New Caledonia.

Notes

1. René de Chambrun, *Mission and Betrayal 1940–1945: Working with Franklin Roosevelt to Help Save Britain and Europe* (Stanford, 1993), 68. Cited in Jean Lacouture, *De Gaulle*, vol. 1: *Le rebelle* (Paris, 1984), 529.
2. Cited in Robert Dallek, *Franklin D. Roosevelt and American Foreign Policy, 1932–1945* (New York, 1981 ed.), 229.
3. P.M.H. Bell, *A Certain Eventuality: Britain and the Fall of France* (London, 1974), 65–66.
4. Secretary of State (Hull) to First Secretary of the Embassy (Mathews) at Tours, 13 June 1940, for the president, *Foreign Relations of the United States* (henceforth *FRUS*), 1940, vol. 1 (Washington, 1959), 248.
5. Biddle to Hull, 14 June 1940, *FRUS*, 1940, vol. 1, 253. A useful analysis of Reynaud's last-minute appeal may be found in Eleanor M. Gates, *End of the Affair: The Collapse of the Anglo-French Alliance, 1939–1940* (Berkeley, 1981), 413–15.
6. The confusion, if not contradiction, in British policy is analyzed in Bell, *A Certain Eventuality*, 71–77.
7. Biddle to Hull, 16 June 1940 (9 p.m.), *FRUS*, 1940, vol. 1, 261.
8. William L. Langer, *Our Vichy Gamble* (New York, 1947).
9. David Fromkin, *In the Time of the Americans: FDR, Truman, Eisenhower, Marshall, MacArthur–the Generation that Changed America's Role in the World* (New York, 1995), 583.
10. Churchill to Franklin D. Roosevelt, 12 June 1940, *FRUS*, 1940, vol. 1, 247.
11. Christopher Thompson, "Prologue to Conflict: De Gaulle and the United States, from First Impressions through 1940," in *De Gaulle and the United States: A Centennial Reappraisal*, ed. Robert O. Paxton and Nicholas Wahl (Providence R.I., 1994), 13–32.

12. De Gaulle, *Discours et messages I: Pendant la guerre* (Paris, 1970), 3.
13. De Gaulle, *Mémoires de Guerre*, vol. 1, *l'Appel 1940–1942* (Paris, 1954), 71–72.
14. Ibid., 269, 275.
15. Martin Thomas, *The French Empire at War 1940–1945* (Manchester and New York, 1998), 40–43.
16. Gen. André Truchet, *L'Armistice de 1940 et l'Afrique du Nord* (Paris, 1955), cited in Robert O. Paxton, *Vichy France: Old Guard and New Order* (New York, 1972), 7n. 6.
17. William A. Hoisington, *The Casablanca Connection: French Colonial Policy* (Chapel Hill, 1984), 174–75.
18. De Gaulle, *Mémoires*, vol. 1, 268–69.
19. Bernard Ledwidge, *De Gaulle* tr. Inès Heugel et Dominique Rist (Paris, 1984) 82.
20. De Gaulle, *Mémoires*, vol. 1, 283.
21. Ibid., 90.
22. Two recent accounts of the rallies of the sub-Saharan African territories may be found in: Jean-Louis Crémieux-Brilhac, *La France Libre: De l'appel du 18 juin à la Libération* (Paris, 1996), 110–23, and Thomas, *French Empire at War*, 49–60.
23. One of the best accounts of these events may be found in de Gaulle, *Mémoires*, vol. 1, 90–95.
24. British Consul, Duala, to foreign office, 28 July 40, in de Gaulle, *Mémoires*, vol. 1, 286.
25. De Gaulle, *The Complete Memoirs of Charles de Gaulle*, tr. Jonathan Griffin, (New York, 1968), 108.
26. A selection of cables with American reactions to the Free-French rallies in Africa may be found in *FRUS* 1940, vol. 2: 636–45.
27. Leopoldville to State, 25 September 1940, U.S. National Archives and Records Administration (USNARA) State Dec. File 740.0011EW/6273.
28. Gauss to State, 21 and 28 August, 3, 9, 14 and 19 September 1940, USNARA State Dec. Files, 851L.00/02, 05, and 740.0011EW 1939/5586, 5819.
29. Arthur J. Marder, *Operation Menace: the Dakar Expedition and the Dudley North Affair* (London and New York, 1976), 11–12.
30. De Gaulle, *Mémoires*, vol. 1, *l'Appel*, 98.
31. Marder, *Operation Menace*, 44–46.
32. Vichy (Huntziger) to Wiesbaden Armistice Commission, 20 September 1940 and Baudouin to Henry Haye, Washington, Ministère des Affaires Etrangères (MAE) Papiers 1940, Papiers Baudouin, vol. 3.
33. De Gaulle, *Mémoires*, vol. 1, 108.
34. Lacouture, *De Gaulle*, vol. 1, 441nn. 16,17.
35. De Gaulle telegram to de Larminat, Leclerc and Éboué, 27 September 1940 in Charles de Gaulle, *Lettres, Notes et Carnets (LNC), juin 1940-juillet 1941* (Paris, 1982), 126.
36. De Gaulle to Mme de Gaulle, 28 September 1940, ibid. 127–28.
37. De Gaulle, *Mémoires*, vol. 1, 111.
38. A. A. Berle, the assistant secretary of state, who paid homage to the "individual heroism" of De Gaulle, but then noted, "we have always recognized that France was bigger than any one man." Memorandum, 1 July 1943, USNARA State Dec. File 851.01/2352.
39. On American and French differences in political symbolism, see Philip G. Cerny, *The Politics of Grandeur: Ideological Aspects of de Gaulle's Foreign Policy* (Cambridge and New York, 1980), 31.
40. Cited in Charles G. Cogan, *Oldest Allies, Guarded Friends: The United States and France since 1940* (Westport, Conn, 1994), 12, 44.
41. Paxton, *Vichy France*, 70.
42. Crémieux-Brilhac, *La France Libre*, 138–39.
43. Henri Michel, *Histoire de la France Libre*, 4th ed. (Paris, 1980), 22.

44. Members of the Empire Defense Council included General Catroux, de Gaulle's emissary to the Middle East in Cairo; René Cassin, Captain Thierry d'Argenlieu, and Admiral Muselier in London; Colonel Edgar de Larminat, the high commissioner for Equatorial Africa, and General Medical Officer Sicé at Brazzaville, Colonel Leclerc, governor of the Cameroon, and, high commissioner for the Pacific, Governor Henri Sautot, in New Caledonia.
45. De Gaulle to Churchill, 3 February 1941, *LNC juin 1940–juillet 1941*, 247.
46. Winston Churchill, *The Second World War*, vol. 2: *Their Finest Hour* (Boston, 1948–1953), 454.
47. Harwood Blocker (vice-consul) to State, 29 June, 30 July 1940, USNARA State Dec. File 851B.00/11 and 851B/00/13.
48. Letter to General de Gaulle from Amicus Madininoe, 4 October 1940 attached to American Consul (Fort-de-France) to State, 11 October 1940, USNARA State Dec. File 851B.00/24.
49. Note to U.S. Consul, Léopoldville, *LNC juin 1940-juillet 1941*, 150–52.
50. Garreau-Dombasle to Col. Fontaine, 1 November 1940, MAE Guerre, Londres CNF, vol. 309.
51. This episode is well told from the American standpoint in Samuel Eliot Morison, *History of United States Naval Operations in World War II*, vol. 1: *The Battle of the Atlantic September 1939–May 1943* (Boston, 1950), 30–33.
52. An account of Vichy's repression in Guadaloupe may be found in Eric T. Jennings, *Vichy in the Tropics: Pétain's National Revolution in Madagascar, Guadeloupe, and Indochina, 1940–1944* (Stanford, 2001), 79–104.
53. Sommerville-Smith to Spaeght, 1 October 1940 with draft telegram, 25 September 1940, United Kingdom Public Record Office (PRO) FO 371/24343 C10826/7328/17, in Bell, *A Certain Eventuality*, 229.
54. De Gaulle to Garreau-Dombasle, 1 February 1941, *LNC juin 1940-juillet 1941*, 245–46.
55. De Gaulle to Sautot, 26 October 1940, *Mémoires*, vol. 1, 341 and same to same, 12 February 1941, MAE Guerre 1939–45 Londres CNF, vol. 79.
56. De Gaulle to Sautot, 28 January 1941, vol. 79.
57. Châtellain and M. Kollen to de Gaulle, 28 December 1940, MAE Guerre 1939–45, Londres CNF, vol. 79.
58. On 21 January 1941, the State Department asked the Vichy ambassador in Washington, Henry Haye, for a visa that would enable MacVitty to become consul in Nouméa with Perry Ellis as vice-consul; permission was granted on 17 February; Haye to Vichy, 6 April 1941, MAE Guerre 1939–45, Vichy Asie E, vol. 372.
59. De Gaulle to Col. Fontaine, 12 November 1940, MAE Guerre 1939–45, Londres CNF, vol. 309.
60. Among the works dealing with the difficulties of the Free French in America see: Julian Hurstfield, *America and the French Nation, 1939–1945* (Chapel Hill, 1986); Raoul Aglion, *De Gaulle et Roosevelt* (Paris, 1984); Guy Fritsch-Estrangin, *New York entre de Gaulle et Pétain: Les Français aux États-Unis de 1940 à 1946* (Paris, 1969), Colin Nettlebeck, *Forever French: Exile in the United States, 1939–1945* (Oxford, 1991); and Jeffrey Mehlman, *Émigré New York: French Intellectuals in Wartime Manhattan, 1940–1944* (Baltimore and London, 2000).
61. Anonymous note, 18 July 1941, MAE Guerre 1939–45, Londres CNF, vol. 309.
62. D'Argenlieu to de Gaulle, 20 April 1941, ibid.
63. Pleven to de Gaulle, 19 May 1941, ibid.
64. Minute on United States Attitude toward the Free-French Movement, Sommerville-Smith to Morton, 16 May 1941, PRO, FO 371/28320 Z3945/56/17.
65. De Gaulle to Pleven, 19 May 1941, *Mémoires*, vol. 1, 471.
66. "U.S. Relations with Free French Colonies," 22 May 1941, PRO, FO371/28320.
67. De Gaulle to Pleven, 28 May 1941, *LNC juin 1940–juillet 1941*, 341.
68. De Gaulle to Pleven, 17 May 1941, MAE Guerre 1939–45 Londres CNF, vol. 309.

69. De Gaulle to Pleven, 20 May 1941, *LNC juin 1940–juillet 1941*, 330–31. De Gaulle's suggestion that he might visit the United States if all went well was edited out of the published version, but may be found in Pleven's papers, Archives Nationales (AN) 560 AP 25 Fonds René Pleven.
70. Biddle to Franklin D. Roosevelt with enclosures, 12 May 1941, 15 May 1941, 26 May 1941, Hyde Park, FDR Library, PSF, Diplomatic Box 34.
71. Pleven to de Gaulle, 26 June 1941, MAE Guerre 1939–45, CNF vol. 309, and same to same, 1 July 1941, *Mémoires:* vol. 1, 472–74.
72. Memorandum Submitted by M. Pleven on Behalf of General de Gaulle and the Council of Defence of the French Empire, July 1941, attached to Memorandum of Conversation (Welles), 8 July 1941, *FRUS*, 1941, vol. 2, 573–78.
73. Pleven to de Gaulle, 13 July 1941, *LNC juin 1940-juillet 1941*, 474–75.
74. Hull to Mallon (Leopoldville), 8 August 1941, *FRUS* 1941, vol. 2, 578, announced Cunningham's appointment as military observer to French Equatorial Africa.
75. Pleven to de Gaulle, 31 July 1941, MAE Guerre 1939–45, CNF vol. 309, and *Mémoires*, vol. 1, 475.
76. De Gaulle to Pleven, 9 August 1941, ibid. 476–77.
77. Pleven to de Gaulle, 26 August 1941, MAE Guerre 1939–45, Londres CNF, vol. 309.
78. Mallon (Leopoldville) to Hull, 9 June 1941; same to same, 10 June 1941, and Welles to Mallon, 28 June 1941, *FRUS* 1941, vol. 2, 572–73.
79. Pleven to de Gaulle, 20 September 1941, MAE Guerre 1939–45, Londres CNF, vol. 309.
80. The demotion of Sieyès, who had become compromised in the factional fighting and touched by a financial scandal in New York, was handled gracefully by de Gaulle. The General thanked his old friend from St. Cyr (Sieyès was one of the few individuals whom de Gaulle addressed in the familiar "tu" form) for his services to the cause "in difficult times" and assigned him to General Catroux's staff in Lebanon. De Gaulle to Sieyès, 3 December 1941, *LNC juillet 1941–mai 1943*, 126.
81. W.H.B. Mack Memorandum, 29 September 1941, PRO, FO 371 282329 Z 8186/56/17, cited in Hurstfield, *America and the French Nation*, 111, which has an astute description of the calculations behind the forming of the Free-French delegation.
82. Pleven to de Gaulle, 20 September 1941, MAE Guerre 1939–45, Londres CNF, vol. 309.
83. De Gaulle to Pleven, 23 September 1941, *LNC juillet 1941–mai 1943*, 80; *Mémoires*, vol. 1, 482; and MAE Guerre 1939–45, Londres CNF, vol. 309.
84. Raoul Aglion, *De Gaulle et Roosevelt*, 36.
85. Hurstfield, *America and the French Nation*, 110–11.
86. Pleven to de Gaulle, 4 October 1941, *Mémoires*, vol. 1, 484–85, and AN 560 AP 25 Fonds René Pleven.
87. Pleven to Atherton, 4 November 1941, MAE Guerre 1939–45, Londres CNF, vol. 309.
88. De Gaulle to Pleven, 11 November 1941, *Mémoires*, vol. 1, 479–80.
89. De Gaulle to Pleven, 11 November 1941, AN Papiers Cassin 382 AP51.
90. De Gaulle to Pleven, 22 September 1941, *Mémoires*, vol. 1 *l'Appel*, 481–82.
91. MacVitty to State, 8 September 1941, USNARA State Dec. File 851L.20/7.

CHAPTER 2

THE NEW CALEDONIAN RALLY TO THE FREE FRENCH

News from metropolitan France always arrived late in New Caledonia. No direct connection linked France with the colony since cables from metropolitan France passed through either Australia or Saigon, and the Caledonian day began eleven hours ahead of Paris. Reports of the German invasion of Poland and the French and British declarations of war in September 1939 reached New Caledonia after a day's time delay. The news was relayed over Nouméa's low watt radio station that an amateur radio enthusiast, Charles Gaveau, had set up in his residence on the rue d'Alma to provide local information, music and sports results.[1] Having heard the declaration of war, the Caledonians responded patriotically to the call to arms.

During the First World War a number of Kanak (Melanesian) and French Caledonians had served in Europe. Losses had been heavy during that conflict. Twenty-three percent of those who had gone to the front in Europe never returned home. Despite this tragic experience, the Caledonians were determined to assume their responsibility in this new conflict and make whatever contribution they could to a victory over the Germans. A partial mobilization of ten eligible classes placed 800 reservists in uniform to join the regular garrison in anticipation of a defense of the island, or possibly to form an expeditionary force for service in the European theater.

On 20 October 1939 a new governor, Georges Pélicier, arrived in Nouméa and was given an enthusiastic welcome. Measures were taken in the name of defense and security. The government imposed a surtax upon exports, as high as 20 percent for iron ore, which was shipped exclusively to Japan, for the purchase of armaments.[2] All exporters had to secure separate licenses for each transaction and had to guarantee that goods would not reach enemy ports. The government confiscated firearms owned by foreigners.[3] A decree forbade speaking any foreign language on the telephone, a ban that was subsequently lifted for those who used English. Foreigners had to register with the police and could not travel outside Nouméa or the villages of their residence without obtaining permission three weeks in advance of the proposed travel. Taxes on foreign residents increased from 125 to 300 French Pacific francs per year (ca. $3.00-7.00).[4] Although there was little that could be done to influence the war in Europe, the French in the South Pacific were confident of victory.

Following the defeat of Poland in September 1939 ensued a phony war on the western front in Europe in which the expected German attack failed to materialize. As this phony war dragged along, Caledonians began to grumble about requisitions, shortages and hoarding, soaring meat prices, and the inadequate state of the island's defenses. The latter consisted of four antiquated cannons of an 1892 model that provided minimal coastal defense and offered no protection from an air attack. Caledonians considered the absence of any means of self-defense to be another example of the French colonial administration's neglect and attitude toward a colony often described as the French "orphan of the Pacific."

In September 1938, the general council had expressed its alarm over the lack of any meaningful coastal defense and had deplored the absence of a naval warship stationed in Nouméa. In August 1939 under pressure from a colonial inspector, the general council agreed to raise Fr32 million in local taxes over two

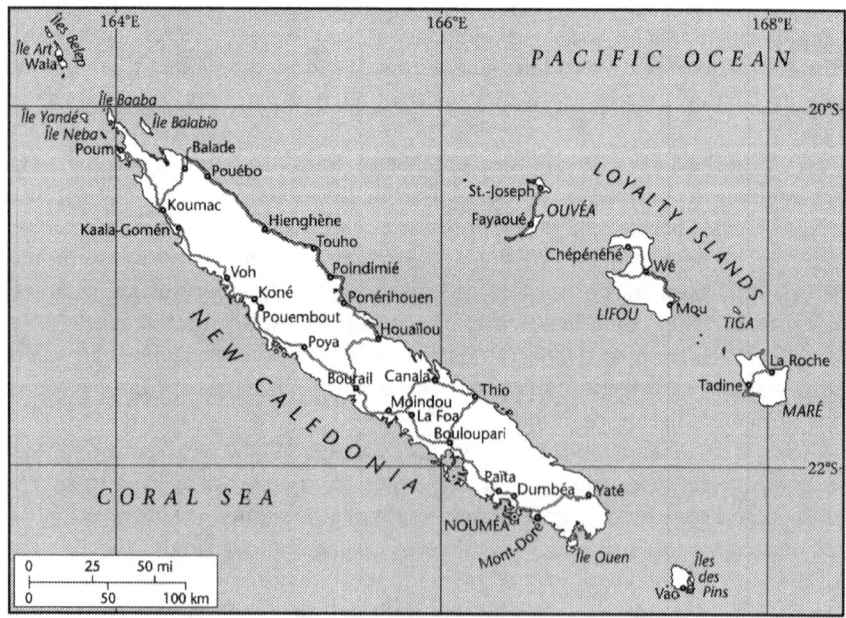

Map 1. New Caledonia.
Source. Cartography Lab, University of Minnesota.

years to improve coastal defenses, but nothing had been done when the war broke out within three weeks of this decision, and the colonial inspector returned to France.[5] War taxes were voted and imposed, but the Caledonians could expect no military reinforcement or support from a beleaguered home government. A familiar gulf between the Caledonians and representatives of centralized French authority reemerged under the strains and anxieties of the phony war. The Caledonians had to fend for themselves. Local authorities had to find customers for nickel ore, the backbone of the Caledonian economy, to replace Germany, which had been a major purchaser before the war. Nickel exports were essential to provide the foreign exchange necessary to purchase imported food and other goods that could no longer be obtained from France. And Le Nickel was a major employer on the island. Anxieties increased with news of France's collapse in May and June 1940.

The first indication of military disaster in Europe came on 15 June 1940. A radio broadcast from Australia announced the German armored breakout from the Ardennes forest, described the cutting off of the British Expeditionary Force and French army units in the north, and reported the subsequent evacuation from Dunkirk. The report also included rumors of an armistice, which were confirmed on 23 June. That afternoon Governor Pélicier hastily called a meeting of all general councilors from the Nouméa region and informed them of his intention to continue the war at the side of the British Commonwealth. The council concurred, although Florindo Paladini, a councilman who also happened to be a leader of the local communist party and a large landowner, urged that New Caledonia place itself under the protection of the United States.[6] Another council member, G.L. Ley, recommended that any decision be postponed until the situation was clarified. This was also the initial position of the general secretary of the colony, André Bayardelle, who was concerned about prospects for the island's mineral exports and its economic future.[7] At the same time, James Daly, president of the veterans' association, cabled Prime Minister Robert Menzies in Australia to assure him of the veterans' desire to continue the struggle against Germany.[8]

The Caledonians were astonished by and outraged about the rumors that circulated in the aftermath of the French collapse in Europe. News of military disaster and capitulation brought a crowd into the streets of Nouméa. The demonstrators gathered outside the Town Hall on 23 June to insist that the war be continued at the side of the British Empire. The next day an estimated five thousand Caledonians, carrying French and British flags, assembled at the war memorial and drew up a petition that asked the council to adopt a resolution that would reject the armistice and support continued resistance.[9] Governor Pélicier responded sympathetically to the crowd's demands. From his perspective, New Caledonia had no choice but to continue its commitment to the British Commonwealth. When news of the defeat reached the interior of the island, Georges Baudoux, a surveyor who assumed that the government would transfer to Algeria and would continue the struggle from there, exclaimed, "No, France has not been defeated, she has been betrayed!"[10] This reaction reflected disbelief over the sudden capitulation and an expectation that the unconquered empire might provide the base for redeeming the defeat in Europe. Rumors circulated that Algeria, Morocco and Tunisia would continue to resist along with Syria and Indochina. On the 21st news that General Mittelhauser in Syria intended to continue fighting reached New Caledonia, and reports from Indochina indicated that General Catroux was committed to continued resistance in that colony. The legend of a 100 million person French Empire so vigorously promoted by French imperial apologists would now be tested. Would the empire and New Caledonia in its modest way become the source for a recovery and renewal of a fallen France? Such was the excited hope of French patriots and colonists overseas, but the signing of Marshal Pétain's armistice, which removed the empire from the war and imposed metropolitan control and neutrality upon all French overseas territories, dashed these hopes.

Disunity in Local Allegiances and Foreign Interests

Soon after the armistice the British Government offered support to those French colonies that might continue to resist the Germans, and Governor Pélicier expressed his gratitude to Australian Prime Minister Menzies for his assistance and promised "to continue the struggle by the side of the British Empire."[11] He admitted that the colony's "helpless situation" meant a continuing relationship with Australia was necessary, but he also expressed "the grave fears he had of interference by another power since the capitulation of the Mother Country."[12] Pélicier's concern over foreign dominance revealed a deep-seated fear among French colonial administrators that the British Commonwealth would exploit the French military defeat for the benefit of the British Empire.

In the meantime the crowd in the streets of Nouméa demanded that the administration commit New Caledonia to continuing the struggle. Pélicier assembled the general council, which unanimously passed a resolution to continue the war and cooperate with British allies. Among the motives that inspired this resolution was a fear that Germany, as part of the armistice agreement, might insist upon a special position for Japan in Indochina, New Caledonia and the New Hebrides. Despite concerns over potential British domination, most Caledonians feared Japanese economic and political ambitions in New Caledonia even more. Telegrams announcing the council's resolution were promptly sent to New Zealand and Australia, and following the announcement the Nouméan crowd marched to the British consul's residence where "La Marseillaise" and "God Save the King" were given rousing renditions.[13]

Michel Vergès, an ambitious lawyer who had his own ideas about the future organization of the colony and who should lead it, drew up a petition with two associates, André Prinet and Émile Moulédous, that called for local autonomy for the island and the election of an assembly to run its affairs for the duration of the war. The name of his political party, the Autonomist Constitutional Reform Party, revealed the lawyer's objective. Vergès also sought to gain support from the frontier farmers of the interior, or Broussards. The Vergès-Prinet-Mouledous petition made no mention of de Gaulle or his call for resistance, which had reached the island by this time. Eventually the petition obtained 1,100 signatures and was presented to the general council at its meeting on 24 July. Two days later the council unanimously passed a resolution that called for the creation of an elected assembly that would, "represent the dynamic forces and the will of the Caledonian population without exception."[14] The move for New Caledonian autonomy and defiance of Vichy and the armistice had gathered momentum under Michel Vergès's energetic push.

The resolution of 26 July reflected a growing suspicion on the part of the Caledonian population that the French administration on the island was beginning to waver in its commitment to continuing the war. There was good reason for this suspicion. A test of true patriotism from a Caledonian perspective had occurred on Bastille Day when the veterans' organization held its traditional parade and ceremony at the war memorial in Nouméa. A large, enthusiastic and patriotic crowd gathered for this occasion, but no representative from the administration appeared. The crowd then marched to the Government House and insisted that someone come out and address them. No one was available. Governor Pélicier had decided to go for a solitary walk along the beach at Anse Vata to contemplate the difficult choices that confronted him. The crowd then moved on to the general secretary's residence and demanded a speech for the occasion. Secretary André Bayardelle, who was present, refused to provide it and remained indoors. The Caledonians began to question the administration's pledge to continue the struggle.

On 21 July a cable arrived in Nouméa from Vichy that required publication of Marshal Pétain's constitutional decrees. A second telegram arrived shortly thereafter ordering all ties with Great Britain terminated; anyone who refused to do so would be mercilessly condemned. Pélicier was crushed by this news and desperately replied to France that a break with Australia would mean famine, unemployment and social unrest for the island, since Le Nickel's smelters at Doniambo depended upon imports of Australian coal to continue operations. New Caledonia, he insisted, had no other choice but to maintain relations with neighboring states of the Commonwealth. He noted that the Caledonians feared the alternative would be increased dependency and eventual domination by Japan.

According to the Vichy minister for colonies, Henry Lémery, there was no Japanese danger. The threat came from Australia, and he warned Pélicier of the threat of British intervention in New Caledonia. The colonial ministry forbade any foreign-policy initiatives without Vichy's approval.[15] Pélicier revealed none of this exchange to the general council, which had reaffirmed its determination to continue the struggle and seek assistance from Australia if necessary.[16]

Caught between the growing independence of the local council and the demands of Vichy, Pélicier became desperate. He cabled Vichy that not only his own authority but that of all colonial officials had been challenged in an unacceptable way. He assured Vichy that he was taking all precautions, but he warned that the local population remained extremely nervous in the face of a potential Japanese threat, and he stated that he had established contacts with Australia to obtain assistance and provisions. He assured his superiors, "In any case we will fight to keep New Caledonia French."[17] The governor faced an insoluble dilemma.

The conflict between the governor and the Caledonians intensified when Pélicier published Pétain's decrees on 29 July. This action provoked an angry response in Nouméa among the population of the capital and within the general council itself. The general council met again on 2 August to express its disapproval of the decrees and decided to contact General de Gaulle. Once more a crowd appeared in the streets of Nouméa, shouting its displeasure at Pélicier's actions. A few days later Governor Pélicier warned the Caledonians that the street demonstrations and disorders were misguided. He called for an end to such disruptions and urged that the people place their trust and confidence in him. If Vichy policies caused difficulties, he promised to try to get them changed.[18]

Suspecting Pélicier and his maneuvers, the Broussards of the interior called for a break with Vichy. They began circulating their own petition for a national rally to the Gaullist movement, not an autonomist movement that would serve the local ambitions of certain political leaders, notably Michel Vergès whom they distrusted. They preferred a calm rally behind a national leader and not what Georges Baudoux described as a ruckus, which would result from the showdown that Vergès and his supporters seemed to favor.[19] News of the rally of the New Hebrides under the leadership of the French Commissioner Henri Sautot had reached New Caledonia by this time, and it was this sort of rally that the Gaullists of the interior preferred. Baudoux wrote to a friend and fellow surveyor, Georges Dubois, in Nouméa to report on the growing support for a rally to de Gaulle that was spreading through the interior. Dubois was popular and trusted by the Broussards. Furthermore, Dubois was a respected member of the veterans' organization who held a reserve commission of lieutenant in the French Army.

Another important addition to the growing Gaullist movement was the politically influential Pierre Bergès, a coffee grower from La Foa, a town some seventy miles northwest of Nouméa. Bergès welcomed the news from the interior, but he argued that the center of the movement and its leadership had to be in Nouméa, where the crucial test and rally would take place, no doubt with support from the Broussards. He wrote to Baudoux that a Gaullist movement was being formed in the capital, composed of "honorable and serious men," who wished to bring about a rally of the island. He reported that cables had already been sent to de Gaulle in London, and they were awaiting instructions.

Already two local patriots, Charles Châtellain and Marcel Kollen, had sent General de Gaulle a letter in which they described the events of the Bastille day celebration and explained the island's economic dependence upon mineral exports. They warned that the land of the rising sun might take over New Caledonia in order to obtain a monopoly of its mineral resources. They asked that de Gaulle urge the Australians to purchase the island's exports in order to counteract the influence of those who wished to strengthen economic ties with Japan.[20] De Gaulle thanked his correspondents for their information, and he urged that they form a committee for French resistance. He promised that he would contact the British and Dominion governments to seek their support.[21]

Following the demonstration on 2 August, Raymond Pognon, a former planter and businessman, wrote to de Gaulle. Not trusting the local censorship, Pognon sent his letters by way of the PanAm clipper service for delivery to his sister in Sydney to be forwarded to de Gaulle in London. In his letters Pognon argued that the Caledonians were fed up with Pélicier's maneuvers, did not recognize Vichy's authority and wished to follow de Gaulle's lead and continue the war effort. Pognon concluded that the Gaullists had to take control of the colonial government and administration. His messages eventually reached de Gaulle in London, but not until nearly a month had passed.[22] Despite these individual efforts and General de Gaulle's urging, a unified Gaullist organization in Nouméa still had not been formed by late August.

In the meantime, anger over Governor Pelicier's double game violently manifested itself on the evening of 18 August when dynamite exploded in the garden of the governor's residence. No one was injured by the blast, but this apparent assassination attempt had so badly shaken Governor Pélicier that he was on the verge of a nervous breakdown. His state of mind scarcely improved when a member of the general council warned him that his and his family's lives were in danger if they remained in New Caledonia.[23] By this time the gulf between colonial officials from metropolitan France and the Caledonian settlers was becoming both obvious and dangerous.

The governor cabled Vichy with a description of the bomb explosion and reported that the demonstration of 2 August had been marked by violence and reflected a hostile mood among the Caledonians. He feared new incidents might occur at any moment. The frightened governor cabled, "I insist that you provide necessary support as soon as possible without which I cannot guarantee the internal security of the colony."[24] The colonial ministry assured Pélicier that help was on the way, and on 23 August *Dumont d'Urville* under Commander Toussaint de Quièvrecourt, an ardent and tough-minded Pétainist, arrived in Nouméa harbor. Although this Vichy warship briefly restored calm to the island's capital, its docking eventually provoked a crisis that led to the colony's rally to the Free-French cause.

While events moved toward a confrontation in New Caledonia, the Australian Government had become concerned about the situation on the island but hoped that the issue of New Caledonia's allegiance could be resolved without any active Australian intervention. This attitude revealed considerable ignorance about affairs on the neighboring French colony and reflected the absence of any official contact in relations between New Caledonia and the government of the British Commonwealth before the war. Australia had no official representative on the island after the recall of the consul in 1922.

There was an economic link with Australia in the purchase of coal to fuel the nickel smelters at Doniambo, but restrictive French tariff policies meant that the bulk of New Caledonia's imports and exports were with France or other parts of the French Empire. As for security matters, New Caledonia did not figure in Australian defense plans before the war, and even during the phony war there had been no formal contact between the governments of New Caledonia and Australia, neither on matters of common defense nor on economic policy.[25]

The French collapse and armistice had led to the first serious discussion in Canberra of developments on the island. The Australian Government, like the Caledonians, feared that armistice terms might have awarded special rights for Japan in Indochina, New Caledonia and the New Hebrides. A Japanese presence in New Caledonia, less than 1,100 miles from Brisbane, would pose a security problem for Australia since most of the Australian fleet had departed for the Mediterranean theater. The chief of staff of the Australian Navy noted that the French Pacific islands could not be defended against Japan should Australia decide to occupy them or place them under a protectorate. The Australians hoped that the United States might warn Japan against any intervention in New Caledonia, as it had with the Netherlands East Indies. Vulnerability in the face of Japanese naval power meant that the Australian Government was reluctant to assume the added burden of New Caledonia's defense. Concerned with a possible Japanese intervention in New Caledonia, Canberra cabled the dominion office in London for advice.[26]

The British Government replied that the limited resources of the empire prevented an occupation of even a portion of the French Empire, although all efforts were to be made to encourage continued resistance by French colonial forces. As for the Pacific, the British agreed that the only meaningful deterrent would be a statement from the United States Government that any alteration of the status quo would be considered a cause for war.[27] R.G. Casey, the Australian minister in Washington, asked if the United States Government would be interested in making a declaration that would call for the maintenance of the status quo in New Caledonia and other French Pacific islands. Two weeks later, Sumner Welles replied that the United States would find that any statement concerning New Caledonia would embarrass the administration.[28] The United States declined to take any action or offer any guarantees.

In the absence of an American assurance, the Commonwealth proposed trade agreements to New Caledonia and Tahiti with the caveat that nothing be done to give complaint to the Japanese and their trading interests. Shortly after the armistice the Australian and New Zealand Governments sent telegrams of sympathy and support to the governor of New Caledonia but made no offers of military assistance. Australia wished to preserve good relations and keep the French Pacific Empire in the struggle without offending the Japanese Government or offering an excuse for Japanese intervention in the South and Southwest Pacific. Prime Minister Menzies carefully backed away from any suggestion that the Australian Government wished to interfere in the political status of New Caledonia.[29] These exchanges took place in June. By August the climate had changed significantly.

In a conversation with the American minister in Canberra, Foreign Minister McEwen reported that the situation in New Caledonia was deteriorating rapidly.[30] The governor and general secretary treated the newly arrived Japanese consul, Takitaro Kuroki, with great deference. The British consul was no longer exempt from the island's tax on foreign residents, although the Japanese consul and his staff had been given this customary exemption. The governor was reputedly ready to offer the Japanese an opportunity to purchase up to 25,000 tons of nickel ore, and by publishing Marshal Pétain's constitutional decrees, Pélicier gave every indication of obedience to Vichy. In these circumstances the Australian Government decided to send a consul to Nouméa. Although the Australian consul's assignment in New Caledonia was ostensibly economic and commercial, the American minister in Australia noted that it would also be increasingly political.[31]

The choice for the Australian consul in Nouméa was B.C. Ballard, a lawyer who had represented Australian interests in the New Hebrides since 1934 and was fluent in French. He proved to be an excellent choice for a difficult assignment. Ballard's instructions reflected the dilemma of Australian policy toward New Caledonia. He was to determine the attitudes of officials, the general council, and the Caledonians toward both Vichy and General de Gaulle's movement. As for overall policy, his instructions summarized the Australian Government's attempt to have a friendly government in Nouméa without provoking trouble with Japan or causing a break with Vichy,

> Every effort is to be made to ensure continuation in New Caledonia of the desire to work with the British Empire in general and the Commonwealth of Australia in particular for the defeat of Germany, but this is to be done by avoiding as far as possible any public activity which could be interpreted as political rather than commercial in character. General stress is to be laid publicly upon trading relationships between New Caledonia and Australia. It is desired to avoid any activity or statement which would make it appear that the Commonwealth wishes to interfere with the maintenance of the political status quo in New Caledonia; otherwise an excuse may be given to Japan for interference in the maintenance of the political status quo of other areas in the Pacific or even in New Caledonia itself.[32]

Ballard received these prudent instructions on 8 August 1940, and on the sixteenth he embarked for Nouméa.

While the Australians cautiously watched the situation, the British Government edged toward favoring a rally to the Gaullist movement in New Caledonia. Sir Harry Luke, the British high commissioner for the Western Pacific in Fiji, had received reports of the 2 August demonstration on the island. Luke concluded that time had come for de Gaulle to send out a warship with Free-French officials to take over the administration: "Otherwise, the influence of the Pétain Government may prove too strong."[33] London agreed and forwarded this recommendation to Canberra. Also, British intelligence had determined that the Japanese consul in Nouméa had been instructed to secure all nickel production on the island.[34] Still uneasy about mixing in local politics, the Australian Government refused to take any action until Ballard had an opportunity to report on developments in New Caledonia.[35]

When Ballard arrived in New Caledonia, he discovered a tense political climate. Pélicier knew that Ballard's presence would cause him trouble with Vichy authorities. At the last minute Pélicier tried to delay Ballard's arrival.[36] At the same time, the island appeared to be in military peril. For three days from 14–16 August a German surface raider, *Orion*, appeared off the southern coast of New Caledonia. A showdown between the various pro-de Gaulle factions and Vichy authorities was rapidly approaching as a result of Vichy's hostility toward Great Britain and the Commonwealth.

Shortly after his arrival, Ballard realized that a choice between Vichy and de Gaulle was rapidly approaching. Popular opinion favored de Gaulle and a continuation of the war effort, but any rally to the Free French would have to begin with the removal of the pro-Vichy officials and military leaders. Careful planning and coordinated action on the part of the Gaullists was essential. The most serious problem was the presence of the Vichy gunboat, *Dumont d'Urville*, in Nouméa harbor. Toussaint de Quièvrecourt was determined to end the vacillation and disorders on the island, and he was firmly loyal to Vichy. Any attempt to bring New Caledonia to join the Free French would have to begin by neutralizing *Dumont d'Urville*.

The Political Showdown Begins

The showdown quickly arrived. On 25 August Vichy's minister of colonies instructed Pélicier to reserve all of New Caledonia's mineral production for the Japanese.[37] This order put Pélicier on the spot, since the governor earlier had obtained Australia's formal commitment to take a large portion of the colony's nickel production. Alfred Rapadzi, the acting head of Société Le Nickel, was fully aware of his company's dependence upon Australian coal. He was also president of the general council and increasingly inclined toward a rally behind General de Gaulle. Under Rapadzi's influence the council decided to ask for the removal of Governor Pélicier. The council suggested that for his own safety the governor should consider leaving the island. When Pélicier seemed uncertain as to his action, the council met with Vergès, Mouládous and Prinet, the authors of the original petition to continue the war, on 28 August. After a discussion of the situation the council unanimously passed a resolution that asked for the governor's recall. A cable to this effect was sent to Vichy.[38]

Pélicier also had lost the confidence of Toussaint de Quièvrecourt, who deplored Pélicier's failure to annul the pro-Gaullist decisions of the council. Despite concessions to the local population, Quièvrecourt reported, events had by-passed the governor, who had lost control of the situation, and he remained unpopular with the Caledonians.[39] The officers of *Dumont d'Urville* shared their commander's view, contemptuously referring to Governor Pélicier as "a wet noodle."[40] Quièvrecourt cabled Vichy and asked that the governor be replaced. He threatened to remove Pélicier from office on his own initiative if Vichy did not reply quickly.[41]

The next day a return message from Vichy via Saigon appointed the commander of the regular military garrison, Lieutenant Colonel Maurice Denis, interim governor in place of the disgraced Pélicier. Vichy instructed Denis to bring order to a population that had fallen under foreign influences, and he was to establish tighter control over the local press.[42] Colonel Denis, backed by Commander Quièvrecourt, assumed effective control of the island on the eve of the visit to Nouméa of Sir Harry Luke, British governor of Fiji and high commissioner for the Western Pacific, scheduled for 30–31 August.

As a British observer later remarked, "Sir Harry had a way of arriving—merely en route from somewhere else—at every opportune moment."[43] His official French hosts received this emissary of the British Empire with a studious and frosty correctness. Although Governor Pélicier had extended an invitation to the British high commissioner to visit New Caledonia, French officials tried to discourage the visit at the last minute by denying landing rights to Sir Harry's seaplane. Despite this rebuff, Sir Harry decided to visit Nouméa anyway, and he arrived on board his official yacht, *Viti,* at noon on 30 August.[44] A large and enthusiastic crowd of Caledonians, who waved Free-French and British flags and sang patriotic songs, welcomed him at the municipal dock.

His official welcome was far less cordial. Much to his surprise, Sir Harry discovered the presence of *Dumont d'Urville* in Nouméa harbor and found that Colonel Denis had replaced Pélicier as governor. Quièvrecourt made a courtesy call on board *Viti* where he delivered what Sir Harry Luke described as a furious onslaught on de Gaulle whom he denounced as an adventurer. Confronted with the unwanted presence of the British high commissioner for the Western Pacific, French authorities quickly arranged an official dinner that evening at which the atmosphere was glacial.[45]

Sir Harry realized that Denis was even more loyal to Vichy than his predecessor, but was uncertain that any fundamental shift in policy was likely at least in the short term. The next day he received a delegation from the general council, which expressed its displeasure at the pro-Vichy stand of Colonel Denis and Commander Quièvrecourt. They feared that the various resolutions of the council would be ignored by the new regime. The council reaffirmed its solidarity with Great Britain and General de Gaulle, and they informed Sir Harry that a majority of the Caledonians wished to obtain an autonomous status for the colony with only a nominal link to France during the war. Sir Harry warned the council members to proceed cautiously in view of the strongly held views of *Dumont d'Urville's* commanding officer on this subject.

Later that morning a crowd of 2,000 gathered at the dock to sing the "Marseillaise" and "God Save the King" in what was now becoming a ritualized performance that more than implied impatience with the colony's administration. After this meeting, Quièvrecourt did not mince words. He threatened to detain all British ships in the harbor, and Sir Harry took the hint and hastily left New Caledonia for the Anglo-French condominium in the New Hebrides where the French resident, Henri Sautot, had already rallied to the Free French.[46] In this more hospitable environment, Sir Harry Luke began to contemplate the need for firm action in New Caledonia.

When Sir Harry Luke reached Port Vila on 3 September, he found a series of telegrams awaiting him. They showed London and Canberra engaged in a frantic diplomatic scramble over the issue of New Caledonia and its allegiance, an exchange of messages that would bring about a decisive change in Australian policy toward New Caledonia. Halfway around the world events were producing a British decision to seek Australian intervention in the affairs of the French colony.

By the end of August de Gaulle concluded that the moment to rally New Caledonia had arrived. On 10 August he warned Henri Sautot that he might be called upon to do so. De Gaulle informed Churchill of the parade and demonstration that had taken place in New Caledonia on 14 July, and he sent the prime minister copies of the petitions that called for a continuation of the war. On 23 August de Gaulle ordered Sautot to go to New Caledonia and rally the population to the Free-French cause, replacing Pélicier as governor of the colony.[47] On the 28th de Gaulle formally requested that the British Commonwealth provide a warship to transport Sautot to Nouméa where he anticipated a bloodless coup could be accomplished. The same day he instructed Pognon in Nouméa to get in contact with Sautot as soon as possible.[48]

The British war cabinet discussed New Caledonia and agreed to support the Gaullist movement, despite lingering Australian reservations about becoming involved in the political affairs of the colony. Officials in London decided that as long as *Dumont d'Urville* remained in harbor the pro-Gaullist majority in New Caledonia would be compelled to adhere to Vichy's directives. Intervention could not be avoided.[49] The British Government requested that an Australian cruiser, H.M.A.S. *Adelaide*, be made available to accompany Sautot to New Caledonia, and on 2 September *Adelaide* sailed for Port Vila in the New Hebrides.[50] Its commander, Captain Henry A. Showers, was to refrain from any use of force. The Australians hoped that the presence of the warship would encourage the pro-Gaullist party on the island and compel Vichy officials to accept a peaceful transfer of power.

The choice of *Adelaide* and the presence of Captain Showers in command of the light cruiser proved to be a good one. At the time of the assignment, though, uncertainty about *Adelaide*'s successful fulfillment of this mission was considerable. Most of Australia's first-line warships had departed for the Mediterranean or the Atlantic, leaving *Adelaide* as one of a handful of ships protecting Australian waters. The cruiser's age was apparent, despite the improvements carried out during its recommissioning in 1938/9. *Adelaide* had been built in 1922 based on a 1908 design and was armed with six-inch guns that officers aboard described as one stage removed from muzzle-loaders.[51] Nevertheless, it was thought that *Adelaide* would outgun and intimidate the more modern but less heavily armed French sloop, *Dumont d'Urville,* which had been commissioned in 1932. Whatever the deficiencies of *Adelaide* as a modern warship, they were more than compensated by the qualities of Captain Showers, who proved himself to be a skilled diplomat whose steady judgment and nerves would be tested in assisting the rally of New Caledonia to the Gaullist cause.

When Showers reached Port Vila on 7 September, his assignment had not yet been confirmed. During *Adelaide*'s passage from Australia diplomatic cables between Canberra and London continued to weigh the risks of active intervention. The cautious Australian ministry for external affairs, still fearful of Japanese complications, persuaded Menzies to hold Showers in port awaiting further instructions.[52] On the other hand, Ballard in Nouméa was convinced that if the attempt were not made, Vichy supporters would consolidate their position and play into the hands of the Japanese and to the disadvantage of the Commonwealth. The British Government had intercepted a radio message from Vichy to Nouméa in which Denis had been ordered to restore a pro-Vichy attitude among the population by temporarily withholding punitive action against the autonomist leaders but to crack down once the crisis had passed.[53]

To reinforce Vichy authority in New Caledonia, the French warship, *Amiral Charner,* was preparing to sail from Saigon.[54] Ballard reported that the arrival of a representative of de Gaulle would be welcomed by a strong majority of the population, although the feeling would not be unanimous. He concluded that the risk in favor of the Gaullist solution was the preferable one.[55] Sir Harry Luke, who had returned to Fiji, agreed that prompt action was necessary.[56]

Optimism soared in London. Much of the French Empire appeared on the verge of rallying to the Free-French cause. The British Government noted "a great and growing basis of pro-de Gaulle feeling in other territories" such as French Equatorial Africa, Cameroon and the French Congo, which had rallied at the end of August. French Guyana and at least part of French West Africa were expected to rally while similar tendencies could be found in North Africa, Syria and the Antilles.[57] In the Pacific Tahiti already had voted overwhelmingly to join the Free French on 3 September. With French Oceania and the New Hebrides in the

Gaullist camp New Caledonia appeared ready to follow suit. By the late summer of 1940 a number of French colonial dominoes were falling in General de Gaulle's favor.

The Australians agreed to intervene when Ballard warned that the situation was getting out of hand.[58] In cooperation with R.D. Blandy, the British resident in the New Hebrides, Showers drew up a plan for escorting Sautot to Nouméa.[59] Sautot would be carried on a Norwegian tanker, *Norden*, accompanied by *Adelaide* to avoid the appearance of a British "takeover." Captain Showers proposed that *Norden* and *Adelaide* would reach Nouméa during the morning hours of 19 September. In the meantime the Gaullists would stage a coup and gain control of Nouméa. Once the Gaullist had control of Nouméa, a boat from the Gaullist committee would rendezvous with *Norden* and take Sautot ashore. Showers would wait until eleven in the morning. If no one showed for the rendezvous, Showers would depart, leaving the Caledonians to sort out their wartime destiny.[60]

Although Sautot was only brought into these plans at the last minute, there was no doubt that he was the one French official in the Pacific who was best suited for taking the lead in a Gaullist rally of New Caledonia. Already he had shown his determination to continue the war at the side of the British Commonwealth. In rallying the French part of the Anglo-French Condominium in the New Hebrides, Sautot became the first ranking French administrator to have brought a French colony into the Gaullist camp, however modest in size that support might have been. He enjoyed great popularity and affection among the British and French residents of the New Hebrides.[61] At fifty-five and approaching retirement this paternal ruler of the French Empire did not hesitate to do what he considered to be his patriotic duty. When informed of the plans for the rally of New Caledonia and aware of the dangers and uncertainties involved, Sautot placed his considerable personal courage at the service of the French resistance. On 13 September General de Gaulle formally appointed Sautot as high resident for the French Colonies in the Pacific and governor of New Caledonia.[62] On the afternoon of 16 September Blandy came to inform his French colleague that *Norden* was scheduled to sail that evening, due to arrive in the early morning hours of the nineteenth.[63]

The two ships sailed toward an uncertain rendezvous since neither Showers nor Sautot had any idea of the reception that awaited them. The presence of *Dumont d'Urville* was a serious obstacle to the peaceful rally of New Caledonia. Sir Harry Luke had warned that Commander Quièvrecourt, whose pro-Vichy determination he had experienced at first hand, would have to be removed. The officers on board *Dumont d'Urville* felt that a rally to de Gaulle was a capitulation to perfidious Albion, which intended to use the occasion of France's humiliation to lay hands upon the weakened outposts of the French Empire. The second officer aboard *Dumont d'Urville* later described the crowd in Nouméa as "a band of agitators paid by Australia."[64] Much depended upon the skills of the Gaullists on the island, for Showers had orders to avoid the use of force to impose Sautot. It was up to the band of agitators to gain control of the town.

There was some hope that the Gaullists might be able to prepare the way for Sautot's arrival. The day before *Adelaide* appeared, Maurice Houssard, a representative of the Vergès group in Nouméa, arrived in Port Vila where he announced that a de Gaulle committee had been formed in New Caledonia. He revealed that Vergès and his associates planned to kidnap Governor Denis and take over *Dumont d'Urville*. Houssard optimistically claimed that half of the crew of the warship was sympathetic to the Gaullist cause and would rally in defiance of their commander.[65] Preparations were under way and Sautot was expected.

While British and Australian diplomatic cables had been discussing what to do about New Caledonia, the settlers had moved to action. Although the departure of Pélicier on a PanAm clipper in the early morning hours of 4 September had momentarily calmed the crowd in Nouméa, the atmosphere of the colony remained tense. Soon the crowd was in the streets again. The dismissal of Pélicier and his replacement by the ardent Vichyite, Colonel Denis, meant that the Caledonians had to move quickly before Vichy authority became consolidated on the island.

Quièvrecourt was prepared to meet the local challenge. He warned his superiors in France that agitation had resumed and a de Gaulle committee was being formed. The commander of *Dumont d'Urville* feared that interim governor Denis was not up to the task of holding the islanders loyal to Vichy. He asked that a French admiral be dispatched to the Pacific aboard a capital ship to assert Vichy's authority.[66] One can only speculate what might have happened had someone like Admiral Georges Robert, who held Martinique firmly in the Vichy camp until June 1943, arrived to take charge of New Caledonia. Furthermore, the situation in Tahiti called for a show of force. Quièvrecourt again requested that *Amiral Charner* be dispatched from Saigon so that he could return to Papeete and restore order there.[67]

The resistors had to move quickly. At the end of August General de Gaulle instructed Raymond Pognon to assume the presidency of a committee that would rally the island to the Free-French cause. He asked that his supporters in New Caledonia get in contact immediately with Henri Sautot.[68] Unfortunately there was a delay that might have proven fatal to the rally. De Gaulle's telegram to Raymond Pognon arrived in Nouméa on 30 August but was held up for nearly a week at the request of the Australian consul, Ballard, whose government remained divided over how or to what extent it wished to become involved in the affairs of New Caledonia. Pognon did not receive his instructions until 6 September. In the meantime Michel Vergès found out about de Gaulle's instructions before Pognon did, and he exploited this information to send his own emissary, Houssard, to contact Sautot at Port Vila.[69] This contretemps would later have repercussions among those who participated in the rally when Vergès would claim that he was the leader of the Gaullist committee.

The delay in getting the message to Pognon caused him to ask that the coup be postponed, for Pognon feared that there was not enough time to organize a Gaullist plot. However, once he was informed that preparations were well along and that *Adelaide* could be in Caledonian waters for only a short time, Pognon began discussions with other opponents of the Pétainists. By the 12th they had consolidated their activities into a single Gaullist committee, and Pognon asked Georges Dubois to establish contacts with the Broussards of the interior. Whatever differences may have existed among the various Caledonian groups temporarily evaporated before the need for serious and concerted action. The Gaullist conspirators had less than a week to prepare. Pognon published an appeal for a Gaullist committee in the local papers, and he needed support from the Broussards. Baudoux and his fellow Broussards abandoned any qualms they may have had over provoking "a ruckus" and decided to act.[70]

During this time Michel Vergès put his "manic energy" to good effect, as John Lawrey has observed.[71] On the sixteenth Vergès, Prinet, Moulédous and another leader of the opposition, Edouard Rabot, issued another manifesto in which they reminded the Caledonians of the government's refusal to agree to a referendum that would permit the Caledonian population to determine its own fate for the duration of the war. Vergès called for the people of the interior to gather at six on the morning of 19 September in Nouméa and be prepared to make whatever sacrifices might be necessary to assure their liberty.[72]

The New Caledonian Coup

News of the impending coup reached the interior the next day. At eight that morning, Georges Dubois arrived at the Baudoux residence in Houaïlou. Dubois asked about Badoux's commitment to the Gaullist cause and if he were prepared to risk his life for its success. Baudoux assured him he was willing to make any sacrifice. Dubois informed him of Sautot's scheduled arrival at five in the morning of the nineteenth on board a Norwegian tanker, accompanied by an Australian cruiser. The plan was to kidnap Governor Denis and detain him until Sautot could get ashore and replace him as governor. Dubois asked Baudoux to bring five to ten Broussards into Nouméa in the early hours of the nineteenth, armed with guns and plenty of ammunition. They were to occupy the Government House and serve as guards for Sautot. The next day several Broussards brought their rifles to the Baudoux property on the pretext that they were planning a deer-hunting expedition.

That night Baudoux was asleep when a car arrived in his front yard shortly after midnight. Baudoux went out to discover Vergès in the yard. Vergès explained that the plot to abduct Denis had been discovered. "Everyone in Nouméa knows about it." He warned that if they went ahead with the existing plan, it would fail. The new plan was to hold a vast demonstration in Nouméa on the nineteenth that would compel the resignation of Denis. He asked that Baudoux persuade all of the Broussards in the region of Houaïlou to come to the capital at five on the morning of the nineteenth. Baudoux agreed, and Vergès continued his tour along the rough roads of the interior, urging the Broussards to come to Nouméa early the next morning.

A crowd of embattled farmers from the backwoods headed for Nouméa on the evening of 18/19 September armed with hunting rifles. Their assembly point was La Foa some seventy miles from Nouméa. When they arrived around eleven that evening, Baudoux and his companions discovered an enormous crowd had already gathered. Reinforced with alcoholic refreshments supplied by the house, these frontiersmen of the South Pacific were determined to win the day in Nouméa. At two in the morning of the nineteenth this boisterous crowd set off for Païta, just outside the capital where Florindo Paladini had an estate that was to serve as a headquarters and final assembly point for the assault upon Nouméa itself. When the Broussards arrived at Paladini's, they discovered that Denis had declared a state of siege and had set up a roadblock with machine guns astride the colonial highway at the bridge crossing the Salt River on the edge of Nouméa. There was no other way into town, and a bloody confrontation seemed likely. They also found out that Denis had drawn up a list of leaders who were to be arrested when they appeared at the roadblock.

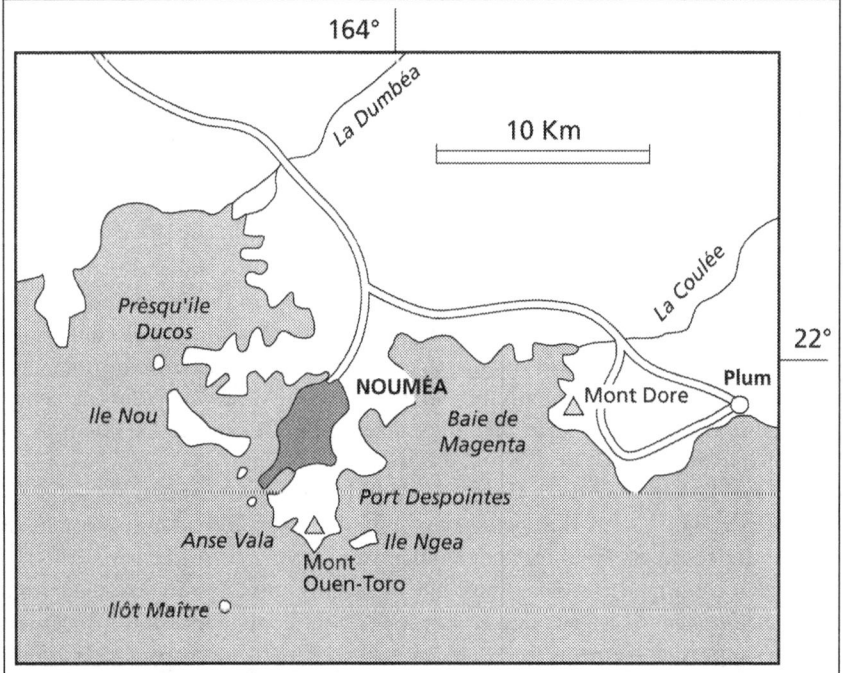

Map 2. Nouméa, New Caledonia in 1940.
Source. Territorial Archives New Caledonia.

One missing figure was Vergès, who had gone to his estate at Dumbea for a few hours rest but a car had gone to fetch him. At four thirty he appeared and asked that the crowd gather in the great room of Paladini's main house to agree upon a course of action. He advised that they leave all weapons and ammunition behind and proceed unarmed to the roadblock, insisting that they came as good citizens who should be allowed to enter Nouméa peacefully. They would be searched and if any weapons or ammunition were found, then they would be turned back or arrested. If they were refused entrance into Nouméa, then Vergès proposed that they return to Païta to set up headquarters and prepare for an armed assault upon the town. Prompt action was essential, Vergès warned, since the Australian cruiser and Governor Sautot would only wait until nine that morning. Once Sautot left with the cruiser, chances of another coup succeeding would be virtually nil. It was all or nothing on the morning of the nineteenth, and the Broussards roared their approval for making the attempt.

Baudoux and three companions led the convoy toward Nouméa, anxiously anticipating the appearance of the soldiers at the checkpoint. Five kilometers from Nouméa they were stopped. The sentries carefully went through the car and frisked the passengers. Not finding any weapons, the soldiers allowed them to pass. After going about a kilometer, Baudoux and his companions discovered that they were alone. Fearful of being caught in Nouméa without any support, they waited anxiously for their companions. Soon a truckload of Broussards arrived, then a second and a third and a fourth.

When they felt they were sufficiently numerous, the convoy continued into Nouméa where the residents came out of their homes to greet them, running alongside the truckloads of Broussards or jumping on the running boards. This convoy of vehicles and excited Caledonians arrived at the Hôtel du Pacifique where a crowd had assembled. The new arrivals received an enthusiastic welcome. The crowd, now swollen to some 3,000 people, abandoned the vehicles and proceeded on foot to the war memorial where a wreath was laid and then headed for the town hall where they hoped to send a message to the commander of the Australian cruiser steaming in the outer harbor. They still did not control the town, and they wanted to delay the departure of Sautot and *Adelaide* until they did and could welcome him ashore. No one knew the *Adelaide's* radio frequency, so a group of volunteers scrambled up semaphore hill to attract the attention of the Australian cruiser.[73]

At first Showers did not see the signal. At 0615 that morning *Adelaide*, followed by *Norden*, had passed the reef through Boulari pass and rounded Amadeus lighthouse south of Nouméa that marked the approach to the harbor.[74] The Australian commander was cautious. He had been spotted by the floatplane from *Dumont d'Urville*, which had ample time to warn the commander of the Australian cruiser's approach. Knowing that *Adelaide* would arrive the next day, Quièvrecourt moored *Dumont d'Urville* with the ship's fore-deck guns trained on the harbor. Showers also feared that the coastal artillery might open fire. He looked for a signal that the town was in the hands of the Gaullists, but the only boat to approach *Adelaide* was a motor launch from *Dumont d'Urville*, which had been sent out by Quièvrecourt to determine Showers's intentions and warn him not to enter the harbor. If he could get aboard *Norden*, First Officer Laveissière had instructions to arrest Sautot.[75]

Showers wisely avoided making any contact with Laveissière's launch and drew next to *Norden* to prevent the launch from reaching the tanker. Showers then spotted the signal station, which was flying a Gaullist flag that signaled "You must not enter harbor," indicating that the Gaullists did not yet have control of the town. Another boat appeared shortly afterward, which was from the Gaullist committee. This delegation informed Showers that Vichy forces, backed by sailors of *Dumont d'Urville*, still controlled the port, the town and all roads four miles beyond. Martial law had been declared the previous night and one member of the Gaullist committee had been arrested, but the rest of the leaders had escaped into the interior and were preparing an assault on the town. The delegate warned Showers that orders had been given for the shore batteries to fire on *Adelaide*. Despite this sobering intelligence Showers decided to hold *Norden* past the scheduled departure of 0900 in the hope that the Gaullists still might gain control of Nouméa. He intended to remain cruising offshore until 1600, at which time he would leave if there were still no sign from the Gaullists ashore.

In Nouméa pro-Vichy forces faced an increasingly difficult and potentially explosive situation. Much depended upon the actions of Colonel Denis. On the sixteenth the governor held a war council of his advisors. There was a lot of brave talk. If Sautot set foot in Nouméa, he and his supporters "would be taken care of." A burst from a well-placed machine gun would disperse "these rabbits who think they are foxes."[76] By the eighteenth the appeal to the Broussards to assemble in Nouméa had gone out. Quièvrecourt appeared at the Government House and insisted that firm measures be taken. Denis then proclaimed a state of siege for that evening, beginning at eight o'clock, and he drew up a blacklist of leaders of the Gaullist movement. Orders were given for their arrest. All businesses in Nouméa were closed. Denis ordered a military detachment, commanded by an officer from *Dumont d'Urville*, to begin patrolling the streets. Scuffles occurred as the crowd greeted the patrolling soldiers with rocks and overripe fruit. A shot was fired over the head of the demonstrators to disperse them but without effect. Another patrol established a roadblock to keep the Broussards from entering town.

By mid-morning it was clear that the crowd controlled the streets of Nouméa, but the government still commanded the military forces. Many of the soldiers were reservists, both European and Kanak, and their reliability or willingness to fire on a crowd of fellow Caledonians was uncertain. The critical test of loyalty came when the crowd learned that Vergès, Dubois and Prinet had been arrested at the roadblock when they had tried to enter town. At seven thirty Pognon, acting as head of the Gaullist committee, led the crowd down the road toward the blockade. When they arrived at the roadblock, the commander of the military detachment, Lieutenant Perrault, asked what they wanted. Pognon demanded that Vergès, Dubois and Prinet be released. Perrault then threatened to arrest Pognon, who was on Colonel Denis's list of traitors.

Gendarmes and soldiers quickly surrounded Pognon. When the crowd realized that their leader had been arrested, a scuffle ensued as the crowd began pressing against the military detachment and broke through the roadblock. Perrault asked for restraint, and Pognon made an appeal for calm to the now enraged crowd. In the midst of this excitement Perrault sent a message back to Colonel Denis with the news that he could not hold the crowd without firing upon them, and the colonial officer was uncertain that the reservists would obey his orders. Denis yielded and ordered the roadblock dismantled. The crowd cheered its victory and embraced the soldiers. Many of the reservists joined them as they marched back into town. The regular colonial forces returned to quarters. Vergès and his colleagues appeared, and the crowd jumped on the automobiles that were now careening toward the center of town in triumph.[77]

A delegation of Gaullists with Vergès as spokesman arrived at the Government House where they met with Governor Denis. They urged him to join those who were rallying to the Gaullist movement. Denis declined, but he agreed that Captain Michel would go out in a pilot launch with a delegation to bring Sautot ashore. As the delegation left, Denis began to lament that he had "betrayed his country." The crowd then marched to the main dock where the launch set off to welcome Sautot. Shortly after 1100 the launch approached *Adelaide* and, according to the pre-arranged signal, raised a tricolor with the cross of Lorraine attached. Sautot boarded the launch with difficulty as a high wind had whipped up a heavy sea. He tried to get some information from Captain Michel, but the colonial officer refused to talk to Sautot on the pretext that he was seasick.

When the launch returned to the dock, an enthusiastic crowd shouted, "Vive de Gaulle! Vive la France! Vive l'Angleterre!" Accompanied by this large, pro-de Gaulle welcoming committee, headed by the ebullient Vergès, Sautot joined the crowd in singing the Marseillaise as they marched to the Government House where a despondent Colonel Denis awaited them. Sautot entered and read Colonel Denis his instructions from de Gaulle that appointed him high commissioner for the Pacific and governor of New Caledonia. Denis threatened to arrest him as a traitor. Sautot then asked if Denis was prepared to announce his arrest to the crowd of 3,000 Caledonians, many of them now armed Broussards, who were milling outside. Denis replied that he would yield to superior force and the presence of "an enemy cruiser" in the harbor. Sautot read his proclamation to the cheering crowd, and he informed Denis that he would return at three o'clock that afternoon to formally take over the office of governor.[78] By then the bloodless coup of 19 September was complete, although there were some anxious moments ahead in the few days following.

Figure 2.1. Governor Sautot, Michel Vergès, Raymond Pognon and crowd sing the Marseillaise as they march from the dock to the Government House to rally New Caledonia to the Free French.
Source. Territorial Archives of New Caledonia.

Pro-Vichy Partisans

One problem had to do with allegiance of the colonial administrators. At five-thirty that afternoon, Sautot gathered the heads of the island's administrative services and asked them to continue at their posts for the duration of the war. He did not insist upon a submission to the Free French or an enlistment in de Gaulle's service. He wished to have a continuation of administrative services on a normal basis to avoid anarchy or any threat of social upheaval that might follow in the wake of that day's events. Speaking on behalf of the colonial administrators, Secretary Bayardelle assured Sautot that they would loyally remain at their assigned posts, that they would not become involved in political activity and that they would respect the authority of the new governor.[79] As it turned out, not all of the administration would agree to serve Governor Sautot, and several of them later asked to be sent to French Indochina.[80]

The attitude and reliability of the military was even less certain. Captain Quièvrecourt and Lieutenant Chardonnet, Colonel Denis's adjutant, remained firmly loyal to Marshal Pétain and had opposed the rally. Quièvrecourt had ordered the landing company of colonial troops back to *Dumont d'Urville* after the events of the nineteenth. These forces might intervene at any time, although the continued presence of the street crowd tempered any thoughts of using French marines to restore Vichy order in New Caledonia. The only obstacle to a counter-revolution was the presence of armed Broussards in Nouméa. Consul

Johnston reported to Showers that the backwoodsmen had been constituted into a civil guard of some 800 men, fully armed and expert shots, who had gained confidence by successfully breaking the state of siege, but they were an undisciplined force without any formal control.[81]

When many of the Broussards began returning home, Captain Showers feared that pro-Vichy military officers might try to overthrow Governor Sautot. And Captain Michel and two non-commissioned officers hatched a plot to abduct Sautot and restore Denis as governor. At the last minute, Sautot avoided a trap laid for him, and the hasty return of some 600 to 700 Broussards, who had been alerted to the plot and were armed with their trusty hunting rifles, foiled the attempted coup. Following this aborted counter-revolution, Captain Michel and the non-commissioned officers of the colonial army's regiment took refuge on board a passenger ship, *Pierre Loti*, which became a temporary residence for Vichy sympathizers awaiting deportation from New Caledonia.

Originally Captain Michel had been offered command of the colonial troops on the island, but he had refused. Of the eighty noncommissioned officers of the colonial army stationed in New Caledonia at the time, only two agreed to serve under the new regime. The rest asked to be transported to Indochina. This attitude on the part of the leaders of the colonial army caused Sautot to despair of the lost fighting spirit of the French "marines." "The spirit of General Mangin has ceased to beat in the heart of the colonial army," he lamented.[82] The unwillingness of the regular troops to serve the new regime meant that officers for the reserve forces in New Caledonia had to be found. Georges Dubois was the preferred candidate, and he was given command of the island's militia with rank of captain.

An additional problem for Sautot emerged from within the Gaullist committee where Michel Vergès intended to play a leading role in the new government and sought to implement his strongly autonomist views on its organization. He considered his own Gaullist organization to be a committee of public safety, and he wished to take drastic measures against all of those whom he considered to be political enemies and Vichy supporters. In the aftermath of the abortive coup, the crowd shouted for immediate justice against the Pétainists. They called for an extensive purge not only of military but also of the colonial administration. Secretary Bayardelle spoke against drastic measures, but his effort at moderation gained him the suspicion of the crowd. On the other hand, Bayardelle had become fearful that the crowd itself wanted a drastic social revolution. At Vergès's instigation, Bayardelle was arrested as an opponent of the rally.

The general secretary's confinement did not last long. When Sautot discovered that Bayardelle had been arrested at Vergès's initiative, he immediately ordered his release. He was encouraged to do so by Showers and the British and Australian consuls, who also feared that promises of safe-conduct for French administrators and officers who wished to be repatriated would not be respected by a crowd out of control. For his part, Sautot resented Vergès's assumption of authority and, in turn, Vergès concluded that Sautot was too soft on the old regime. This episode began what was to become a bitter quarrel between these two men, recently allies in the successful rally of the colony. The quarrel between Maître Vergès and Governor Sautot would cast a shadow over subsequent events in wartime New Caledonia.

Sautot knew that the situation was far from stable. He asked Captain Showers to remain in harbor for at least forty-eight hours until matters calmed down and arrangements could be made to deport the Pétainists. In his telegram of congratulation to Sautot de Gaulle had approved Sautot's request to deport those who refused to rally to the Free-French movement either to France or to Indochina. Many Vichy supporters already had sought refuge aboard *Pierre Loti*, and this passenger ship was to convey all who wished to leave for Saigon by way of Australia.

By this time Showers had received further instructions from the Australian Naval Board, which had become concerned about the continued presence of a Vichy French warship at Nouméa. His superiors in Melbourne informed Showers that *Dumont d'Urville* was not to be allowed to interfere with the freely expressed desire of the Caledonians to join the Free-French movement. The continued threat posed by the presence of *Dumont d'Urville* had to be removed.[83] Time was pressing, for *Amiral Charner* apparently was on its way to New Caledonia.

Much to Showers's dismay, he discovered that Sautot had no plan for compelling the departure of *Dumont d'Urville*, and he promptly dictated a letter to Captain Quièvrecourt.[84] Showers wished to avoid any conflict with the French vessel, and he expressed his willingness to resolve any differences peaceably. He invited Captain Quièvrecourt to come aboard *Adelaide* for a discussion of issues, including arrangements for the French ship's departure and the transport of all Pétainists who wished to leave the colony.[85]

The discussion between Commander Quièvrecourt and Captain Showers aboard *Adelaide* was "cordial and correct." A number of issues were discussed. They reached a tentative agreement on the departure of *Dumont d'Urville* with a stipulation that the French be allowed enough provisions for the eighteen-day voyage to Saigon and an assurance that all who wished to leave New Caledonia would be permitted to do so. Quièvrecourt cabled Vichy that the British would fight to maintain those colonies that had rallied to de Gaulle.[86] Although he had asked for reinforcements, it was clear that *Amiral Charner* would not arrive in time. On the eve of his departure Quièvrecourt thanked Showers for having intervened to secure release of those officers who had been interned and for obtaining assurance of the repatriation of all officers, men and their families who wished to leave on *Pierre Loti*.[87]

Despite relative cordiality in these negotiations, the possibility of an engagement between the two warships had not been removed. That afternoon officers of *Dumont d'Urville* learned of the conflict at Dakar in which Vichy ships had opened fire on an Anglo/Free-French expedition. A radiogram from Admiral Darlan authorized Quièvrecourt in light of these events to attack and sink the Australian cruiser if circumstances permitted. Fearing that the Australians had intercepted this message, Laveissière stood the early morning watch convinced that *Adelaide* would open fire at any moment. Nothing of the sort happened. Instead, Australian sailors on board the cruiser were sunning themselves on deck when Quièvrecourt hoisted anchor, and Showers sent no shells but signaled "Bon Voyage" as the French ship steamed out of the harbor, "in a very seamanlike manner," according to Showers's report.[88] French officers on board *Dumont d'Urville* took this gesture not as a signal of maritime courtesy and respect, as it was intended, but as Anglo-Saxon exulting over another French naval and colonial defeat.[89]

Showers still had more to do, particularly in calming belligerent spirits in Nouméa. Vergès called for a rearrest and expulsion of Bayardelle aboard *Pierre Loti,* and he insisted upon further arrests and internment of pro-Vichy suspects. Showers explained to the de Gaulle committee that as a British officer he was honor bound to fulfill the commitment he had made to Quièvrecourt to permit the departure of all who wished to sail aboard the passenger liner *Pierre Loti.* He insisted that all provocative and retaliatory speeches be curtailed in the interests of a calm resolution of the deportation issue, a clear warning to Michel Vergès. After some discussion, Vergès assured him that the de Gaulle committee would cooperate.

As for Bayardelle, the secretary declared his loyalty to de Gaulle but asked to serve the cause anywhere but in New Caledonia where he claimed that his life was in danger. Bayardelle then warned Sautot that in two months' time "either a Britisher will be sitting in that chair or there will be a revolution."[90] Bayardelle subsequently made his way to London where he ingratiated himself with the Gaullist leadership and became resident expert on interpreting events on the island of New Caledonia. Later in London he would express his disdain for the Caledonians and his profound suspicion of Australian intentions toward New Caledonia.

On 27 September Showers intercepted orders from Vichy that instructed both *Dumont d'Urville* and *Amiral Charner,* which was one third of the way to New Caledonia, to return to Saigon. Showers informed Sautot that *Adelaide* could not remain in Nouméa any longer. His mission was completed. He assured Sautot that he would return to defend New Caledonia if there were any Vichy attempt to overturn the Free-French Government on the island. If such an attempt were made, Sautot would need assistance. Showers toured the island's defenses and reported, "The visit to the forts was most illuminating and disclosed a deplorable state of affairs to exist in the fixed defences of Nouméa, which at present can only be described as useless."[91] The Australian government advised the governor that if he should encounter further difficulties, he should intern any dissident troublemakers and deport them to Indochina by way of Australia.[92] With some measure of calm established and with Sautot apparently in control of the situation, Captain Showers sailed *Adelaide* out of Nouméa harbor on 4 October, bound for Australia. Sautot and the crowd on the municipal dock waved farewell.

The rally of New Caledonia to the Free-French movement had been concluded successfully, but the colony's future remained as uncertain as the outcome of the war.

Notes

1. Jacqueline Sénès, *La Vie quotidienne en Nouvelle-Calédonie de 1850 à nos jours* (Paris, 1985), 253.
2. Order #1209, 7 November 1939, in Australian Archives, Canberra (AA), A609, 552/176/1, General: New Caledonia Commerce.
3. They were subsequently returned to all but Japanese residents, a decision that the Japanese in New Caledonia protested as discriminatory.
4. W.A. Johnston, British consul, Nouméa, to Lt. Col. W.R. Hodgson, secretary of external affairs, Canberra, 4 February 1940, AA CRS A981, Japan 160.
5. André Bayardelle, "Le rapport Bayardelle sur le ralliement de 1940," *Bulletin de la société d'études historiques de la Nouvelle-Calédonie*, no. 20 (1974): 4.
6. Bayardelle, "Rapport," 8–9.
7. John Lawrey, *The Cross of Lorraine in the South Pacific: Australia and the Free French Movement 1940–1942* (Canberra, 1982), 8–9; John Lawrey, "A Catch on the Boundary: Australia and the Free French Movement in 1940," *Journal of Pacific History* 10, 3 (1975): 67–68.
8. James Daly, président, Ancien Combattants to Menzies, 25 June 1940, AA A816, 19/311/74, part 1.
9. Testimony of M. Roger Gervolino, "Le ralliement de la Nouvelle-Calédonie à la France Libre" (taken 29 May 1945), Archives Nationales, Section Contemporaine (henceforth ANSC) 72AJ 225, folder 3 (New Caledonia).
10. Georges Baudoux, "Le Rapport Baudoux sur le ralliement de Georges Baudoux (fils de l'écrivain)," *Bulletin de la Société d'Études historiques de la Nouvelle-Calédonie*, no. 24 (1975): 19.
11. Pélicier to Menzies, 26 June 1940, doc. 439, in *Documents on Australian Foreign Policy, 1937–49* (henceforth *DAFP*) vol. 3: *January-June 1940*, ed. H. Kenway, H.J.W. Stokes & P.G. Edwards, (Canberra, 1979).
12. Johnston to Lord Lloyd, under secretary for foreign affairs, 28 June 1940, United Kingdom Public Record Office (henceforth PRO), FO371/24338, New Caledonia 1940, 997/7327/17.
13. Johnston to Lloyd, 28 June 1940, PRO FO371/24338, New Caledonia 1940, 997/7327/17; Gervolino, "Le ralliement," ANSC, 72AJ 225, folder 3 (New Caledonia) and Bayardelle, "Rapport," 13–15.
14. Bayardelle, "Rapport," 23.
15. Lémery (Vichy-Colonies) to Governor, Nouméa, 22 July 1940, Archives of the Service Historique de l'Armée, Château de Vincennes (henceforth SHA), Outre-mer, Pacifique, carton 5. The crisis in late July that erupted between the general council and Governor Pélicier is detailed in Bayardelle, "Rapport," 18–22.
16. Prime Minister, New South Wales, to Prime Minister Menzies, 20 August 1940, "Summary of Extra-ordinary Session of general council, 22 July 1940," AA CRS 981, New Caledonia 1B, part 6.
17. Pélicier to Colonies, 27 July 1940, SHA, Outre-mer, Pacifique, carton 5.
18. Johnston to Sir Harry Luke, high commissioner for the Western Pacific, Fiji, 9 August 1940, containing copy of Pélicier's speech of 5 August, AA A981/N-C/B, part 3.
19. Baudoux, "Rapport Baudoux," 20–24.

20. Châtelain and Kollen, Nouméa, to General de Gaulle, London, 14 July 1940, Ministère des Affaires Etrangères (MAE) Guerre 1939–45, Londres CNF, vol. 79.
21. Charles de Gaulle, *Lettres, notes et carnets (LNC): juin 1940–juillet 1941* (Paris, 1981), 47, 82.
22. Copy in translation of Pognon's letter annexed to Prime Minister, New South Wales, to R.G. Menzies, Canberra, 20 August 1940, AA A981/N-C/1B, pt. 6. De Gaulle's reply to Pognon, dated 28 August 1940, may be found in de Gaulle, *LNC: juin 1940–juillet 1941*, 105.
23. Bayardelle, "Rapport," 31.
24. Pélicier to Colonies via Decoux (Indochine), 19 August 1940, MAE Guerre 1939–45, Vichy, Asie ser. E, vol. 372; also SHA, Outre-mer, Pacifique, carton 5.
25. Lawrey, *Cross of Lorraine*, 18.
26. War Cabinet Minute, and Commonwealth Government to Lord Caldecote, U.K. secretary of state for dominion affairs, both 18 June 1940, docs. 399 and 400, in *DAFP*, vol. 3.
27. Caldecote to Sir Geoffrey Whiskard, U.K. high commissioner in Australia, 19, 20, and 21 June 1940, docs. 406 413 415, ibid.
28. McEwen to Casey, 26 June 1940, doc. 443, ibid. Cited in Margot Simington, "Australia and the New Caledonia Coup d'Etat of 1940", *Australian Outlook*, 30, 1 (1976): 77 and n3.
29. Mr. W.A. Johnston, U.K. consul in Nouméa, to Mr. R.G. Menzies, prime minister, 24 June 1940 and Mr. R.G. Menzies, prime minister, to Mr W.A. Johnston, U.K. consul in Nouméa, 27 June 1940, docs. 428 451, *DAFP*, vol. 3.
30. Ernest Oughton to McEwen, Min. Ext. Aff., Canberra, nd (August 1940), New Zealand National Archives (NZNA), Wellington.
31. C.E. Gauss, American minister, Canberra, to State Department, 21 August 1940, "The Situation in New Caledonia: Relations with Australia," and 13 August 1940, "Memorandum of Conversation with Mr. J. McEwen, Minister for External Affairs," U.S. National Archives and Records Administration (USNARA), State Dec. File 851L.00/2; also, Menzies to High Commissioner, London, 13 August 1940, AA A816 19/311/74, part 1.
32. Instructions drafted by department of external affairs for Mr. B.C. Ballard, official representative in New Caledonia, n.d. (early August), doc. 45, in *DAFP*, vol. 4: *July 1940–June 1941* ed. W.J. Hudson & H.J.W. Stokes (Canberra, 1980).
33. Sir Harry Luke, U.K. high commissioner for the Western Pacific to Lord Lloyd, U.K. secretary of state for colonies, 9 August 1940, doc. 58, *DAFP*, vol. 4, and Luke to Menzies, 30 July 1940, AA A816 19/311/74, part 1.
34. S.M. Bruce, high commissioner in London, to Menzies, 2 August 1940, doc. 48, *DAFP*, vol. 4.
35. Commonwealth Government to Lord Caldecote, U.K. secretary of state for dominion affairs, 11 August 1940, doc. 62, ibid.
36. Lawrey, "A Catch," 75.
37. Lawrey, *Cross of Lorraine*, 30, citing interview with Albert Rapadzi, September 1974; and Julien-Joseph Legrand, *L'Indochine à l'heure japonaise* (Cannes, 1963), 40.
38. Bayardelle, "Rapport," 31–33.
39. *Dumont d'Urville* to Naval and Colonial Ministry, Vichy, 26 August 1940, Archives Nationales Section d'Outre-mer (ANSOM), Nouvelle-Calédonie, carton 230 and same to same, 25 August 1940, MAE Guerre 1939–45, Vichy, Asie ser. E, vol. 372.
40. Pierre Laveissière, "Introduction à la lecture d'un journal et extraits d'un journal tenu à Nouméa en septembre 1940," *Neptunia*, no. 139 (1980): 44.
41. *Dumont d'Urville* to Naval Ministry, 28 August 1940, MAE Guerre 1939–45, Vichy, Asie ser. E., vol. 372.
42. Lémery, Vichy, to Lt. Col. Denis, Nouméa, 28 August 1940, MAE Guerre 1939–45, Vichy, Asie ser. E., vol. 372.
43. Lieutenant J.A. Templeton, Report No. 6, "The Mission of Rear Admiral Thierry d'Argenlieu to the French Pacific," (n.d., ca. March 1943), PRO FO371/46307.

44. Lawrey, *Cross of Lorraine*, 36.
45. Bayardelle, "Rapport" 34.
46. "The Situation in New Caledonia and French possessions" C.E. Gauss, Canberra to State Department, 3 September 1940 and C.E. Gauss, Memorandum of conversation with Lt. Col. W.R. Hodgson, secretary of the department of external affairs, 2 September 1940, USNARA, State Dec. File 740.0011/ EW 1939/5819.
47. Telegram, de Gaulle to Sautot, 23/8/40 in Charles de Gaulle, *Mémoires de Guerre*, vol. 1: *L'Appel, 1940–1942*, 288.
48. De Gaulle, *LNC: juin 1940–juillet 1941*, 77–78, 80–81, 105.
49. Under-secretary of state for dominions to Australia and New Zealand, 30 August 1940, PRO FO371/133994/Z4338.
50. Menzies to high commissioner for dominions, London, 31 August 1940; instructions to Commanding Officer, *Adelaide*, 2 September 1940, AA A816 19/311/74, part 1; A.R. Nankervis, secretary of department of the navy to Mr. F. Strahan, secretary of prime minister's department, 2 September 1940, doc. 92, *DAFP*, vol. 4.
51. Lawrey, *Cross of Lorraine*, 41.
52. Gauss conv w/Col W.R. Hodgson, 9 September 1940, NARA State Dec. File 851L.0015/5819.
53. Caldecote, U.K. secretary of state for dominion affairs to Menzies, 6 September 1940, doc. 105, *DAFP*, vol. 4.
54. *Amiral Charner* remained in port until 17 September when it departed Saigon for Nouméa. Admiral Découx, Indochina to Colonies, Vichy, 14 September 1940, MAE Guerre 1939–45, Vichy, Asie ser. E, vol. 372, and French Admiralty to *Dumont d'Urville*, 19 September 1940, AA A981, New Caledonia, part 6. At this point Quièvrecourt intended *Amiral Charner* as a replacement so that he could return to Tahiti and re-establish Vichy authority; he was not anticipating Sautot's arrival or any serious uprising in New Caledonia. *Dumont d'Urville* to Colonies and Admiralty, Vichy, 18 September 1940, AA A981, New Caledonia, part 6.
55. Ballard to external affairs, 8 September 1940, doc. 110, *DAFP*, vol. IV: *July 1940–June 1941*.
56. Luke to Menzies, 7 September 1940, doc 107, *DAFP*, vol. 4. The Australian representative in London, Alfred Sterling, referred to this telegram, noting that Sir Harry Luke had "completely changed his mind" and now urged intervention in a cable that again presented British arguments for intervention. Sterling to external affairs, Canberra, 8 September 1940, AA A2937, New Caledonia. Once converted, Sir Harry insisted on quick action. Luke to Blandy, 10 September 1940, AA A981, N-C 1B, part 3.
57. Ibid.
58. Lawrey, *Cross of Lorraine*, 43.
59. Blandy to external affairs, 10 September 1940, AA A981/New Caledonia/B, part 3.
60. *Adelaide* Operational Plan, Appendix 1, "H.M.A.S. *Adelaide*—Letter of Proceeding for Operations at Nouméa," 8 October 1940, AA CP290/2, Bundle 1.
61. Raoul Aglion, *l'Epopée de la France combattante* (New York, 1943), 156; and M.L. Dubois, Nouméa to M. et Mme Maurice Dubois, Le Fay (India), 12 December 1940, ANSOM, Nouvelle-Calédonie, c 233.
62. Mr. A.R. Nankervis, secretary of department of the navy, to Mr. F. Strahan, secretary of prime minister's Department, 13 September 1940, doc 118, *DAFP*, vol. 4; telegram to Sautot, 11 September 1940, de Gaulle, *LNC, juin 40–juillet 41*, 113.
63. Henri Sautot, *Grandeur et décadence du Gaullisme dans le Pacifique* (Melbourne, 1949), 40.
64. Laveissière, "Extraits d'un journal," 44.
65. Luke to Menzies, 7 September 1940, doc 107, *DAFP*, vol. 4. Sir Harry Luke also reported that one-half of the ship's company of *Dumont d'Urville* was sympathetic to the Free-French movement and some of them had inquired about service in the British navy. Luke to High Commissioner for Colonies, London, 3 September 1940, PRO FO371/24338.

66. *Dumont d'Urville* to Naval Ministry, 9 September 1940, MAE Guerre 1939–45, Vichy, Asie ser. E, vol. 372.
67. Telegrams (intercepts) of 10 and 17 September 1940, *Dumont d'Urville* to French Admiralty, AA A6445, 2/40.
68. Telegram to R. Pognon, 28 August 1940, de Gaulle, *LNC: juin 1940–juillet 1941*, 105.
69. Sautot, *Grandeur et décadence*, 36–37; Ballard to ext affairs, 8 September 1940, doc. 110, *DAFP*, vol. 4.
70. Baudoux, "Rapport Baudoux," 27.
71. Lawrey, *Cross of Lorraine*, 44.
72. There are two versions: Baudoux, "Rapport Baudoux," 38 and de Gaulle *Mémoires de Guerre*, vol. 1, 294–95.
73. Ibid. 31–34.
74. Showers' account is detailed in "H.M.A.S. *Adelaide*—Letter of Proceeding for Operations at Nouméa," 8 October 1940, AA CP290/2, bundle 1.
75. Laveissière, "Extraits d'un journal …," 49n. 16.
76. Bayardelle, "Rapport," 37.
77. Baudoux, "Rapport Baudoux," 34–35.
78. Sautot, *Grandeur et décadence*, 44–45.
79. Bayardelle, "Rapport," 38–40.
80. Commanding Officer, in "H.M.A.S. *Adelaide*," appendix 20, 8 October 1940, AA CRS CP290/2, Bundle 1.
81. Ibid.
82. Sautot, *Grandeur et décadence*, 60.
83. Based on Lawrey, *Cross of Lorraine*, 47–50; Showers to Commonwealth Naval Board and Commonwealth Government to Caldecote, 21 September 1940, docs 130 and 131, *DAFP*, vol. 4.
84. *Adelaide* draft letter to be dispatched by Governor to *Dumont d'Urville*, appendix 3, "H.M.A.S. *Adelaide*," 8 October 1940, AA CP290/2, bundle 1.
85. Laveissière, "Extraits d'un journal …," 52.
86. *Dumont d'Urville* to Colonies, 22 September 1940, AA 6445 3/40.
87. Lawrey, *Cross of Lorraine*, 50; Laveissière, "Extraits d'un journal …," 53.
88. Lawrey, *Cross of Lorraine*, 51.
89. Laveissière, "Extraits d'un journal …," 54.
90. Lawrey, *Cross of Lorraine*, 52, citing Showers, "Letter of Proceeding."
91. "H.M.A.S. *Adelaide*," 8 October 1940, AA CP290/2, bundle 1.
92. External affairs to Ballard, 2 October 1940, doc. 150, *DAFP*, vol. 4.

CHAPTER 3

NEW CALEDONIA IN LIMBO: PREPARING FOR WAR IN THE PACIFIC

Once Captain Showers sailed away the Caledonians had to deal with immediate and pressing issues. They were elated over their accomplishment in overturning the Vichy Government, in asserting their patriotic determination to continue the war, and in thwarting a threatened counter-revolution. But when the Broussards drifted back to their country farms, they left the task of assuring order and providing for the colony's security and welfare to Governor Henri Sautot. The governor faced a demanding task, given the excitement and high expectations that the rally had aroused.[1] Governor Sautot had to organize and sustain the new Free-French regime, provide for the island's security, and assure exports needed for survival.

Local and Foreign Anxieties over New Caledonia's Defense

Concerns about whether or not Vichy would try to regain control of New Caledonia and, beyond that, a fear that Japan might seek a dominant influence on the mineral rich island lingered over the colony. Although Captain Showers had departed with *Adelaide*, the island's security rested upon the good will of the Australian Government. This military dependency created an opportunity for Vichy to claim that New Caledonia, as other parts of the French Empire that had rallied to the Free French, was no more than a British client colony soon to be swallowed by British imperialists. New Caledonia reflected the uncertainties of choice and consequent anxieties that pervaded French colonial territories following the 1940 armistice. Despite the enthusiasm of the rally, some Caledonians were uncertain about the colony's future as part of a Free-French movement led by an unknown general in London. These Caledonians considered the break with Vichy an opportunity to gain a measure of autonomy for themselves.

In his report on events in New Caledonia, Captain Showers assessed the chances for additional rallies based upon what he had observed in New Caledonia. Showers claimed that "practically every Frenchman" was anti-German and desired to see an ultimate British victory that would free France of German domination, but the French wanted to obtain their freedom on their own terms with limited and discreet support from the British Commonwealth. He also warned that the psychological shock of defeat had produced "a condition of tension and intrigue which clouds the judgment and direction given to [a] practical, immediate and balanced war effort. Confidence in leadership is not attainable whilst this mental instability persists," he warned.[2] Indeed, Sautot's task was to create a sense of stability and confidence with respect to both his own and General de Gaulle's leadership.

Sautot had to improvise and reconstruct much of the island's colonial bureaucracy and public services since most of the colonial bureaucrats maintained their allegiance to the government of Marshal Pétain. Over two hundred officials, including most of the civil service and several gendarmes, were among the first wave of deportations sent aboard the passenger ship *Pierre Loti* to Australia for eventual transportation to Indochina. To replace such key personnel, Sautot recalled former officials who were living in retirement and pressed war veterans into service to maintain internal order.[3]

The regular military forces also strongly supported the Pétain Government in its hostility toward Great Britain, and most officers remained firmly opposed to General de Gaulle and requested repatriation. The garrison on New Caledonia was from the French Colonial Army, which shared the traditional Anglophobic prejudices of the French Navy, a view that the British attack on the French fleet at Mers-el-Kebir in Algeria in July and the events at Dakar in September had reinforced. On the other hand, a number of local troops called to the colors were reservists who had served during the First World War and were strongly anti-German patriots. Many of these veterans came from the countryside and had marched on Nouméa in September 1940 to support the rally and Governor Sautot. They favored continued resistance, but their future role, either in defense of the island or in service with Free-French Forces elsewhere, remained unclear.

In addition to administration and defense there was a question of economic survival after the metropolitan connection had been broken. The economy of the island depended upon the export of minerals, particularly nickel and, to a lesser extent, chrome. The hard pressed Broussards also needed to export coffee, hides and canned beef from their ranches to survive and meet their debts to the commercial interests in Nouméa. Sautot had to find markets to sustain New Caledonia's economy for the duration of the war.

In his appointment General de Gaulle gave Sautot extensive powers in fiscal matters to address these issues. The General recognized New Caledonia's dependence upon economic and military support from Australia, a dependency that Vichy would exploit. De Gaulle urged that Sautot be prudent and refute all rumors that New Caledonia might become a British protectorate. The governor needed to make clear that, as de Gaulle put it, cooperation with the British Commonwealth and His Majesty's Government "does not infringe on the rights of French sovereignty, which is complete for the French possessions in the Pacific."[4] With de Gaulle's warning in mind, Sautot assumed that he had full backing and authority from London to deal with local complexities in the Pacific, including relations with Australia, and to establish Free-French authority on New Caledonia in his own person.

Although considered a hero for his role during the rally, Sautot had still to confirm his authority in New Caledonia, particularly within the context of Caledonian local politics and rivalries. Sautot was well aware of New Caledonia's reputation as a "graveyard for governors" in the colonial service, stemming largely from the Caledonians' strong sense of individualism and their equally intense desire to govern themselves. His major challenge came from the ambition of Michel Vergès, who had his own ideas about how to run the colony. Vergès was determined to become the de facto leader of the colony and bring it into an autonomist era, freed from either metropolitan constraints or the overweening pressures of the British Commonwealth. Vergès seemed to be driven by a potent combination of pride, ambition and paranoia. He was highly suspicious of foreigners and foreign designs upon New Caledonia, beginning with his distrust of the Australians. And he conceived an implacable hatred for his former ally in the rally, Governor Sautot. Sautot and several of his successors, as well as the Americans after 1942, would feel the sting of his invective and xenophobic passion. Since the Vergès-Sautot quarrel had such an important influence on the wartime history of New Caledonia and eventually clouded relations between the Americans and the Free French, the origins of this dispute need to be told.

A serious disagreement with Vergès arose from Governor Sautot's creation of an administrative council to help him manage the affairs of New Caledonia for the war's duration. Under normal circumstances the governor of New Caledonia ruled in consultation with two local institutions: a private or "privy" council appointed by the governor that was largely an advisory body, and a governing council that was elected on the basis of European adult male suffrage. This elected body did not have powers of initiative, but members discussed and approved the program and budget that the governor presented to them. In a negative way it could have a powerful influence, and in the past the obstructionism of the general council had frustrated several governors of the colony. The frequent comings and goings of the island's governors became known as "the waltz of the governors," but many of them had stalked rather than waltzed away from New Caledonia in their frustration over the governing council's obtuse independence.

The ambiguous attitude of the existing governing council at the moment of New Caledonia's rally disturbed Sautot and was another reason why he wished to have a new council. Some influential members of the council feared that a rally in which Broussards played a crucial role might overturn the established political and social order on the island. No member of the general council participated actively in the events of 19 September, and several resigned from the council following the rally. Consequently, Sautot decided to dissolve both the governing and privy councils and replace them with a single appointed body that would represent various interests on the island to provide him with advice and support in governing the colony. A key member of the new administrative council was Nicholas Rapadzi, acting director of Le Nickel. Sautot sought a balance between the populist Broussards of the interior and cooperation with the economically dominant Le Nickel.[5]

Sautot's appointment of an administrative council greatly upset Michel Vergès. The important role that Vergès had taken during the rally raised the possibility, at least in his own mind, that he might emerge as the most powerful figure in, if not acknowledged head of, the colony in the weeks following the rally. The means for achieving that ambition was the de Gaulle Committee that had been hastily formed in early September to bring the colony into the Free-French camp. Vergès intended that the de Gaulle Committee would govern the colony during the war, and he would become the de facto ruler of the island with Sautot fulfilling a largely symbolic role.[6] When it became apparent that Sautot would not agree to this arrangement, Vergès denounced Sautot's "inept" leadership. Vergès and his colleague, André Prinet, spread rumors that Sautot and his supporters were nothing but paid agents of Australia.[7] In an effort to placate Vergès and Prinet, Sautot offered them positions on the administrative council, but they refused; from this point Michel Vergès regarded Governor Sautot as his bitter enemy.

To cut short Vergès's intrigues Sautot asked de Gaulle's permission to dismiss the old governing council and replace it with a "more representative" administrative council. Sautot warned de Gaulle that autonomist extremists hoped to gain control of Caledonian politics and wished to decide on all matters including elimination of the compulsory expenses that had been required by the metropolitan government in the past. Sautot warned that such a move would cause executive authority to pass from the governor's office into the hands of the administrative council, undermine his authority and make his task impossible. He informed de Gaulle that Vergès hoped to use the de Gaulle Committee to implement his autonomist program.[8]

General de Gaulle quickly approved Sautot's request to dismiss the old council and appoint a new one. Authority could not be divided. "The Committee, which has no official role to play, cannot claim to keep the governor dependent upon it nor under its control."[9] Sautot assured de Gaulle that the new council reflected "various categories [of] social and economic activity [in the] colony." Elections would be held as soon as circumstances permitted. De Gaulle agreed and emphasized that the suppression of elections was to be presented as a measure imposed by wartime conditions. The future political structure of the empire remained to be determined in the postwar period.[10] With support from Gaullist headquarters Sautot was able to isolate Michel Vergès and his allies by mid-December.[11]

An equally pressing problem was to provide for the island's defense and at the same time fulfill Sautot's desire that New Caledonia should send Free-French Forces to North Africa. This was a difficult assignment, given the limited resources at hand. With the departure of most of the regular colonial troops New Caledonia had no more than a battalion, reduced to two infantry companies, one European and the other Melanesian, available for the island's defense. With the repatriation of most of the regular colonial troops, Sautot appointed the highly respected reserve lieutenant, Georges Dubois, to head military forces in New Caledonia, awarding him the temporary rank of captain. Dubois began organizing a militia force of infantry and riflemen from both European and Melanesian veterans and volunteers.

The first contingent of the Pacific Battalion to be sent to Africa was to consist of six hundred troops drawn from Tahiti and New Caledonia. Major Broche from Tahiti, whom de Gaulle had appointed commander of all Free-French Forces in the Pacific, was to command this Pacific Battalion.[12] He was scheduled to arrive in New Caledonia with the Tahitian volunteers in late October or early November where they would train and be sent to the European theater as soon as they were ready. By the end of the year the enrollment for both the militia and the Pacific Battalion came to a total of 1,200 European and 1,500 Melanesians in addition to the 300 Tahitians and 40 volunteers from the New Hebrides.[13]

Kanak were particularly enthusiastic. Chief Naisseline from the Loyalty Island of Maré sent a contingent for training on the main island. Consul MacVitty had high praise for these Kanak volunteers, noting that "the native New Caledonian makes an excellent soldier."[14] Given this display of Kanak loyalty and support for the Free French, both Governor Sautot and Governor de Curton in Tahiti argued that all indigenous peoples who served with the Free-French Forces should automatically be given citizenship. René Cassin, de Gaulle's legal advisor, largely on the advice of former general-secretary Bayardelle, rejected this proposal as premature but promised to bring the matter up for discussion at the end of hostilities.[15]

This show of support from New Caledonia pleased General de Gaulle. He cabled General Catroux that Sautot was organizing a battalion of 700 European and Melanesian soldiers who were to depart for Egypt as soon as transportation could be arranged.[16] Australian authorities assured Sautot that funding would be provided to equip the Pacific Battalion and urged that the matter go forward rapidly as "de Gaulle is anxious that these recruits should proceed quickly" to the Mediterranean theater.[17] Difficulties in obtaining shipping, however, delayed the Pacific Battalion's departure until 5 May 1941. Sautot considered the Pacific Battalion to be evidence of Caledonian patriotism and commitment to the Free-French cause.

Creation of the Pacific Battalion led to further conflict between Sautot and Vergès, who was adamantly opposed to sending any troops out of New Caledonia. He wished to retain them for the island's defense. Polemics erupted in the local press when Vergès and his followers accused Sautot and his supporters of trifling with the island's security by making its protection dependent upon the Australians. Vergès began discouraging volunteers, particularly the Broussards, from engaging in the Pacific Battalion. At one point Captain Dubois and Major Broche accused Vergès of crossing names off the enlistment rolls.[18]

Vergès's concern about New Caledonia's ability to defend its shores was not misplaced and was shared by the Australians. After agreeing to provide transportation for the Pacific Battalion, the Australian Government began to worry about New Caledonia's weak defenses, particularly when the Japanese threat intensified at the beginning of 1941. Prime Minister Menzies cabled London, "that due to general weakness of defense position in South Pacific and extreme importance that New Caledonia *not* fall into hands of Japan, the dispatch of troops from New Caledonia should be discouraged, and that local defense troops should in fact be reinforced."[19]

When Vichy officials in Indochina proclaimed their intention to send an expedition to reclaim New Caledonia early in 1941, de Gaulle also became concerned about defending New Caledonia.[20] Eventually he agreed that an initial contingent of 600 men would be the only one sent to the Mediterranean theater and that all other Free-French troops recruited, equipped and trained with British and Commonwealth support would remain in the Pacific. De Gaulle feared that a Japanese takeover in Indochina was imminent, and he noted that Japan considered New Caledonia to be within a Japanese sphere of influence.[21] To reassure the Caledonians, the Australians agreed to send a military mission to consult with Sautot on his defense requirements.[22] General de Gaulle agreed to this proposal, which also had Sautot's enthusiastic support.[23]

The Japanese threat to French interests in the Pacific was serious. The Australian minister in Japan, Sir John Latham, warned that Japan's siding with Thailand against Indochina in their border dispute revealed increased Japanese prestige in the area and showed that Indochina had definitely fallen under Japanese sway. Already the Japanese presence in Indochina created strategic problems for Singapore; Japanese control of Thailand "would be fatal" since Singapore lacked the military resources to resist a land-based attack.[24]

Warnings of possible Japanese action also arrived from London and Washington at this time. R.G. Casey, the Australian minister in Washington, announced that the Japanese appeared ready to make a major move south in the near future. A Japanese push appeared to have been decided upon "even if this means war."[25] This move was expected as soon as German actions in Europe created favorable conditions and as soon as the Japanese resolved the dispute between Thailand and French Indochina. These alarms created something of a war scare and led to an Australian reaction that revealed anxieties about the country's precarious situation.

The Australians wanted to improve New Caledonian defenses and needed to have direct discussions with Sautot and his representatives on the island's needs, but they had to do so without offending Gaullist sensitivity over the question of New Caledonia's independence from British domination. They also encountered French preference for centralized control. General de Gaulle's requirement that all communications from the South Pacific pass through his office in London hampered the ability of Australia to provide assistance to New Caledonia or to find out what equipment and military supplies were needed. The Australians complained that they were in the dark as to de Gaulle's plans or Sautot's requirements for the defense of New Caledonia. Prime Minister Menzies impatiently suggested to London, "that the piece-meal communications now passing between de Gaulle and Sautot are *not* leading to a clarification of the present position and that it is essential the whole matter be placed on a proper footing and based on a definite plan without delay."[26]

Presumably the Australian military mission to New Caledonia would provide this information and produce a plan for the island's defense. Control of New Caledonia was essential for securing air and sea lines of communication to the United States and for obtaining reinforcements from that source in the event of hostilities in the Pacific.[27] On 20 January the British war cabinet approved a request that financial assistance be given to French Forces in the South Pacific. Staff conversations were to begin directly with Sautot to determine how aid to New Caledonia might strengthen the security of both the Free-French colony and protect Australia's line of supply in the event of war with Japan.[28] With de Gaulle's approval, two Australian officers, Lieutenant-Colonel R.E. Fanning of the army and Lieutenant-Commander G.A. Gould from the navy, departed for Nouméa by way of Auckland, New Zealand on 14 February.[29]

Colonel Fanning reported that the political situation on the island was stable, although "an air of intrigue" continued in Nouméa. The European population of the capital was 60 percent for the Free French, and in the countryside the farmers were 90 percent in favor of the rally. The Broussards were armed with hunting rifles and admired as tough fighters who knew the countryside well. As for organized military manpower, 1,100 troops had been recruited, one-half of them native Melanesians, and of these 300 were to be sent to the Mediterranean with an additional 300 Tahitians in the Pacific Battalion. Two thousand additional reservists could be called up and another two thousand might be available, but they lacked training and weapons. These forces provided little realistic prospects for resistance against a modern and well-equipped military force. The report recommended that Australia immediately offer assistance to remedy the military weaknesses on the island.[30]

Six weeks later final approval was given after a meeting in Australia in which Dubois and Ballard assured the Australian Government that Sautot's Free-French administration in New Caledonia was stable and was unlikely to be overthrown by any pro-Vichy coup. The local population would welcome the presence of an Australian military mission on the island to assist in the training of local military personnel. The Australians agreed to provide arms and equipment for another 1,200 men in New Caledonia. They would establish a seaplane base on Ile Nou adjacent to Nouméa and install two six-inch modern artillery guns on the heights overlooking Nouméa to cover the harbor and its approaches. Engineers would be provided to survey land for construction of two air bases, one at Tontouta thirty-five miles northwest of Nouméa and another at the Plaine des Gaiacs one hundred fifteen miles further up the west coast. An Australian contingent of forty officers and men would be stationed on the island to operate the base, and additional personnel would be brought in temporarily to train local troops in the use of the artillery battery. The Australian Government agreed to fund these measures in accordance with the financial agreement that Churchill and de Gaulle had signed in August 1940.[31]

The Australians reaffirmed their willingness to provide a market for New Caledonian exports. "New Caledonia should be treated on the same basis as an Australian State or Territory insofar as purchases from Australia are concerned, and that export licenses should be granted in accordance with this principle."[32] A solid foundation for cooperation between New Caledonia and Australia seemed to be at hand. As the American consul reported to Washington, the majority of the population was heart and soul for de Gaulle, despite the loyalty to Vichy of some businessmen and persons of the better class.[33]

Even with these agreements, concern over the British Commonwealth's intentions persisted at de Gaulle's headquarters in London. The Australians had hoped that most matters on defense could be settled directly between Canberra and Nouméa, but de Gaulle insisted that London was the place to coordinate policy in the South Pacific in the face of the Japanese threat.[34] Mindful of French authority and sovereignty, de Gaulle insisted that French officers approve the use of Australian aircraft that were to be stationed in New Caledonia. This demand, Lawrey notes, revealed de Gaulle's hypersensitivity on issues of French sovereignty and what he called the near-paranoid attitude pervading Free-French headquarters in London.[35] Even a cordial discussion between de Gaulle and Menzies during the Australian leader's visit to Great Britain, in which they discussed the need for better local communication and avoidance of any appearance of an Australian domination of New Caledonia, failed to reassure the General.[36] As tensions mounted in the Pacific during the early months of 1941, de Gaulle decided to send a mission to assess the ability of New Caledonia to defend itself from the Japanese and to resist the suspected ambitions of the colony's neighbors and allies.

De Gaulle's Desire for Centralized Control and the Brunot Mission

General de Gaulle's desire for central control over all decisions that affected French territories became an issue for the British foreign office in discussion of defense and other policy matters. Lord Cranborne, British secretary of state for dominion affairs, warned that relations with French territories "give rise to somewhat delicate problems. These originate," he noted, "mainly from divergence between the French conception of highly centralized control from Europe and our system of decentralization coupled with dominion responsibilities for Free-French colonies in the Pacific." De Gaulle had only a few administrators to manage the colonies that had rallied to his leadership, and they were accustomed to a highly centralized system. Working through the Empire Defense Council would be an effective answer to accusations that Great Britain was using the Free-French movement as "a smoke screen to conceal [its] own designs on the French Colonial Empire."[37] Regardless of the cumbersome procedure that would result, the British and Australian Governments accepted de Gaulle's demand that London approve all of Sautot's negotiations and agreements on financial, military and economic matters.

De Gaulle's insistence upon centralized control would be the source of considerable misunderstanding and friction in subsequent months. Although Sautot had amply demonstrated his loyalty and commitment to the Free-French cause, de Gaulle's anxieties about independent initiatives on the part of his subordinates lay behind his decision to send his own representative to evaluate the situation in the Pacific. This representative would demonstrate the grandeur and authority of the Free-French movement to the local population and assure that French rights and interests would be respected. In addition, General de Gaulle suspected that a desire for local autonomy could be found in New Caledonia and Tahiti. The rallies of these two colonies resulted from local initiatives, and certain leaders of the rallies hoped to use the conditions of war to obtain a greater measure of self-rule and escape the constraints of a highly centralized colonial administration.[38] Thus for both local political reasons and as a result of his global strategy, as the General recalled in his memoirs, "an authority as strong and centralized as possible was to be imposed in Oceania." In his loftiest manner de Gaulle informed Sautot by cable that "the complexity of the political and economic problems that are emerging in the Pacific and the need for direct contact with Australia and New Zealand" caused him to appoint Richard Brunot to lead a mission to the South Pacific.[39]

Brunot was high commissioner of Cameroon when he joined de Gaulle after some moments of hesitation in 1940. He was among the highest-ranking colonial officials to join the Free French, and he was ambitious. The conflict that developed between Brunot and Sautot would have a lasting impact upon relations between the Caledonians and General de Gaulle's representatives, as the

Americans would later discover. Brunot's mission was to assert Gaullist authority in response to international pressures that were emerging in the South Pacific. Evidence of an American interest in New Caledonia was one of the reasons, along with his suspicions about local autonomist sentiment, why General de Gaulle wished to strengthen Free-French authority on the island. The American consul's arrival in New Caledonia nearly coincided with the appearance of Brunot, who was accompanied by his wife and an aide, Captain Fatoux.

Sautot suspected that Governor Brunot's main purpose in coming to New Caledonia was to obtain his own post. Brunot's intention to replace Sautot became apparent when Mme Brunot rather indiscreetly commented upon the deplorable appearance of the governor's mansion and indicated that she would soon have it redecorated properly when her husband was "Lord and Master" of the island.[40] As the American Consul MacVitty observed, Brunot's actions revealed his malevolent desire "of securing the post of governor and high commissioner for the territories of Free France in the Pacific for himself."[41] Two of the original Caledonian Gaullists shared this impression and informed General de Gaulle that the local population would greatly resent Sautot's replacement by an outside official.[42]

Disagreements over administrative details led to immediate confrontations between Sautot and General de Gaulle's emissary. Brunot found Sautot's somewhat lax methods of administration to be wanting, according to the Australian consul.[43] Sautot for his part regarded Brunot and his entourage as a wasteful and unnecessary expense. In his memoirs Sautot complained that Brunot showed little appreciation for the prudent economies that he had introduced into his administration, claiming that Brunot stated he should not worry so much over costs since "money no longer counts."[44] Brunot then tried to discredit the governor in the eyes of Carlton Gardens by informing London that Sautot was seriously ill, had lost control of the situation, and was not up to the task of administering the Free-French possessions in the Pacific.[45] Brunot's reports seriously damaged Sautot's reputation among the Free French in London, and his intrigues poisoned relations between the Caledonian patriots and General de Gaulle's representative.

Sautot tried to salvage his reputation among Free-French officials in London. He cabled de Gaulle that his health had been restored, and he had matters in hand. As for Brunot, Sautot denounced his treachery and slander and accused him of being a political schemer. He warned de Gaulle that the Caledonian population had sized him up as nothing but an ambitious and dangerous political operator. Hostility toward Brunot was so strong that Sautot disclaimed any responsibility for his safety.[46] Rather than strengthening the authority and prestige of the Free-French movement in New Caledonia, the Brunot mission had exactly the opposite effect.

Having stirred Sautot's anger and alienated many Sautot supporters in New Caledonia, Brunot then continued his mission to Tahiti where a series of political conflicts had been reported to General de Gaulle's headquarters in London. Some brief account of Brunot's actions and the comic opera events in Tahiti is necessary, since they had a decisive impact upon the role of the Free French in the South Pacific. These events compelled de Gaulle to send out another mission to salvage the Free-French movement's reputation, which was becoming badly tarnished by Brunot's actions and by the personal squabbles that ensued in both Free-French colonies.

When Brunot had been sent out to the South Pacific, the Gaullists realized that difficulties might be brewing in Tahiti. Although the lush tropical paradise had rallied to de Gaulle with an overwhelming vote of support on 3 September 1940, behind this near unanimity were several intrigues that reflected strong political, ideological and personal differences. On the extreme left there was a small but noisy communist group led by two automobile mechanics who had the support of some younger Papeetans, a disgruntled official in the public health service and the head financial officer in the administration. At the other end of the scale an extreme rightist group, the Comité des Français d'Océanie, declared itself in favor of Petain and called for the removal of all "half-breeds" from the French administration. This group consisted of Doctor Florisson, their leader, two other doctors, a "non-conformist" critic of the French colonial administration, the legendary sailor and explorer Alain Gerbault, and Hubert Rusterholtz, who was an ardent admirer of Nazi doctrines. Following the rally, a Gaullist administration had been established under the leadership of Dr. Emile de Curton with the backing of colonial officers who had rallied and a group of moderate business and political leaders in Tahiti. Passions ran high, and rumors of continuing intrigue and rivalries had reached Carlton Gardens.

General de Gaulle also suspected that a desire for local autonomy could be detected behind these Tahitian political rivalries and Brunot was sent to Tahiti to assert Free-French authority, as in New Caledonia. André Bayardelle, the former Secretary-General of New Caledonia who was then in London, informed de Gaulle that while the situation in New Caledonia was now satisfactory, conditions were more difficult in Tahiti and he recommended that Brunot be sent there as quickly as possible.[47]

Shortly after he arrived in Tahiti, Brunot took sides in these local rivalries. On 10 June Brunot indicated that he wished to replace the elected local councils and substitute a government of his own choosing. Governor de Curton feared that Brunot's new appointees would be drawn from among his political opponents, which would make his task of governing difficult if not impossible.[48] He and his political allies on the council concluded that Brunot's actions exceeded his authority as head of a mission of inspection, and they cabled de Gaulle on 13 June to ask his recall.

Brunot got wind of this, and the next day he ordered the arrest and jailing of de Curton and his council. In a cable to de Gaulle Brunot reported that he had unearthed a plot by de Curton and others, who "aimed to arrest me and put me on a boat, if not even to kill me," and he had no choice but to move quickly. Brunot claimed that this was a Vichy plot, although he admitted the reasons were "still obscure." When Etienne Davio, who was a member of the communist faction, and five other citizens published an open letter to protest the arrests and high handed actions of Brunot, the governor-general arrested them and accused Davio of fomenting a communist revolution in Tahiti. As the American consul in Papeete observed, Brunot "was able to see sinister motives in the most casual actions or remarks."[49] Brunot's alarming reports of events in Tahiti brought an anxious response from London where the Empire Defense Council asked Brunot to account for his actions, which they noted were serious and seemed to contradict the information that he had previously provided.[50]

Brunot's behavior provoked a bitter resentment among Governor de Curton's supporters in Tahiti, who regretted that their adherence to the cause of General de Gaulle, "should have subjected them to the capricious tyranny of such an irresponsible maniac as Governor General Brunot."[51] News of Brunot's behavior in Tahiti soon reached London. The Empire Defense Council warned General de Gaulle, who was in Egypt at the time, that they were increasingly alarmed over mounting evidence of Brunot's state of mind in which they detected tendencies toward megalomania.[52] Informed of what had taken place, de Gaulle announced that Brunot had no authority to imprison a governor whom he had appointed.[53] The council recommended sending another mission to the Pacific to sort out the chaos produced by Brunot and refurbish the now tarnished image of Free France in the South Pacific.[54]

On 9 July de Gaulle replied that he was appointing Captain Thierry d'Argenlieu to be high commissioner for the Pacific, replacing Sautot, since the time had come to establish the authority of Free France in the Pacific. He ordered d'Argenlieu to place Free-French territories in a state of defense that would enable them, in concert with their allies, to meet any potential dangers. He granted d'Argenlieu full powers to act in his name, and he urged d'Argenlieu to take any necessary measures concerning personnel, including, if necessary, "to replace Governor Sautot in Nouméa as governor of New Caledonia."[55]

Governor Sautot was understandably upset at his demotion, and news of d'Argenlieu's appointment provoked an angry telegram to London in which he denounced Brunot's "treachery." Sautot reminded de Gaulle that he had been the first to rally to the General's noble cause to which he remained loyal, "whatever may happen," but he asked that de Gaulle give him a vote of confidence. Sautot argued that Nouméa, or even New Caledonia, was not big enough for two individuals holding high office and there were bound to be clashes over authority. Sautot even offered to resign all of his offices and serve the cause as a reserve sergeant in the Pacific Battalion, despite his fifty-six years of age.

De Gaulle refused Sautot's offer and asked that d'Argenlieu award the governor the Cross of Liberation and make him a Companion of the Liberation in recognition of his services. These flattering gestures masked de Gaulle's reservation about Sautot's abilities, expressed in his condescending observation that while "Sautot lacks the necessary capacities for his tasks," he had served France well and deserved some reward.[56] One historian has suggested that a further motive for Sautot's demotion was his rather unimpressive appearance and the fact that he had risen from the ranks and, therefore, lacked the status and standing necessary to represent the *grandeur* of France.[57]

D'Argenlieu sympathized with Sautot's feelings, and he asked Gaulle not to appoint him to replace the loyal governor.

> In such a troubled atmosphere it is morally impossible for me to agree to take Sautot's place against his will, even if only his position as high commissioner. This would be to play Brunot's game and make me an accomplice to the serious injustice done to the reputation of one of my colleagues on the [Empire] Defense Council who has earned the esteem and gratitude of Free France.[58]

D'Argenlieu urged that either his mission be annulled or that, if de Gaulle persisted in the appointment, his responsibilities be more carefully defined, presumably to avoid a slap in Sautot's face. But General de Gaulle could not avoid sending another mission, whatever Sautot's feelings.

The d'Argenlieu Mission

The damage to Free-French prestige and authority in the South Pacific had to be repaired, particularly in light of the growing tensions in that part of the world it was "extremely urgent" for d'Argenlieu to take up his post. He was "to go directly to the Pacific where it is essential to restore the situation."[59] De Gaulle feared that Japan, and "perhaps other foreign countries" might exploit the "cesspool of intrigues" in Tahiti or autonomist sentiments in New Caledonia for their own advantage.

New Caledonia was the most important of the Free-French holdings in the Pacific and a bastion of French presence in the area. From a Gaullist perspective threats to the integrity of an already divided French Empire were to be found not only in Japanese expansionism and in Vichy's appeasement but also in the potential imperial ambitions of the British Commonwealth and, increasingly, the security requirements of the United States. Firm and centralized Free-French authority had to be clearly established as the world conflict entered a new and decisive phase in the Pacific. The d'Argenlieu mission with its retinue and full authority to prepare the island's defense was essential "to reinforce the military position of France in the Pacific in the face of a critical international situation."[60]

To strengthen the admiral's hand he confirmed d'Argenlieu's appointment with full authority in all civil and military affairs. D'Argenlieu was to assure Sautot that the reason for his mission was to lift morale and strengthen the military situation of these colonies in light of the attitude of Japan. The Japanese threat made defense a question of the greatest importance, he informed Sautot, particularly when measures for protecting the Free-French colonies would require cooperation with the British Empire and the United States. This decision did not in any way weaken his confidence in the governor. "You are and you will always be the great Free Frenchman of the Pacific, my companion of the first hours, the able and brave Sautot."[61]

The choice of Georges Thierry d'Argenlieu to head the Free-French mission to the South Pacific reflected the high degree of trust that de Gaulle held for one of his earliest and most ardent supporters. D'Argenlieu came from a family in Mayenne of the petty nobility, and he had followed a tradition of his social class by entering the conservative École Navale. After receiving his commission he saw service aboard the cruiser *Du Chayla*. During the First World War d'Argenlieu served with distinction in the French Navy, but he retired from active service after the war to devote himself to the Church. He assumed the name of Father Louis de la Trinité and eventually became a provincial superior in the Carmelite Order.

When the Second World War broke out in 1939, he was recalled to active service with the rank of lieutenant commander and was placed in charge of the naval facility at Cherbourg. At the time of the armistice he was ordered to surrender the Cherbourg supply depot to the Germans, but he refused to do so. After the Germans arrested him, he escaped and made his way in disguise to London where he joined de Gaulle and the Free French. De Gaulle welcomed this conservative, authoritarian but fervently patriotic man who had instinctively rebelled against the armistice decision, and he developed a very high regard for d'Argenlieu's integrity, moral qualities and personal courage.[62]

Captain d'Argenlieu's devotion to the Free-French cause and his bravery were fully demonstrated during the Dakar episode when he had gone ashore to negotiate transfer of French West Africa to the Free-French movement. Subsequently d'Argenlieu participated in the rally of Gabon in November 1940. The following year he undertook a delicate diplomatic mission to Canada to impress the Quebecois, whose sympathies appeared to lie with Vichy, with the strength, spiritual value and true patriotism of the Free-French movement. His mission was successful, or at least many Quebecois became more receptive to Gaullism, and d'Argenlieu gained a reputation for diplomatic skill and forceful leadership. D'Argenlieu's qualities and status among the Free-French elite recommended him for the task of liquidating the Brunot mission and restoring some luster to the tarnished prestige of the Free-French movement in the South Pacific. To strengthen his hand, de Gaulle raised Captain d'Argenlieu to the rank of rear admiral and made him plenipotentiary delegate of the French National Committee with full authority in civil and military affairs.

Whatever Admiral d'Argenlieu's impressive personal qualities, it would be difficult to find an individual among the Free French, other than perhaps de Gaulle himself, whose behavior, comportment and attitude would stand in sharper contrast with the man he was to replace as high commissioner, the easygoing Governor Sautot. Governor Sautot was rather unimpressive in his personal appearance, and his manners were casual and familiar. He rather enjoyed discussing the affairs of the moment with the people of New Caledonia, and his unpretentious ways and simplicity greatly endeared him to his listeners. He was quick to express his feelings, sometimes in bursts of outrage but more often with a profusion of tears and sentiment, particularly when it came to expressions of loyalty to France and faith in the ultimate victory of the allies over Germany. His speeches at the war memorial were always emotional and very moving expressions of loyalty to de Gaulle and conviction in a final victory for democratic France.

Admiral d'Argenlieu could not match Sautot's popular appeal nor would he be able to play the "man of the people" that was Sautot's strength. In his public manner d'Argenlieu tended to be formal and aloof; he preferred to keep his own counsel and seldom confided in others. His appearance was austere, reflecting his background; he could be quite eloquent and later impressed the Americans with formidable powers of oratory, but this talent was more formal than familiar, more measured than emotional. Where Sautot appeared to act upon impulse, d'Argenlieu always seemed to be calculated in his gestures as well as in his actions. His sense of mission, suspicion of foreigners, and his sense of responsibility, rank and importance contrasted with Sautot's modesty, simplicity and strong admiration for Free-French allies in the Pacific.

Beyond such personal contrasts in style and manner were substantial differences in attitudes, particularly when it came to dealing with allies and their relations with the Free French, and these differences would erupt shortly after the Americans arrived in New Caledonia. Admiral d'Argenlieu had a profound, Gaullist suspicion of foreign intentions toward France and the Free-French cause. Sautot, on the other hand, was very popular with his British and Australian colleagues, who frequently expressed support and admiration for him both publicly and in communications with Canberra and London. Both Consul MacVitty and Sir Harry Luke equally admired the governor and could not understand his demotion. MacVitty believed that Sautot had become a victim of intrigues in London.[63] Sir Harry Luke described Governor Sautot as "the lynchpin" of the Free-French position in the Pacific. He warned that French settlers of New Caledonia and New Hebrides looked upon Sautot as a local hero and would resent his removal as high commissioner. Sautot, he argued, was a true patriot "with a hero-worship for General de Gaulle."[64]

Those qualities that the Anglo-Americans so admired in Sautot were precisely those that may have made him appear less than adequate to represent the full power, authority and grandeur of the Free-French cause in the Pacific from a Gaullist perspective. His willingness to work so readily with his Pacific allies became suspect in the eyes of de Gaulle, who was at that moment locked in a furious dispute with Churchill over Syria and Lebanon. In a cable to Sautot de Gaulle stated that while he did not have time to go into the details, d'Argenlieu would inform him of the difficult diplomatic and military efforts to place Lebanon and Syria under Free-French control in the face of British maneuvers.[65]

He again asked d'Argenlieu to assure Sautot "that I hold him in high esteem, [and] that I shall never forget anything that he has accomplished."[66] But Free-French authority had to be reinforced. The fiasco of the Brunot mission explains de Gaulle's anxiety about the vulnerability of Free France in the South Pacific.

Threats to French imperial interests in the Pacific had mounted dramatically during the summer of 1941 when the Japanese Government demanded in July 1941 that Vichy allow Japanese forces to be stationed in southern as well as in northern Indochina. The Japanese promised to respect French sovereignty in Indochina, and Admiral Decoux retained his ability to impose Vichy's "National Revolution" in the French colony.[67] However, the agreement of 21 July between Vichy and Tokyo confirmed the Caledonians' belief that they would have suffered the same fate had they not rallied to the Gaullist cause. Previously the American consul reported that Japanese ships arriving in Nouméa displayed charts of the South Pacific on which red lines had been drawn, showing New Caledonia to be within a Japanese sphere of influence. When the Japanese moved into southern Indochina in late July, Governor Sautot immediately requested that de Gaulle allow him to join the American, Dutch, and British responses to the Japanese move by freezing Japanese funds in New Caledonia. The American consul reported that such action would be welcomed by all elements of the population, even among those sympathetic to Vichy, "for if there is one thing in which the entire population appears to be in agreement it is their hatred and fear of the Japanese."[68]

The Japanese ultimatum and occupation of Indochina was a decisive moment in the course of international relations in the Pacific, leading directly to increased tensions that would culminate in the Japanese attack upon Pearl Harbor and the entry of the United States into the Second World War. In response to the Japanese move in Indochina, President Franklin Roosevelt had imposed an economic embargo on oil shipments to Japan and had frozen Japanese assets in the United States. These measures placed the Japanese in the position either of yielding to American demands that they give up their war of conquest in China or of turning toward Southeast Asia to obtain the resources necessary to continue that war. A southern strategy ran the risk of war with Great Britain and the United States, but this was the decision taken by the Japanese Government in the summer of 1941. As these war clouds gathered in the Pacific, de Gaulle was driven to strengthen the Free-French hand in order to assure that French interests the South Pacific would not be further harmed.

Both the American and Australian representatives in New Caledonia looked forward to Admiral d'Argenlieu's arrival. B.C. Ballard, the Australian consul, hoped that the presence of d'Argenlieu's mission would give a much-needed sense of urgency to the Caledonians.[69] In his report to the State Department MacVitty observed that de Gaulle was probably right to have appointed a military officer to the post of high commissioner, and he expected that Admiral d'Argenlieu would be welcomed.[70]

After sorting out matters in Tahiti and sending Brunot to London to face a court of inquiry, Admiral d'Argenlieu reached Nouméa on 5 November. A retinue of twenty officers and wives accompanied him. A large crowd that the American consul estimated to be 90 percent of the town's population gave d'Argenlieu and the Free-French mission an enthusiastic reception.[71] The admiral was pleased with his welcome. The population of New Caledonia was "ardently patriotic" and Nouméa reminded him of a small, provincial village in France. He quickly established cordial relations with Governor Sautot, whose patriotism had by no means been diminished as a result of d'Argenlieu's appointment to replace him as high commissioner. Even with certain shortcomings Sautot remained enormously popular with the Caledonians and with his British and Australian colleagues, d'Argenlieu observed. He also sensed divisions of a personal character on the island, even among the Gaullists, but he did not expect these quarrels to hamper his task.[72]

This initial welcome soon turned to disenchantment. Before reaching New Caledonia, d'Argenlieu had asked Sautot to make housing available for his staff, and he specifically requested the main residence in Nouméa overlooking the town as appropriate for his status as high commissioner.[73] Sautot had replied that, in addition to the costs of the mission, these housing requirements were unreasonable demands to ask of the Caledonians. He asked the Admiral to reconsider his request, but d'Argenlieu refused. Upon arrival Admiral d'Argenlieu and his staff remained on board *Cap des Palmes*, the Free-French ship that had brought them to New Caledonia, for ten days while they requisitioned housing, wine supplies, and automobiles by what the American consul described as "drastic means."[74]

The high-handed behavior of the mission quickly alienated the local population. The newly arrived Free-French officers seemed more interested in parties and driving rapidly through the streets of Nouméa in their requisitioned cars than in fighting the war or preparing the island's defense. At a time when the Caledonians felt they were making sacrifices, even if outside observers may have felt they were not terribly onerous, and had experienced shortages on the island, the mission's high living seemed particularly inconsiderate. In a letter to a friend with the Free-French movement in London a Caledonian woman described the luxurious living of the mission. They had taken over the military baths, using soldiers of the Caledonian reserves to haul sand from the beach at Anse Vata "so that the fair ladies of the Mission need not walk on pebbles." Lights from their requisitioned cars illuminated the baths while "all the mission disports itself in the water."[75] Members of the mission tended to look down upon the colonials.

The Caledonians seldom were invited to the mission's parties. A social gulf emerged between the rustic colonials, presumed to be descended from the criminal prisoners or revolutionary Communards deported to the colony in the nineteenth century, and the officers of the mission, many of whom, as one Caledonian sourly noted, carried an aristocratic particule before his name.[76] The d'Argenlieu mission quickly aroused Caledonian sensitivity to an all-too-familiar pattern of metropolitan disdain and a disposition to exploit the colony for its own benefit. An Australian airforce officer in Nouméa reported that growing resentment toward the mission was having a bad effect upon morale in the island, and the British resident in New Hebrides later claimed that an incipient revolt against the mission was averted only by the arrival of the Americans.[77]

The Caledonians were further dismayed when the local *Journal Officiel* published de Gaulle's ordinance of 2 August that gave the high commissioner of France in the Pacific far broader powers than granted to Sautot. What most upset the local population was that article 5 of the ordinance established that 60 percent of the costs of maintaining the mission would come from the Caledonian budget with the balance to be covered by the budgets of Tahiti and New Hebrides.[78] The worst Caledonian fears were confirmed. Since the officers of the mission showed a well-developed taste for luxury, the bill was likely to be high.

Admiral d'Argenlieu had no intention of playing to local political sensitivities. Shortly after his arrival he concluded that Sautot had conceded too much authority to the administrative council when he had appointed it. He informed General de Gaulle that he would brook no resistance from the council, particularly on financial matters, and he asked authority to veto any actions of the administrative council in New Caledonia that he did not approve.[79] Having rallied to the Gaullist cause in 1940 and having thought that this action had won them some measure of authority to manage their own affairs, the Caledonians now found themselves subordinated to the old system of central authority.[80]

Gaullist insistence upon centralized control and subordination of local needs and interests to those of France, broadly conceived, also reflected a concern over the imperialistic ambitions of de Gaulle's allies. On his passage through Fiji Admiral d'Argenlieu reminded Sir Harry Luke that he and General de Gaulle were determined to preserve French rights in the South Pacific.[81] Apprehensions over an Australian takeover or domination of New Caledonia had been present from the first days of Free-French rule. By the time d'Argenlieu reached New Caledonia a growing Gaullist fear was that an American presence in New Caledonia might prove fatal for the independence of the French colony. Suspicions of Australian and British intentions toward the French Empire became an even stronger suspicion of American imperialistic ambition in wartime New Caledonia.

Planners in Washington realized that New Caledonia was strategically located along the sea-lanes linking the United States to Australia, and they began to gather information about the island as the threat of war in the Pacific developed. Beginning in May 1941 the State Department asked Consul MacVitty to provide information on the strength of the island's defenses, a map of Nouméa, and an estimate of the size of the Japanese population living in New Caledonia. Military authorities also wanted to know the number and size of all airfields on the island, and they requested an assessment of the political attitudes and general morale of the Caledonian people.[82] With the entry of the United States into the war, the war department hastily assembled a military expedition to be sent to defend New Caledonia from the Japanese threat. Brigadier General Alexander M. Patch was appointed commander of this expedition, code named "Poppy Force." The Americans were coming, although Admiral d'Argenlieu had no knowledge of Washington's plans for the defense of the Free-French colony.

The first major test of American/Free-French cooperation was at hand in New Caledonia, setting the stage for a profound misunderstanding. Free-French dispatches show that de Gaulle expected that American cooperation would lead to recognition of the French National Committee and d'Argenlieu would command all Allied military forces on New Caledonia.[83] As General de Gaulle subsequently observed in his memoirs,

> ... whatever might be Washington's juridical position and feelings towards us, the entry of the United States into the war obliged them to co-operate with Free France. This was the case, immediately, with the Pacific where, by reason of the lightning advance of the Japanese, our possessions—New Caledonia, the Marquesas, Tuamato, the Society Islands and even Tahiti—might from one day to the next become vital to allied strategy.[84]

When they arrived, the Americans would be welcomed by most, but not all, of the French settlers. Governor Sautot would cheer their arrival and offer his enthusiastic support. Admiral d'Argenlieu would accept their presence with reservations. One of those who definitely did not welcome the American forces was Sautot's political adversary, Michel Vergès. "What the hell has this bunch of Americans come to do here?" he demanded. "We did not ask for them and we do not need them to defend our colony."[85]

General Patch would need all the cooperation he could get in preparing New Caledonia's defense and in dealing with the antagonism that existed between the Caledonian settlers and the d'Argenlieu mission, which would produce a riot six weeks after the Americans landed in New Caledonia.

Notes

1. B.C. Ballard (Nouméa) to External Affairs, 14 October 1940, Australian Archives (AA) ACT, 1975/215 item 3/40.
2. Remarks upon the "Free France" Movement and Frenchmen by Commanding Officer, H.M.A.S. *Adelaide*, transmitted 21 December 1940, U.K. Public Record Office (PRO) FO371/24338, 133994.
3. Wing Commander Alexander to Secretary of the Air Board, Melbourne, 19 October 1940, AA A1196 22/501/29; Henri Sautot, *Grandeur et décadence du Gaullisme dans le Pacifique* (Melbourne, 1949), 66–68.
4. De Gaulle to Sautot, 5 October 1940 and 7 October 1940, Ministère des Affaires Etrangères (MAE) Guerre 1939–45, Londres CNF, vol. 79; latter telegram reproduced in Charles de Gaulle, *Lettres, Notes et Carnets (LNC), juin 1940–juillet 1941* (Paris, 1981), 134.

5. Nicholas Rapadzi replaced Paul Vois as interim director of Le Nickel in New Caledonia following Vois's capture by the Germans after sinking the *Noitou* on 16 August 1940. The twelve members of the new administrative council included: Jean Audrain, accountant in Nouméa; Pierre Bergès, planter at La Foa; Clement Brumelet, miner from Nouméa; Leon Dévillers, cattle grazer at Houaïlou; August Henriot, planter from Kone; Maurice Janisel, planter at Pouébo; Just Mayet, representative from the Union of Employees in Nouméa; Émile Moulédous, merchant from Voh; Georges Morlet, merchant at Bourail; Henry Rolly, planter from Gomen; Dr. Trubert from Nouméa; and Albert Rapadzi, Director of Société Le Nickel in Nouméa. Listing from U.S. National Archives and Records Administration (USNARA), State Department, OSS Research and Analysis (R&A) Branch, Report 710, dtd. 22 September 1943.
6. Ballard to External Affairs, 12 November 1940, AA A816 19/311/74 File 3.
7. B.C. Ballard noted the curious alliance of Vergès, Prinet and some Nouméan business interests born of a common dislike for Australia and the British Commonwealth. Ballard to External Affairs 8 March 1941, AA 1975/215 (A6445) item 3/40. Vergès denounced Sautot as a tool of the Australians.
8. Sautot to de Gaulle, 18 January 1941, Archives Nationales, Section d'Outre-Mer (ANSOM) Nouvelle-Calédonie, carton 163.
9. De Gaulle to Sautot, 4 January 1941, *LNC juin 1940–juillet 1941*, 218.
10. Ballard to External Affairs, 29 October 1940 and 12 November 1940 AA A816 19/311/74 File 3; Sautot to de Gaulle 4 November 1940 and 17 November 1940, and de Gaulle to Sautot, 13 and 21 November 1940 in Archives Nationales (AN) Papiers Cassin 382 AP52; Châtellain and Kollen to Ccommandant Fontaine, 25 November 1940, MAE Guerre 1939–45, Londres CNF, vol. 79.
11. Châtellain and Kollen to de Gaulle, 28 December 1940, ibid.
12. De Gaulle to Captain Broche, 24 September 1940, *LNC juin 1940–juillet 1941*, 122–23.
13. Sautot, *Grandeur et décadence*, 89–94.
14. MacVitty to State, 7 May 1941, USNARA State Dec. File 851L.20/1.
15. Note du Professeur Cassin sur l'attribution de la qualité de *citoyen* aux indigènes de Tahiti et de la Nouvelle-Calèdonie," 16 August 1941, AN Papiers Cassin 382 AP52.
16. De Gaulle to General Catroux (Cairo), 18 December 1940, *LNC juin 1940-juillet 1941*, 204.
17. Commonwealth Government to Lord Cranborne, U.K. secretary of state for dominion affairs, 14 December 1940 doc. 224, and Cranborne to Commonwealth Government, 3 January 1941, doc. 244 in *Documents on Australian Foreign Policy (DAFP)*, vol. 4: *July 1940–June 1941*, ed, W.J. Hudson & H.J.W. Stokes, (Canberra: 1980).
18. Châtellain and Kollen to de Gaulle, 7 December 1940, MAE Guerre 1939–45, Londres CNF, vol. 79.
19. Mr. R.G. Menzies, prime minister, to Lord Cranborne, U.K. secretary of state for dominion affairs, 23 January 1941, doc. 255, *DAFP*, vol. 4.
20. In a radio broadcast, Colonel Denis boasted that he would arrive in New Caledonia in January or February aboard a French ship and would return the island to Vichy's control. Telegram from Naval Institute, Melbourne to Singapore, 27 December 1940, MAE Guerre 1939–45, Londres CNF, vol.79.
21. De Gaulle telegram to Sautot, 28 January 1941, in Charles de Gaulle, *Mémoires de Guerre*, vol. 1: *L'Appel, 1940-1942* (Paris, 1954), 341; and same to same, 12 February 1941, MAE Guerre 1939–45, Londres CNF, vol. 79.
22. Memorandum by Department of Internal Affairs, 13 January 1941, doc. 250; R.G. Menzies, PM, to Lord Cranborne, 23 January 1941, doc. 255; A.W. Fadden, Acting PM to P. Fraser, New Zealand PM, 10 February 1941, doc. 281, in *DAFP* vol. 4.
23. De Gaulle to Australian Government, 27 February 1941, *LNC juin 1940–juillet 1941*, 238.
24. Sir John Latham to Dept External Affairs, 4 February 1941, doc. 272, *DAFP*, vol. 4.

25. Lord Cranborne, U.K. secretary of state for dominion affairs, to Sir Geoffrey Whiskard, U.K. high commissioner in Australia, 7 February 1941, doc. 277; same to same, 12 February 1941, doc. 290; and Mr. A.S. Watt, first secretary of the legation in Washington, to Mr. R.G. Casey, minister to the United States, 12 February 1941, doc. 288, ibid.
26. Mr. R.G. Menzies, prime minister, to Lord Clairborne, U.K. secretary of state for dominion affairs, 23 January 1941, doc. 255, ibid.
27. Commonwealth Government to Cranborne, 15 February 1941, doc. 300, ibid.
28. John Lawrey, *The Cross of Lorraine in the South Pacific: Australia and the Free French Movement 1940–1942* (Canberra, 1982), 54–55; Menzies to Cranborne, 23 January 1941, doc. 255, *DAFP*, vol. 4.
29. Mr. A.W. Fadden, acting prime minister, to Mr. P. Fraser, New Zealand prime minister, 10 February 1941, doc. 281, War Cabinet Minute, 12 February 1941, doc. 284, *DAFP*, vol. 4.
30. "Report of the Australian Mission to New Caledonia, February–March 1941," AA A4311 66/2.
31. Lawrey, *Cross of Lorraine*, 57–58; Sautot to de Gaulle, 16 February 1941, De Gaulle, *Mémoires*, vol. 1, 362.
32. Cited in Lawrey, *Cross of Lorraine*, 56.
33. MacVitty to State, 10 May 1941, USNARA State Dec. File 851L.00/10.
34. De Gaulle telegram to Garreau-Dombasle, Free-French Rep. to the United States, 13 February 1941, *Mémoires*, vol. 1, 354.
35. Lawrey, *Cross of Lorraine*, 58.
36. De Gaulle telegram to Sautot, 7 March 1941, *Mémoires*, vol. 1, 358–59; Menzies to McFadden, acting prime minister, 16 March 1941, doc. 357, *DAFP*, vol. 4.
37. Secretary of State for Dominion Affairs to Prime Minister, 23 February 1941, AA CRS A981, New Caledonia 1B Part 6; French version, MAE Guerre 1939–45, Londres CNF, vol. 79.
38. Jean-Marc Regnault and Ismet Kurtovitch, "Les ralliements du Pacifique en 1940. Entre légende gaulliste, enjeux stratégiques mondiaux et rivalités Londres/Vichy," *Revue d'histoire moderne et contemporaine*, 49, 4, (octobre–décembre 2002): 75–76.
39. De Gaulle, *Mémoires*, vol. 1, 188; Francelib (London) to Sautot, 10 February 1941, MAE Guerre 1939–45, Londres CNF, vol. 79; also same to same 11 February 1941 in *LNC juin 1940-juillet 1941,* de Gaulle, 253.
40. Sautot, *Grandeur et décadence,* 101.
41. Ballard reported Sautot's illness to Canberra with the comment, "If his health breaks down seriously a major problem will be created, as there is nobody here who could replace him." Ballard to External Affairs, 30 April 1941, AA 1975/215 (A6445) item 3/40. MacVitty to State, 9 August 1941 USNARA State Dec. File 851L.00/16.
42. Châtelain and Kollen to de Gaulle, 1 April 1941, MAE Guerre 1939–45, Londres CNF, vol. 79.
43. Ballard to External Affairs, Memorandum 8 July 1941, AA CRS A981, New Caledonia IB Part 8.
44. Sautot, *Grandeur et décadence,* 101.
45. Brunot to Pleven, 15 May 1941, AN, Papiers Cassin 382 AP52. Sautot, *Grandeur et décadence,* 98; Secretary State Colonies to Luke, 15 July 1941, PRO FO371 28403 Z5931.
46. Sautot to de Gaulle, 21 July 1941 quoted in *Grandeur et décadence,* Sautot, 100; same to same, 2 August 1941, AN, Papiers Cassin 382 AP52; Sautot to Brunot, 28 July 1941 in *Grandeur et décadence,* Sautot, 100–101.
47. Telegram to de Gaulle (Brazzaville), 24 April 1941, ANSOM, CNF Telegrams, carton 811. The story of the Tahiti intrigues may be found in François Broche, *Le bataillon des guitaristes, l'épopée inconnue des FFL de Tahiti à Bir-Hakeim, 1940–1942* (Paris, 1970), 79–82, 89. See also Emile de Curton, *Tahiti 1940: Récit du ralliement à la France libre des Établissements français d'Océanie* (Paris, 1973) annexes 30, 31.

48. Rapport de Curton (to Commander d'Argenlieu), October 1941, Annex 1 Part 3 "L'Affaire Brunot-de Curton," in Broche, *Bataillon des Guitaristes*.
49. R.M. de Lambert to State, Summary of Events from June 1940 to January 1942, 2 February 1942, USNARA State Dec. File 851M.00/17.
50. Brunot to de Gaulle, 18 June 1941, and Muselier and Members of the Empire Defense Council for de Gaulle (then in Egypt) to Brunot, PRO FO371/28402 Z5149.
51. C.H. Archer (British consul) to Foreign Office, 4 December 1941, PRO FO371/32053 Z1586; Archer noted with understatement that this was not his term but that of the French citizens; he added that he felt compelled "to revise the opinion of the governor-general more than once in an adverse sense;" Davio also called Brunot "a dangerous maniac."
52. Muselier, Cassin, d'Argenlieu to de Gaulle, 30 July 1941, AN Papiers Cassin 382 AP52.
53. De Gaulle to d'Argenlieu, 4 August 1941, AN Papiers Cassin 382 AP52, and *LNC juillet 1941–mai 1943*, 40.
54. Muselier, d'Argenlieu, Cassin to de Gaulle, 17 June 1941, AN Papiers Cassin 382 AP52.
55. The instruction enabling Sautot's dismissal is in Broche, Annex 1 Part 4 "L'Affaire Brunot-Sautot" in *Bataillon des Guitaristes*, Broche, as noted by Lawrey, *Cross of Lorraine:* 69, de Gaulle omits this instruction from the published telegram from de Gaulle to the Free-French delegation in London, 9 July 1941, de Gaulle, *Mémoires*, vol. 1, 474.
56. De Gaulle to d'Argenlieu, 4 August 1941, AN Papiers Cassin 382 AP52 and de Gaulle, *LNC juillet 1941–mai 1943*, 40.
57. Georges Pisier, "Le Ralliement de la Calédonie et l'intervention Britannique (juin–octobre 1940)," *Bulletin de la société d'études historiques de la Nouvelle-Calédonie*, no. 62 (1er trimestre) 1985: 41, describes him as "un personnage courtaud, lourdaud, moustachu, jovial, bavard, qui ne payait pas de mine."
58. D'Argenlieu to de Gaulle (Cairo), 24 July 1941, AN Papiers Cassin 382 AP52.
59. De Gaulle to d'Argenlieu, 26 July 1941, *LNC juillet 1941–mai 1943*, 19; de Gaulle to Sautot 30 July 1941, AN Papiers Cassin 382 AP52, and de Gaulle to d'Argenlieu, 2 August 1941, *LNC juillet 1941–mai 1943*, 35.
60. De Gaulle to Sautot, 4 September 1941, and Council for Pacific to Sautot, 12 September 1941, PRO FO371 28406 Z7462.
61. De Gaulle to d'Argenlieu, 4 August 1941, and de Gaulle to Sautot, 6 September 1941, ibid. 40, 57.
62. Lieutenant Commander Tracy B. Kittredge, "Free French Interpretation of the New Caledonia Situation," (nd) Cincpac Box 110, file NB/105, case 198, Operational Archives, Naval History Center, Navy Yard, Washington, D.C. (Op Arch, NHC).
63. MacVitty to State, 19 August 1941, USNARA State Dec. File 851L.0018.
64. Luke to Sir Cosmo Parkinson (colonial office), 16 July 1941, forwarded to Foreign Office (Sommerville-Smith), 24 August 1941, PRO FO371 28406 Z7264.
65. De Gaulle to Sautot, 12 September 1941, AN Papiers Cassin 382 AP52.
66. De Gaulle to d'Argenlieu, 4 August 1941, ibid.
67. Eric Jennings, *Vichy in the Tropics: Pétain's National Revolution in Madagascar, Guadeloupe, and Indochina 1940–1944* (Stanford, 2001), 130-33.
68. MacVitty to State, 31 July 1941, USNARA State Dec. File 851L.00/12.
69. B.C. Ballard to External Affairs, 21 November 1941 AA ACT, CRS A981, New Caledonia 1A Part 9.
70. MacVitty to State, 19 September 1941, USNARA State Dec. File 851L.0022.
71. MacVitty to State, 7 November 1941, USNARA State Dec. File 851L.00/22; Ballard also reported that d'Argenlieu was "well received" on his arrival. Ballard to External Affairs, 21 November 1941, AA ACT CRS A981, New Caledonia 1A Part 9.
72. D'Argenlieu to de Gaulle, 21 November 1941 and 24 November 1941, AN Papiers d'Argenlieu AP517.

73. D'Argenlieu to Sautot, 19 August 1941, AN Papiers Cassin 382 AP52.
74. MacVitty to State, 3 December 1941, USNARA State Dec. File 851L.00/23.
75. Letter from Mrs. Beer to "Zezette," 20 May 1942, tr. (crudely) from the French and made available to U.S. military intelligence, USNARA War Dept, RG 165, regional file, "NC" Box 1793.
76. E. Cane to Sautot, 2 May 1942, appendix BB to Flight Lieutenant Evan McColl, "Revolution in New Caledonia," USNARA, OSS RG 226.
77. Air Intelligence, Nouméa to Air Intelligence, Melbourne, 8 February 1942, AA A816 item 19/311/138; R.D. Blandy, via Sir Harry Luke to Colonies, 6 February 1942, PRO 371/32053/Z3646.
78. MacVitty to State, 3 March 1941 with annexed copies of the decree in French and English, USNARA State Dec. File 851L.00/23.
79. D'Argenlieu to CNF, 12 April 1941, MAE Guerre 1939–45, Londres CNF, vol. 328, and same to same, 12 May 1941 AN Papiers Cassin 382 AP 59, and d'Argenlieu to de Gaulle, 1 December 1941, AN Papiers d'Argenlieu 517AP.
80. In April Admiral d'Argenlieu warned that "an excess of centralization … risks leading us, I fear, into the old mistakes from which our colonies in the Pacific in particular have suffered." D'Argenlieu to CNF, 7 April 1942, MAE Guerre 1939–45, Londres CNF, vol. 328.
81. D'Argenlieu to de Gaulle, 26 October 1941, AN Papiers d'Argenlieu 517AP.
82. See MacVitty to State, 4 November 1941, USNARA State Dec. File 851L.20/11.
83. CNF to Tixier, 27 January 1942, MAE Guerre 1939–45, Londres CNF, vol. 120.
84. De Gaulle, *Mémoires*, vol. 1, 187; translation is from Charles de Gaulle, *War Memoirs*, vol. 1: *The Call to Honor 1940–1942* tr. Jonathan Griffin (London, 1955): 220.
85. Sautot to Patch, 30 April 1942, Administrative History Appendices 34(10)(C), Op Arch NHC, Washington D.C.

Chapter 4

Going to Pieces: The 1942 Riot

Although war clouds had formed over the Pacific, the surprise Japanese attack on Pearl Harbor on 7 December 1941 came as a shock out of the blue. The Americans were in the war, but were they prepared? Most of the Pacific Fleet had been immobilized, and prospects for halting a Japanese advance into Southeastern Asia and the South Pacific were not promising. The American Army in 1940 had been roughly the size of the Bulgarian Army. President Franklin Roosevelt had embarked upon an expansion program with a peacetime draft and a gearing up of war industries, but the Americans were far from ready for the demands of a global struggle. Yet the entry of the United States, even under the tragic circumstances of Pearl Harbor, seemed to assure eventual victory over the Axis in the eyes of Prime Minister Winston Churchill. The full industrial might of the United States was on the side of the Allies. With the Russians stopping Hitler's army at the gates of Moscow and with the Americans at war, the combination of American material strength and Soviet manpower would be decisive.

Like Churchill, General de Gaulle was convinced after Pearl Harbor that the eventual victory of the Allies was assured, despite continued but short-term military setbacks.[1] The Gaullist concern was that France and the French Empire should not be overwhelmed by American power and that the United States should treat Free France as a full-fledged ally. He did not hesitate to join the Allies in the fight in the Pacific. He promptly declared war upon Japan, despite the limited resources available to defend Free-French possessions in the South Pacific. He was uncertain, but he hoped that American assistance would be forthcoming, given American interest in air bases in Polynesia and New Caledonia.

Admiral d'Argenlieu awaited the arrival of the Americans with mixed emotions. The General's declaration of war and Japanese interest in New Caledonia's mineral resources, he rightly suspected, made New Caledonia an objective of Japanese expansion. Vichy might try to recover New Caledonia and Tahiti with Japanese support, reversing the rallies of 1940. In January 1942 Admiral Jean Decoux, governor-general of Indochina, proposed an expedition to regain control of the dissident colonies. Radio Saigon claimed that New Caledonia could avoid the horrors of war if the colony would return to neutrality and Vichy control.[2] From Tahiti Governor Georges Orselli warned that he might not be able to count on the support of the local population against a Vichy expedition from Indochina supported by the Japanese.[3] Vichy subsequently vetoed Admiral Decoux's project, but Admiral d'Argenlieu had no way of knowing this in the anxious weeks that followed the Pearl Harbor attack.

He also well understood that the island could provide no more than a token defense against a Japanese force. As the Japanese drive southward gathered momentum at the beginning of 1942, the Free-French colony was in serious danger. Australian promises of assistance seemed inadequate, and the Australians faced a very real possibility of invasion and could spare no naval forces to protect a French possession, however strategically important that colony might be. The only realistic hope for defending New Caledonia was assistance from the United States, but that meant Free-French and New Caledonia's further dependence upon a foreign power.

In August two American seaplanes had visited Nouméa to size up the situation on their way to and from Australia. This visit was kept as quiet as possible with the censorship forbidding any mention of their presence to avoid Japanese

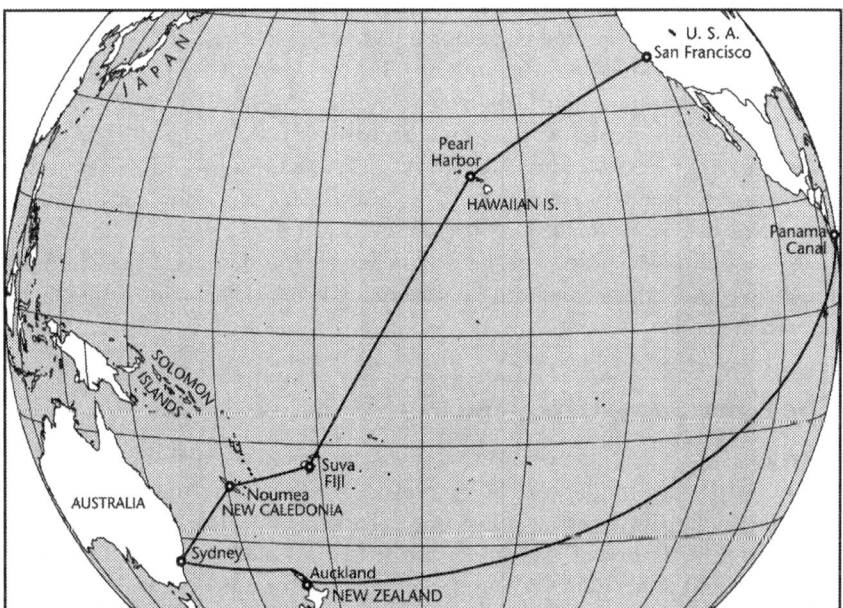

Map 3. U.S. Supply Routes to South Pacific, 1942.
Source. Cartography Lab, University of Minnesota.

suspicions.⁴ Three months later the U.S. Army's Hawaiian Department sent an officer to New Caledonia on an intelligence mission without bothering to inform or even establish any contact with Admiral d'Argenlieu. When Admiral d'Argenlieu learned that an American officer was travelling about the colony without informing him, he became upset at this cavalier disregard of Free-French authority. He ordered the Australians to cease all construction work at Tontouta and to have nothing to do with the Americans. In a cable to de Gaulle d'Argenlieu complained bitterly of American technicians on the island acting largely on their own without consultation.⁵ Consul MacVitty also complained to the State Department about the surreptitious activities of American military representatives. He asked that General Short in Hawaii be reminded that his officers were on foreign soil as guests. Their ignoring diplomatic courtesies had greatly complicated the situation.⁶

To assure that the French National Committee would have a significant role in the defense of French Pacific territories, de Gaulle insisted that all matters of policy be negotiated through London. He warned d'Argenlieu that any American attempt to deal with local authorities on the spot, as had occurred with Admiral Robert in Martinique, was more or less calculated meddling and nothing less than a deliberate plot to break up the French Empire.⁷ De Gaulle admonished d'Argenlieu, "As far as the use of our Pacific bases by the Americans is concerned, carry out the commitments we have made, but go no farther."⁸

The construction of airfields at Tontouta and Plaine des Gaiacs, which the Australians had begun, made New Caledonia an even more tempting target for Japanese strategists. Admiral d'Argenlieu had to be reassured of American plans for military support. On 15 January 1942 he informed General Carleton Emmons of the Hawaiian Department that if Emmons could not promise immediate reinforcements, he would stop work on the airfields.⁹ Admiral d'Argenlieu cabled General de Gaulle that the Americans had not responded to his request for military equipment. The local population feared an immanent attack and anxiety was high. The "irresponsibility of the Americans" did not help the situation in New Caledonia, he glumly reported. A defense of the island was impossible under these conditions, but he assured de Gaulle that he would do his duty to the end.¹⁰

The Americans Arrive: January–March '42

American help was on the way. After some debate as to where troops headed for the South Pacific might best be employed, the war department decided to commit the largest American force in the Pacific, other than in Australia and Hawaii, to the defense of strategically located New Caledonia. New Caledonia's size also would provide an excellent training ground for American troops, and the Americans were anxious to deny the Japanese access to its nickel resources.

With the prospect that the United States might be engaged in a global conflict, information about distant places became important and in 1941 the understaffed American intelligence services hastily expanded. One new recruit to what would become the Office of Strategic Services (OSS) was David Pinkney, a recent Ph.D from Harvard, who was given the assignment of gathering as much information about New Caledonia as possible. In addition to the information that Consul MacVitty had provided, he made good use of information to be found in the Library of Congress, and on 31 January 1942 produced a two hundred-page report that detailed the geography, harbor facilities, population, and resources of New Caledonia.[11] This document was available to General Patch, who flew to the South Pacific after the Poppy Force had sailed from Charleston, South Carolina on 23 January 1942.

The intelligence document informed General Patch that New Caledonia had been a French colony since 1853. Its principal economic activity was nickel mining, but the growing of coffee for export and cattle ranching were also important for the local economy. The strategic location of New Caledonia and its size and mineral resources gave New Caledonia its importance. Since New Caledonia was sparsely populated, its open fields offered good training sites, and the plain that stretched along the 250 mile West Coast was ideally suited for the construction of airfields. Although Nouméa was a small town of only 18,000 inhabitants, it had an excellent harbor that could be exploited, even if the dock facilities were limited.

According to extrapolations from recent census information, the population of New Caledonia was approximately 57,000 individuals. This population was divided between 29,000 native Melanesians, or Kanak, 17,000 European settlers, and 11,000 Asians. The latter included just under 10,000 Javanese and Tonkinese indentured laborers, who had been brought in to work in the mines or on the large ranches, and 1,100 Japanese iron mine workers and truck farmers who supplied produce to Nouméa.[12]

The European settlers included a small, relatively prosperous elite, who controlled the mining industry, the large cattle ranches and the commercial trading companies in Nouméa. Most of the European settlers were the Broussards, small farmers of the interior who scratched a harsh, marginal existence on the rocky plain along the West Coast of the island or worked as supervisors at the mines. Some of these Broussards were involved in raising coffee for export while others were small shopkeepers in the towns and villages of the interior. Many of them were descendants of prisoners, including Communards from the 1871 Parisian uprising, sent to New Caledonia in the late nineteenth century when the island was a penal colony. Others had come as the result of government sponsored settlement programs. The social gulf between the Broussards and the wealthy elite was a significant characteristic of New Caledonia's French settlers.

The non-European population included the majority Kanak, whose best lands had been taken from them by the Europeans. They had been confined to a small number of reservations and lived in relative isolation, frustration and despair. During the first years of the European occupation of New Caledonia, the Kanak population had gone into a severe decline, due to disease and demoralization. On two occasions in 1878 and 1917 Kanak had risen in revolt against the colonizers, uprisings that the French military had brutally suppressed. By 1936 Kanak birth rates had begun to rise and mortality declined so that a Kanak demographic recovery was under way by the time the Americans arrived. As for the indentured Asian workers, they worked for low pay and lived in misery in the inadequate housing provided by mining companies.

For reasons of security the Americans provided General de Gaulle and Admiral d'Argenlieu with no specifics as to the expedition's size or command structure.[13] In general terms the State Department informed de Gaulle that the American and British general staffs had commenced taking measures to assure New Caledonia's defense, and they asked that Admiral d'Argenlieu be informed in absolute secrecy of this decision.[14] Not until a month later did d'Argenlieu learn that recently promoted Major General Alexander Patch would command the expedition and he would contact him.[15] Meanwhile General de Gaulle would try to send reinforcements, but he urged Admiral d'Argenlieu to do his utmost to defend French territory to the last. "One can say that the honor of the French flag and that of Christianity are in your hands out there."[16] This was a heavy assignment for a commander with limited means at his disposal.

While the effective defense of New Caledonia depended upon the arrival of the Americans, Admiral d'Argenlieu feared that they would pursue their own interests at the expense of the Free French once they appeared. "The Americans," he warned de Gaulle, "seem to want to get what they need from us without providing us with any compensation."[17] He understood, although he could not confirm, that there was a secret agreement between the Americans and Australians to land American troops without getting prior approval from the Free French. If so, he then feared the Free French would be brushed aside and ignored. He noted that General de Gaulle had ordered him to resist such action, and he promised to execute his orders. If the Americans came to New Caledonia, Admiral d'Argenlieu suspected that they might prefer dealing with Vichy rather than the Free French. He predicted that if American forces confronted those of Vichy, the Americans would make an arrangement with them on the pretext that French sovereignty was being preserved.[18] In a letter to Governor Orselli in Tahiti he observed that the difficulty in dealing with the Americans was that they remained attached to their Vichy policy. Free France did not count in American eyes. A lack of military means, he lamented, caused the Americans to treat the Free French "like very poor relations."[19]

American recognition of Free-French control of New Caledonia provided Free-French authorities with some reassurance that the United States would not deal separately with Vichy in New Caledonia. On 15 January the Free-French representative in Washington, Adrien Tixier, signed an agreement that allowed the United States to establish military bases on French possessions in the Pacific as long as French rights and sovereignty were respected.[20] The State Department issued a declaration that the United States recognized Free-French authority in those territories that had rallied to the Gaullist cause and repeated its promise regarding "the maintenance of the integrity of France and the French Empire and the eventual restoration … of all French territories." A week later Consul MacVitty gave d'Argenlieu the statement for publication in Nouméa.[21]

De Gaulle expressed satisfaction with this announcement and claimed it was "tantamount to a promise to restore the complete independence of all French territories, whether at home or in the empire."[22] He ordered d'Argenlieu to cooperate with the American military expedition that soon would arrive in New Caledonia. Admiral d'Argenlieu thanked Consul MacVitty when he was informed that the Americans recognized only the authority of the French National Committee in those French territories of the South Pacific that had rallied to Free France. In a gesture of solidarity Admiral d'Argenlieu reaffirmed and praised the traditional friendship that historically had bound France and the United States.[23]

While the State Department's declaration satisfied General de Gaulle, there was still the matter of who would command the Allied troops in New Caledonia. General de Gaulle proposed that Admiral d'Argenlieu should assume command of all Allied Forces stationed on French territory to ensure that French sovereign rights would be respected. However, if General Patch arrived with considerable numbers of troops under his command, de Gaulle conceded that d'Argenlieu might work under Patch as part of an inter-Allied command structure in the South Pacific theater.[24] And General Patch, who flew into Nouméa five days ahead of the Poppy Force as it was code-named, had a substantial number of troops and an impressive amount of equipment at his command—substantial and impressive at least to Caledonian eyes.

The astonished Caledonians discovered on the morning of 12 March 1942 that a flotilla of American troop ships and their escorts was entering Nouméa harbor. The first fifteen thousand of an eventual force of over forty thousand soldiers were soon coming ashore, unloading equipment, setting up tents, and seeking training facilities for what eventually was to become the Americal Division that would relieve the Marines on Guadalcanal six months later. One observer noted that the supplies were piled so high on the docks that you could not see the roofs of the adjacent warehouses. The American arrival hid the confusion of their shipping in which equipment had been hastily loaded in a willy-nilly fashion that required unloading and re-loading in Australia. The official American historian has called Task Force 6184 a military stew of men and equipment, but the stew when it arrived looked reassuring and comforting to the nearly defenseless Caledonians.[25]

Admiral d'Argenlieu was overwhelmed. His expectation of commanding allied forces in New Caledonia suddenly appeared misplaced, even a bit humiliating. "It seems obvious," he ruefully cabled de Gaulle, "that command of allied forces in New Caledonia can only belong to Patch, whose troops and resources are crushing in comparison with ours."[26] The equipment and personnel that the Americans brought with them made a painful contrast with the modest resources available to the admiral. In addition to the twenty members of the d'Argenlieu mission there were only fourteen hundred men, including Kanak, who had been called up or had volunteered for active duty and some two thousand Caledonians, mostly Broussards, who had been organized into a militia under the command of Captain Dubois. These limited resources made the Free-French contribution to New Caledonia's defense pale by comparison with what the Americans could provide.

Figure 4.1. General Patch and Admiral d'Argenlieu reach agreement on defending New Caledonia.
Source. U.S. National Archives (111-SC-151186).

After some discussion Admiral d'Argenlieu formally turned over command to Patch, who assumed responsibility for New Caledonia's defense.[27] In a message to General de Gaulle he expressed his profound emotion in having to turn responsibility for the defense of French imperial territory to a foreigner. The very presence of the Americans was a painful humiliation for France, causing him to lament "our powerlessness to assure our own security," and he deplored the almost total abandonment in which the metropolis had left the colony. Despite his feelings, he reported that his relationship with the American commander was excellent and that he would try to work out matters with the well-equipped Americans who had arrived.[28]

From the beginning of their time in New Caledonia the material resources of the United States not only overawed the d'Argenlieu mission but deeply impressed the Caledonians, whether European settlers or Kanak living on the reservations of the interior. The first wave of Americans required three days and nights to unload their equipment. Caledonians have retained vivid memories of the quantity and size of the trucks and jeeps, "the avalanche of material unloaded was stupefying," and they were equally impressed with the speed and organization that made the task possible. Arnold Daly, a long-time resident of Nouméa, observed that the size of the equipment, notably the trucks and tractors, was "monstrous" and the Americans themselves appeared to be from another planet. "If Martians had landed among us, we would not have been more surprised."[29]

"One might have said the Martians had landed" was also how Gabriel Païta, a young Kanak student in a Catholic missionary school, reacted when the Americans appeared. He recalled studying American history, but he was unprepared for the amount of weapons, the sizes of the trucks, jeeps and bulldozers associated with the image of "Lafayette and all of that." The Americans established a camp near his school in Canala, and not long after the students began to receive shoes, clothing and GI rations. What had been a remote village suddenly was less remote as American broadcasts brought news of the outside world. Soldiers handed out chewing gum, peanuts, and cans of corned beef. The head of the school, Father William, even received a "precious jeep." This abundance and spontaneous generosity created a lasting impression, to the point that Gabriel Païta, looking back over fifty years, insisted, "It was the Americans who led to the advancement of the Kanak people."[30] American casual generosity contrasted vividly with the distant, formal relations that Admiral d'Argenlieu and his staff adopted toward not only Kanak but also toward Caledonian settlers from whom they requisitioned cars and homes for their own use. Free-French officials feared that American material resources would tempt Caledonian and Kanak alike to look to the Americans rather than to the Free French for their defense, welfare and possibly even liberation from the rigors of French colonial rule.

If the Caledonians were astonished at the arrival of the Americans, the soldiers of the Poppy Force were no less surprised to find themselves in New Caledonia. Many of the soldiers aboard the troopships, most of them members of the

National Guards of Massachusetts, New Jersey and Tennessee, did not know the name of the island, what language would be spoken, or even if it were friendly. The commanding officers, including General Patch, were better informed, but their briefing on New Caledonia had been of recent vintage since not much was known in the United States about New Caledonia, its location, its population, or its size.

General Patch knew that the island had rallied to General de Gaulle in 1940 and that he was coming to friendly territory. His assignment was to prepare his

Figure 4.2. "One might have said the Martians had landed," Gabriel Païta.
Source. U.S. National Archives (111-SC-163689).

troops to defend the island and engage Japanese forces advancing into the South Pacific. New Caledonia would become a crucial staging ground for American forces. He had some awareness of the social divisions on the island, including the important role that the Broussards had played in the rally. He would have to establish good relations with the local population as well as with General de Gaulle's representative in New Caledonia, Admiral d'Argenlieu.

Initial contacts between Admiral d'Argenlieu and the Americans went smoothly enough with receptions and luncheons. Both sides offered toasts to the traditions of Franco-American friendship and cooperation. Admiral d'Argenlieu informed General de Gaulle that his relations with General Patch were as cordial as possible.[31] To coordinate defense planning and preparation Patch asked that Captain Dubois, commander of the local militia, be attached to his staff and be responsible for their training under Patch's supervision. Admiral d'Argenlieu agreed to this arrangement. In addition to 2,000 militia troops, forces on the island consisted of some 320 Australian commandos whose morale was good and who were well trained. Of the 1,400 French reserve troops, however, only 600 could be considered a capable fighting force, and these were located mainly in the Nouméa region. They were equipped with outmoded Lebel rifles, although they had a good supply of light machine guns. A battery of 65mm mountain guns and a battery of 95mm coastal guns protected the harbor, but they would be of little effect against modern warships.[32]

The militia provided useful assistance to the Americans as they moved into the countryside since they knew the backcountry well, but getting American forces into the interior would not be easy. General Patch noted the poor condition of roads, including the main road along the western coast of the island, which was narrow and cut by several rivers that could be crossed only with ferries. Despite such obstacles some 22,000 American soldiers had dispersed throughout the countryside by late March.

In addition to difficulties of the terrain General Patch encountered problems with the d'Argenlieu mission. Relations between the American command and Admiral d'Argenlieu began to go sour within three weeks of the American arrival. On the Free-French side Admiral d'Argenlieu concluded that the Americans showed no respect for French sovereignty or for his authority and status as Free-French high commissioner. Patch retained control over all military supply and its distribution, including Lend-lease equipment, which he made directly available to Captain Dubois for the militia. D'Argenlieu resented that he was little consulted on defense preparations. He began to be less and less accommodating.

New Caledonia in Political and Military Crisis: April '42

Admiral d'Argenlieu deplored the tendency of Governor Sautot, Captain Dubois, the administrative council, and Mayor Ernest Massoubre of Nouméa to make arrangements with American authorities without consulting him or obtaining his prior approval. Minor episodes assumed cosmic proportions. Traffic circulation in Nouméa, for example, was changed with one-way streets created to facilitate unloading. That proved too much for d'Argenlieu. One afternoon he telephoned Sautot and in an angry voice asked, "Have you seen what is going on in town? *Eh bien!* These one-way street signs are in one language only, the English language! I have already warned you, it is the American takeover of New Caledonia, and you have not wanted to do anything about it; you allowed it to happen."[33]

But it was about more than traffic signs. D'Argenlieu complained to de Gaulle that the Americans were exceeding the authority that he had voluntarily yielded in turning over command of the army and air forces on the island. The Allies had changed the command structure for the Pacific without consulting him, and a military conference on the Pacific had been held in Washington without Free-French representation.[34] In their rather casual and thoughtless manner, the Americans failed to take account of d'Argenlieu's pride and sensitivity on the subject of French authority. The Americans tended to work problems out as they developed, and they scarcely suspected that the honor and prestige of the Free-French movement or that the unity of the French Empire was at issue in the admiral's insistence that he constantly be consulted. The Americans became impatient with his insistence that he and he alone had the right to authorize or

Figure 4.3. "It is the American takeover of New Caledonia," Admiral d'Argenlieu.
Source. U.S. National Archives (111-SC-244037).

deny American requests over seemingly minor decisions that the Americans considered necessary to facilitate the war effort.

These slights wounded d'Argenlieu personally and, as he saw it, showed disregard if not contempt for the Free French and what they represented. In a letter to de Gaulle, he thanked the General for his insistence that Free France be respected by the Allies as the legitimate representative of a France that was rich in one thousand years of history and tradition. He believed that it was important in a distant place such as New Caledonia to resist the domineering tendencies of arrogant Allies.[35]

The Americans were oblivious to the potential problems that a disregard for French formal procedures and slights to Free-French prestige might create. The British Foreign Office, which had a longer experience in dealing with the Gaullists, noted that "the Australians and Americans will have trouble with Admiral d'Argenlieu if they do not pay the greatest attention to his position and rights." D'Argenlieu's tactic was to become increasingly uncooperative in the face of what he thought to be American indifference to the Free French. The Foreign Office, which had been sympathetic to the d'Argenlieu appointment, observed with annoyance and surprise that "Admiral d'Argenlieu is showing more pettiness than one would have expected from him."[36] American intelligence indicated that the Japanese were preparing a major offensive thrust in the direction of Port Moresby in New Guinea and toward New Caledonia to cut American communications with Australia. In these circumstances, Patch could not await a lengthy decision-making process. D'Argenlieu's punctilio was getting in the way of the war effort.

Admiral d'Argenlieu's pettiness increased with his growing animosity toward Governor Henri Sautot whom he accused of being too cooperative with the Americans. The Americans, he later reported sarcastically to General de Gaulle, preferred to make local arrangements with a Sautot who was, "so friendly, so obliging, so understanding."[37] In the admiral's eyes Sautot was completely subservient to the Americans to the detriment of French interests and even French sovereignty. De Gaulle agreed, and he stated that the American liking for Sautot came from a preference for dealing with a more malleable France.[38] The governor's willingness to cooperate with the American forces in New Caledonia brought a showdown with Admiral d'Argenlieu, who decided to get rid of Governor Sautot, barely two weeks after the arrival of the Americans.

On 31 March he cabled General de Gaulle that beneath Sautot's facade of sentimental and superficial patriotism, the governor was cultivating his own popularity among the Caledonian population by orchestrating a campaign to get rid of the d'Argenlieu mission. D'Argenlieu complained that Sautot was playing to Caledonian's long-standing hostility to centralized French authority. Sautot reportedly claimed that the arrival of the Americans meant that the mission's presence for the defense of New Caledonia no longer was necessary. Furthermore, Sautot blamed all of the inconveniences the Caledonians suffered upon the mission and its activities. As a result of his "demagoguery" d'Argenlieu considered Sautot's presence in the colony to have become "intolerable and dangerous." Sautot had played the British card in the New Hebrides, he noted, the Australian one in New Caledonia and now was preparing to play the American one against French interests. The admiral asked that de Gaulle put an end to this state of affairs by ordering Sautot to London to report to the French National Committee on the situation in the Pacific.

Once Sautot left the colony, d'Argenlieu was confident that he would be quickly forgotten. He warned, though, that Sautot's removal might cause some agitation among the volatile elements of the local population. D'Argenlieu implied that such difficulties could be avoided if the matter were handled diplomatically. Out of respect for the prestige of France and in the presence of American allies, Admiral d'Argenlieu hoped that the governor's departure could be accomplished in a dignified and correct fashion, particularly if Sautot were lavishly praised for his accomplishments. With the approaching danger he was certain that the local population would understand this change.[39] In any event, as Admiral d'Argenlieu subsequently assured de Gaulle, the presence of American troops would guarantee that order would be preserved.[40]

On 8 April General de Gaulle ordered Sautot to return to London for reassignment to "an important post." To soften the blow, de Gaulle instructed d'Argenlieu to express publicly his satisfaction over the way in which Sautot had accomplished a particularly difficult and deserving mission. He also asked that before carrying out this order Admiral d'Argenlieu should try to work out his relations with Sautot and make the governor understand his duty. If d'Argenlieu judged that this breach could not be closed, then he would be justified in ordering Sautot to London for consultations. Admiral d'Argenlieu complied and waited three weeks before he gave General de Gaulle's order to Sautot after concluding that their relationship remained intolerable.[41]

Patch's distant manner toward Admiral d'Argenlieu stemmed from his impatience with the Admiral's delaying tactics and obstructionism.[42] When he had been sent to New Caledonia, Patch's instructions were simple in their brevity. His assignment was to hold New Caledonia in cooperation with all Allied Forces in the face of Japanese aggression, and he was to do so without any guarantee of additional reinforcements. He would have to make do with what was at hand. He answered directly to the American war department in Washington. The situation was critical as Japanese naval and land forces had overrun the Dutch East Indies and had captured Rabaul in New Britain in the Bismarck Archipelago at the western end of the Solomon Islands. His task was a difficult but straightforward military assignment.

Before d'Argenlieu issued de Gaulle's order recalling Sautot, Consul MacVitty and General Patch had concluded that d'Argenlieu's unpopularity on the island, combined with his aloof manner and uncooperative attitude, was a liability. A month after his arrival General Patch warned Washington that the d'Argenlieu mission was proving to be uncooperative due to resentments over Sautot's popularity with the local population. Frustrated by Admiral d'Argenlieu's lack of cooperation General Patch cabled Washington that matters would go more smoothly in preparing the defense of New Caledonia if Admiral d'Argenlieu could be persuaded to move his headquarters elsewhere, and he suggested Tahiti.[43]

In exasperation MacVitty informed the State Department that the admiral showed little interest in preparing to defend New Caledonia. He reported, "D'Argenlieu has consistently shown that he desires to impress all and sundry with his importance and that this attitude seems of more paramount importance to him than the present dangerous situation in this part of the Pacific."[44] The Americans in Washington were now convinced that Admiral d'Argenlieu placed his own rank and prestige, and what d'Argenlieu apparently believed was the status of Free France, ahead of the war crisis and the immediate military danger.

In view of his attitude and behavior, General Marshall cabled Patch for guidance on how to deal with the Free-French admiral, "Should he be flattered, pampered or treated in a firm, positive manner?" Patch's reply was measured:

> High commisioner d'Argenlieu is an intelligent, dignified, and very formal Frenchman, but is vain, meticulous, devious, and ambitious. Our governmental agencies should deal with him in a polite but very firm and positive matter. Vast majority of New Caledonians strongly resents d'Argenlieu and his personal staff. On the other hand, Free French Governor Henri Sautot is liked and trusted. If d'Argenlieu were located elsewhere the local military and political situation would be materially improved.[45]

Whether or not this amounted to a conspiracy by MacVitty and Patch to get rid of him and take over the Free-French colony, as Admiral d'Argenlieu claimed, is difficult to determine, but it was Sautot rather than d'Argenlieu who was relocated. The political and military situation on the island of New Caledonia was not improved, quite the contrary.

In his hostility toward Governor Sautot and his conviction that the Americans intended to take over the island d'Argenlieu received encouragement from Michel Vergès, who found an opportunity to get revenge upon Sautot and secure his removal from the island. Vergès had quickly ingratiated himself with members of the d'Argenlieu mission and had successfully persuaded d'Argenlieu that he and his colleague, André Prinet, were the only true and sincere supporters of General de Gaulle on the island. Just as he had argued that Sautot was selling out to the Australians in 1940/41, Vergès now claimed that the governor was in the pay of the Americans.

Admiral d'Argenlieu was apparently impressed with Vergès's version of the events of September 1940. In his telegram to de Gaulle requesting Sautot's recall and again in his full report on the events of May, d'Argenlieu passed along Vergès's claim that Sautot hesitated at a crucial moment in the rally. It was Vergès, not Sautot, who was responsible for New Caledonia's rally.[46] Even though Vergès's denigration of Sautot's role in the rally was at odds with the accounts provided by the British and Australian consuls and by Sir Harry Luke, who had praised his personal courage and devotion to the Free-French cause, this slander against Sautot was an additional reason to justify the governor's removal.

The crisis broke at the end of April. According to Admiral d'Argenlieu's account, an extraordinary session of the administrative council was held and a motion passed that asked for the departure of d'Argenlieu and the Free-French mission.[47] The Free-French admiral got wind of this maneuver in the evening of 27 April and decided to put an end to such intrigues. The next day he handed Sautot General de Gaulle's telegram of 8 April recalling him to London. Sautot regretted having to leave New Caledonia at a time of growing danger, but in the national interest he bowed to de Gaulle's wish and indicated that he would comply with the General's order.[48] However, when d'Argenlieu informed Pierre Bergès, the president of the council, of this order, Bergès decided to take the lead in opposing the popular governor's removal. Admiral d'Argenlieu detected a maneuver on the part of Bergès, whom Michel Vergès claimed was the leader of the Caledonian autonomist party, to secure rights to self-government for the colony under American protection. As d'Argenlieu later put it, "The old autonomist leavening was about to cause the entire Caledonian pastry to rise up."[49]

Things Go Awry: May '42

News of Sautot's recall spread in Nouméa the following day, 1 May. A Labor Day parade was held in the morning, and afterward a crowd of four to five hundred gathered outside the Government House. Sautot assured the demonstrators that his reassignment was in the best interests of the Free-French cause. Later that afternoon a delegation of Broussards arrived at the governor's office and urged Sautot to remain at least until the Japanese danger had passed. At the same time Sautot learned that Michel Vergès was running through the streets of Nouméa loudly boasting that he had obtained his dismissal. Sautot then reconsidered his decision to accept General de Gaulle's order.[50] In the meantime a delegation that included Bergès, Moulédous, Pognon and Rapadzi from the administrative council and Captain Dubois of the militia asked General Patch to send a telegram to General de Gaulle requesting that Governor Sautot be allowed to remain on the island. The Caledonians were convinced that General de Gaulle would recall Admiral d'Argenlieu rather than Governor Sautot if he were informed of the admiral's arbitrary dismissal of the popular Governor Sautot.

Patch refused to send the message on the ground that he wished to remain neutral in the conflict. Instead, he sent three officers from his staff to inform Admiral d'Argenlieu that he had declined to send the telegram. Patch's representatives also expressed their regret that the decision to recall Governor Sautot had been taken at such a poorly timed moment with New Caledonia facing the possibility of a Japanese invasion. His refusal to send the message from the Caledonian notables cost Patch some popularity with the Caledonians, but it somehow convinced the admiral that General Patch was part of a plot against him. The American Consul MacVitty also declined to send the message, and MacVitty also would be accused of plotting against d'Argenlieu and his mission. Eventually the British consul forwarded the delegation's telegram to London. When it reached General de Gaulle's headquarters, it was dismissed out of hand as coming from a tainted source and misrepresented what was actually happening on the island.[51]

Sautot also sent a telegram warning that the situation was serious and he feared his departure would provoke disturbances since a great majority of the Caledonian population in Nouméa and the interior was upset at his recall. In light of a possible uprising, he had decided to delay his departure.[52] D'Argenlieu agreed to forward Sautot's request, adding that he would include his own comment for the General. On 2 May Admiral d'Argenlieu sent Sautot's appeal to General de Gaulle in London along with his request that de Gaulle confirm his order. In his post-riot report d'Argenlieu claimed that maintaining the order was a matter of "French sovereignty and the dignity of our LEADER."[53] D'Argenlieu insisted that his departure, not Sautot's, would be disastrous for French authority in New Caledonia. The next day General de Gaulle again ordered Sautot to come to London for consultation.[54]

By this time feelings over Sautot's recall were running high on the island, particularly among the Broussards who could not understand why the popular governor and hero of the 19 September rally should be removed from his post, a view shared by his colleagues from the administrative council. On 2 May the same delegation of four members from the administrative council, who had unsuccessfully asked Patch to send their telegram to de Gaulle, presented a petition to the high commissioner. They demanded the departure not of Sautot but of the d'Argenlieu mission "with all the honors it should wish." In his account of this episode, Sautot claimed that d'Argenlieu hinted that he and his staff might leave.

The next day another member of the administrative council, Dr. Eduard Trubert, a man in whom Admiral d'Argenlieu had confidence and who was widely respected on the island, visited Admiral d'Argenlieu. During a lengthy discussion Trubert bluntly informed d'Argenlieu of his unpopularity, and Trubert came away from the interview with d'Argenlieu's assurance that he would leave the island if the demonstration against him were called off and he were permitted "to leave with the dignity and respect due his office."[55] The Australian naval liaison officer reported on 3 May and again on 4 May that Admiral d'Argenlieu would accept the will of the people and leave the colony.[56]

D'Argenlieu's version differs slightly from the Australian naval officer's account. In his report to de Gaulle he noted that Dr. Trubert had warned him that an insurrectionary committee had been formed under the leadership of Bergès, Moulédous, Dubois, Pognon and Solier, a member of the judiciary.

Figure 4.4. The Caledonian crowd hears General Patch's declaration of neutrality.
Source. U.S. National Archives (111-SC-151166).

This committee was going to ask him to leave the island either voluntarily or by force. If he went voluntarily, he would be accorded all honors. Otherwise four-hundred militia members backed by the Broussards would expel him forcibly. Dr. Trubert had advised him to leave, and he admitted that he had promised to do so.[57] But it would not be Admiral d'Argenlieu who would leave the island. Instead, he had Governor Sautot and four members of the administrative council abducted.

Matters came to a head on 5 May, the first anniversary of the Pacific Battalion's departure for North Africa. After mass in the cathedral, Sautot and General Patch reviewed the French, Australian and American troops. D'Argenlieu was absent since he had been forewarned that his presence might provoke a hostile demonstration. Sautot made a patriotic speech, and he returned to his office where he once more received a delegation of Broussards. Later that afternoon he received a message from d'Argenlieu that requested his presence at the Government House.

When he arrived, Sautot found d'Argenlieu, Captain Cabanier, who was d'Argenlieu's chief-of-staff, and an ensign in full dress uniform waiting, all wearing revolvers. D'Argenlieu showed Sautot de Gaulle's reply in which he again ordered Sautot to return, once more expressed his appreciation for his services, and called upon the colony to display, "for all, union and discipline. That is the password, more necessary than ever."[58] "You are going to plunge [New] Caledonia into fire and blood," Sautot warned the Admiral.[59] In light of de Gaulle's order d'Argenlieu asked what the governor proposed to do. Sautot answered that he would turn over his office to the general secretary the next day after conferring with the administrative council. D'Argenlieu replied that there was not time for that since he was going to dissolve the administrative council.[60] He ordered Cabanier to escort Sautot to his residence to pick up some belongings while d'Argenlieu broadcast a message to the Caledonian people asking for calm and understanding.

After Sautot had packed his suitcase Cabanier then escorted the hapless governor to the dock where a Free-French gunboat, *Chevreuil*, was waiting. That evening d'Argenlieu asked that General Patch in his capacity as military commander prevent the Broussards from coming into Nouméa.[61] Instead, Patch sent a military guard to the residence of Captain Dubois, who feared his own arrest and claimed that his life was in danger. In the meantime four members of the administrative council, who had presented d'Argenlieu with the petition for his departure, were invited for an aperitif at the High Commissioner's residence, where they were arrested and taken aboard *Chevreuil*. Only Captain Dubois was missing. All of this activity at the dock took place before the astonished eyes of Lieutenant Templeton, a British liaison officer on board *Chevreuil*.[62]

The next day *Chevreuil* picked up a contingent of French soldiers after spending the night out of sight of Nouméa. On the morning of the seventh, the gunboat sailed with its political passengers for an unknown destination. An hour and a half after clearing the light, an SOS signal was received on board *Chevreuil* from a Greek freighter, which reported that it had been torpedoed and was being shelled by a Japanese submarine. The American military station in Nouméa also picked up this distress signal and relayed it to *Chevreuil*. The gunboat's captain requested permission to respond to the SOS. That *Chevreuil* might have intervened to halt the attack, destroy a Japanese submarine or at least pick up survivors is confirmed by reports at the time. Lieutenant Templeton, who was on board and observed the performance, estimated that *Chevreuil* was no more than twenty miles from *Chloe* at the time of the attack, and General Patch reported that the Greek ship was under fire from 0700 to 0945. *Chevreuil* had recently been fitted with the latest British submarine detection equipment and carried forty depth charges aboard.

Admiral d'Argenlieu denied the *Chevreuil* captain's request to go to the aid of the Greek freighter, for he saw in it an American plot. He cabled de Gaulle, "On military pretexts Patch is pressing me to divert *Chevreuil* from her mission and make her come back to Nouméa. The return of Sautot is strictly impossible ... *Chevreuil* is pursuing her mission."[63] He took Patch's request as evidence of American interference in French affairs. He consulted Captain Cabanier, who advised him that *Chevreuil* would be of little help. In his report to de Gaulle d'Argenlieu stated that he had replied with all courtesy to General Patch, informing him that *Chevreuil* was on its way to Auckland. As for Patch's behavior, d'Argenlieu claimed the American commander was as discourteous as possible toward Captain Cabanier.[64] The French behaved correctly and the Americans were at fault. He would later claim that the Americans exploited reports of the "inexperienced and garrulous" Templeton in order to slander the record of a Free-French warship.

In his reply to d'Argenlieu de Gaulle asked the High Commissioner to inform Patch that neither he nor the French National Committee could accept Patch's interference in an internal French matter.[65] De Gaulle fully accepted that Patch's request was motivated by political rather than military reasons and was a subterfuge to bring Sautot back to New Caledonia. From the American record there is no evidence that General Patch had anything in mind except a military situation in which an allied ship had been torpedoed and shelled within the vicinity of a Free-French warship. Patch denied any political motivation or intention to become involved in French political disputes. Admiral d'Argenlieu had General de Gaulle's injunction against Patch's interference sent to Patch, who replied that he was "glad to know that he [General de Gaulle] concurs in my attitude of strict neutrality in connection with the recent political happenings here. This attitude is in accordance with the instructions from my government."[66] Despite Patch's statement d'Argenlieu would persist in his thesis that the Americans wanted to get rid of him and bring back Governor Sautot for their own benefit and Patch's neutrality masked his intention.

After receiving d'Argenlieu's order to continue without responding to the SOS, the captain of *Chevreuil* reportedly locked himself in his cabin. Admiral d'Argenlieu's refusal to answer another vessel's distress signal was a serious violation of maritime etiquette. Equally serious was his refusal to allow the French captain to go to the aid of an allied ship under enemy attack or even to search for survivors. After observing *Chevreuil's* performance "as a political yacht," Templeton concluded, "it now seems quite unlikely that the ship will ever intentionally take an active part in any military operation."[67] This judgment proved premature, for *Chevreuil* was instrumental in the Free-French rally of Wallis and Futuna three weeks later.[68]

Chevreuil's steady course took the ship and passengers to Walpole Island, a windswept and barren plateau covered with guano some one hundred forty miles east of Nouméa, where the four administrative councilors were placed under the armed control of a military detachment. *Chevreuil* continued to New Zealand with Sautot, accompanied by Lieutenant Albert Renard from the d'Argenlieu mission. In New Zealand the governor enjoyed the warm hospitality of Prime Minister Peter Fraser. Two weeks later he sailed for New York aboard *SS Waiatapu*, accompanied by the watchful Renard.[69]

While *Chevreuil* fulfilled its mission, the abduction of Sautot and the arrests of the four councilors had provoked a massive demonstration in Nouméa. The crowd marched to General Patch's headquarters and shouted for the return of Sautot and his companions. Patch listened to their complaint but declined to intervene in what he perceived to be an internal French matter. At the same time d'Argenlieu asked Patch to provide protection for him at the Government House, which he feared might be seized by the Caledonian mob. Patch also declined this request, stating that U.S. troops would remain neutral. In his report to General George Marshall, Patch insisted that had he taken action against the crowd he would have alienated 90 percent of the settler population. With the Japanese Navy pressing into the Coral Sea he could not risk provoking the civilian population and alienating the militia of New Caledonia. Patch feared that if he used his forces against the Caledonian people and their demonstration he would lose their good will, which he could not afford to do.[70] What Patch believed to be a neutral stand d'Argenlieu of course considered a conspiracy against him.

D'Argenlieu cabled de Gaulle that the American game was obvious: to push the French authorities aside and gain control of the island. "The Americans," he cried out, "increasingly have revealed their intentions to supplant French authority for all practical purposes" in New Caledonia. Local interests, he claimed, had been impressed by the deployment of military forces and were now tempted to enter the orbit of the dollar having previously been lured by the Australians. He called upon the French National Committee to enlist the assistance of Churchill and the Dutch to dampen the "imperialistic wave of the United States in the Pacific."[71] This American imperialistic wave still seemed a greater danger to Admiral d'Argenlieu and to the Free-French movement than did the Japanese Navy that had swept into the Coral Sea and was engaged against American and Australian naval forces at that very moment.

By this time New Caledonia was in a state of near revolution. When they heard of Sautot's abduction, Broussards from the interior tried to march on Nouméa, but Michel Vergès and Prinet, remembering the earlier role of the upcountry people, persuaded d'Argenlieu to set up seven roadblocks between Païta and the capital. This precaution had the effect of stopping some five-hundred Broussards outside of town. In the meantime, a general strike was called in Nouméa and normal business came to a standstill. The streets filled with a tumultuous crowd carrying portraits of Sautot. Many of the demonstrators were women, since the male Broussards had been prevented from entering Nouméa by the roadblocks. As one participant noted, when they realized that the prisoners on Walpole Island were not being returned and "that the mission didn't give a damn for us, the women simply went off the handle."[72]

When d'Argenlieu's car was spotted, some women in the crowd jumped onto the running board and began shouting insults at d'Argenlieu. They then marched on the American headquarters where Patch was cheered. D'Argenlieu claimed that all of this was the work of fifth columnists, encouraged by the Americans.[73] Why the Americans would be favoring the work of fifth columnists at this moment is one of the puzzling aspects of d'Argenlieu's account.

Figure 4.5. The crowd calls for Governor Sautot's return.
Source. U.S. National Archives (111-SC-15172).

When General Patch informed the crowd that he intended to remain neutral in the dispute, a group of leading citizens drew up a petition that demanded the return of the hostages on Walpole Island and the departure of the d'Argenlieu mission. No reprisals against anyone involved in the demonstrations would be taken. They asked for a restoration of freedom of the press and a statement that the Caledonian patriots had never been in the pay of a foreign power and were not part of any fifth column. A copy of this appeal was given to the general secretary of the colony, Jan Bourgeau in his capacity as interim governor.[74]

The demonstration became violent that evening when a crowd marched to the radio station in Nouméa and demanded access to broadcast facilities. The person in charge of the station refused, whereupon the demonstrators entered the building, seized the microphone, and broadcast a message to the inhabitants of the interior informing them that the protest was continuing and that they needed the Broussards in Nouméa to support their action. At the conclusion of this broadcast a military detachment of sixty soldiers from the d'Argenlieu mission appeared. The soldiers, all reservists and many of them Kanak, refused to fire on their fellow Caledonians. Caledonian soldiers had guarded the admiral and manned the roadblocks, but as Mrs. Beer put it, "if he thinks he is safer with them, he is mistaken, for nobody here, neither whites nor blacks, would fire on their Caledonian brothers. Let them get that into their heads." The crowd promptly seized the officers of the detachment and took them to "a safe place."

Then Captain Cabanier arrived on the scene. He was the highest ranking member of the mission in Nouméa, because d'Argenlieu had gone to the interior to calm a population that, Cabanier claimed, had been aroused and "deceived by a propaganda campaign orchestrated by foreigners" against the admiral and his mission. "The women went to work on Cabanier," Mrs. Beer reported, "one bit him on the arm, others kicked his behind; others tore off his belt and insignia. He declared that he'd rather face fifty men than five Calédoniennes."[75] After this scuffle Cabanier got to the microphone long enough to announce that troublemakers and rebels had attacked him. The crowd detained Cabanier for four hours at the station during which time they presented the petition demanding the return of Governor Sautot. Cabanier refused to agree to these demands. At midnight they all went home and Cabanier was released. The whole episode, Cabanier glumly reported to General de Gaulle, took place before "the derisive gaze" of American photographers, reporters and military personnel who looked on but did nothing as his uniform was torn.[76]

Admiral d'Argenlieu's encounter with the Broussards of the interior took place at what Cabanier described as the admiral's "mountain command post in La Foa."[77] However, La Foa happened to be a stronghold of the militia and hometown of Pierre Bergès, president of the administrative council, who was one of the hostages on Walpole Island. When d'Argenlieu arrived in La Foa, he was immediately recognized, and the commander of the local militia placed him under house arrest. Worse yet, as Mrs. Beer's colorful account put it, de Gaulle's representative "got into the clutches of our Mme Bergès who grabbed Mr. d'Argenlieu and shook him like a plum tree and gave him a piece of her mind."[78] He was held prisoner in a room at Banuelos's inn, which had served as a site for the 1940 Broussard rally.[79]

Following five days of abductions, a general strike and demonstrations, Patch decided on the tenth that order had to be restored. He received a report that a Japanese aircraft carrier was within striking distance of New Caledonia, and he cabled Washington for permission to declare martial law on the island if necessary. This request led to negotiations between de Gaulle in London and Admiral Harold R. Stark, the commander of United States naval forces in Europe, who was serving as one of two American military representatives to de Gaulle's French National Committee. Stark listened respectfully to de Gaulle's complaints against Patch and the Americans, but he insisted that the immediate danger required that order had to be established and that Patch was responsible for the island's security. He also gave General de Gaulle a different version, based on reports from General Patch and channeled through Washington, of what de Gaulle would dismiss then and later as "the American thesis" about events in New Caledonia.

Reluctantly de Gaulle consented to martial law being declared, if necessary, but he stressed the need to preserve French sovereignty on the island and insisted that any action by Patch would be strictly for military security. He informed Captain Cabanier that General Patch was authorized to declare a state of siege on the condition that Patch make clear that his action was due to the immediate military crisis and was taken with General de Gaulle's consent. Admiral d'Argenlieu was to have free communication with London, and he insisted that Patch would not have any civilian function, nor would he be allowed to act as governor of the island. Above all he insisted that a strict censorship be maintained on the events that had occurred on the island. He asked that Admiral d'Argenlieu send a full report on these events by code. He also expected that Admiral Ghormley, Commander of American Naval Forces in the South Pacific, would inquire into the complaints he had made to the American Government concerning the attitude and actions of the American occupation forces in New Caledonia during these troubles.[80]

To make sure that French sovereignty over New Caledonia remained intact, General de Gaulle appointed Auguste Montchamp to replace Sautot as governor of New Caledonia. In his telegram to Montchamp, de Gaulle stressed the need for someone with experience, firmness, tact and an understanding of "the Anglo-Saxon mentality" to resist the Americans and their overwhelming material resources. He urged that Montchamp work closely with Admiral d'Argenlieu in fulfilling this assignment.[81] As he later told d'Argenlieu, he perfectly understood the ins and outs of recent events, and he had let the Americans know about the "foul trick" that Patch had played upon him. He ordered d'Argenlieu to remain at his post.[82]

De Gaulle sent stern messages to the now abducted councilors, reminding them that their strict duty under the circumstances was to support Admiral d'Argenlieu as the highest representative of French authority on the island. He refused their appeal to have Governor Sautot return to New Caledonia. He asked that they not compromise the patriotic endeavor that they had undertaken in rallying to the Free-French cause. As for Sautot himself, he cabled that in light of the crisis then developing with the British over their occupation of Madagascar in the Indian Ocean, the ex-governor should understand why he was being recalled. De Gaulle asked that he remind his friends in New Caledonia that any demonstration would be an unjustified, criminal act.[83]

Sautot loyally obeyed and sent a message to his supporters in which he stated that in the interest of France and the Empire, he had placed himself under General de Gaulle's orders and was prepared to assume any new task asked of him. He urged "all my New Caledonian friends to whom I am affectionately attached, to put aside their personal opinions and to consider only the superior interest of our country which is to be saved. I ask you personally in order to restore calm in the territory."[84] Admiral d'Argenlieu thanked Sautot for his message to the Caledonian population and wished him a bon voyage on his way to London by way of the United States.[85]

As for General Patch, de Gaulle asked Washington to invite its representatives in New Caledonia to support the high commissioner, and he asked d'Argenlieu to re-establish relations with Patch and show some leniency toward the troubled population of New Caledonia. He asked d'Argenlieu to assure General Patch personally of de Gaulle's confidence in "the brave American troops under [his] orders." However, he insisted that the difficulties Patch faced as commander on the island would "disappear if [he made] it clear that [he is] marching hand in hand with d'Argenlieu, who has my full confidence and is responsible for the sovereignty and authority of France in New Caledonia."[86] From de Gaulle's perspective, it was up to Patch to restore order and fully support Admiral d'Argenlieu in his conflict with the local population.

Patch did not declare martial law on the island. Instead, he ordered the militia to release d'Argenlieu and other members of the mission who had been detained. Patch feared that there might be a repeat of the 1940 revolution just at the moment when the island was clearly in danger. The militia took up its defensive posts on the island, and the strike ended. In calling off these demonstrations Patch lost some more popularity among certain Caledonians, who may have hoped that the anti-d'Argenlieu riot and demonstration would enable them to reassert their own authority against what they felt to be the oppressive power of the centralized colonial administration. According to the Australian naval observer, the restoration of calm was due in large measure to the "immobilizing of [the] Militia as a revolutionary force due to incorporation in General Patch's command." As for de Gaulle's complaint that Patch had interfered in the internal affairs of New Caledonia, the naval observer concluded, "General Patch's attitude since [the] crisis developed has been strictly correct" and the presence of American troops probably had prevented bloodshed in this Franco-French quarrel.[87]

After a week of turmoil, the situation in New Caledonia settled down. Admiral d'Argenlieu returned from La Foa, and Captain Cabanier reported that General Patch's attitude had improved. On 17 May the exiled councilors returned from Walpole Island. When the U.S. Navy and units from the Royal Australian Navy stopped the Japanese Navy's advance into the Coral Sea, the immediate military danger temporarily eased. At exactly the time when the Free French were fighting among themselves before the astonished eyes of General Patch, his soldiers, and their Commonwealth allies, this important battle played itself out and became one of the decisive turning points of the war in the Pacific. Yet the allies were astonished at the way in which the French were more concerned about the political issues in New Caledonia than the immediate military danger. Here was a basic source for the Franco/American *mésentente* in which the American concern was with the war effort while the French seemed entirely focused upon specifically French political problems.

Calm is Restored, but *Mésentente* Sets In: May–July '42

The ways in which the French and the Americans have recorded this historic moment reveals the underlying differences that divided them over their respective roles during the Second World War. Two different versions have emerged. For the

French at the time and in the Gaullist-inspired histories that have subsequently been written, the preoccupation is with the threat that the American presence posed for French sovereignty in New Caledonia. They were convinced that the American game was to discredit the Free French, undermine their authority and prepare a takeover of New Caledonia. A weak and compliant France, the Gaullists were convinced, would best serve the United States and its intention to dominate the postwar world at the expense of the French Empire. For this reason the Gaullists insisted that the Americans had to respect and support French authority in New Caledonia, as elsewhere. D'Argenlieu and his staff rejected Patch's argument that military necessity required him to avoid any clash with the majority of the French settler population or with the Caledonian militia. According to this version, the Americans had produced the agitation in the first place by meddling in New Caledonia's internal affairs.[88] De Gaulle insisted that there had been no trouble in New Caledonia before the arrival of American troops. However their appearance "gave the turbulent elements in this colony the impression that a game could be played with the foreigner, and unfortunately the American authorities did nothing to cut short this game."[89] The Americans and General Patch in particular have been held responsible for causing the riot at a crucial moment. The battle of the Coral Sea and the Japanese threat to New Caledonia receive scant notice in Gaullist accounts.

On the other hand, the Americans were astonished at the French preoccupations that were harming the war effort. Admiral d'Argenlieu's timing in the removal of Sautot raised serious questions in the minds of both British and American officials about High Commissioner d'Argenlieu's judgment and the advice that he received concerning matters in New Caledonia. A heated conversation took place in London over the New Caledonia riot between Maurice Dejean, Free-French commissioner for foreign Affairs, René Pleven, commissioner for colonies, and William Strang of the Foreign Office and Charles Peake, British representative to the French National Committee. The British officials did not mince words. They deplored the situation that "had been wantonly created by the Free French on the very edge of the battle" in the South Pacific. In no uncertain terms Strang stated that matters had to be put back in order. He told Dejean that French actions in New Caledonia would have a calamitous effect upon Free-French relations with the United States and would influence how the British and Americans dealt with the Free French in Madagascar, Martinique and elsewhere.[90]

At the beginning of the rioting in Nouméa, Admiral d'Argenlieu had stated that he would be willing to leave New Caledonia, but General de Gaulle refused to sanction his departure until Sautot's replacement arrived.[91] A hasty retreat of the mission would have been damaging to the authority of the Free French. Admiral d'Argenlieu and his staff were convinced that the Americans were responsible for the humiliation that the Caledonians had inflicted upon Captain Cabanier and the entire mission, and he would harbor a deep hatred for the Americans generally and General Patch in particular. Following the riot and the alleged American complicity in the events General de Gaulle declared that he no longer believed that Free-French reconciliation with the Americans was possible. Some officers of the mission claimed that they would shoot at the Americans rather than allow themselves to be bullied by "these occupiers." Others swore that they would never fight at their side.[92]

Taking up Admiral d'Argenlieu's denunciations of "a democratic country with imperialistic ambitions," de Gaulle decided to resist what he believed to be American designs upon the French Empire. Although his attitude would occasionally soften, General de Gaulle remained intransigent toward what he perceived to be American domineering tendencies. From this point on he repeatedly referred to "American imperialism," language that previously had been used by the French Left or by Vichy to denounce American policy.[93] Should it come to a break with the Americans, Admiral d'Argenlieu assured de Gaulle that he was prepared to leave New Caledonia, taking his mission and all administrative and military personnel with him, for Tahiti where there were no Americans. With the resources at his disposal he would deny them or others access to this French colony.[94]

Free-French resentment toward the Americans reflected General de Gaulle's belief that the Americans wished to see his movement fail. The General was deeply depressed after his interview with Admiral Stark on 9 May, fearing that events in New Caledonia were leading to a collapse of the Free-French movement. During the crisis the French National Committee insisted that the Americans impose a strict censorship on news from New Caledonia to avoid any publicity that might discredit the Free-French movement.[95] The news ban was broken when articles in the *New York Times* reported the conflict in New Caledonia between Admiral d'Argenlieu and Governor Sautot.[96] This news report infuriated General de Gaulle who saw it as a deliberate violation of the censorship that he had requested, but the news had been deliberately leaked to the American press by officials in Washington who were anxious to discredit the Free French. The existence of the Free-French movement, de Gaulle argued, depended upon absolute unity and the unambiguous support by the Anglo-Saxon powers. "We exist morally only to the extent that our companions in arms realize that our allies are with us."[97] From his perspective the Americans had not shown unambiguous support for Free-French authority in New Caledonia, and Vichy was all too ready to exploit allied differences.

Yet the Americans, despite General de Gaulle's suspicion, were not anxious to see a break-up of the Free-French movement. A.A. Berle, often a critic of the Free French, argued that despite the "free-for-all row" in New Caledonia and the apparent "failure of the Free French to make a political go of it […], we cannot allow the movement to go to pieces. De Gaulle's name is current throughout the world, and so is the Lorraine Cross."[98] He feared that if the movement broke up in the colonies, enemies of the allies would take advantage of it. The Americans actually wanted the Free French to succeed and blamed the Gaullists for causing the troubles in New Caledonia that led to Vichy's criticism.

From London Admiral Stark tried to convey the Free-French position to Washington. He noted that the Free French deeply resented the State Department's continued relations with Vichy, and this policy, he speculated, might have skewed the Gaullist view of the nature of the opposition in New Caledonia. Patch's support of Dubois and the militia as well as his sympathy for Sautot were seen to have a political motive that encouraged separatist tendencies. Although Stark listened and tried to understand the Gaullist perspective, he concluded that "their judgment may be wrong on certain points," and added that "... the Free-French headquarters in London cannot know all of the facts of all aspects of the local situation in a place as far removed as New Caledonia."[99] Each side reconstructed and interpreted the events in New Caledonia to suit its own particular interest, which for the French was a political and for the Americans a military one.

The Americans were bewildered by the hostility that their presence in New Caledonia evoked among the Gaullist Free French. One officer, commenting upon the events of May 1942, finally could find no reasonable explanation for the attitude of the d'Argenlieu mission other than as a kind of paranoia. "Unlike the straight-forward colonials," he wrote, "some of the metropolitan Fighting French—particularly those in highest positions—have been so touchy, so arrogant, so nearly impossible to get along with, that their behavior can hardly be described except in psychiatric terms." The attitudes of the Caledonians, on the other hand, were far more comprehensible within the context of American values. The Americans looked upon the Caledonians as frontier types whose behavior was familiar and understandable. The same intelligence report described the Broussards as rustic, frontier farmers with a strong streak of independence and self-reliance. In emergencies, "they are inclined to take matters into their own hands, not unlike the 'embattled farmers' of American Revolutionary days."[100] Here was an American preference for behavior that was less formal and more casual. The Broussards appeared to be more "American," more direct, rugged and masculine than the arrogant, authoritarian, and emotionally irrational Gaullists.

Patch tried to calm the anti-French feelings among his own officers, who resented the accusations and generally hostile attitude of d'Argenlieu's entourage toward them. He reminded his troops that they were in New Caledonia as guests, and he stressed that the Americans were there to protect the island and its inhabitants and not because of any designs upon it. Patch recognized that the humiliation resulting from the defeat of 1940 was a sore point for the Free French and might account for some of their touchiness. In a letter to his fellow officers, Patch asked for understanding and tolerance:

> The Free French ... should command our respect and admiration and we should treat them as allies who have been willing to sacrifice everything for our own common cause. Naturally they are sensitive about [the] humiliating defeat they suffered and the apparent ease with [which] their country was beaten and over-run, but they have offered their lives to wipe out that shame and if possible to bring back to their country the victory that they fight for. No man can do more.[101]

It seems clear, at least to an American observer, that Patch wished to ease any tensions that had developed by showing both respect and sympathy to the Free French and their cause. The Gaullists, however, took Patch's statement as evidence that Washington had ordered Patch to work with them in New Caledonia, and his statement was an admission that he was at fault in his actions at the time of the riots and in his behavior toward Admiral d'Argenlieu. In his memoirs General de Gaulle claimed that General Patch "went to see d'Argenlieu to excuse himself for the 'misunderstandings' in which he had become involved."[102] From the French perspective an American attempt to understand was tantamount to an apology and an admission of guilt and responsibility and not, as Patch and his staff intended, an attempt to put differences aside. Instead, the d'Argenlieu mission continued to denigrate Patch, and General de Gaulle continued to blame the Americans for their treatment of the Free French in New Caledonia.

At the end of July Auguste-Henri Montchamp arrived as governor, making Admiral d'Argenlieu's presence less necessary to maintain French authority in New Caledonia. D'Argenlieu's departure apparently fulfilled the promise to leave the colony that he had given five months earlier during the riot in May, although for face-saving reasons d'Argenlieu let it be known that he was only going temporarily "en mission" and would be returning at some point. He retained his title of high commissioner for the Pacific and left behind his deputy, Frédéric Fourcade, to represent his office.

Admiral d'Argenlieu's departure did not mean that his differences with Patch were forgotten. He persisted in a single-minded effort to get revenge upon his nemesis. While General Patch was training and preparing the troops of the Americal Division to replace the Marines on Guadalcanal, d'Argenlieu proposed that de Gaulle and the French Committee of National Liberation pressure Washington to have Patch removed from his command. In a long cable to de Gaulle from Tahiti, where d'Argenlieu had taken up residence in October, he continued to denounce Patch's behavior once more and asked de Gaulle to make "a vigorous intervention" in Washington to bring Patch to order and obtain his transfer elsewhere.[103]

D'Argenlieu left the Pacific by way of the United States. When he reached Washington, d'Argenlieu met with American officials to obtain some idea of American policies and to explain the situation in New Caledonia to A.A. Berle and Secretary of State Cordell Hull. Berle commented that d'Argenlieu was reputed to be a nice man but "he appears to have gone to pieces in the South Pacific."[104] Berle and Hull tried to convince Admiral d'Argenlieu and Adrien Tixier, the Free-French representative in Washington, that American policy was not hostile to the Free French. On his side Admiral d'Argenlieu gave the impression of an extremely cordial relationship between the Americans and the Fighting French (the term General de Gaulle preferred) in the Pacific.[105] The Admiral stated that he returned from the Pacific "with the most happy impressions of his cooperation with the American forces in the Far East." He admitted that there had been some difficulties during the first "two or three days" after the arrival of the Americans, but rumors of friction between himself and General Patch were distorted. An "extremely cordial relationship" had developed with American officers in New Caledonia and elsewhere. There were no clouds on the horizon. He even reported that he enjoyed "the closest relationship" with the American consul in New Caledonia, the despised MacVitty.[106]

Hull was also in a conciliatory mood. The secretary explained that American policy toward Vichy was driven solely by concern over the status of the French fleet, not out of any sympathy for Marshal Pétain's Government. He praised General de Gaulle as someone who "stood for something very special to all Americans in the French situation", and it was "the prayer" of the American people that all French would contribute to a military victory that would "restore France to her independence." After the meeting Tixier told Ray Atherton that the secretary's explanation of America's Vichy policy, "was a perfect answer to all or any Fighting-French apprehensions" concerning any American intention to deal separately with Vichy. For his part Admiral d'Argenlieu informed General de Gaulle that he came away from this encounter "with a good impression."[107]

Despite the courteous tone of the interview between Hull and d'Argenlieu, the *mésentente* persisted. Within a month Tixier cabled London that d'Argenlieu's troubles in New Caledonia resulted from Patch's deliberate and calculated intrigue in local Caledonian politics for the purpose of detaching New Caledonia from the Free-French movement. The Free-French view was that the Caledonians had been dragged into the war against their will. Only the timely arrival of Admiral d'Argenlieu prevented them from lapsing back under Vichy control. D'Argenlieu's firmness had forced American recognition of Free-French control of the island, but Patch had then begun his game with certain local interests.[108] This was a rehearsal of an old argument, and it reinforced Gaullist suspicions of Patch and American policy toward the Free French. Here was the basis for a *mésentente* of significant proportions and duration.

In the absence of High Commissioner d'Argenlieu, responsibility for defending Free-French interests in New Caledonia thus fell upon Governor Montchamp. On his way to New Caledonia Montchamp met briefly with ex-governor Sautot in New York where Sautot tried to warn him of the difficulties he would face in his new assignment. However, Montchamp's instructions reflected d'Argenlieu's rather than Sautot's perspective on the situation in New Caledonia. "We have only one objective in Nouméa," High Commissioner d'Argenlieu had emphasized, "which is to see that the island remains French while at the same time assuring its defense."[109] The new governor also had to restore the credibility of the governor's office by overcoming Caledonian suspicions of yet another representative from the central power of Free France. And he would have to deal with the Americans.

While in Washington Governor Montchamp paid a courtesy call to A.A. Berle. He assured Berle that his primary interest was to win the war. He had heard of the recent difficulties in New Caledonia, and he would make every effort to assure tranquility on the island. Berle agreed that stabilizing the political life of New Caledonia was a delicate task that would require all of his diplomatic skills, but it was one that was important since it would contribute to the United Nations' successful war effort in the Pacific. Berle assured Montchamp that General Patch was anxious to cooperate, was willing to discuss candidly any issues that the governor wished to raise, and that General Patch "had no desire to mix into questions of internal administration."[110]

Between cooperating with the Americans and protecting French sovereignty in New Caledonia, Governor Montchamp was aware that ahead he had a difficult assignment.

Notes

1. Several authors have cited Passy's account of de Gaulle's reaction to news of Pearl Harbor: Colonel Passy (André Dewavrin), *Souvenirs*, vol. 1 of 3: *Le Bureau de Londres* (Monte Carlo, 1947), 236.
2. "Free French Interpretation of New Caledonia Situation," 27 June 1942, in "U.S.–Free French Relations, 1942–44," Appendix B, Op Arch, Naval History Center (NHC), Washington D.C.
3. P. Lissington, "New Zealand Relations with French Possessions in the Pacific," n.d. but postwar, New Zealand National Archives (NZNA) Wellington, WAII 21/21a.
4. MacVitty to State, 8 September 1941, U.S. National Archives and Record Administration (USNARA) State Dec. File 851L.20/7.
5. D'Argenlieu to de Gaulle, 25 November 1941, Archives Nationales (AN) Papiers Cassin 382 AP59.
6. MacVitty to State, 3 December 1941, USNARA State Dec. File 851L.00/23; cited in John Lawrey, *The Cross of Lorraine in the South Pacific: Australia and the Free French Movement, 1940–1942* (Canberra, 1982), 87.
7. De Gaulle to d'Argenlieu, 24 December 1941, in Charles de Gaulle, *Lettres, Notes et Carnets (LNC), juillet 1941–mai 1943* (Paris, 1982), 148–49; and Ministère des Affaires Etrangères (MAE) Guerre 1939–45, London CNF, vol. 328.
8. De Gaulle to d'Argenlieu, 4 January 1942 in Charles de Gaulle, *Call to Honor 1940–1942: Documents*, trans. Jonathan Griffin (London, 1955), 226.
9. Louis Morton, *Strategy and Command: The First Two Years* (Washington D.C., 1962), 208.
10. D'Argenlieu to de Gaulle, 24 January 1942, AN, Papiers d'Argenlieu AP517, and same to same, 20 January 1942, Charles de Gaulle, *Mémoires de Guerre*, vol. 1: *l'Appel, 1940–1942* (Paris, 1954), 515.
11. Interview with David Pinkney, Santa Barbara, November 1989.
12. These approximations were extrapolated from the 1936 census, which showed 15,400 Europeans (29 percent), 28,800 Kanak (Melanesians) (54 percent) and 9,000 others (17 percent).
13. Dwight D. Eisenhower to Delos Carleton Emmons (Commanding General, Hawaiian Department) 4 March 1942, in Alfred D. Chandler, et al., *The Papers of Dwight David Eisenhower: The War Years* (Baltimore, 1970), vol. 1, #168, 163–65.
14. Comité National Français (CNF) to d'Argenlieu, 25 January 1942, in Charles de Gaulle, *Mémoires*, vol. 1, 521.
15. De Gaulle to d'Argenlieu, 25 February 1942, ibid. 527.
16. Same to same, 27 January 1942, ibid. 522.
17. D'Argenlieu to de Gaulle, 20 January 1942, ibid. 516.

18. Same to same, 31 January 1942, AN Papiers d'Argenlieu AP517.
19. D'Argenlieu to Lieutenant Colonel Orselli, 29 January 1942, AN Papiers d'Argenlieu AP517.
20. Adrien Tixier to CNF, 15 January 1942, *Mémoires*, vol. 1, 512.
21. Atherton to Tixier, 23 February 1942, USNARA State Dec. File, 851L.01/11; d'Argenlieu to CNF, 28 February 1942, MAE Guerre 1939–45, London CNF, vol. 75.
22. CNF to Beirut, Cairo, and other diplomatic posts, 2 March 1942, MAE Guerre 1939–45, London CNF, vol. 75.
23. D'Argenlieu to MacVitty, 26 February 1942, AN Papiers d'Argenlieu AP517.
24. De Gaulle to d'Argenlieu, 25 February 1942, *Mémoires*, vol. 1, 527.
25. Morton, *Strategy and Command*, 209. See also Francis D. Cronin, *Under the Southern Cross: The Saga of the Americal Division* (Washington D.C., 1951), 4–5, 10–11, 14–15.
26. D'Argenlieu to CNF, 12 March 1942, *Call to Honor: Documents*, 275; MacVitty later attributed d'Argenlieu's hostility toward Patch to the admiral's failure to have full command of the Allied Forces on New Caledonia. MacVitty to State, 3 June 1942, USNARA State Dec. File 851L.01/22.
27. D'Argenlieu to Patch and Patch to d'Argenlieu, 12 March 1942, USNARA Mod Mil Branch, OPD 381 New Caledonia, and AN Papiers d'Argenlieu AP517; d'Argenlieu to CNF, 19 and 24 March 1942, MAE Guerre 1939–45, London CNF, vol. 77.
28. D'Argenlieu to de Gaulle, 26 March 1942, AN Papiers d'Argenlieu AP517.
29. Quoted in Gérard Lacourrège and Pierre Alibert, *La présence américaine en Nouvelle-Calédonie* (Nouméa, 1981), n.p.
30. Gabriel Païta, *Témoinage Kanak: D'Opao au pays de la Nouvelle-Calédonie 1929–1999, Récit autobiographique de Gabriel Païta*, recueilli, ed. Jérôme Cazaumayou et Thomas de Dekker, (Paris, 1999) 42–43.
31. D'Argenlieu to de Gaulle, 19 May 1942, AN Papiers d'Argenlieu AP517.
32. Cronin, *Under the Southern Cross*, 14.
33. Henri Sautot, *Grandeur et décadence du Gaullisme dans le Pacifique* (Melbourne, 1949), 126.
34. D'Argenlieu to de Gaulle, 16 April 1942, U.K. Public Record Office (PRO) FO371/31884.
35. D'Argenlieu to de Gaulle, 12 April 1942, AN AP517, Papiers d'Argenlieu.
36. Covering notes to d'Argenlieu's cable to de Gaulle, which passed through British channels, 21 April 1942, ibid.
37. D'Argenlieu to de Gaulle, 19 May 1942, ibid.
38. De Gaulle to d'Argenlieu, 16 May 1942, *LNC juillet 1941–mai 1943*, 277.
39. D'Argenlieu to de Gaulle, "very secret and personal," 31 March 1942, AN Papiers d'Argenlieu AP517.
40. D'Argenlieu to de Gaulle, 30 April 1942, AN Papiers d'Argenlieu AP517.
41. De Gaulle to d'Argenlieu, 8 April 1942, *Call to Honor*, 281, same to same, 8 April 1942, *LNC juillet 1941–mai 1943*, 243–44, and d'Argenlieu to de Gaulle, 28 April 1942, AN Papiers d'Argenlieu AP517.
42. D'Argenlieu to de Gaulle, 19 May 1942, ibid.
43. Patch to General Marshall, 17 April 1942, USNARA Mod Mil Branch, OPD 381 New Caledonia.
44. MacVitty to State, 15 April 1942, USNARA State Dec. File 851L.01/13.
45. Marshall to Patch, telegram 25 April 1942 and Patch's reply, "Report on Franco-American Relationship," Ad Hist Append 34(L)(C), Op Arch, NHC, Washington D.C.
46. D'Argenlieu to de Gaulle, 31 March 1942 and same to same, 19 May 1942, AN Papiers d'Argenlieu AP517.
47. D'Argenlieu to de Gaulle, 19 May 1942, Papiers d'Argenlieu AP517. There is no evidence other than this assertion that the Americans had any relationship with the administrative council, much less offered its "tacit support" for the council's action.
48. D'Argenlieu to de Gaulle, 30 April 1942, *Call to Honor: Documents*, 281–82.

49. D'Argenlieu to de Gaulle, 19 May 1942, AN Papiers d'Argenlieu AP517. According to Captain Dubois's account, Vergès is also reported to have boasted that he would next get rid of High Commissioner d'Argenlieu. "Report by Captain Dubois of Events Occurring in New Caledonia 5–10 May 1942," USNARA, OSS RG 226.
50. Gouverneur de la Nouvelle-Calédonie et Dépendances (Tallec) à M. le Ministre des Colonies, Direction Politique, 5 November 1944, Archives Nationales, Section d'Outre-Mer (ANSOM) AP, c. 509.
51. This was the message from the four notables held on Walpole Island, plus Captain Dubois, sent just before their arrest, 6 May 1942 PRO FO371/31884.
52. D'Argenlieu telegram to de Gaulle, 2 May 1942, *Mémoires*, vol. 1, 536.
53. D'Argenlieu to de Gaulle, 19 May 1942, AN Papiers d'Argenlieu, AP517.
54. De Gaulle to Sautot, 3 May 1942, *Mémoires*, vol. 1, 248.
55. "Recent Disturbances in New Caledonia," July 1, 1942, HQ Americal Division, Append to "Report on Franco-American Relationship," Ad Hist Append 34(10)(C), Op Arch, NHC, Washington D.C; and Flight Lieutenant Evan McColl, "Revolution in New Caledonia," 6, USNARA, OSS RG 226.
56. Australian Naval Liaison Officer (ANLO) Nouméa to Department of Naval Intelligence (DNI), 8 May 1942, NZNA, EA ser. 1, 86/19/1, pt. 1a General New Caledonia. This promise to leave has been confirmed by other sources, including a young Australian diplomat, John Lawrey, who was in New Caledonia at the time and was acting head of mission while Consul Ballard was in Australia. L.J. Lawrey to secretary external affairs, 16 May 1942, AA CRS A981, N-C, 1A, part 9.
57. D'Argenlieu to de Gaulle, 19 May 1942, AN Papiers d'Argenlieu AP517.
58. De Gaulle to d'Argenlieu, 2 May 1942, *Call to Honor*, 282.
59. D'Argenlieu to de Gaulle, 19 May 1942, AN Papiers d'Argenlieu AP517.
60. In any event, as d'Argenlieu admitted, Bergès, Moulédous, Pognon and Solier were already "out of the way." D'Argenlieu to de Gaulle, 19 May 1942, ibid.
61. D'Argenlieu to de Gaulle, 19 May 1942, ibid.
62. Lieutenant John Templeton, "Report of British Naval Liaison Officer, *FS Chevreuil*," 20 May 1942, Ad Hist Append 34(10)(C), Op Arch, NHC, Washington D.C.
63. D'Argenlieu to de Gaulle, 7 May 1942, *Call to Honor*, 283.
64. D'Argenlieu to de Gaulle, 19 May 1942, AN Papiers d'Argenlieu AP517.
65. De Gaulle to d'Argenlieu, 8 May 1942, *Mémoires*, vol. 1, 537.
66. Patch to d'Argenlieu, 10 May 1942, AN Papiers d'Argenlieu AP517.
67. Australian Naval Liaison Officer, Nouméa, to Melbourne and Wellington, 10 May 1942, NZNA, EA ser 1, 86/19/1, pt. 1a, General New Caledonia.
68. A brief and laudatory account of *Chevreuil's* wartime career may be found in René Auque, "Le 'Chevreuil' bâtiment FNFL," *Revue de la France Libre*, no. 258 (2ème trimestre 1987): 14, which makes no mention of this episode. Mention is made of one occasion during *Chevreuil's* career on convoy patrol in the North Atlantic in the summer of 1941 when the Free-French vessel picked up eighteen survivors from two torpedoed cargo ships.
69. C.A. Furlong, internal affairs department, "Entertainment of Messieurs Henri Sautot and Albert Renard of Free French Forces," 22 May 1942, NZNA, EA ser. 1, 86/19/1, pt. 1a.
70. Patch to Marshall, 7 May 1942, USNARA State Dec. File 851L.01/18; report forwarded to CNF, MAE Guerre 1939–45 London CNF, vol. 83; ANLO to DNI, 8 May 1942, NZNA, EA ser. 1, 86/19/1, pt. 1a.
71. D'Argenlieu to de Gaulle, telegram #65, 8 May 1942, AN Papiers d'Argenlieu AP517.
72. Letter from Mrs. Beer to "Zezette," 20 May 1942, USNARA War Dept, RG 165, regional file, "NC" Box 1793.
73. D'Argenlieu to de Gaulle, 19 May 1942, AN Papiers d'Argenlieu AP517.

74. Statement signed by notables, including Mayor Massoubre, and five members of the administrative council and two members of the militia, a similar version may be found in Sautot, *Grandeur et décadence*, 173.
75. Letter from Mrs. Beer to "Zezette," 20 May 1942, USNARA War Dept, RG 165, regional file, "NC" Box 1793.
76. Cabanier to de Gaulle, 8 May 1942, AN Papiers d'Argenlieu AP517 and same to same, *Mémoires*, vol. 1, 539 and *Call to Honor*, 285.
77. Cabanier to CNF, 10 May 1942, MAE Guerre 1939–45, London CNF, vol. 82.
78. Letter from Mrs. Beer to "Zezette," 20 May 1942, USNARA War Dept, RG 165, regional file, "NC" Box 1793.
79. Cabanier to de Gaulle, 10 May 1942, AN Papiers d'Argenlieu AP517. D'Argenlieu claimed that American soldiers had placed oil drums behind his car, thereby holding him hostage in La Foa. When told of this accusation, Patch ordered an investigation that revealed only six U.S. soldiers to have been in La Foa at the time, and they took no part in d'Argenlieu's detention.
80. De Gaulle to Cabanier, 9 May 1942, *LNC juillet 1941–mai 1943*, 260–61.
81. De Gaulle to Montchamp, 8 May 1942, ibid. 259–61.
82. De Gaulle to d'Argenlieu, 11 May 1942, ibid. 261.
83. De Gaulle to d'Argenlieu and same to Sautot via d'Argenlieu, 8 May 1942, ibid. 258–59. De Gaulle's reference to Madagascar had to do with the British decision to invade the island at exactly the same moment that the New Caledonia situation was erupting. See Martin Thomas, *The French Empire at War 1940–1945* (Manchester, 1998), 144–50.
84. Sautot to High Commissioner, 13 May 1942, NZNA, EA ser. 1, 86/19/1, pt. 1a, General New Caledonia.
85. D'Argenlieu to Sautot (Auckland), 21 May 1942, NZNA, EA ser. 1, 86/19/1, pt. 1.
86. De Gaulle to d'Argenlieu, 8 and 9 May 1942, *Call to Honor*, 284.
87. ANLO (McColl) to DNI (Department of Naval Intelligence), Melbourne and Wellington for information, 12 May 1942, NZNA, EA ser. 1, 86/19/1, pt. 1a.
88. "De la part de M. Pleven" (an account of Stark's meeting with de Gaulle), 9 May 1942, and d'Argenlieu to CNF, 7 May 1942, ibid.
89. De Gaulle to Tixier, 9 May 1942, *Call to Honor*, 285; Gaullist condemnation of Patch continues to this day. See Jean Lacouture, *De Gaulle*, vol. 1: *Le Rebelle* (Paris, 1984), 519.
90. Strang, memo of conversation with Dejean, 9 May 1942, PRO FO371/31884; this row is described by Lawrey, *Cross of Lorraine*, 106–107.
91. De Gaulle to d'Argenlieu, 11 May 1942, *LNC juillet 41–mai 43*, 261.
92. Jean-Louis Crémieux-Brilhac, *La France Libre: De l'Appel du 18 juin à la Libération* (Paris, 1996), 304.
93. Ibid., 305.
94. Ibid., 313n. 4 citing d'Argenlieu to de Gaulle, 29 June 1942, AN Papiers d'Argenlieu AP517.
95. D'Argenlieu to de Gaulle, 23, 24 and 26 May 1942, MAE Guerre 1939–45, London CNF, vol. 80.
96. *New York Times*, 21 May 1942, 1:6.
97. De Gaulle to Tixier, 9 May 1942, MAE Guerre 1939–45, London CNF, vol. 82; most of this document is reproduced in *Call to Honor*, 284–85.
98. Diary entry 2 May 1942, *The Adolf A. Berle Diary* (Hyde Park, N.Y., Franklin D. Roosevelt Library: 1978), roll 4, frames 103–104.
99. COMNAVEU to COMINCH, 9 May 1942, USNARA RG 165, 381 New Caledonia, and Kittredge, "U.S.-Free French Relations 1942–44," Appendix B, Part I (Correspondence May-October 1942), Op Arch NHC, Washington D.C.
100. "Fighting French in the Pacific, June 1940-September 1943," 22 October 1943, Central Pacific Branch, Theatre Group, Military Intelligence Division, USNARA Operational Plans Division (OPD), 336 France.

101. "Memorandum to All Officers," 10 September 1942, MAE Guerre 1939–45, London CNF, vol. 80.
102. De Gaulle, *Mémoires*, vol. 1, 192.
103. High Commissioner to de Gaulle, 24 October 1942, MAE Guerre 1939–45, CNF London, vol. 80.
104. Memorandum of Conversation on "New Caledonia" between Maurice Schwob and A.A. Berle, 11 August 1942, USNARA State Dec. File 851.01/625/1/2 PS/TL.
105. After the Free-French success in holding up General Rommel's troops at Bir-Hakeim for ten days in the Egyptian desert, an event in which the Pacific Battalion played a major role, General de Gaulle decided that henceforth the Free French would be referred to as the Fighting French. Both terms are used here interchangeably.
106. Memorandum of Conversation between Hull, Tixier, d'Argenlieu and Atherton, 8 December 1942, USNARA State Dec. file, 851.01/658-2/5.
107. D'Argenlieu to de Gaulle, 9 December 1942, AN Papiers d'Argenlieu AP517.
108. Tixier to Pleven, 6 January 1943 MAE Guerre 1939–45, CNF London, vol. 121.
109. "Instructions du Commissaire National aux Colonies pour le Gouverneur Montchamp," 2 July 1942, AN d'Argenlieu Papers AP517.
110. Memorandum of Conversation, Governor Montchamp, Captain Dacosta, A.A. Berle, 2 July 1942, USNARA State Dec. File 851L/001/5.

Chapter 5

The Rooster and the Eagle: Governor Montchamp, Admiral Halsey, and the American Occupation

When Governor Montchamp arrived in Nouméa, he began the process of mending fences with the various factions that had emerged from the riot. He showed great deference to Admiral d'Argenlieu and the members of his mission, assuring d'Argenlieu that he was prepared to obey the high commissioner's every order. He made a tour of the interior of the island and shook the hand of Captain Dubois, which gained Montchamp a measure of tolerance among the Caledonians but alarmed members of the d'Argenlieu mission. Toward the Americans he displayed a mixture of good humor and firmness in response to their constant requests. In private Montchamp deplored continuing American pressures for additional space to house their rapidly expanding staffs and accommodate their officers, requests that Montchamp rightly complained were often presented in a rude and aggressive fashion by junior officers sent over from American headquarters.[1]

American requirements led to numerous disputes with Governor Montchamp, resulting in lengthy and often bitter communications between Nouméa, London and Washington. The need for space increased dramatically when the Americans decided to move the headquarters of the commander of the Allied Forces in the South Pacific from Auckland to Nouméa, which was over one thousand miles closer to military operations in the Solomon Islands. While Admiral Ghormley had accepted the inconvenience of having his headquarters aboard a ship anchored in Nouméa's harbor, his successor, Admiral William S. ("Bull") Halsey was not at all willing to endure such hardship, particularly when he believed that adequate space for his large staff could be found ashore. Halsey's eye fixed upon the Nouméa residence, now vacant, of Admiral d'Argenlieu. Although in need of refurbishment, it had sufficient space to house Halsey's staff, and the sizeable grounds would allow junior officers to set up tents there, if French officials would make the residence available. When they were unwilling to do so, or at least delayed giving a positive response to Halsey's request, a dispute developed that again underlined differences in style, sensitivity and priorities that existed between the Americans and the Fighting French. Halsey's appointment changed both the tone and the nature of relations between the American military leadership and local Fighting-French authorities in New Caledonia.

Admiral Halsey's Arrival

Halsey arrived in Nouméa in mid-afternoon of 18 October and immediately read the orders that Admiral Chester Nimitz, the commander of the American Fleet in the Pacific, had sent to him in Nouméa after his departure from Pearl Harbor. "Jesus Christ and General Jackson," the American admiral exclaimed upon reading his orders. "What a hot potato they have handed me!" The "hot potato" was Halsey's appointment as Commander of Allied Forces in the South Pacific Theater, replacing the disheartened Admiral Robert Ghormley.

The decision to send Halsey to Nouméa to relieve Admiral Ghormley was a difficult and painful one for Admirals Nimitz and Halsey, since both were close friends of Ghormley and respected him as a naval officer. Ghormley had finished fifth in his class when he graduated from Annapolis, and his career in the Navy had been impressive, including most recently an assignment as naval representative to the British Government in London from 1939 to 1942. He had been recalled from this post and replaced by Admiral Harold Stark upon his appointment as commander of Allied Forces in the South Pacific. However Ghormley appeared overwhelmed by the responsibilities of his command, particularly when confronted with the serious naval loss suffered at the Battle of Savo Island, one of the worst defeats in U.S. naval history. His severely depleted forces made the task of protecting and supplying the beleaguered Marines on Guadalcanal extremely difficult. Both the battle on land to preserve control of Henderson Field and naval engagements in the waters of the Solomon Islands were taking their toll. It was by no means certain in August and September 1942 that the United States would be able to hold Guadalcanal, much less inflict a defeat upon the Japanese.

In late September Admiral Nimitz made an inspection tour of the South Pacific, and he was shocked by the sense of discouragement and obvious strain that had weakened morale at Ghormley's headquarters in Nouméa harbor. When Nimitz returned to Hawaii, he consulted with his staff and reluctantly concluded that Ghormley would have to be replaced by a fighting admiral.[2] The choice was "Bull" Halsey, who had a reputation in the Navy as a crusty and charismatic sailor's admiral.

Among the qualities that made Halsey popular with American sailors was his impatience with formalities and red tape; he liked to roll up his sleeves and "get the job done" in a rough and ready, positive manner, but he lacked Ghormley's patience and diplomatic finesse. Where Ghormley was a worrier, reflective and understated in his manner, Halsey was by nature optimistic, an extrovert to the point of braggadocio, and he imparted an air of breezy confidence to those under his command. Halsey's appointment gave a tremendous boost to American morale in the South Pacific, but it did not augur well for easy or graceful relations with sensitive Fighting-French Allies in New Caledonia, who would have to deal with this aggressive and impatient all-American admiral. Halsey would be far more blunt, direct and dismissive in his dealings with the French than either Admiral Ghormley or General Patch had been.

To facilitate negotiations, the navy department in Washington asked that General de Gaulle allow Governor Montchamp to negotiate directly with Halsey.[3] In these negotiations Montchamp gave Halsey the impression that he was anxious to accommodate the Americans but was unable to reach agreement without London's approval, although de Gaulle initially had authorized direct negotiations between Montchamp and Halsey in New Caledonia.

Montchamp warned London that the Americans were threatening to take over all facilities on the island. He feared that yielding to Halsey's request for French government residences in Nouméa would produce a serious morale problem and further diminish Fighting-French prestige on the island.[4] In subsequent telegrams Montchamp's tone became even more alarmist. He asked that de Gaulle inform Washington that "the imperious and constantly increasing requests of the allied commanders ... are making the situation impossible."[5] If the U.S. Army would occupy other locations in New Caledonia, additional space would be freed in Nouméa for the navy. As it was, there was no more space for lodging American officers in town. To support his contention that everything possible had been done to accommodate the Americans, Montchamp sent a list of the housing and facilities that had been turned over to them.[6] French concessions, the governor argued, had reached a maximum limit.

From Tahiti, d'Argenlieu backed Montchamp's resistance to American requests. He complained that in their high-handed way the Americans had already occupied all of the new buildings that had been constructed by the French Government. "Sautot always gave in to their requests," he lamented. After Sautot's departure, d'Argenlieu insisted that he and Governor Montchamp had always given the Americans satisfaction with the greatest good will, but he warned that the day was coming when the Americans "will throw out the Governor himself to occupy his residence."[7] He repeated his conviction that the Americans sought to end all French civil and military authority in New Caledonia.

In response to these warnings de Gaulle informed Montchamp that he wanted d'Argenlieu to keep the residence and asked the governor to make Halsey understand the reasons for this refusal. He urged that other villas and the residence of the former Japanese consul be placed at Halsey's disposal. "Admiral d'Argenlieu and Government Montchamp have the feeling of being completely overwhelmed by the Americans,"[8] de Gaulle lamented to Washington. He asked that American authorities take into account the sensitivities of local opinion in New Caledonia on the issue of French sovereignty.

The U.S. position was that these were matters that could and should be resolved in New Caledonia between Governor Montchamp and the American commanders without constant reference back to London and Washington for resolution.[9] The underlying source of misunderstanding remained: a French insistence upon centralized decision making, a concern that French sovereignty embodied in the Free-French movement should be preserved intact, and a fear of an American tendency to make arrangements with local authorities at the expense of French interests. The Americans considered these procedures to be obstructionist, delaying tactics that impeded the war effort, and they thought that French concerns over their rights and sovereignty to be excessive and little more than bureaucratic punctilio or misplaced egoism.

Halsey accepted to forego the high commissioner's residence in the event of his return. He took up residence in the house of the former Japanese consul, as de Gaulle had proposed, which gave Halsey a certain amount of satisfaction. "The house is thoroughly comfortable and modern, for this place, and it has a wonderful outlook over the harbor. Four other members of my staff are with me. The remainder of the staff is living in great discomfort in town. This will be corrected as soon as we can erect some Quonset huts."[10] If the Americans could not obtain any more housing from Free-French authorities, they would build temporary housing of their own, since Halsey was reluctant to build permanent structures as he hoped to move forward soon.[11]

In the meantime, American demands for space continued, but Montchamp steadily denied these requests, which exasperated Admiral Halsey. "It appears to be just an entire lack of desire to cooperate," Halsey reported to Washington. He claimed that French barracks and military buildings were all over Nouméa but were hardly used. Given the small number of French troops in Nouméa, Halsey believed that their activities could be concentrated in one building. But, as he put it with the sarcastic and demeaning language that he customarily employed in discussing the French, "this would not uphold the dignity and sovereignty of the Fighting (not here) Free French. You can figure this one out as well as I can. It makes no sense by any known standard." He blamed his troubles in getting his way to a combination of French "dilatoriness" and the fact that the Americans in the South Pacific were "on the receiving end from the Darlan incident in North Africa." Halsey's patience, never his strong suit, was fast running out, and in his exasperation he stated that he wished "we could take the place over. They would starve to death if it were not for our 'Lend-lease' and assistance."[12] While this statement was contained in a letter to Nimitz, similar careless and ill-considered remarks could be heard from other American officers in New Caledonia at that time, and they alarmed the French in the colony and in London.

Montchamp replied that if it were possible to give full satisfaction to Admiral Halsey's requests, he would do so "but the order of General De Gaulle is fixed." He agreed that the size of the French force in Nouméa "is far from equal to yours" but he assured Halsey that the French had squeezed themselves into space that was "neither large nor comfortable" as Halsey had claimed. He reminded the American commander that the resources of Nouméa had been strained prior to the arrival of the Halsey's staff. He could go no further in offering facilities to the Americans.

The language and substance of these exchanges were typical of the Franco-American wartime *mésentente*; on the one hand, an American attitude that was condescending and paternalistic towards the French and were regarded as wards unable to take care of themselves and acted in a peevish manner by not yielding to all American requests; on the other hand, an extreme sensitivity on the part of the French who found in their demands evidence of an American intention to push them aside as a people who no longer mattered and who commanded little respect. French refusals became acts of defiance, independence and rebellion against domination. American requests and the American manner of presenting them were seen to be insults to French honor, prestige and sense of grandeur that could only be defended by saying "No!" either directly or in evasive, courteous language that achieved the objectives of denial and an assertion of independence.

Beyond the dispute over space was an equally serious concern on the part of the French governor: that of preserving a French way of life in the face of massive American presence in the French colony. Montchamp believed that further concessions would have a disastrous effect upon French prestige in New Caledonia. He warned Halsey that American requests encouraged "tendentious rumors [and] bad intentions of people who are opposed to us," an oblique reference to the presumed autonomists who wished to weaken, if not break, ties with French central authority. He portrayed himself as gallantly struggling against pernicious claims that the Americans were "trying to kill French life, by suppressing little by little through requests based on military considerations, all our organization—to substitute for it some American form which would lead to the ruin of all that is French." His duty as governor required him to be vigilant in defending "all that is French" against this American onslaught. He asked Halsey's understanding and support in assuring its preservation against the day when further American victories would enable "your force to follow your victorious troops to a base nearer a new theater of operations."[13]

Admiral Halsey had little sympathy for Montchamp's belief that the Americans were ruining a French way of life in the South Pacific, and in any event the Americans had a job to do, which was to win the war. From Halsey's perspective the French had to accept the inconveniences of the American presence and should grant what he believed were reasonable and necessary requests. In a letter to Frank Knox, the secretary of the navy, Halsey expressed his feelings about Montchamp and his superiors. "Our principle difficulty," he wrote, lies in the non-cooperative 'business as usual' attitude of the French. They are jealous of their prerogatives and anxious to preserve, war or no war, French traditions and customs, allegedly so that French influence in the Colony will not be weakened in the post-war period, but really I think they desire to avoid the mental discomfort of changing their habits and the physical discomfort of contracting their installations to make room for us.[14]

The trouble stemmed not so much from Montchamp, whom Halsey still considered "anxious to play ball with us," but from High Commissioner d'Argenlieu to whom Montchamp still had to answer. Halsey stated that Admiral Stark had obtained agreement in October from Fighting-French headquarters that de Gaulle would authorize Montchamp to deal directly with him. He suspected that the telegram authorizing Montchamp to do so had never been sent or was never given to Montchamp since d'Argenlieu's chief of staff, Frédéric Fourcade, alone held the French code and may not have given Montchamp the message. Halsey complained that Montchamp still had to refer all matters, major and minor, to d'Argenlieu whose replies were always "delayed and unsatisfactory". This was not surprising, Halsey noted, since d'Argenlieu, "despite the fact [that] his life was saved at one time by General Patch, is asserted by all hands to be obstructionistic and anti-American." In his comments Halsey displayed little sympathy for French anxieties and sensitivities on the issue of their prestige, and he regarded their fears of American domination to be no more than anti-Americanism and a desire to avoid cooperation and its inconveniences. From this perspective, the Fighting French were more obstacles than allies in the war effort, and the impatient Halsey was even prepared to push the French aside if necessary to obtain what he felt was required to win the war in the South Pacific.

Montchamp eagerly anticipated the moment when the Americans would move on, no longer threatening a French way of life in New Caledonia and no longer needing more quarters for their officers or space for their staff operations. However, the date of the American departure did not arrive as quickly as Montchamp might have wished, despite Halsey's own hope to be able to move forward as the Solomons campaign progressed. Nouméa would remain the location for the South Pacific Naval Commander's headquarters throughout the Solomons campaign, which continued for over a year after the American defeat of the Japanese forces on Guadalcanal in February 1943.

Guadalcanal, the Solomons Campaign, and the Expansion of U.S. Military Presence: August '42–August '43

The battle for Guadalcanal had been precarious from the moment of the American landing on the island and nearby Tulagi on 7/8 August 1942. The decision to seize the airfield that the Japanese had begun was a risky one, given the limited resources of the Americans, and it nearly turned to disaster during the first days when protective naval cover, particularly Admiral Fletcher's aircraft carriers, were withdrawn from Guadalcanal shortly after the landing. This decision left the Marines exposed to Japanese counterattacks. Fortunately the Americans were able to hold and use Henderson airfield, and American pilots operating from the field established superiority during daylight hours that limited the Japanese capacity to reinforce their troops on Guadalcanal.

At sea the Americans also had some good fortune after suffering heavy losses at the Battle of Savo Island during the evening of 8/9 August. Had the Japanese Navy pressed its advantage at that time, American Marines on Guadalcanal would have been in serious difficulties and the U.S. Navy hard pressed to relieve them. The Japanese force withdrew after Savo Island, enabling the unprotected transports to complete unloading of troops and supplies. Subsequent naval engagements during September and October led to a stalemate between the Americans and the Japanese in the struggle to control the waters of the southern Solomons. Generally the Americans had the advantage during the day while the Japanese were able to run "the Slot" between the islands to reinforce Guadalcanal by night.

The decisive turning point for the Americans came during a series of naval and air engagements that were fought between 12 and 15 November 1942, when the Japanese brought in elements of their Combined Fleet, including three formidable battleships, to pound Henderson Field and support a substantial troop reinforcement. American warships and aircraft inflicted heavy losses upon

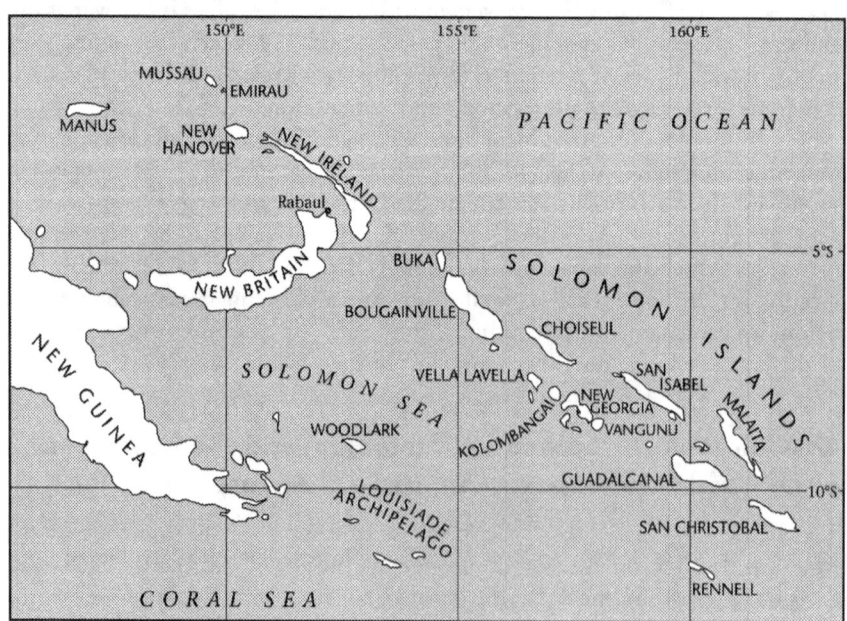

Map 4. The Solomon Islands.
Source. Cartography Lab, University of Minnesota.

the Japanese, including two battleships sunk, and only one-fifth of the ten-thousand Japanese troops sent to Guadalcanal arrived after the Americans sank seven of their transports and forced four others to run aground with a full loss of equipment and supplies.

Although the Americans suffered another disastrous engagement off Tassafaronga Island at the end of November, by December it was clear that the Japanese would not recapture Henderson Field. Reinforcements from General Patch's Americal Division began arriving in large numbers beginning in October to relieve the Marines, which meant that the Japanese could not expect to match the size of the American Forces on Guadalcanal. The Marines had held, and American pilots and sailors had regained their confidence. It was a tremendous victory for the Americans, and it indicated that the limit of Japanese expansion in the South Pacific had been reached.

On 12 December the Japanese Naval command recommended that Guadalcanal be abandoned, a recommendation accepted at Imperial headquarters on the thirty-first. In a series of night operations, the Japanese successfully evacuated ten-thousand troops from Guadalcanal with the loss of only one destroyer in the process. By 8 February the last living Japanese soldier had left the island, now in the hands of forty thousand American troops. Guadalcanal was an impressive victory, particularly for the Marines who had defended Henderson Field for four hellish months before being relieved. But there remained another sixteen months of fighting before the end of the Solomons campaign, and Montchamp and his successors would experience sixteen more months of American requests before Halsey would leave New Caledonia for good.

As the battle for Guadalcanal was coming to an end, Admiral Halsey and his colleagues realized that they would be in New Caledonia for longer than expected. In 1943 New Caledonia became the main staging area for the Solomons campaign. American military headquarters continued to be located in Nouméa, rather than going forward as Halsey had anticipated. The buildup of American and New Zealand forces meant that accommodations had to be built and tent cities created throughout the island as well as in the area around Nouméa. Warehouses to store the vast amounts of goods and equipment were needed, and empty space in Nouméa was leased by the military for the construction of Quonset huts. Open spaces also became storage depots for ammunition and military equipment. An extensive construction program began in late 1942 and early 1943 that was to transform the landscape of New Caledonia.

Halsey's persistent requests for space led to exchanges with Free-French authorities in Nouméa and London that again revealed contrasts in Free-French and American attitudes. For example, Halsey wanted additional space for a supply depot, and he requested that certain French naval buildings near his headquarters be made available. Montchamp replied that since these facilities were under the control of Admiral d'Argenlieu he would have to cable London. Halsey saw this as another stalling tactic and offered to cable London himself, adding with his habitual lack of subtlety that if the governor was overwhelmed by the tasks of administering the island, "the American government will take over the civilian administration"; to which Montchamp replied, "such action would be considered as inconsiderate on the part of the American force."[15] While Montchamp might be willing to cooperate with U.S. authorities, Halsey reported, local representatives of Admiral d'Argenlieu blocked the governor's ability to do so. This additional dispute over space was forwarded to London to be sorted out by Admiral Stark in negotiations with the Fighting French.[16]

Stark took the issue directly to de Gaulle in a letter that stated wartime conditions did not permit the long, time-consuming bureaucratic procedures that might be customary in time of peace. He noted that if there were no competent authority in New Caledonia able to respond to demands that required quick action and if all decisions on local matters were routinely referred to London for adjudication, then unpleasant incidents would be inevitable. In the hope of avoiding such misunderstandings he had requested that authority be given to de Gaulle's local representative, Governor Montchamp. He doubted those decisions about a war zone as distant as New Caledonia could be made from London. Stark bluntly informed de Gaulle:

> There is no officer of the U.S. Government in London with adequate knowledge of the military programs and local conditions in the South Pacific to discuss local questions with you or with other members of the French National Committee. I should be surprised if even your very distinguished colleagues have the wide and necessary knowledge and understanding of the current local situation and of the military problems arising from operations in this area to enable them to reach wise and appropriate decisions on purely local questions.[17]

The American concern was to win the war in the Pacific and not be distracted by political maneuvers between Nouméa and London.

As Halsey lost patience with continuing French refusals to meet his space requests, he asked and obtained Washington's permission to declare Nouméa and its surroundings to be a military district, "within the limits of which there would be American military control."[18] Halsey could then requisition any buildings he deemed essential for the security of the island. The American threat to create a military district in Nouméa was a serious challenge to French sovereignty and would have brought strong protests from Montchamp and de Gaulle had it become known, but the military district was never implemented. Halsey himself recognized that such a step would have serious diplomatic and practical repercussions "with its consequent popular reaction" and drain upon American military forces and administrative staffs.[19] Although never applied, Halsey's authorization to declare a military district was a more serious threat of an American takeover of New Caledonia than General Patch's request for the right to declare limited martial law in 1942.

Relatively minor or practical matters related to the conduct of the war became major matters of sovereignty and prestige when transferred to London. These differences confirmed the American view that Gaullists continued to be more interested in the politics of prestige than they were in the war effort or in cooperation with their allies. Montchamp himself urged that either the governor or the local representative of the high commissioner be given authority to act and make decisions. Such authority, he argued, would give the ranking French official in New Caledonia weight in dealing with the Americans rather than creating the impression that he could only send messages and await replies from the central authority in London, diminishing the prestige and authority of the governor's office.[20]

As a result of Admiral Stark's letter to de Gaulle, the situation in New Caledonia became an issue at Free-French headquarters. Admiral d'Argenlieu responded to Admiral Stark with a statement of the Gaullist position on the problem of maintaining French sovereignty in the empire in the face of an American military occupation. He informed Stark that the instructions given to Montchamp explicitly excluded making available any locations belonging to the high commissioner's office and any French military sites that were necessary for Free-French troops and support services. He added that American complaints about a lack of cooperation were unjustified. From the very day of the arrival of American troops French authorities had shown "a fully cooperative spirit to achieve the common goals that we pursue and in testimony to the friendship that the French people have always shown toward the American people."[21]

Nouméa was a little town with limited resources, and d'Argenlieu recommended that the Americans construct their own buildings as they had done in Australia. He then made a list from memory of buildings and facilities that had been made available to the American Forces. He insisted that French Forces had to keep all of their barracks and military facilities and would henceforth refuse all additional requests. D'Argenlieu observed that if the French gave in to all American requests they would abandon the protection of the interests of the population, and such abandonment would have harmful effects upon the local political situation. From a Gaullist perspective the American military presence in New Caledonia was a threat to Free-French control and constituted deliberate slights that revealed an underlying drive toward domination.

Stung by d'Argenlieu's claim that the Americans had not constructed any buildings, Halsey ordered his staff to make a survey of how the Americans were housed in New Caledonia as of 1 May 1943. The report of Halsey's staff revealed the extent of American military construction and facilities in the Nouméa area. As the report noted, D'Argenlieu's claim that no barracks or other new structures had been erected in Nouméa or elsewhere showed his "lack of familiarity with the present situation" since the end of September 1942.[22]

Figure 5.1. "This photograph 'entirely refutes the impression Admiral d'Argenlieu gave us'."
Source. U.S. National Archives (111-SC-231351).

According to the survey the total number of buildings constructed by or for American Forces on the island was 2,186. The Army Service Command had constructed 271 warehouses so far with an area of 409,284 square feet and had planned 336 more that would provide an additional 1,043,305 square feet of storage space. For every one thousand U.S. troops on the island, the report noted that 905 were "under canvas," ninety were housed in buildings constructed by or for U.S. forces, and five were billeted in French buildings, mostly ranking officers, which included those renting houses, living in hotels or rooming with French families. The majority lived two or more to a room. Between twenty-five and thirty private houses in Nouméa were occupied exclusively by Americans. The number of such lodgings was limited and a French rental commission controlled prices to avoid escalating rents that might result if American officers got into a bidding war with the civilian population. A joint service board reviewed all requests for private housing, and no officer could obtain private quarters without the board's approval. Thus, a cooperative French-American effort functioned to ration housing in a way that would limit the impact and hardships of the housing crisis.

The Americans noted that French officers in both private accommodation and in their barracks were less crowded than their American counterparts. Elsewhere on the island housing had been constructed for soldiers, often Kanak-type long houses built by American or New Zealand forces, the latter being housed almost exclusively in these quarters. The extent of the construction impressed General Barrowclough, the commander of the New Zealand Third Division, stationed on the island. He told the Americans, "I think I can confidently say that I have never seen any force in any part of the world in which I have served which has made less use of the buildings belonging to the local inhabitants."[23] The report noted that requisitioning procedures were employed only in "a very rare number of instances" and claimed that no undue or unnecessary hardship had resulted.

In response to d'Argenlieu's claim that practically all French government warehouses, offices, barracks, etc. were occupied by Americans, the American report listed eight buildings occupied in their entirety by French forces. The only buildings occupied by the Americans on the Ile Nou were the French artillery barracks, which were taken over after the French had voluntarily withdrawn, the meteorological station, and a private house formerly occupied by French officers. The hospital and prison buildings continued to be under the French. When Halsey's report with accompanying photographs arrived in London, Stark promptly asked Kittredge to present the material, including the photographs to René Massigli. The report and photographs, he bluntly stated, "entirely refute the impression Admiral d'Argenlieu gave us."[24]

Despite all efforts to mitigate its inconveniences the American occupation of New Caledonia was overwhelming and intense. Nouméa had become the main port of assembly for the remainder of the Solomons campaign, which, the Americans knew, was far from over. After Guadalcanal, followed by the occupation of the Russell Islands, a lull ensued in the South Pacific, in part imposed by the shipping, manpower and supply requirements for the landings in North Africa, which had taken priority. Nevertheless, the American Navy was able to command enough shipping to begin the build-up for the island hopping up the Solomons chain toward the major Japanese base at Rabaul. The strategy was to link up with General MacArthur's American Forces and the Australians coming across Papua New Guinea. Gearing up for the final phase of the Solomons offensive meant a continued influx of war material, soldiers and sailors into the already crowded port of Nouméa. In 1943 the amount of shipping tonnage passing through Nouméa was second only to that of San Francisco as a Pacific port, surpassing both Seattle and Los Angeles in overall activity. Bottlenecks were inevitable and ships were often in port for weeks without being able to unload. Anchored cargo ships that could not be unloaded were used as supply depots, but this was an impractical method given the constant demands for shipping in all theaters of war.

The situation began to improve at the beginning of 1943 when Halsey informed Nimitz that the rate for unloading tonnage had risen dramatically from 1500 tons/day in November to over ten thousand tons six weeks later.[25] The construction of Quonset huts on vacant land near the docks greatly expanded storage capacity ashore. These improvements meant further inconveniences for the Caledonians since the Americans now occupied and used virtually all of the dock space in Nouméa and a priority for military delivery often meant delays in distribution of necessities for the civilian population. As Ballard reported there was no provision for an orderly handling of unloaded civilian goods. The French administration seemed overwhelmed by problems of distribution; price control was "only a phrase" as prices mounted and inflation increased dramatically; the rationing scheme, he reported, was poorly controlled.[26] While some of the difficulties in supplying civilian needs might be blamed on the shortage of qualified French personnel, Americans and their military priorities became the main targets for civilian complaints.

Nouméa and its surroundings became filled with tent camps, supply depots, and infirmaries. The population of Nouméa tripled with the arrival of the American headquarters for Halsey's command as well as becoming headquarters for the army and army air corps in the South Pacific. "The town and peninsula were totally swamped by this unprecedented military occupation."[27] This massive presence brought inconveniences that the local population began to resent. Water supply and electrical service became severely strained. Fresh meat, fruit and vegetables were in short supply and often not available, although staples such as flour and rice could be obtained. Delays in unloading produced rumblings of discontent.

On the other hand, the Caledonians discovered unexpected and welcome opportunities for exploiting the American military presence. "All is overshadowed by the prevailing occupation of making money out of the Americans," Ballard reported to his superiors in Canberra, "there must be few people, white or black, who are not benefiting from them directly or indirectly."[28] An underground market emerged for goods, some obtained by unusual means from American military sources, and there was widespread production of moonshine liquor that was sold to the military personnel at a substantial mark-up. As prices rose, Caledonians on fixed salaries began to suffer economic hardship, while those who could engage in entrepreneurial activity enjoyed their newly found prosperity. Even members of the administration, whose salaries were fixed, engaged in secondary activities to supplement their incomes.

The demand for labor and services was heavy, particularly for laundry services and for snack and soft drink bars to slake the hungers and thirsts of swarms of American soldiers, sailors and marines. As long as French shopkeepers held a monopoly of such activities, they prospered by charging high prices. The Americans responded by placing shops accused of price gouging off-limits, and they established post exchanges in town that sold cokes and sandwiches for five cents apiece. The Americans hired labor to work in these establishments, and they also employed native Melanesians and Asians to assist them with the unloading of equipment and supplies. These employees received generous salaries by local standards, much to the dismay of certain Caledonians business leaders who now faced competition for labor services. The Fighting-French administration feared a total disruption of the economy as a result of this induced prosperity and accompanying inflation.

The massive American military presence provided further occasion for critics to denounce a form of occupation that threatened to undermine Fighting-French authority and prestige in the colony. "One is obliged to observe," Montchamp lamented, "that the very presence of our allies in our colony has brought restrictions upon the principle of French sovereignty to the point of a deprivation of our sovereign rights."[29] He noted that in disputes or claims against the American military forces for damages the Americans reserved the right to determine amounts to be awarded in their own military hearings. He protested that French law should prevail on French territory, and he urged that French officials in London negotiate an indemnity from the Americans for this loss of French rights in a French colony.

But the loudest and most public campaign against the American presence in New Caledonia spilled from the mouth and pen of Michel Vergès, who denounced the disruptive effects that the American occupation had upon New Caledonia. He accused Montchamp, along with Secretary Bourgeau and d'Argenlieu's own representative, Fourcade, of having sold out to the Americans. Military intelligence reported that a group of dissatisfied Caledonians headed by Michel Vergès was intent upon stirring anti-American feelings among the Caledonians.[30] These were d'Argenlieu's supporters from the time of the May disturbances, who looked forward to the return of the high commissioner who would put the overbearing Americans in their place. Against this background, rumors of American designs upon New Caledonia began to circulate in Nouméa once more, encouraged by Michel Vergès and by what the American consul described as the careless talk of American military personnel.

Newspaper reports of misbehavior on the part of some troops, including trespassing and slaughtering cattle for their own use, gave ammunition to the anti-American campaign in the pages of the *Bulletin du Commerce* and brought protests in letters to the editors. As one American report noted, the local population had cause to be annoyed "... that their cattle have been killed, their fences torn down, roads built over their property, trees cut down and many other things done ... .The feeling is increasing, and unless the destruction and stealing by the U.S. forces here is curbed there may be difficulty."[31] An anonymous report to Australian intelligence noted the rise of anti-American sentiments. "There are many insular and bone-headed Babbits, possibly even more among the officers than enlisted men," the informant warned, "who think nothing of insulting the French openly, and of discussing in public whether or not America will have the bounty to take over New Caledonia now, or after the war."[32]

To silence talk of an American ambition to take over the French colony, General Rush Lincoln, commander of the First Island Command, used the occasion of the first anniversary of the arrival of American troops to make a radio broadcast to the Caledonians. He assured them that U.S. forces had come to the colony only to protect it. The American Government had no desire to replace the sovereignty of France, and the American people did not enter the war for conquest. He recognized the inconveniences caused by the American military presence, but he declared that whatever measures had been or would be taken were the result of military needs and nothing else. He thanked the people for their hospitality and understanding in a difficult time. A French version of the speech was read immediately afterward, and both French and English versions were published the next day in *France Australe*, the other newspaper on the island and one that was generally more sympathetic to the Americans.[33] General Lincoln's speech was well received although not all anxieties about American intentions were fully removed.[34]

In an effort to improve relations and remove sources of conflict and dissatisfaction, the army's public relations office instituted weekly conferences between officers of the First Island Command and members of the local press, which the American consul claimed removed some of the misunderstandings that had arisen.[35] In response to claims for damages caused by American military personnel, the military authorities established and published procedures whereby the Caledonians could register their claims and apply for reimbursements for losses. As Colonel Freby reported to Governor Montchamp, American officials had begun to pay for certain of these damages, and he added that the population should not continue to allow rumors to circulate "that our allies are not interested in rectifying the faults committed by their soldiers."[36] These efforts failed to reassure either the Fighting French or the local Caledonian population. A military intelligence report observed a cooling of the local population's friendliness and cooperation toward the Americans.

The report also noted a problem that would become acute and a major source of tension with the arrival of Montchamp's successor as governor: the issue of race relations. According to this report, a significant source for growing friction and hostility toward the Americans stemmed from what were described as "several regrettable incidents caused by colored members of the United States Armed Forces."[37] During the latter part of 1943 tensions mounted as fights broke out between white as well as black American troops on the one hand and French civilians and members of the French military forces in New Caledonia on the other. The American recruitment, legally and illegally, of native Melanesian labor and of Javanese and Tonkinese indentured workers who had escaped from the mines, provided further grievances from both the population and the administration.[38] The social and economic impact of the American military presence produced tensions that aggravated differences between the Americans, Fighting-French representatives, and some Caledonians.

American military commanders understood that the tremendous expansion of military and naval facilities and personnel in New Caledonia meant that the civilian population was now in a minority on the island. There was a danger that rights of the colonists, including their property rights, might be violated and lead to a reaction that would have a negative effect upon Caledonian attitudes toward the Americans.[39] The Americans tried to alleviate some of these hardships by improving the colony's services and infrastructure. The American consul reported that American military authorities had assumed partial or full responsibility for harbor facilities, road maintenance, public health and hygiene, the Nouméa water supply and sewage disposal, and improvements and repairs for the overburdened electrical supply system in Nouméa.

These measures were impressive, although they barely kept pace with the demands imposed by American military requirements, and they also became sources of concern to the Fighting-French administration. Day noted that while such services were appreciated, there was a danger that elements hostile to the American presence would point to these measures as evidence of an intention to take over the governance and administration of the island.[40] Fighting-French authorities feared that this impressive deployment of resources would tempt some autonomists into seeking the creation of a government that would be nominally independent but in fact would be under American control.[41]

The Americans faced an almost insoluble dilemma. The presence of a large military population, even if presumably transient, brought with it both inconveniences and benefits. It also presented the Americans with a situation in which efforts to relieve the hardships and inconveniences caused by military needs could also be interpreted as an intention to take over the island. The impressive construction of facilities consciously or unconsciously highlighted the sense of abandonment and resentment toward central authority that had been characteristic of New Caledonia's political culture. The more the Americans tried to help and provide services the more their actions looked like an investment in New Caledonia, perhaps to be recouped at the end of the war. An abundance of material, mostly war goods, but also health services, better sanitation for Nouméa, electricity and telephones, even chicken and egg production served to emphasize the comparative prewar neglect of New Caledonia by successive colonial administrations under the Third Republic. Impressive quantities of military equipment, hundreds of airplanes unloaded, a harbor filled with battleships, cruisers, aircraft carriers, destroyers as well as supply and cargo ships in unimagined profusion all emphasized the discrepancy of resources at the disposal of the Americans compared with the modesty of the Fighting-French military presence in New Caledonia. The American presence was overwhelming.

However, Montchamp's troubles in governing the colony were not all of American making. He also had to contend with the attitude and intrigues of d'Argenlieu's representatives on the island, notably the Fighting-French admiral's deputy, Frédéric Fourcade.[42] And there were local political issues, including a persistent resistance and resentment on the part of the governing class in New Caledonia toward any representative of central, Fighting-French administration, whether the governor or the High Commissioner's representative. These conflicts would literally exhaust Governor Montchamp.

The Governor's Graveyard: Montchamp, d'Argenlieu and Vergès

The d'Argenlieu mission closely scrutinized Montchamp's behavior, always wary that the new governor might forget himself and become another Sautot. In his usual blunt fashion Admiral Halsey informed secretary of the navy Frank Knox that one of the governor's problems in being more forthcoming was "the presence of other members of the d'Argenlieu group who I believe act as stool-pigeons for everything the Governor does."[43] Having earlier sung Montchamp's praises at the time of his appointment, d'Argenlieu soon began to criticize him for various faults and weaknesses. Admiral d'Argenlieu later admitted to René Pleven, commissioner for colonies, that if he had known more about Montchamp as Sautot's successor, he would have preferred to keep the latter.[44] This remarkable admission once more revealed Michel Vergès's influence upon the high commissioner, shaping his view of events in New Caledonia. Vergès had been one of Admiral d'Argenlieu's staunch supporters during the May 1942 riot, sharing his ardent patriotism and his anti-American sentiments.

That the d'Argenlieu mission distrusted Montchamp and tracked his activities may be seen in a comic episode. On one occasion Montchamp, who had promised Sautot that he would convey the former governor's best wishes to his close friends in Nouméa, the Garcia sisters, decided to do so one Sunday morning following mass in the Cathedral. The Garcia sisters' apartment was nearby, and upon leaving the Cathedral Montchamp ordered his driver to take him to see Sautot's favorites, staying there, according to Templeton, no more than "a purely formal ten minutes" to convey Sautot's affectionate greetings after which the governor returned to his residence.

His visit was observed by one of Fourcade's agents, the same M. Lavoix who had tried to arouse anti-American sentiments among the Broussards following the May 1942 riot. Lavoix wrote a lengthy report in which he contended that Montchamp was behaving in an immoral fashion and was consorting with the low life that had been cause of Sautot's undoing in the eyes of Admiral d'Argenlieu. "By some extraordinary means," Templeton reported, Lavoix's report was placed on the desk not of M. Fourcade but on that of the governor, and when Montchamp discovered it, "The rage and fury of His Excellency was too majestic to be described."[45] Montchamp summoned Fourcade to his office: "Vous êtes arrivés ici comme un tout petit administrateur, et, mon Dieu, vous l'êtes toujours!" This outburst was followed by a second one directed toward Lavoix, who had followed Fourcade into Montchamp's office. "Je déteste les flics," the governor proclaimed and had Lavoix transferred out of New Caledonia.

The most serious damage to Montchamp resulted from Michel Vergès's return to New Caledonian politics through a venomous letter-writing campaign. Vergès repeated his claim to be the true voice of Gaullism in New Caledonia, the only one who had truly "national interests" at heart, and he denounced his political enemies as being at once Vichy collaborators, pro-American and anti-French. A major target was Montchamp, whom he criticized for having taken up with people compromised, he alleged, in the May events. Vergès's bombast and the intemperance of his language did not prevent Admiral d'Argenlieu from taking seriously his interpretations of events in New Caledonia.

Vergès warned that Sautot's "anti-national" policies, upset by the arrival of d'Argenlieu and his mission, had been resumed under Montchamp and Frédéric Fourcade "with even more intelligent duplicity and local deceptions." He accused the Montchamp administration of undermining the national cause in New Caledonia.[46] What was wanted in New Caledonia and, he claimed, "UNANIMOUSLY demanded here," was the return of Admiral d'Argenlieu who would restore a firm and truly French authority.[47] He called for a purge of Montchamp's "immoral" and "anti-national" administration, which was supported by local profiteers and foreign interests.

Vergès claimed that Montchamp failed to forward his letters to London. But American intelligence reported that Captain Cabanier, who was in Nouméa during March and April 1943, had spent some time in the company of Vergès and had carried his messages back to d'Argenlieu and to General de Gaulle.[48] That d'Argenlieu received Vergès's communications and took them seriously may be seen in his sending Colonial Commissioner Pleven a copy of a letter from Vergès to Fourcade.[49] D'Argenlieu used this letter to denounce Montchamp as someone who "displayed a scandalous private life in the midst of a population that already has risen up" against Free-French authorities. The admiral considered the matter serious enough to recommend that Montchamp be sanctioned.[50] Decisive and irreparable damage had been done to Montchamp's reputation among the Gaullists in London, and his prospects for remaining as governor of New Caledonia were slim, given d'Argenlieu's hostility fed by the feverish denunciations of Michel Vergès. In combining his hostility toward his political enemies with a strong anti-Americanism, Vergès skillfully played upon Admiral d'Argenlieu's suspicions and, through him, those of General de Gaulle.

In addition to his difficulties with d'Argenlieu, Montchamp also found himself frustrated by local Caledonian political resentments, which ultimately drove him from the colony. Montchamp had arrived in New Caledonia determined to restore the tarnished prestige of Free France and impose some discipline upon recalcitrant Caledonians, sharing d'Argenlieu's view that Sautot had given the administrative council excessive powers that hampered the ability of the governor or the high commissioner to administer the colony. The leader of the opposition within council was Pierre Bergès, whom Montchamp described as a convinced autonomist.[51] Bergès of course was one of the councilors whom Admiral d'Argenlieu had abducted, and he had been leader of the faction asking for the high commissioner's departure. Montchamp decided to rid himself of the council and limit the political influence of Bergès. On 2 February 1943 he announced that new elections would be held on 21 March for a council of fifteen members to replace the council that Sautot had appointed. A major consideration in calling for new elections was Montchamp's determination to find a more sympathetic council in anticipation of the return of Admiral d'Argenlieu to New Caledonia, which the council and most Caledonians strongly opposed.[52]

Foreign observers were divided over the wisdom of holding elections. Consul Day feared that elections would serve no useful purpose and might provoke further disturbances that would have a harmful effect upon the military effort. B.C. Ballard felt that while the appointment of the Gaullists to the council by Sautot had been a good idea at the time, those appointed were generally individuals of little distinction and it was now more important to have members of some ability on the council. In Washington the State Department also argued that an election might actually be useful, noting that there had been "constant petty squabbles between different French factions in New Caledonia … and … an election might be helpful rather than harmful" as a way of clearing the air.[53] However, the election was not held. René Pleven, commissioner for colonies, reminded d'Argenlieu that the wartime ban on elections remained in force.[54]

Had elections been held Pierre Bergès and his faction would have won an impressive victory, which might have revealed the unpopularity of Free-French representatives in New Caledonia. Fourcade sent an intelligence mission into the countryside to sound out opinion among the Broussards. M. Banuelos, a supporter of Bergès and the owner of the hotel in La Foa where the Caledonian militia had held Admiral d'Argenlieu prisoner during the May riots, claimed that the Bergès list, which called for "Caledonia for the Caledonians," would be elected. If not, "a general strike will take place in the colony." The agent tried to discredit Banuelos's testimony by noting that he had close ties with American military officers in the region and had been given a silver cup by the Americans for his services.

The Broussards were unsympathetic to Governor Montchamp on the ground that he did not have the interests of the Caledonians at heart and had openly expressed his desire to leave the colony as soon as possible. "The present governor is a zero," went one comment, and another witness stated that all members of the mission should leave immediately since their only purpose in coming to New Caledonia was "to make war from the arm chair." The report's conclusion was a sobering one for the Fighting-French representatives in New Caledonia. "In all the districts through which I have traveled," the anonymous author reported, "I have had the clear impression that the people are against the present administration [and] against the officers of the French Army who have come here in too great numbers. They are awaiting the elections in order to have demonstrations against them."[55]

The agent also claimed that the Americans were encouraging such sentiments and that they had gathered a stock of clothing and supplies that they would make available in a crisis to demonstrate that the United States was prepared to come to the aid of the Caledonians. This report is the only evidence of such stockpiling for political purposes. Of course the American military had supply depots throughout New Caledonia; that they were intended to be used in support of some future Caledonian revolution cannot be established and may well have been the figment of the intelligence reporter's imagination. Instead, the Americans were concerned that further demonstrations would have a disruptive effect upon the war effort. Nevertheless, a Free-French belief in an American intention to interfere in the affairs of New Caledonia for their own long-term profit remained very much alive and was read into any sign of trouble in the colony.

Montchamp accepted with relief Pleven's instruction not to hold the election. In his report to d'Argenlieu, he admitted that the campaign was off to a bad start and would have resulted in an even more hostile environment. He observed that the Bergès faction might have been contained had he been allowed to appoint twelve additional members, who would have given the governor a majority on the council, but he had abandoned the idea for fear it would provoke trouble. Montchamp confessed that members of the administrative council held a profound antipathy toward him, and he declared that he had become thoroughly worn out by "this electoral stew." He became afflicted with insomnia, and his doctor recommended two months of rest and recuperation in Australia. He asked Admiral d'Argenlieu to relieve him of his duties. "I most ardently hope, Admiral, never to return here and wish to be assigned to a combat unit."[56] He felt that his services merited favorable consideration, and the time was right for him to leave.

In his final report to the high commissioner, Montchamp claimed he had fulfilled the assignment that Admiral d'Argenlieu had given him. He was to defend the island against an enemy attack, to maintain the population in its loyalty in the face of Vichy intrigues and autonomist ambitions, and to assure French sovereignty with respect to the American allies. He assured d'Argenlieu and Pleven that he had been vigilant in protecting French interests and that Admiral Halsey, unlike General Patch, no longer played the autonomists' game. If a foreign flag should be raised over New Caledonia, he was confident that the entire population would rise up in revolt.[57] On the other hand, he remained convinced that local politics made the task of governing New Caledonia difficult, if not impossible. During his ten months on the island Montchamp had come to regard the colony and its residents with ill-disguised disdain. He despised the Caledonians and believed that his opposition in the administrative council came from a group of narrow-minded, self-serving mediocrities.[58]

Despite his problems with the Caledonians, he noted that relations with the Americans were much improved since his arrival. He assured London that Jan Bourgeau could handle three or four months' interim until a replacement could be sent out. The contentiousness of New Caledonian politics and his disputes with Fourcade and Admiral d'Argenlieu, more than American behavior, had defeated Governor Montchamp. He now understood New Caledonia's reputation as a "graveyard for governors" under the Third Republic. It also had become a "graveyard for governors" under the Gaullists. With great relief Montchamp departed New Caledonia in June for his rest in Australia. Temporarily Jan Bourgeau became responsible for everyday administrative affairs in New Caledonia. The Caledonians wondered who would replace Governor Montchamp; rumor had it that Admiral d'Argenlieu might return.

The choice of Montchamp's replacement was important since a strong Fighting-French authority was needed to deal with a difficult situation. As Consul Henry Day observed, the absence of a strong single authority produced some confusion and a division of French authority in which Secretary Bourgeau had responsibility for the colony's current and urgent affairs alongside Fourcade, who represented the high commissioner's office and authority. He warned that if no successor to Montchamp were appointed for some time, a divided and relatively uncertain local French authority might give the impression that the Americans were assuming responsibility for the management of the island's affairs.[59]

The only way to regain some control of the local economy and assure order, Bourgeau insisted, was through the creation of a strong local government with a governor "having the necessary skill to avoid becoming involved in local intrigues." The new governor would also have to gain the support of a new council recognized by the population of the island. Finally, he argued that the governor had to be given responsibilities and needed the backing of central authorities. The high commissioner's office, he observed, should be a support and not an obstacle for the governor in the exercise of his duties.[60] The selection of a new governor was urgent and, given its importance, was a decision that very much involved High Commissioner d'Argenlieu whose views on New Caledonia and relations with the Americans carried great weight at de Gaulle's headquarters in London. What d'Argenlieu wanted for New Caledonia was a strong governor who would impose Free-French authority and withstand American pressure.

The choice fell on another colonial administrator, Christian Laigret. Although his initial appointment was that of interim governor, Laigret came to New Caledonia filled with an ambition to succeed and a determination to continue the assertion of French authority and prestige against the threat of American domination. In his hostility to the Americans, Laigret very much represented d'Argenlieu's xenophobic suspicion of Free-French allies in the Pacific. Through Laigret, Admiral d'Argenlieu would have another fling at the Americans. Laigret's brief tenure as governor brought American relations with the Free French to a crisis in New Caledonia.

Notes

1. Commander Templeton, "The Mission of Rear Admiral Thierry d'Argenlieu to the French Pacific," 51, United Kingdom Public Record Office (PRO) FO371/46307.
2. E.B. Potter, *Bull Halsey* (Annapolis, 1985), 159.
3. Correspondence log, 21 October 1942, U.S. National Archives and Record Administration (USNARA) RG 38, COMNAVEU Box 29, folder 69, which records the exchanges of telegrams requesting that Admiral Halsey be allowed to negotiate directly with Governor Montchamp; and Governor, New Caledonia, to CNF, 2 October 1942, Ministre des Affaires Etrangères (MAE) Guerre 1939–45, London CNF, vol. 80.

4. Governor Montchamp to CNF, 25 October 1942, ibid.
5. Same to same, 26 and 31 October 1942, ibid.
6. As of mid-November 1942, Montchamp reported that Americans had requisitioned forty-three private residences, seventeen "mixed" buildings with shops, twenty-nine dock storage warehouses, eight state-owned dock storage warehouses, three municipal buildings, plus the Bernheim Library, the "internat" or boarding school for girls, new offices that had been built for the governor, the army's "cercle militaire" space, a part of the military quartermaster's supply building, and two main hotels in town, including the Hotel du Pacifique where Patch had his headquarters; in addition space had been provided on the customs dock, three other dock spaces, the PTT dock space, and half of the municipal wharf. The colony retained the governor's residence and offices, buildings in Nouméa used by the veterinary services, the police, the gendarmerie, public works, mining and survey offices, and the army retained use of the infantry and artillery barracks and the local lycée, College Lapérouse. Montchamp noted that there were 1,800 private homes in Nouméa to accommodate 8,000 Europeans, 1,400 Melanesians, and approximately 2,000 Javanese and 1,000 Tonkinese indentured workers. He stated that even before the arrival of U.S. troops, Nouméa suffered from a shortage of housing. Montchamp to CNF, 14 November 1942, ibid.
7. High Commissioner d'Argenlieu to CNF, 24 October 1942, ibid.
8. De Gaulle to Montchamp, 26 October 1942, and de Gaulle to Tixier, 1 November 1942, ibid.
9. CNF to Tixier, 3 November 1942, and J.G. Bray, U.S. Forces in Europe, to M. Paris, Carlton Gardens, 4 November 1942, and CNF to Montchamp, 6 November 1942, ibid.
10. Halsey to Nimitz, 29 November 1942, Halsey Papers, carton 15, Library of Congress (LC), Washington, D.C.
11. Halsey to Captain Henkle, base CO New Caledonia, 20 December 1942, Halsey Papers, carton 15, LC.
12. Halsey to Nimitz, 20 December 1942, ibid.
13. Montchamp to Halsey, 11 January 1943, ibid.
14. Halsey to Knox, n.d. but post 17 February 1943, Halsey Papers, carton 14, LC.
15. Montchamp to CNF, 7 March 1943 MAE Guerre 1939–45, London CNF, vol. 80.
16. Correspondence log, 7 March 1943, USNARA RG 38, COMNAVEU Box 29, folder 69.
17. Stark to de Gaulle, 16 March 1943, PRO, FO 371/36062.
18. Knox to Halsey, 17 February 1943 and State Department Memo, 2 February 1943, Halsey Papers, carton 14, LC.
19. Halsey to Knox, 17 March 1943, Halsey Papers, ibid.
20. Montchamp to d'Argenlieu, n.d. but late March, 1943, Archives Nationales Section d'Outre-mer (ANSOM), New Caledonia, c. 163.
21. D'Argenlieu to Stark, 11 March 1943, AN Papiers d'Argenlieu, 517AP.
22. Halsey to King, "Construction and Use of Buildings by U.S. Forces in New Caledonia," 8 May 1943, Op Arch NHC, New Caledonia, Misc., microfilm reel.
23. Barrowclough to Army HQ, NZ, 30 October 1944, NZ National Archives (NZNA), Nimitz-Barrowclough conversation, EA ser 1, 86/1/13 pt. 1.
24. Stark to Kittredge, 10 June 1943, Hoover Institute Archives, Stanford California, Kittredge Papers, carton 38.
25. Halsey to Nimitz, 11 November 1943, Halsey papers, carton 15, LC.
26. B.C. Ballard to Ext. Affairs, Canberra, 19 February 1943, AA ACT CRS, A989, 43/610/11.
27. Templeton, "The Mission of Rear Admiral Thierry d'Argenlieu to the French Pacific," 51, PRO FO371/46307.
28. B.C. Ballard to External Affairs, Canberra, 19 February 1943, AA ACT CRS, A989, 43/610/11.
29. Montchamp report to Pleven, 24 February 1943, MAE Guerre 1939–45, CFLN, vol. 679.

30. HQ, 1 Island Command, annex no. 2 to weekly Intelligence (G-2) Report no. 9, 27 February 1943, USNARA RG 338.
31. Transcript of interview with Colonel Brown Rolston by Mr. Robert Hall of the Lend-lease Mission, 23 March 1943, USNARA RG 338.
32. Director Naval Intelligence to Department External Affairs, Canberra, 23 October 1942, annex. "The Growth of Anti-American Feeling in New Caledonia," 1 October 1942, AA, CRS A981, New Caledonia 9, "Relations with the U.S."
33. Day to State, 22 March 1943, USNARA State Dec. File 851L.01/34.
34. HQ, 1 Island Command, annex no. 2 to weekly Intelligence (G-2) Report no. 11, 13 March 1943, USNARA RG 338.
35. Day to State, 20 July 1943, USNARA State Dec. File 851L.00/38.
36. Freby to Montchamp, 31 March 1943, Archives of the Service Historique de l'Armée, Château de Vincennes (SHA), Outre-mer: Pacifique, c. 6.
37. HQ, 1 Island Command, annex no. 2 to weekly Intelligence (G-2) Report no. 27, 2 July 1943, USNARA RG 338.
38. Bourgeau, general secretary, to d'Argenlieu, 11 August 1943, ANSOM New Caledonia, c. 163.
39. HQ, 1 Island Command, annex no. 2 to Weekly Intelligence (G-2) Report for week ending 2 January 1943, USNARA RG 338.
40. Day to State, 20 July 1943, USNARA State Dec. File 851L.00/38.
41. Bourgeau, general-secretary, to d'Argenlieu, 11 August 1943, ANSOM New Caledonia, c. 163.
42. Templeton, "The Mission of Rear Admiral Thierry d'Argenlieu to the French Pacific," 45, PRO FO371/46307.
43. Halsey to Knox, post 17 February 1943, Halsey Papers, carton 14 LC.
44. D'Argenlieu to Pleven, 5 December 1943, AN Fonds René Pleven, 560AP/27. After Montchamp's arrival in New Caledonia in August 1942 Admiral d'Argenlieu, who was still on the island at the time, cabled de Gaulle that he was "an excellent choice" and had his full confidence, d'Argenlieu to de Gaulle, 8 August 1942, AN Papiers d'Argenlieu 517AP.
45. Templeton, "The Mission of Rear Admiral Thierry d'Argenlieu to the French Pacific," 45, PRO FO371/46307.
46. Vergès to Fourcade, 18 January 1943, AN Papiers d'Argenlieu 517AP.
47. Vergès to Fourcade, 23 February 1943, Vergès to Montchamp, 2 March 1943, and Vergès to Fourcade, 15 March 1943 in which he quotes fully Montchamp's reply to his letter of 2 March 1943, ANSOM Affaires Politiques, c. 509.
48. HQ, 1 Island Command, annex no. 2 to weekly Intelligence (G-2) Report no. 14, 3 April 1943 and to Report no. 96, 28 October 1944, USNARA RG 338.
49. D'Argenlieu to Pleven (Colonies), 25 May 1943, ANSOM CNF c. 3.
50. D'Argenlieu to Pleven (Colonies, Alger), 15 September 1943, ANSOM New Caledonia, c. 162.
51. Montchamp's grievances against the council are contained in a lengthy report sent to Admiral d'Argenlieu at the end of March 1943, ANSOM New Caledonia 163.
52. Day to State, radiogram 4 February 1943, USNARA State Dec. File 851L.00/30.
53. B.C. Ballard to External Affairs, Canberra, 19 February 1943, AA ACT CRS, A989, 43/610/11; Day to State, radiogram 4 February 1943, and memo by Berle, 18 February 1943, USNARA State Dec. File 851L.00/30.
54. D'Argenlieu to Pleven, 9 April 1943, and Pleven to d'Argenlieu, 13 April 1943, ANSOM New Caledonia, c. 163.
55. Rapport de l'Emissaire D en éxécution de l'ordre de Mission No. 24 du X à Y Avril 1943," SHA, Outre-mer: Pacifique, c. 6.
56. Montchamp to d'Argenlieu, n.d. but late March, 1943, ANSOM New Caledonia, c. 163.

57. Montchamp to Pleven, "Rapport au sujet de la Nouvelle Calédonie," 28 December 1943, ANSOM New Caledonia, c. 162.
58. Templeton, "The Mission of Rear Admiral Thierry d'Argenlieu to the French Pacific," 45 PRO FO371/46307.
59. Day to State, 20 July 1943, USNARA State Dec. File 851L.00/38.
60. Bourgeau to d'Argenlieu, 11 August 1943, ANSOM New Caledonia, c. 163.

Chapter 6

Governor Laigret and the American Economic and Cultural Challenge

Governor Montchamp's departure left Fighting-French authority in New Caledonia both weak and divided, reflecting the difficulties that Governor Sautot had predicted at the time of d'Argenlieu's appointment as high commissioner for the Pacific in 1941. Throughout the subsequent two years there had been ongoing tension that at times led to sharp confrontations between the governor's and high commissioner's offices. While technically the highest authority was that of the high commissioner, de Gaulle's direct representative, the daily administration of the colony, including relations with the Caledonians and with American military officials, was the governor's task. Lines of authority continued to be blurred as long as d'Argenlieu and de Gaulle were unwilling to delegate much responsibility to the governor. What was needed, according to General Secretary Jan Bourgeau, was a governor "who would really govern."[1]

Local Politics and the Arrival of Governor Laigret

Rumors that d'Argenlieu himself might resume residence in the empty villa greatly alarmed members of the administrative council. Rather than unifying the Caledonian political elite in opposition to d'Argenlieu's return, however, these rumors produced a split within the administrative council. This division stemmed from a reverse political direction for Pierre Bergès, who had been one of the four councilors abducted by Admiral d'Argenlieu. Bergès's change in attitude toward the admiral began shortly after the confrontation with Montchamp over the issue of elections for a new governing council.

At first Bergès had opposed a new election. When he discovered that he had an excellent chance of winning the election and strengthening his own authority, he decided that the Caledonians should be allowed to vote in a referendum to determine whether or not elections should be held. Bergès cabled d'Argenlieu that this referendum would show respect for the democratic traditions of New Caledonia and provide a way to strengthen Fighting-French authority by restoring confidence between the people and de Gaulle's representatives.[2] He also concluded that the overwhelming American presence required closer cooperation with the central authority of General de Gaulle's Committee of National Liberation, which had moved its headquarters from London to Algiers as of June 1943. Bergès realized that de Gaulle would become the leader of France and it would be with him that the Caledonians would have to negotiate at war's end.

D'Argenlieu also sought conciliation rather than continued conflict with the Caledonians. He forwarded Bergès's communication to Commissioner for Colonies René Pleven, noting the Caledonian's desire to find a way toward better cooperation between the Caledonians and the French National Committee.[3] He also sent a very diplomatic and flattering cable to Bergès in which he thanked his former antagonist for his kind personal message. He assured Bergès that he, General de Gaulle, and the French National Committee agreed fully with the Caledonian leader's desire for the "qualified population" to have a wider voice in managing New Caledonia's affairs. The high commissioner informed Bergès that he was studying his proposal to hold a referendum on elections in New Caledonia, reassured by Bergès's statement that the voting would take place in a calm atmosphere. He also stated that the governor of the colony should, as apparently Bergès had requested, be completely devoted to the interests of this faithful province of France and fulfillment of the great national task before the French National Committee.[4]

D'Argenlieu's conciliatory approach to Bergès revealed his own shift in dealing with the Caledonians. Continued friction between central authority and the Caledonian political leaders might allow the Americans to exploit local grievances. In his reports on the situation in New Caledonia, which he had observed during his visit in April, Captain Cabanier warned d'Argenlieu that Montchamp's policy of confrontation with Bergès and the administrative council had produced a sense of discouragement among the honest folk of New Caledonia. This friction had encouraged "dubious elements" in the population to think of autonomy if not full independence from French authority. French governments could no longer neglect their possessions in the Pacific, he warned, particularly when confronted with "an invasion by Allies who are well supplied with goods and money that they dispense with a smile." These colonists would turn to the United States unless there were changes in French methods of administering and governing these distant possessions. He favored holding a referendum as the "least bad" solution to the problem of restoring faith in the central French authority and overcoming the "disastrous" effects of Montchamp's administration.[5]

When Pierre Bergès's political allies learned of his communication with d'Argenlieu and d'Argenlieu's cordial response, they insisted that Bergès account for his behavior. The meeting between Bergès and his political allies was tense. Bergès defended himself by stating that it was not his fault if the central power happened to be that of d'Argenlieu. This position satisfied none of his colleagues, and they proposed that a telegram be sent to Algiers informing the authorities that the population of New Caledonia did not want d'Argenlieu's return. All agreed to do so with the exception of Bergès. Two of his former allies called Bergès a traitor who had let down the population of New Caledonia. The cable, which was signed by several political notables, asked that Admiral d'Argenlieu not return to New Caledonia in light of the disturbance that his previous actions had provoked.[6] After the stormy meeting with Bergès, Émile Moulédous resigned from the administrative council upon disagreement with the new political line taken by Bergès in his contacts with Algiers.[7]

Pierre Bergès had lost some of his old allies, but he had found new friends. Bergès attended a reception and dinner given by Fourcade at the high commissioner's residence shortly after this confrontation. The reception was attended by an influential group of Caledonian businessmen who had connections with the economically powerful Le Nickel. Some of these notables were suspected of having had Vichy sympathies but were evolving in their loyalties as a result of the agreement in Algiers between Generals de Gaulle and Giraud over the creation of a jointly led French Committee of National Liberation (FCNL). Shortly thereafter Bergès was given a suite of rooms and an office in the high commissioner's residence for his use whenever he was in Nouméa. He also obtained use of an automobile with chauffeur.[8]

Bergès then took his case to the Caledonian public with an open letter. Although denying his request for d'Argenlieu's return, he insisted, in light of the impasse that had developed between the administrative council and Governor Montchamp, that it was necessary to improve relations with the central Fighting-French authority. A smooth administration could be accomplished, and he noted that these conciliatory tactics already had resulted in a lifting of some censorship restrictions. He agreed to meet with Captain Cabanier of the d'Argenlieu mission to improve relations.[9]

Although the quarrel between Bergès and some of his former allies revived memories of the May upheaval, from the American standpoint this was, according to Consul Day, a purely local affair without any serious consequences for American interests.[10] On the other hand Day feared that a return of d'Argenlieu or the appointment of a governor of his choice would not foster a spirit of cooperation with American military authorities.[11] The Americans had had enough of Admiral d'Argenlieu's overt hostility.

Various candidates for governor were rumored to be under consideration. One was Frédéric Fourcade and another was Jan Bourgeau. Neither of these prospects pleased d'Argenlieu. According to Michel Vergès, Fourcade was allegedly the choice candidate of the Americans, since Fourcade was considered less hostile and more easily manipulated by them.[12] Fourcade learned from a staff member of the U.S. Army headquarters that the American military commanders had supposedly received instructions to intervene to obtain his nomination as governor of New Caledonia, and he immediately cabled d'Argenlieu denying any connection with such a maneuver and stating that he was not foolhardy.[13] Fourcade knew very well that an American blessing would be a poisoned endorsement at de Gaulle's headquarters.

As for General Secretary Jan Bourgeau, Admiral d'Argenlieu's negative evaluation again revealed Michel Vergès's influence, who accused Bourgeau of being involved in the bootleg liquor trade with American soldiers and sailors, of having a "scandalous" private life and of being too much involved with local business interests.[14] D'Argenlieu informed Pleven that while Bourgeau might have administrative skills, his lack of judgment resulted from "an excessively long stay in the Pacific where even the soundest minds become unsettled."[15] A fresh governor would bring a single voice to represent French authority in New Caledonia.

Shortly after Montchamp's departure from New Caledonia d'Argenlieu informed Pleven that he was sending out Christian Laigret with the rank of interim governor. He urged Governor Laigret to work with Pierre Bergès toward improving relations with the administrative council, calling for new elections if needed.[16] Clearly Laigret was d'Argenlieu's man in New Caledonia, and Bergès had become an accomplice who would work closely with the new Gaullist representative in the interests of a more effective relationship with the Fighting-French central authority. To whom was Governor Laigret responsible? Although Laigret was soon to be directly responsible to Pleven, the commissioner for colonies, he acted as the high commissioner's representative in New Caledonia. During his stormy tenure Laigret did not hesitate to employ forceful measures in the assertion of French rights and sovereignty in New Caledonia. In so doing he followed the d'Argenlieu policy.

Laigret received his appointment and headed to New Caledonia by way of Washington, where he visited the Pentagon. He assured the Americans that he wished to work for complete harmony between the Fighting French and the Americans. He intended to increase New Caledonia's agricultural contribution to the war effort, and he hoped to arrange for participation of French troops in the Pacific war.[17] After a stopover in Hawaii where he paid a call upon Admiral Nimitz at Pearl Harbor, Laigret arrived in New Caledonia on 28 August. His initial appointment was as head of the high commissioner's office in New Caledonia, replacing Frédéric Fourcade in that post; two weeks later he was confirmed as interim governor.

American military intelligence reported that Laigret's arrival was enthusiastically received, and initial relations with the Americans were extremely cordial. Admiral Halsey and General Rush Lincoln, commanding officer of the

First Island Command, heartily welcomed Governor Laigret. The Americans were pleased by what appeared to be a friendly and cooperative attitude on the part of the interim governor.[18] They also appreciated the appointment of Lieutenant Charles Stehlin, a Frenchman who was also an American citizen, as the governor's liaison officer with the American forces. Laigret reported to Algiers that U.S. commanding officers had made extremely complimentary speeches.[19] Earlier Governor Laigret had joined Admiral Halsey for a dinner in honor of Eleanor Roosevelt on 15 September when she visited the island on a brief, incognito visit.[20] In a gesture of good will Governor Laigret removed M. Ricard from the head of the French information and propaganda department, because of his anti-American propaganda.[21]

Turning to Caledonian political issues, Governor Laigret called a meeting of the full administrative council, which had not met with the governor for over six months. Although he recognized there were those opposed to him and his office, he wanted to work with all factions in New Caledonia. Governor Laigret held out the promise of reforms, including an increase in family allotments and pay for dependents whose husbands were serving with the Pacific contingent in the Mediterranean theater. He also promised adjustments in salaries for government officials to keep pace with inflation in the colony. As for his authority, Laigret assured the council that he was chosen for his task because he possessed the confidence of "those who on 18 June 1940 took over the government of France."[22] While Laigret's relationship with the administrative council and with the Caledonians remained warm throughout his tenure, the era of good feelings between the governor and the Americans proved to be of short duration.

Soon after his arrival Governor Laigret reported that conditions in New Caledonia were deplorable from the standpoint of French prestige and from the neglect of French interests that had occurred under his predecessor. His efforts to reconcile the various political factions on the island had encountered difficulties. A common, united French front was absolutely essential in New Caledonia, Laigret insisted. The major problem stemmed from the presence of Allied troops who were spending money freely and had completely upset the economy of the colony. "No one likes the Americans," he claimed, "but they go along because they owe everything to them."[23] The American presence threatened to corrupt French values and destroy a French identity in this distant colony.

Many Caledonians were engaged in illicit trade in alcohol or prostitution. He lamented that no one wanted to work any more. Workers were leaving their places of employment and farmers were abandoning their fields to accept higher pay from the Americans; there were divisions between the townspeople and the Broussards, who resented the relative ease with which the townspeople were able to gain money from the Allied troops. He claimed that American intelligence officers were furthering dissension and sowing a spirit of resistance and hostility to French authority among the population by pointing to the weakness of the French administration. On the excuse of war needs, the Americans imposed their will everywhere. Resistance was necessary. "Whoever acts as a real leader here will have the Americans against him, but will save the country."[24] Montchamp, he noted, had let things slide, but he would be vigilant. Governor Laigret had found his mission.

Laigret outlined a program to restore order and respect for French authority in New Caledonia. First, he intended to reduce the divisions between partisans of Vichy and General de Gaulle's supporters. Already he noted with satisfaction that both the Catholic Bishop and the Protestant pastor had attended the military review on the anniversary of the rally to Free France. He would, though, take firm action against "the zealous agitation of troublemakers who under the pretext of 'Gaullism' are pursuing autonomist ambitions, such as M. Vergès or communists such as Paladini." These were precisely those individuals whom d'Argenlieu had thanked at the beginning of the year for having supported the high commissioner during his travails.[25] He tried to warn Pleven about the tempestuous lawyer when he observed that "the ultra-Gaullist intransigence of Vergès camouflages anti-French tendencies."[26] Laigret would later mend his fences with Vergès, who became one of his staunchest supporters, but he remained suspicious of the communist group that assembled regularly in Rabot's grocery store for political discussions, although they too would prove useful in his anti-American campaign.[27]

As for the Americans, he intended to pursue an aggressive policy of claims for damages that they had caused, to regain control of the port of Nouméa and its docks, and to obtain the evacuation of certain houses and buildings. "Firmness is the best method," he proclaimed. He asked that French authorities intervene to obtain the recall of certain American officers whose attitude he found disagreeable. He called for a massive reinforcement of the French police, since the presence of 100,000 Americans meant that responsibility for maintaining order fell to the military police and shore patrol from the American services. He would request more troops and a naval squadron to allow France to take an active role in the Pacific war and show the French flag. The inclusion of French elements in the Pacific campaign was essential "to reduce the arrogance of the Americans" who claimed that the French were contributing nothing to the war effort and justified their interference in French affairs on the basis of their own military requirements.[28]

In local politics Laigret stated that there would be neither elections nor a referendum in the near future, although subsequently he would promise elections for the spring of 1944. He claimed that all elements, even Pierre Bergès, now opposed holding elections, particularly in the absence of volunteers in the Pacific Battalion who would be unable to exercise their political rights. He proposed to satisfy local coffee growers by increasing the government's subsidy in the face of a price for coffee set by the Americans that he said was too low, and he promised subsidies for other agricultural products. A sharp increase in taxes on excessive profits would pay for these subventions. Laigret called for a nationalization of

Le Nickel and an increase in production as soon as cargo ships could be sent out to assure exports. Without better transportation for nickel and other goods for export and for the import of food and other essentials, the colony's economy was threatened with asphyxiation. An obstacle to the local economy, he noted, resulted from American control of the docks and shipping authority. After calling the administrative council at the beginning of October to outline his program, which was well received, he set out on a twelve day tour of the interior to sell himself, his program and the French Committee of National Liberation to the Broussards.

Pierre Bergès accompanied Laigret on his tour of the interior, lending the governor the support of his prestige and popularity among the country people. The tour was a success by all accounts. American military intelligence reported that Laigret's enthusiasm, his interest in the needs of the people, who had long felt neglected, his promised financial assistance, and his democratic manner endeared him to the Broussards. "There is no doubt," the intelligence report concluded, "that Governor Laigret has been able to obtain a larger personal following than his predecessors."[29] Championing the welfare of the average Caledonian, Laigret's appeal was a populist one.

Laigret repeated his promises of improvements that would benefit the Broussards, including an extension of roads into remoter regions, better telephone, telegraph and postal services, more country doctors, better medical facilities, new construction of schools and housing for teachers. Claims against the Americans for destruction of property would be vigorously pursued. In order to control the labor problem caused by unauthorized departures of workers for American employment, he would require registration of all employees with employment cards that workers would have to keep with them at all times. Governor Laigret assured the Broussards that taxes to pay for these improvements would fall upon those merchants and small businesses, such as laundries, barber shops, and taxi services, that had profited from the presence of Allied troops in New Caledonia.[30]

Grievances and Complaints against the Americans

Governor Laigret immediately displayed firmness toward the Americans. Upon his return, the Americans observed an increasingly critical and hostile attitude.[31] To build his case against the Americans, the governor began compiling a thick dossier of grievances. In the next few months the file became filled with letters sent to General Lincoln or members of his staff in which Governor Laigret detailed the sufferings of the Caledonian people under "a foreign occupation."[32]

The governor's firmness seemed to pay off when the Americans evacuated the girls' orphanage and returned it to its original users. Laigret gave considerable publicity to this gesture as an example of his ability to defend French interests, and in a letter to a member of General Lincoln's staff he expressed his appreciation for the evacuation.³³ At the same time he challenged American press releases that claimed New Caledonia had materially benefited from its occupation by U.S. armed forces. On the contrary, during his tour of the interior he observed the extent of destruction caused by American troops and their installations, damage that in some instances could never be repaired.³⁴

In both private communications and in public the governor revealed his displeasure with the American allies. On Armistice Day a French military chaplain, Captain Brocard, broadcast a message to the French people stating that "we have suffered at the hands of the Germans, and we have also suffered, for other reasons, at the hands of our allies."³⁵ The American censorship officer at the radio station asked that the last part of this statement be removed since it would cause antagonism toward the American forces, but the French officer in charge refused.

When the Americans protested, Laigret responded by reminding the Americans that this was a war to assure freedom of expression, one of Roosevelt's four freedoms, and in any event, he insisted, this was "purely a French affair."³⁶ Admiral Shafroth replied that the Americans wished to live in a friendly environment. They had no desire to alienate the local population, and he argued that there was a difference between providing information and making statements that were intended to provoke hostility toward the Allies with the approval of the governor's office.³⁷ The Americans suspected that the governor's antagonistic policy in dealing with American military representatives reflected directives that had been sent out from the French Committee of National Liberation in Algiers.³⁸

There were few episodes that escaped the governor's notice. He passed along several complaints of aircraft that buzzed low over fields, villages and roadways. He complained that several episodes had occurred in the past but little had been done to reprimand the pilots or to assure that such practices ceased.³⁹ American military trucks that were piled too high with equipment had caused breaks in the telephone lines at several locations causing a disruption in telephone service.⁴⁰ Other complaints had to do with the often random and thoughtless actions of troops stationed in the interior that caused property damage on Caledonian farms and cattle ranches. American soldiers would occasionally shoot cattle while ostensibly looking for deer that were in such abundance in New Caledonia that they were considered a nuisance. Caledonian farmers complained of trespassing and objected to soldiers using their stock for target practice or to obtain the makings of a barbecue. Workers on cattle ranches operated in an atmosphere of fear and danger, according to one rancher.⁴¹

All events, major and minor, that caused friction between the Americans and the Fighting French were blown out of proportion in terms of French rights, dignity and even sovereignty, which seemed to be called into question by thoughtless and at times rude or inconsiderate American actions. Under Laigret French sensitivity became ever more touchy and shrill. These issues were not in themselves of great significance, but the governor's exploitation of each and every grievance was part of a deliberate campaign to discredit the Americans and present their behavior in the most unfavorable light. In his many letters to American commanders and in his public statements published in the local press, Laigret presented himself as a champion of French rights and as advocate for Caledonians seeking relief from the oppression and suffering that the American occupation of New Caledonia had caused. These letters of complaint required American responses, sometimes at the highest levels of command.

Consul Henry Day regretted that letters from Laigret's office insisting upon rectifying misdeeds constantly harassed American staff officers concerned with public relations. These letters were written, as he put it, "in a spirit and manner which do not appear to be primarily motivated by a desire for elimination of causes of friction or to be constructive in character." He added that to the extent that real or imagined grievances had been publicized, relations with the local population had suffered.[42] The governor's less than constructive approach toward French-American relations could be seen in his insistence that American policy toward France was deliberately hostile and provocative. In one letter to the American command, he protested that newspapers published for American servicemen in New Caledonia had shown photographs of anti-Gaullist demonstrations in Lebanon and Egypt. Overlooking his earlier claim that this was a war for freedom of expression, Governor Laigret demanded that this "anti-French" propaganda be censored. He suspected that the Americans had publicized these events with a thought to encouraging the same kinds of demonstrations in New Caledonia.[43]

Laigret emerged as champion of Caledonian interests in supporting Caledonian claims against the Americans for damages caused by troop activity. At the beginning of 1943 an agreement between the Americans and Governor Montchamp established a procedure that enabled New Caledonian residents to present claims with American military authorities for accidents or property damage. Under this arrangement damages of $1000 or less could be settled relatively quickly in a military hearing that acted as a claims court. Laigret found this arrangement to be unsatisfactory since it operated purely under an American administration in accordance with American law.

The trouble resulted from discussions between General Patch and Admiral d'Argenlieu in June 1942 when Patch indicated that Congressional legislation stipulated that only American military courts could judge American military personnel. In property disputes or cases of crimes between military personnel and French citizens or subjects, American military authorities alone reserved right of judgment, and plaintiffs had no rights of appeal. The result, Laigret lamented, was that in all disputes between Caledonians and American military the colonists felt that Fighting-French authorities failed to protect their material interests and that they were powerless before American decisions. Laigret preferred the arrangement that had been made with the New Zealand military authorities in which complaints and cases were heard by mixed panels that included members of the French judiciary.[44] In taking this position Laigret's primary concern was one of principle as much as a complaint over the judgments rendered. The absence of any French role or participation in the judicial process upset him since French sovereignty was at stake. Such practices reinforced Laigret's contention that the Americans behaved as if they occupied the territory.

When informed of Governor Laigret's unhappiness with the American military judicial process, the Americans looked into the matter and concluded that the system had functioned effectively and that most cases had been found in favor of the plaintiffs.[45] René Pleven tried to calm Laigret's annoyance. He recognized the issue of sovereignty involved in these cases but argued that a rapid and equitable settlement of Caledonian claims was the main concern.[46] A neutral observer, B.C. Ballard, noted that the claims commissions in fact acted speedily in response to claims made and the system seemed satisfactory. Sentences given were publicized in the local press, and American military authorities held weekly meetings with French administrators and members of the public in which local grievances and irritations could be discussed. Action was taken in response "with satisfactory results" in most cases.[47]

Whatever the fairness of the findings, Governor Laigret claimed that dependence upon a purely American system was evidence of further disrespect for French rights and weakened Fighting-French prestige in the eyes of the Caledonian population. Unlike Ballard, Laigret insisted that the procedures were slow and unsatisfactory.[48] For Laigret the delays showed the flaws of the system and caused great dissatisfaction among the civilian population. His pursuit of these claims again presented the governor as an active and aggressive defender of the Caledonians in the midst of their sufferings at the hands of the American military occupation. Laigret pursued a policy of "constant vigilance," which the Americans considered to be little more than a policy of constant harassment.

A major complaint that stirred considerable controversy and led to intense exchanges and a painful search for a solution had to do with cases of assault and rape. Laigret deplored the dangers faced by women of Nouméa when confronted with American soldiers and sailors on shore leave, particularly the aggressive and offensive attitude and behavior of African-American servicemen. In a letter to General Lincoln, Governor Laigret claimed that women lived in fear as African-Americans appeared on the streets of Nouméa and the highways of the interior looking "for adventures."[49] He cited one rape, two assaults with intent to rape, and two other assault cases (aggressions) that involved African-American servicemen during the first two months of his office to support his argument.[50] His charge that African-American soldiers and sailors were frequently and noticeably involved in disorderly conduct, including fights with French soldiers, was supported by the newspaper, *Bulletin du Commerce*, which published a series of articles and letters on the problem.

At one point, following a fight between French gendarmes and French Melanesian troops, a purely Franco-French conflict, Laigret imposed a curfew on his own Kanak troops, and he requested that General Lincoln place the city of Nouméa off limits for all African-American servicemen after nine in the evening. Although American services were segregated according to race at this time, General Lincoln refused this request on the basis that any ban would have to apply equally to white and African-American military personnel.[51] Laigret's charges against African-American servicemen compelled the base command to investigate the incidence of rape and assaults that had come before the military courts.[52] These inquiries then led U.S. Army officers to propose a solution that revealed underlying differences between French and Americans on issues of race, sexual relations, particularly miscegenation, and what the French had long deplored as hypocritical American puritanical values.

Between 4 February 1943 and 19 November 1943 there were eighteen cases of rape, of attempted rape or assault with intention to commit rape, or of attempted assault in which a total of twenty-five individuals were involved. Of these twenty-five, eighteen were African-American and seven were white. Given the higher proportion of white to black soldiers and sailors in the service generally (approximately ten to one), African-Americans in New Caledonia were far more likely to be arrested for rape, attempted rape, or assault than were whites, and African-American serviceman were more likely to be given harsher sentences.

Accusations of rape and assault, particularly against African-American servicemen, caused the Americans to search for a remedy to the problem by requesting the establishment of a separate "maison de tolérance" for soldiers and sailors of color. African-American servicemen were excluded from the facilities and services provided in Nouméa's established house of prostitution, known as the "Pink House," by reason of American segregationist practices and prejudice against miscegenation. While the ensuing negotiations revealed differences in American and French attitudes toward issues of race and sexual comportment, they also offered French officials, including Governor Laigret, an opportunity to criticize American behavior and values with a certain amount of sarcasm.

The Pink House was a residence that the French Army had purchased in May 1940. The French Army then leased the premises to Mme Benitier, who operated it as a house of prostitution. It was a legally established activity, and Mme Benitier's employees received regular, weekly visits from the French medical service. With the arrival of American armed forces, business at the Pink House became brisk; by December 1942 the house was receiving approximately two hundred customers daily at a price of four dollars per visitor. Half of this revenue went to the pensioners of the Pink House, and the other half went to Mme Benitier.[53] Although white American soldiers and sailors used the Pink House, it was off limits to officers and African-Americans who began arriving in New Caledonia with the buildup of American forces in 1942 and 1943.

When Laigret's complaints reached American headquarters in November 1943, American commanders decided to find a solution by providing a separate facility exclusively for their use. This "maison de tolérance" would reduce the number of reprehensible acts committed by African-American troops by providing "a release for a life force that otherwise had no outlet." They proposed that the inhabitants of the residence opposite the Pink House be expelled since they were involved in illegal liquor trade and had been cited for disorderly conduct in the past. This house would then be placed under the management of Mme Benitier, who would be authorized to recruit Kanak women to work in this racially segregated establishment.[54]

The French were astonished at this proposal. Colonel Freby declared that he could not expel a French family, however rowdy they might be, to make room for a "maison de tolérance." The head of the French medical service, Colonel Sellier, and Lieutenant Mas, head of the service for native affairs, strongly opposed the recruitment of female Kanak to become prostitutes for African-American enlisted men. Such action, they argued, would bring unanimous protests from all of the missionaries in the colony, would provoke hostility and perhaps touch off an uprising among the Kanak population, and it would offend Kanak soldiers serving as volunteers in the Pacific Battalion. The French officers suggested that the Americans set up tents on the outskirts of Nouméa for this purpose and that they should "bring Negresses from the United States" for the benefit of African-American servicemen. They understood the need for such establishments for White or African-American troops, "… but if the prudish mentality of our American allies prevents them from dealing with such matters, this is not a reason for the French to take on the assignment."[55] Laigret fully agreed, and he authorized the Americans to establish their own facility outside the city limits of Nouméa, employing their own resources.[56] The French were opposed to helping the Americans solve a problem that was a result of American racial and sexual prejudices that the French simply did not share.

When informed of the French suggestion that the Americans create their own "maison de tolérance" in a tent city, Colonel Stead declared that this was impossible since it would mean using government equipment for such activities and would cause a furor if it became known back home. This reply caused Colonel Freby to reflect that "the puritanism of the Anglo-Saxons understands very well the advantages of a house of prostitution for their armies, but it can not tolerate that one of them should lift a finger in order to put such an institution into operation." The Pink House continued to operate, much to the dismay of one Anglo-Saxon observer who reported that "the uniform of our country's service is being discredited every day in this foreign land by the spectacle of American troops standing in a long line in front of the 'Pink House.'"[57] As a way of controlling aggressions on the streets of Nouméa, the American command agreed to increase the activity of the military police and shore patrols, which included both African-Americans and whites.[58]

One of Governor Laigret's strongest complaints about the American military presence in New Caledonia had to do with the way in which the influx of dollars and requests for services disrupted New Caledonia's economy. He held the Americans responsible for the island's shortages of labor, of goods, and for the inflationary rise in prices. The impact of this influx of soldiers and sailors was almost immediate since the Americans lost no time in establishing recreation and refreshment centers for servicemen. Within ten days of arrival in March 1942, the army established a Post Exchange in a warehouse in Nouméa. A week later the Red Cross set up a small canteen and recreation center on the site of a store that previously had been leased by a Japanese merchant. Both the PX (Post Exchange) and the Red Cross service club quickly became popular, and by May an estimated eight thousand men were using the Red Cross facility daily. Weekly dances were held that were also popular, attended by servicemen, nurses and French women as well.[59] A year later three more post exchanges had opened in Nouméa, equipped with self-contained refrigeration units that were capable of supplying thirty-thousand cokes each day to thirsty GIs. The trade was profitable enough so that the equipment had been paid for within two months of operation. Another example of the scale of consumption may be seen in results from the Trade Winds bar and restaurant, which by 1944 was selling 18,000 beers and 5,100 hamburgers daily.[60]

As American and New Zealand troops moved into the countryside, other demands for services provided possibilities for Caledonians to engage in lucrative activities, such as providing laundry services. American intelligence reported the story of the Orcan family from Pouambout to illustrate the phenomenon. The large Orcan family included fourteen children, and they eked out a frugal, impoverished existence on a farm in the interior. They could not afford, for example, to travel to Nouméa, and their home was a small structure with no amenities. To provide some income, the father worked for a mining company, but life was harsh. Then came the Americans. An American aviator discovered that there was a field suitable for landing near the Orcan farm, and he began to fly in his laundry and that of some of his friends in a light plane twice a week. Soon there was so much laundry that the Americans stationed at Plaine des Gaiacs airbase had to resort to truck transportation to deliver it. Madame Orcan put her family to work and soon had cornered the market for the 75th Bomb Squadron.

Income from the laundry produced the equivalent of $16,000/year, a substantial income in those days, and Mr. Orcan gave up his modest salary as a miner to devote himself to the laundry business. Since the 75th Bomb Squadron represented only one-eighth of the personnel stationed at Plaine des Gaiacs, even the large Orcan family could not meet the demand for laundry services, and other local laundries appeared. By the fall of 1943 American intelligence estimated these laundries were collectively earning $2,500 per week. The result of the creation of "this highly lucrative industry, which is available to families without capital or specialized training of any kind, has established a purchasing power ... which can in no way be satisfied by the supply of consumer goods."[61]

Figure 6.1. French Caledoniennes serving thirsty GIs on Bastille Day, 1942.
Source. U.S. National Archives (111-SC-163390).

Consequently in the remote regions and in Nouméa goods such as sheets, pillowcases, shoes and clothing had become unavailable.

The influx of American service personnel and the circulation of dollars benefited some Caledonians but created hardship for those on fixed incomes who lacked means to supplement their earnings. One intelligence report an estimated 300 percent inflation since the arrival of the Americans.[62] Those with access to new sources of income or who could obtain scarce items for sale did extremely well. The illicit liquor trade and bootlegging from various sources gave advantages to those individuals who were well placed to exploit new opportunities. Vegetable farming to supply the American and New Zealand troops, particularly those stationed in the remoter regions of the interior, also brought good returns. Some farmers abandoned coffee growing for truck farming, an activity that formerly had been dominated by the Japanese. American assistance in the form of seeds and equipment encouraged this transition so effectively that in the space of two months production of vegetables had grown from nothing to thirty tons per week.[63]

As a result of these activities an impressive increase in savings occurred. Deposits in the Bank of Indochina had tripled in value from Fr43,000,000 on 1 July 1940 to Fr131,000,000 as of July 1943, and the total savings, with postal savings included, were estimated at Fr200 million. As one newspaper put it,

"Never has New Caledonia been so rich." Although Laigret deplored the effects of American spending and claimed that it did not produce any lasting benefit for New Caledonia, the dollar induced prosperity continued on the island with postal savings rising by Fr8 million in the month of April 1944. With this unexpected rise in savings, the government allowed the maximum deposit to be increased from Fr25,000 to 60,000. As the Australian consul noted, it was difficult to sympathize fully with the complaints of the New Caledonians who were taking their share of this prosperity.[64] The increase in money available, combined with shortages of goods, meant both inflation and a growing black-market economy for scarce goods and commodities.[65]

From the outset the Americans realized that their presence would have an effect upon the local economy. A system of controls was established to ameliorate the impact. Many consumer goods in New Caledonia, such as sugar, rice, meat, wines, various dry goods, clothes, shoes, oil, gasoline and kerosene were rationed, and stores were forbidden to sell such necessities to soldiers and sailors, reserving limited supplies to the civilian population. Nevertheless, the expansion of soft drink and sandwich shops sharply increased demand for sugar and flour, which in turn led to shortages of such necessities. Farmers were also forbidden to sell fruits and vegetables to servicemen, but this restriction was honored mainly in the breach. GIs had the advantage of access to transportation and non-rationed gasoline, which allowed them to use jeeps and trucks to search far and wide for supplies of fresh produce, eggs and poultry. Shortages plagued the civilian markets of the island. There were shortages of fish, which had been supplied by Japanese before the Americans arrived. The deportation of Japanese and a ban on night fishing for security reasons caused a curtailment of the catch, and the ability of the Americans to outbid the locals for limited amounts of fish meant that they were able to corner the market.[66]

An additional problem that applied in almost every area of economic activity had to do with demands for labor caused by the American presence. Upon arrival in New Caledonia American military officers sought workers to help unload the transports and troopships that arrived in Nouméa harbor. A labor force was also required to help with the construction of airfields and other military facilities in Nouméa and the interior.[67] Most of those hired were either French settlers or native Kanak; Asians who had obtained free resident status were not extensively employed. Free-French authorities had formally agreed that the Americans could employ 1,154 Melanesians as laborers and guides. Food, housing, clothing, and medical care were furnished by the armed forces.[68] These workers were to be rotated back to the reservations after four months' employment and replaced by new workers in order to distribute the benefits.

This employment provided unaccustomed revenue to the Melanesians. They also received American clothing, either as issue or from American soldiers, who in their generosity offered gifts of clothing, liquor and rides to the Melanesians they encountered. Kanak in American military employment were housed at

The American Economic and Cultural Challenge

Figure 6.2. Kanak working for the Yankee dollar at Camp Joe Louis.
Source. U.S. National Archives (111-SC-172728).

"Camp Joe Louis" in minimal conditions that were nevertheless an improvement over conditions on the reservations. Finally, it was not uncommon for American truck drivers to offer rides to Melanesians walking along the roads in the interior. A casual familiarity with the Melanesians upset many Caledonians who complained of the increasingly "arrogant" manner of Kanak who, they felt, were becoming spoiled by the Americans.

The labor question brought further confrontation with Governor Laigret, who informed the Americans that they illegally employed Kanak workers beyond the numbers agreed upon, often keeping them in service long after the completion of the tasks for which they had been recruited. This practice deprived the colony of necessary labor services. While he acknowledged the requirements of the war effort, he insisted that the Americans show a greater awareness of New Caledonia's needs.[69] The Americans acknowledged that in some instances they had assigned native workers to tasks other than those for which they had been recruited. American military officials insisted that they had not hired more than the authorized numbers permitted by agreement. Despite American denials, Governor Laigret remained convinced that Americans recruited and hired natives illegally, and he believed that a willingness to pay them well and reward them with gifts ruined their morale.[70]

The governor also blamed Americans for difficulties that the French administration faced in controlling the indentured Asian workers. There were only thirty-eight Asians officially employed by American military personnel in 1943. Yet the attraction of the dollar had an impact, even if there was little direct hiring. There was a large discrepancy between wages paid to the indentured laborers, who earned $6.00/month, and Kanak hired by the Americans at 46 cents/day.[71] The indentured workers began to express their dissatisfaction by refusing to work or by escaping from the mines or from Le Nickel's housing for workers in Nouméa to engage in the underground economy.

The Americans became aware of the discrepancy between the earnings of the Melanesians and the indentured Asians. Not wishing to create difficulties for the management at Le Nickel, they began to pay a portion of Kanak wages in goods, such as clothing, cheap jewelry, or rice and tea. This payment in goods, it was hoped, would avoid putting "too big a gap between their wages and the wages, fixed by contract, of the indentured labor, making it very nearly impossible for the indentured labor to purchase anything."[72] This tactic failed to satisfy growing discontent among the indentured workers, who quickly realized that they could supplement their meager pay by doing laundry or making grass mats and curios for the Americans. Absenteeism began to be a major problem. At one point Le Nickel had to shut down one smelter when 120 indentured servants escaped.[73] Albert Rapadzi, manager of Le Nickel, noted difficulties with Asian laborers. "There is but one object with all of these, be they Tonkinese or Javanese: to leave the mine in order to come to Nouméa, where the distractions are more numerous and above all where the secret trade is easier."[74]

By encouraging an underground economy, the American military presence contributed to the disruption of the traditional labor structure and relations in New Caledonia. The Australian consul, B.C. Ballard, felt that Asians and Kanak had been ruined by the generous sums that the Americans offered for laundry services and souvenirs.[75] Casual contacts with the Kanak population, provision of rides and gifts, relatively generous pay, and a willingness to purchase ice cream or other goods from the Asians alarmed French officials, who saw in these actions a corruption of traditional colonial practices. The governor faulted the Americans for their casual disregard for the status of the Asian workers, and he passed along complaints from Caledonians that American GIs had given rides to Javanese laborers at various locations, including some escapees from the mine at Voh.[76] What offended Governor Laigret as much as the behavior of the Americans in New Caledonia was their manner, or what he continually referred to as their arrogance in their disregard for French laws on French territory.

Laigret's Anti-Americanist Campaign and Increasing *Mésentente*

Laigret's calculated anti-Americanism took expression in the dismissal or transfer of those French officers whom he considered too friendly or too cooperative with the Americans. In this policy he carried on a technique employed by Admiral d'Argenlieu and members of his mission in which French officers deliberately showed coolness and hostility toward their American counterparts. The Australian Air Force observer informed his superiors that American intelligence learned that Governor Laigret was given explicit instructions from de Gaulle not to mix freely with Americans and to always be difficult with them. He reported that Laigret's attitude toward the Americans confirmed this assessment since the governor's remarks at times were extremely anti-American.[77] Early in Laigret's term René Pleven approved his request to have Major Artigues relieved of his duties for having been too friendly with the Americans, and he applauded Laigret's policy of surrounding himself with only those "who wish to assure the maintenance of French sovereignty in New Caledonia."[78]

American intelligence was aware of this anti-American campaign, noting several reassignments that resulted from what was considered to be an unduly friendly or cooperative attitude toward the Americans. One of those was Colonel Freby, who was considered by Americans to be helpful and cooperative although he also had been critical at times of American actions. Colonel Freby was ordered to Algeria by the French Committee of National Liberation. He informed American intelligence that he suspected the governor had requested his recall because Laigret believed he acted "too independently for the good of French sovereignty and collaborated too closely with the Americans."

Another recall was that of Major Houssin, who also showed an understanding of American problems and maintained good relations with his American counterparts despite occasional disagreements. Lieutenant Charles Stehlin decided at the end of December 1943 that he "could no longer silently bear Governor Laigret's verbal abuse of the Americans, his unreasonable requests on the Americans, and his refusal to cooperate with the Americans." Stehlin resigned from the governor's military cabinet and was placed under military surveillance awaiting transportation back to Algiers. Lieutenant de Montaudoin, a long time resident of New York City, who had worked well with the Americans as head of the censorship board, also resigned from Governor Laigret's military cabinet and was reassigned as head of the French Army's artillery park in New Caledonia. The Americans compiled a list of eight officers who were being reassigned apparently as punishment for having worked cooperatively with them.[79]

Perhaps the most striking case of Laigret's retribution toward French officers who were too friendly with the Americans was the case of Captain Charles Boucher, judge advocate in the French Army and also attorney general and public prosecutor at the high appeals court in Nouméa. Boucher came to New Caledonia with orders from the commissioner of justice, François de Menthon, to adjust French law to local conditions. He was also charged with responsibility for prosecuting certain anti-Allied elements among the local population, and he obtained several convictions for black-market trading. Boucher acquired many friends among American and French military circles. He gave a large party in December for lawyers with the U.S. Armed Forces that was a great social success.

Boucher ran into conflict with Governor Laigret, however, not as a result of his social activities but as a consequence of an effort to mediate differences between the Americans and Governor Laigret. Colonel Sherman of the American intelligence staff asked Captain Boucher to arrange a meeting with Governor Laigret in which they would have a frank discussion to straighten out French-American differences. Boucher approached the governor's aide-de-camp, who thought the governor would agree to such a meeting, but the answer was a flat refusal.

Laigret informed de Gaulle that Boucher was trying to arrange this meeting and was playing "the American game." This led to a stormy meeting between Boucher and Laigret in which Laigret called Boucher a traitor to his country and accused him of giving confidential information to American G-2.[80] Shortly after this encounter Captain Boucher was relieved of his duties as attorney general and all other functions for reasons of "ill health." Although the official explanation was that Captain Boucher had become ill as a result of food poisoning, Governor Laigret had him confined to the hospital to undergo mental tests. Boucher informed his American friends that he was being sent back to Algiers to explain his actions to the FCNL and had been eliminated from his post for talking too much to them. He claimed that the real reason that Governor Laigret wished to remove him was that he knew too much of the governor's activities.[81]

Governor Laigret's anti-American campaign immediately increased tension between American military personnel and French troops and civilians. At the beginning of 1944 a series of ugly fights developed, and there is evidence that these conflicts were deliberately sought and provoked by Governor Laigret's head of the French military police, Sergeant Pierre Duval. Duval was a former member of the French Foreign Legion who supposedly had served in the Austro-Hungarian Army during the First World War before joining the legion where he served for twenty-four years. He was a tough customer who liked brawls and fights, according to Major Houssin.[82] Duval was personally loyal to Governor Laigret under whom he had served when Laigret was head of the police force in the Cameroon. Laigret, who was upset to discover that the American military police and shore patrol dominated the security forces active on the island, brought Duval to New Caledonia to form a detachment of French military police that would be directly responsible to him.[83] The purpose of this police force was to track down bootleg and moonshine liquor dealers. Initially Laigret and Duval had difficulties finding recruits for this force since many local prospects had family ties with those involved in the liquor trade. Eventually a corps of thirty special military police was formed under Sergeant Duval's leadership.

At the beginning of January a series of confrontations and fights developed in French-owned sandwich and soft-drink shops between French and American military personnel. According to the American report on these episodes, U.S. military police quickly intervened to disperse the crowds, but the French military police at the scene were reported to have been indifferent to the affair. The

Americans received a report from Major Houssin, who said he knew that one incident had been organized by Duval himself and that antagonistic actions of French military personnel toward the Americans were designed to discredit the reputation of U.S. armed forces stationed on the island.[84] A French intelligence officer, Captain Dequen, confirmed this assessment when he reported that on explicit orders from Governor Laigret, Sergeant Duval had deliberately caused the recent disturbances in an attempt to incite French public opinion against the Americans.[85]

These encounters led to a discrediting of the reputation of American forces on the island, at least in the eyes of certain prominent Caledonians, who complained of the way in which American servicemen conducted themselves on the streets of Nouméa and in French establishments. In one instance their grievance had substance. A serious fight and confrontation occurred at the Hôtel de France on the evening of 5 January 1944. The events of that evening brought a vigorous protest and complaint from Jean Audrain, a local notable who was a member of the administrative council, judge of the commercial court, and a veteran of the First World War.

The episode began when two American naval officers, who were intoxicated, tried to break into a bar that was closed. Two French officers told them to go away. The sailors then began to denounce the French officers, calling them names. In his report to Governor Laigret, Audrain observed that such improper and offensive insults could be heard daily from the mouths of American servicemen, including officers as well as enlisted personnel. He stated that such remarks were particularly painful for the people of New Caledonia, who by their bravery, guts, determination and patriotism had risen up during a tragic period before the Americans were engaged in the war to deny this strategic island to the Japanese.[86]

The Americans, while realizing that everyday relations had become strained and that there were bound to be incidents of this sort, somehow failed to comprehend how their actions offended the French population or how their lack of restraint and discipline produced a negative image. The tendency was to explain their behavior as responses to the provocative policies of Sergeant Duval. As one American report put it, the demonstration in front of the Hotel de France was the first incident of major conflict in New Caledonia, and it was significant that it occurred shortly after the special French military police corps made its appearance under Duval's command.[87] Whether provoked, or a result of rude and aggressive behavior on the part of certain American service personnel, or simply the inevitable consequence of a lengthy stay and crowded conditions in New Caledonia, relations had become strained between American and French military personnel on this tight little island. Still the behavior of American military personnel in New Caledonia as elsewhere reflected a pattern of excessive drinking, belligerence and rowdy behavior that often shocked host countries. There was first of all the question of discipline, self-restraint and a sense of order and authority, not only within the military organizations of each society but generally.

The Americans tended to be casual and even defiantly independent of authority and hierarchy. A casual disregard for formality could be found in the tendency of local commanders to brush the French aside in the name of getting the job done. In the process these individuals displayed little regard for matters of courtesy or sensitivity toward French interests, practices and customs. American soldiers in New Caledonia tended to "make themselves at home" without considering that they were guests in a foreign country.

The French had a greater respect for order, restraint and a certain formal courtesy in their relations with each other and in relations with outsiders. The manner was not casual and familiar, as it was with the Americans. The lack of restraint in American patterns of behavior and attitudes sometimes stunned even sympathetic Caledonians.

The *mésentente* between Americans and French rested at least in part upon the American feeling that their presence was a favor and a benefit for the security of the Caledonians and that they had saved them from a Japanese invasion. They believed that they had come to New Caledonia to defeat a common enemy but felt that they were little appreciated for this sacrifice. The Caledonians and the Free French believed that they had opened their doors and provided a benefit to the Americans, even making the Solomons campaign possible, but had been rewarded for their effort by allies who failed to take them seriously or even show respect. Both sides thus felt under-appreciated by the other and therefore experienced a sense of grievance that had erupted in a minor but perhaps symbolic outburst of violence and frustration in the streets of Nouméa at the beginning of 1944.

Anxious to avoid further incidents, both sides tried to defuse the situation. Conditions also improved after it was announced that Sargent Duval would be leaving New Caledonia along with Governor Laigret, who had been recalled by Algiers for another assignment. This decision to recall Governor Laigret caught the Caledonians and the Americans by surprise and provoked Laigret to attack the American presence and impact in New Caledonia with increased hostility. According to American intelligence few Caledonians attributed his recall to his conflicts with American military authorities, but the recall became the occasion for Laigret's "last fling" at the Americans.[88] It is possible however that the recall did reflect a concern in Algiers that Laigret's anti-Americanism had gone too far.

The French Committee of National Libertion had begun to question Laigret's judgment before he made public his hostility toward the Americans in New Caledonia. The first doubt came from René Pleven when he questioned Laigret's diplomatic skill and sensitivity.[89] A month later General de Gaulle's minister of justice, François de Menthon, sent a telegram to Pleven in which he reported "further serious flaws already apparent in his [Laigret's] previous correspondence."[90] Pleven informed d'Argenlieu that a recent telegram from Laigret, while indicating a great deal of activity and the best of intentions, "worries General de Gaulle and me by a certain lack of level-headedness in his judgement."[91] For this reason Pleven decided that Laigret's appointment should not be extended.[92] On the eve of Laigret's speech to the administrative council his successor had been found: M. Jacques Tallec, who would remain in New Caledonia for "several years."[93]

Knowing that his term was ending but before his recall had been publicly announced, Laigret launched an attack upon the Americans on two occasions. The first came during a lengthy speech to the administrative council on 20 November, presenting the prospect of reform and prosperity under a French administration and implying that a new era for the colony was at hand. Governor Laigret obviously intended to assure the European settlers that their interests would be advanced through their continued loyalty to the FCNL. He laid out an ambitious and impressive program of reforms for improvement that echoed the reforms first outlined in his October address to the council and preached during his tour of the interior. The issue of labor control was important in light of complaints about ways in which the Asian and Melanesian populations had gained a small measure of independence as a result of the American presence.

In contrast with the reforms and improvements that Caledonians could expect from France, Laigret stressed the damage and harm to New Caledonia that the Americans had caused. Various charges were leveled, including:

> … dislocation of the colony's economy as a result of the American troop presence, shortages and diversion of labor, damage to farming and grazing lands, illicit sale of liquor, profiteering by the dollar-mad, lack of building and foodstuffs, increases in penal cases in the courts, derogation of sovereignty in the administration of justice, requisitioning of buildings and houses and shortage of housing, currency inflation.[94]

Consul Day regretted that Governor Laigret had mentioned the negative side of the American presence but failed to mention the reasons why it was necessary for these troops to be in New Caledonia. Day deplored the fact that the sacrifices, including the Americans killed and wounded in Guadalcanal and the Solomons campaign, went unrecognized. There was no mention of the American war effort in the Pacific, nor did Governor Laigret make any mention of what the Americans had done to mitigate some of the impact of their large military presence in the colony. Many of these contributions had benefited the colony, Day noted.

Laigret's speech won the approval of a wide range of opinion. Former Vichy supporters seemed to be coming around, if only for opportunistic reasons. An American intelligence report noted that Henri Millaud, head of the Ballande firm and long suspected of Vichy sympathies, had for the first time entertained Gaullist naval officers.[95] Consul Day reported that Governor Laigret had successfully won back the support of those who had rallied to de Gaulle but had wavered during the time of d'Argenlieu and Montchamp.[96] The governor believed that a newly found unity among the Caledonians had resulted from his anti-American effort, which caused a backlash against the Americans among the Caledonian population.

The president of the administrative council, Pierre Bergès, warmly applauded the speech. Colonel Freby sent Laigret a letter in which he congratulated him for the brilliant explanation to the administrative council, calling it a personal triumph. From another direction, Mme Tunica y Casas, an unorthodox communist, wrote to a colleague stating that she was greatly impressed with Governor Laigret and his program for the improvement of educational and medical services in the interior. She liked his willingness to work for the welfare of the proletariat and praised his determination to force the large commercial concerns to pay increased taxes and relieve the ordinary people of their burdens. She fully approved of Laigret's policy toward the Americans, for she found that "our dear Allies are a little bit too much at ease here and too often forget that they are on French territory." She claimed to be neither anti-American nor anti-this nor that, but simply "anti-nazi, anti-fascist, anti-reactionary and anti-idiotic." Since present American policy in her eyes was "reactionary and idiotic," she could only draw the logical conclusion. She noted with satisfaction that American news and opinion publications on the left and even *Life* magazine, blamed Roosevelt's hatred for de Gaulle for undermining Franco-American friendship. She took comfort that among the Americans in New Caledonia there were some, "but not too many of them," who knew how to see things accurately and be farsighted in their understanding.

Governor Laigret received an enthusiastic "Bravo!" from Michel Vergès for "a magnificent speech that was fully national and very French" in its message. Vergès asked that a copy of the speech be sent to Admiral d'Argenlieu to convince the government in Algiers that Laigret should remain in New Caledonia as governor. Another communist, Louis Forest, praised Laigret's efforts to defend French culture on a small, distant island colony, stating that French culture had been "crucified" by the Americans and a strong governor had brought the martyr down from the cross.[97] Using anti-Americanism as a way of unifying different factions on the island appeared to have been successful for Governor Laigret.

Boosted by these encouraging messages, Laigret defended himself and made a last minute, desperate appeal to Pleven to be allowed to remain in New Caledonia and continue his good work of defending French interests. Laigret observed that he had gone to New Caledonia with the understanding from Admiral d'Argenlieu that his assignment was to be of long duration to assure the Caledonians that the colony was to remain French. He stated that French sovereignty could be preserved only if representatives of central authority were given the support and assurance that they had the long-term interests of the colony at heart and were capable of carrying out a lasting program of assistance. He believed Montchamp's failure resulted from the fact that he seemed no more than another short-term governor. "If you want New Caledonia to remain French," he declared, "you must not, I repeat you must not, recall me at least for the moment, for that would be a repudiation in the eyes of the local population and of the Americans."[98] This message apparently reached the highest levels in Algiers. A note at the bottom of Laigret's long dispatch to Pleven carried an instruction that it was to be given to Major Courcel for transmission to General de Gaulle.

Laigret clearly had been shocked by the conditions he found during his earlier tour of the interior and saddened by the harsh existence that was the fate of most Broussards. In a lengthy report he stated that France had not done in New Caledonia one-tenth of what it had done for certain African colonies. He believed that something had to be done quickly. He observed that the inhabitants of the colony had become aware, because of the presence of American troops, "of the facilities that modern equipment offers as much from the point of view of clearing forests, as in the building of roads, water conveyances, etc." His program was designed to provide an alternative to an American agrarian dream of mechanical efficiency. The negative side was to disparage the American-induced prosperity as having little real benefit for the ordinary Caledonian, concluding that American influence upcountry was harmful.[99]

At the same time Governor Laigret appealed to Caledonian patriotism to demonstrate the commitment of the colony to the cause of France. He persuaded the administrative council, normally resistant to making any financial contribution to London, to set aside Fr5 million from its own budget surplus for the benefit of the FCNL, which brought a telegram of appreciation from General de Gaulle. In addition to the offered financial support this gesture had, Pleven noted, "a considerable political importance with regards to foreigners, particularly after the speech of Senator Russell," in which the American senator proposed that New Caledonia might be acquired by the United States as compensation for American financial aid and unpaid loans that had been granted to France during two world wars.[100] An apparent menace to French sovereignty in New Caledonia had arisen in Washington.

American Ambitions for New Caledonia?

American ambitions for New Caledonia, or what one historian has called an "hour of temptation," emerged during Laigret's tenure. From July-September 1943 Senator Richard Russell of Georgia led a delegation of five senators on a round the world tour to see how the American taxpayer's money was being employed and to determine what kind of return might be expected on this investment after the war. When he returned, Senator Russell proposed that New Caledonia be transferred to the United States in return for canceling French debts still outstanding from the First World War and in payment for Lend-lease assistance that had been granted in the current conflict.[101] This proposal touched off alarm bells for the Free French in Algiers and Nouméa and confirmed Governor Laigret's suspicion of the Americans.

Pleven tried to calm Laigret, who was incensed over Russell's speech, by stating that Senator Russell had spoken only of U.S. control, not sovereignty, over certain bases after the war, including Nouméa. He assured the governor that the National

Committee was keeping a close watch on developments in Washington and was aware of the difficulties that Laigret faced. He urged the governor to keep him informed of relations with American military authorities and to "develop by every means in your power, French national sentiment" in New Caledonia.[102] Laigret's response was to hold a press conference in which he stressed Caledonian loyalty and again gave vent to his grievances against the Americans, their behavior and their attitudes.

Laigret's press conference was his farewell address, since the public announcement of his replacement by Jacques Tallec had been made on 11 December, and it was a final public blast at the Americans. Laigret opened his press conference on 16 December by reminding the Americans of how New Caledonia became French. He observed that the French flag had flown over the island for ninety years and that the Kanak population had been "entirely civilized according to French colonial methods." In addition, a substantial Indochinese population also had been civilized, and a Javanese population, which he described as "refugees from the Netherlands Indies," had been brought in as laborers. Presumably all were living contentedly as a result of a benevolent French administration. He noted that the French elements of the island had settled, populated and developed New Caledonia for generations. He reminded Americans of Caledonian sacrifices in both world wars, and he extolled their contributions to the victory over Germany in 1918, particularly their acts of courage at Verdun and the Somme.

What stung the Americans most was Laigret's insistence that the Caledonian population was suffering under a hostile American occupation. According to Laigret the Caledonians felt injured in their pride by the arrogant, insensitive manner of American soldiers. "The inhabitants of New Caledonia suffer considerably in their interest and too often in their legitimate feeling from the attitude that is often shown without respect by the American troops toward them." Returning to the theme of a conqueror's mentality that had been aired in the Armistice Day broadcast on 11 November, Laigret reminded the correspondents and the Americans that "there is a big difference between the occupancy of a friendly country and the occupation of an enemy country." He hoped that Jacques Tallec would find more sympathetic understanding on the part of the American military commanders.[103]

Not surprisingly Governor Laigret's press conference provoked strong reaction from several quarters. In Nouméa the local anti-American newspaper, the *Bulletin du Commerce,* published a prepared statement issued at the conference which summarized his responses to questions from the press. The editor of the paper, M. Legras, had been present at the conference and appeared thoroughly pleased with the governor's remarks. While not commenting specifically on the content of this blast at the Americans, Pierre Bergès expressed his regret at Governor Laigret's departure.[104] The announcement of this change came as a surprise to several people in New Caledonia who had come to believe that Governor Laigret would be in office for a long time. The programs that he had outlined in his meetings with the administrative council and on his tour of the interior were extremely popular.

The American reaction was one of shock and bitter anger. After Laigret's November speech to the administrative council Henry Day had been generally enthusiastic in reporting Laigret's desire to improve conditions in the colony. His assessment of Laigret's reform program was positive, and he considered Laigret to be sincerely interested in the welfare of the Caledonians, having overcome some of their traditional suspicion of governors as representatives of a distant and uncomprehending central authority. He believed that Laigret's tactic was to restore the prestige of the governor's office and secure greater loyalty to the FCNL in Algiers. He admired Laigret's vigorous approach. But Governor Laigret's negative December portrayal of the impact of the American presence during the December press conference upset him, and Day decided that Laigret had embarked upon a calculated, deliberate anti-American campaign to curry favor in Algiers. Laigret's statements, Consul Day regretted to say, "indicate that for purely political reasons he is prepared to stir up anti-American feeling and pose as the defender of French sovereignty against encroachments by the American armed forces on the island."[105]

Regardless of whether Laigret's anti-Americanism was designed to gain political favor with his superiors in Algiers, he did achieve unity on the island by defining the Americans as a common enemy: there were no other people "who hate the Americans as much as the Caledonians."[106] Thanks to his efforts, the Caledonians had regained a sense of national pride.[107]

Laigret's attack and denunciation of the Americans in his 16 December press conference had repercussions in the United States. The 3 January 1944 issues of *Time* and *Newsweek* magazines carried scathing attacks upon Laigret and included critical remarks about the seedy, rundown qualities of Nouméa. These American press attacks upon New Caledonia, its governor and the French population of what they described as a godforsaken place, came back to New Caledonia when translated copies of the articles began to circulate in Nouméa in January. In turn, Caledonians were now insulted, and even locals who were sympathetic began to spurn Americans and would not speak to them on the streets.

The strongest reaction to Governor Laigret following his press conference came from Admiral Halsey, who returned to the United States at this point for a high-level conference to work out the final strategy for the Pacific war. Before his departure Halsey ordered his staff to compile a dossier that would make plain Governor Laigret's anti-American campaign and provide evidence for removing New Caledonia from French administration at the end of the war. Based upon American intelligence reports, military authorities compiled a list of over twenty occasions where Laigret had given vent to his anti-Americanism and refused to cooperate.[108] Laigret had proved an obstructionist to the war effort, and his actions helped the enemy, according to the authors of the report. The Japanese had picked up reports of Laigret's news conference and used it as a propaganda weapon in a broadcast from Saigon to show the oppressive nature of American military presence in the French colony. Just as de Gaulle had earlier complained that American publicity surrounding the 1942 disturbances in New Caledonia had been used against the Free French, the Americans now returned the complaint. Halsey concluded that:

> ... In his opinion Governor Laigret has failed utterly to appreciate the necessity for cooperation in the war effort, has deliberately attempted to sow the seeds of dissension between French residents of New Caledonia and the American forces stationed here, has utilized the powers of his office to intimidate those who have been friendly toward the Americans, and has thus prevented the friendly cooperation that should prevail.[109]

He informed Roosevelt that it was impossible to work with the French and "under no circumstances should New Caledonia be handed back to the French; its administration is a disgrace."[110] Yet the reality was that the United States, despite the casually possessive language of Admiral Halsey, was not in possession of New Caledonia. But such was American indifference to French sensitivity on matters of sovereignty and postwar presence that the Free French felt that the Americans were determined to humiliate them and deny them a place as an important ally.

When Halsey offered his advice, Roosevelt had just returned from conferences in Cairo and Tehran where he had stated that parts of the French Empire should be placed under an international mandate and trusteeship, much to the alarm of Churchill but to the agreement of Stalin. At the beginning of the year Roosevelt met with the Pacific War Council to report the results of his conversations with Churchill and Stalin at Tehran and with Churchill and Chiang Kai-Shek in Cairo. He expressed the view that all territories in the Pacific, including those controlled by Japan as well as the Dutch East Indies and the Pacific Islands south of the equator, should be governed on a trusteeship basis. He specifically mentioned the French territories and declared that French interests in the Pacific should be transferred to other people, possibly placed under Australian and New Zealand oversight. Indochina was another area that Roosevelt wished to place under international control. As far as New Caledonia was concerned, Roosevelt reported Halsey's advising him that it was impossible to work with the French "and the only logical thing to do was to ask them to give up possession of the island."[111]

Despite all of Governor Laigret's efforts, the future status of New Caledonia as a French possession, along with other parts of the French Empire, was in more doubt than ever, and the Free French did have reason for concern.

Notes

1. Bourgeau to Colonial Commissioner, Algiers, 11 August 1943, Archives Nationales Section d'Outre-mer (ANSOM), New Caledonia, c. 163.
2. Bergès to d'Argenlieu, 21 May 1943, Archives Nationales (AN), Papiers d'Argenlieu 517AP.

3. D'Argenlieu to Pleven (Algiers), 4 June 1943, ANSOM, New Caledonia, c. 163.
4. D'Argenlieu to Fourcade, "Message for Bergès," 22 June 1943, AN, Papiers d'Argenlieu 517AP, and d'Argenlieu to Bergès, rec'd 29 June 1943, Enclosure #1, Day to State, 20 July 1943, U.S. National Archives and Record Administration (USNARA) RG 59, State Dec. File 851L.00/38, and appendix A to Royal Australian AF officer's report to RAAF Intelligence, 9 December 1943, Australian Archives (AA), ACT CRS A 989, 44/610/6.
5. Cabanier to d'Argenlieu, 2 August 1943 and "Memorandum sur les Possessions Françaises du Pacifique," 17 September 1943, AN, Papiers d'Argenlieu 517AP.
6. RAAF officer's report to RAAF Intelligence, 9 December 1943 and appendix B, AA ACT CRS A 989M 44/610/6. The signed copy of this protest reached Algiers, but whether it was the decisive element in the decision not to send d'Argenlieu back to New Caledonia is unclear. ANSOM, New Caledonia, c. 177.
7. Day to State, 20 July 1943, USNARA RG 59, State Dec file 851L.00/38.
8. RAAF officer's report to RAAF Intelligence, 9 December 1943, AA, ACT CRS A 989, 44/610/6.
9. Cabanier also had been in contact with Michel Vergès at this time. HQ 1 Island Command, annex no. 2 to weekly Intelligence (G-2) Report no. 14, 3 April 1943, USNARA RG 338.
10. Day to State, 8 August 1943, USNARA RG 59, State Dec File 851L.00/39.
11. Day to State, 29 July 1943, ibid. 8.
12. Vergès to Fourcade, 23 July 1943, ANSOM, Affaires Politiques, c. 509.
13. Fourcade to CNF, 25 June 1943, Ministère des Affaires Étrangères (MAE) Guerre 1939–45, Londres CNF, vol. 80. The author has found no evidence of such an instruction in the American archives.
14. D'Argenlieu to Pleven, 8 September 1943, AN, Papiers d'Argenlieu 517AP.
15. Same to same, 15 September 1943, ANSOM, New Caledonia, c. 162.
16. Same to same, 23 June 1943 and 28 August 1943, AN, Papiers d'Argenlieu 517AP.
17. Lieutenant Colonel Coulter (War Department) to Bonbright (State), 17 August 1943, USNARA RG 59, State Dec. File 851L.01/36.
18. Report ComSoPac to Secretary of Navy, 12 February 1944, Navy Yard 34(10)(D).
19. Laigret to Pleven, 20 October 1943, ANSOM, Tel. 841.
20. Same to same, 16 September 1943, ibid.
21. HQ 1 Island Command, annex no. 2 to weekly Intelligence (G-2) Report no. 38, 18 September 1943, USNARA RG 338.
22. HQ 1 Island Command, annex no. 2 to weekly Intelligence (G-2) Report no. 41, 9 October 1943, USNARA RG 338.
23. Laigret to Pleven and d'Argenlieu, 21 September 1943, ANSOM, telegr. 841 and AN, Papiers d'Argenlieu 517AP.
24. Ibid.
25. D'Argenlieu to Vergès, Prinet and Rabot, 5 January 1943, AN, Papiers d'Argenlieu 517AP.
26. Laigret to Pleven, 12 October 1943, ANSOM, New Caledonia, c. 163.
27. A month later Laigret informed d'Argenlieu of a reconciliation with Vergès with whom he now enjoyed "excellent" relations and expressed his appreciation for the collaboration and support that the lawyer accorded him. Laigret to d'Argenlieu 13 and 25 November 1943, AN, Papiers d'Argenlieu 517AP.
28. Laigret to d'Argenlieu, 12 October 1943, ibid.
29. HQ 1 Island Command, annex no. 2 to weekly Intelligence (G-2) Report no. 44, 30 October 1943, and No. 45, 6 November 1943, USNARA RG 338.
30. Day to State Department, 24 November 1943, USNARA RG 59, State Dec. File 851L.00/42.
31. HQ 1 Island Command, annex no. 2 to weekly Intelligence (G-2) Report no. 43, 23 October 1942, USNARA RG 338.

32. There are four large folders filled with eighty-one letters of grievance or complaint against the Americans in the archives of Overseas France compiled by Governor Laigret, ANSOM, New Caledonia, c. 177, and another fairly thick folder on "Litigation with U.S. Army," ANSOM, New Caledonia, c. 169.
33. Laigret to Major Field, Adjutant General, 5 November 1943, ANSOM, New Caledonia, c. 177.
34. HQ 1 Island Command, annex no. 2 to weekly Intelligence (G-2) Report no. 45, 6 November 1943, USNARA RG 338.
35. Citation from radio broadcast, 11 November 1943, ANSOM, New Caledonia, c. 177.
36. Laigret to Pleven, 25 November 1943, ANSOM, Tel. 841.
37. Shafroth to Laigret, 13 November 1943, ANSOM, New Caledonia c. 177.
38. HQ 1 Island Command, annex no. 2 to weekly Intelligence (G-2) Report no. 46, 13 November 1943, USNARA RG 338.
39. Laigret to Colonel Hadsell, 6 and 15 November 1943, ANSOM, New Caledonia, c. 177.
40. Laigret to Lincoln, 25 November 1943, and Laigret to Colonel Hadsell, 24 November 1943, ANSOM, New Caledonia 64.
41. Mr. Magnin to Laigret, 3 November 1943, forwarded to Lincoln, 22 November 1943, ANSOM, New Caledonia, c. 163.
42. Day to State, 20 December 1943, USNARA RG 59, State Dec. File 851L.01/39.
43. Laigret to Pleven, 29 November 1943, ANSOM, New Caledonia c.163, and same to same, 19 November 1943, ANSOM, New Caledonia, c.158.
44. Laigret to Pleven, 21 September 1943, ANSOM, New Caledonia, c. 169.
45. HQ 1 Island Command, annex no. 2 to weekly Intelligence (G-2) Report no. 49, 4 December 1943, USNARA RG 338.
46. Pleven to Laigret, 20 January 1944, ANSOM, New Caledonia, c. 169.
47. Ballard to External Affairs, 17 November 1943, AA ACT, CRS A6445, 392/47.
48. Laigret to Lincoln (I Island Command), 25 November 1943, ANSOM, New Caledonia, c. 163.
49. Laigret to Lincoln, 9 November 1943, ANSOM, New Caledonia, c. 177. Laigret also complained of the same behavior among the white troops of the New Zealand Third Division. Laigret to Dove, NZEF, IP, 9 November 1943, ibid.
50. Laigret to Lincoln, 29 November 1943, ANSOM, New Caledonia, c. 163.
51. HQ 1 Island Command, annex no. 2 to weekly Intelligence (G-2) Report no. 49, 4 December 1942, USNARA RG 338. Lincoln to Laigret, 20 November 1943, ibid.
52. "Rape Cases Involving Military Personnel," ComSoPac CIU Report, 8 January 1944, Wash D.C., Navy Yard, "New Caledonia Miscellaneous," microfilm.
53. Freby to Montchamp, 19 December 1942, SHA Outre-mer, c.6.
54. Note from Freby to Laigret, 30 November 1943, ANSOM New Caledonia, c.177.
55. Lieutenant Mas to Head, Governor's military cabinet, 4 December 1943, ibid.
56. Laigret to Lincoln, 8 December 1943, ibid.
57. Captain Daniel L. Schlafly, 3414th Ordnance Company to Commanding General, I Island Command, 28 June 1943, Ad Hist Append, Op Arch, Naval History Center (NHC) Washington D.C. See also History of the "Pink House," annex (a) to HQ, I Island Command, "Report of Special Investigation Number 6, rue Paul Bart [sic], Nouméa, 15 September 1944, ibid.
58. Interview with Mr. Andrew Vrtjak, retired lawyer from Chicago who served on the Judge Advocate General's staff in New Caledonia during the war.
59. Historical Record of HQ Service Command, 12 March 1942 to 5 May 1942, USNARA RG338.
60. HQ SoPac Base Command, minutes of staff meeting, 6 December 1944, USNARA RG 407, box 620.

61. HQ 1 Island Command, annex no. 1 (economic) to weekly Intelligence (G-2) Report no. 41, 9 October 1943, USNARA RG165.
62. HQ 1 Island Command, annex no. 1 (economic) to weekly Intelligence (G-2) Report no. 42, 16 October 1943, ibid.
63. HQ 1 Island Command, annex no. 1 (economic) to weekly Intelligence (G-2) Report no. 41, 9 October 1943, ibid.
64. HQ 1 Island Command, Intelligence (G-2) periodic report for week of 22–29 July 1944, USNARA, RG338, and Australian Consul to Canberra, 18 April 1944, AA, CRS A989, item 44/610/6.
65. HQ 1 Island Command, annex no. 1 (economic) to weekly Intelligence (G-2) Report no. 33, 14 August 1943, USNARA RG165.
66. Norman Read to Phillip Amram, Chief So Pac Is Project, 29 March 1943, USNARA RG 59, State Dec. File 851L.24/27.
67. Patch to Marshall, 17 April 1942, USNARA RG165.
68. HQ 1 Island Command, appendix A to annex no. 1 (economic) to weekly Intelligence (G-2) Report no. 41, 9 October 1943, USNARA RG165.
69. Laigret to Lincoln, 26 January 1944, ANSOM, New Caledonia, c. 177.
70. Lincoln to Laigret, 14 October 1943, and Laigret to Lincoln 10 and 16 November 1943, ibid.
71. HQ 1 Island Command, annex no. 1 (economic) to weekly Intelligence (G-2) Report no. 41, 9 October 1943, USNARA RG165.
72. Memorandum, "Trade Goods as Incentive to Natives to Work," 29 March 1943, ibid.
73. HQ 1 Island Command, annex no. 1 (economic) to weekly Intelligence (G-2) Report no. 30, 24 July 1943, USNARA RG165.
74. Colonel Roger Taylor, Metals and Minerals Representative in New Caledonia, forwarding a letter from Rapadzi (in translation) to H.J. Fraser, Foreign Economic Administration, Washington, 20 October 1944, USNARA RG59, State Dec. File 851L.504/11-1444.
75. Memorandum, "American Activities in Pacific Islands," n.d. but ca. late 1943, AA ACT, CRS A989, item 43/735/310/3.
76. Jean Lubet, Head of Union of Immigrants, to Head Immigration Service, 3 November 1943 and Laigret to Lincoln, 23 November 1943, ANSOM, New Caledonia c. 64.
77. Australian Liason Officer, "New Caledonia Potpourri" to RAAF Dir of Intelligence, 9 November 1943, AA, ACT, CRS A989, item 44/610/6.
78. Pleven to Laigret, 28 November 1943 ANSOM New Caledonia c. 163.
79. HQ 1 Island Command, annex 2 (political) to Intelligence (G-2) Report no.53, 1 January 1944, RG338, and "M. Christian Laigret, Governor pro tem of New Caledonia and Dependencies, Anti-American Attitude of," 12 February 1944, Ad Hist Append, Op Arch, NHC.
80. Australian Liaison officer to Director of Intelligence, 9 December 1943, AA ACT, CRS A989, item 44/610/6.
81. HQ 1 Island Command, annex 2 (political) to Intelligence (G-2) Reports no. 50, 11 December 1943 and no.53, 1 January 1944, USNARA RG 338.
82. HQ 1 Island Command, annex 2 (political) to Intelligence (G-2) Report no. 55, 15 January 1944, USNARA RG 338.
83. "M. Christian Laigret, Governor pro tem of New Caledonia and Dependencies, Anti-American Attitude of," 12 February 1944 Ad Hist Append, Op Arch, NHC.
84. HQ 1 Island Command, annex 2 (political) to Intelligence (G-2) Report no. 54, 8 January 1944, USNARA RG338.
85. HQ 1 Island Command, annex 2 (political) to Intelligence (G-2) Report no. 57, 29 January 1944, ibid.
86. Laigret to Lincoln, 17 January 1944, covering letter for Audrain to Laigret, 9 January 1944, ANSOM, New Caledonia c. 177.

87. HQ 1 Island Command, annex 2 (political) to Intelligence (G-2) Report no. 55, 15 January 1944, USNARA RG 338.
88. HQ 1 Island Command, annex 2 (political) to Intelligence (G-2) Report no. 56, 22 January 1944, ibid.
89. Pleven to d'Argenlieu, 7 September 1943, AN, Papiers d'Argenlieu 517AP.
90. De Menthon to Pleven, 6 October 1943, ANSOM, New Caledonia c.177.
91. Pleven to d'Argenlieu, 22 October 1943, AN, Papiers d'Argenlieu 517AP.
92. Pleven to Laigret, 16 November 1943, ibid.
93. Pleven to Laigret, 15 November 1943, ANSOM, New Caledonia c. 162.
94. Translation of Speech given by M. Laigret ... at the Opening Session of the administrative council in Nouméa, New Caledonia, 20 November 1943, USNARA RG 338; Day to State, 24 November 1943, USNARA RG 59, State Dec. File 851L.00/42.
95. HQ 1 Island Command, annex 2 (political) to Intelligence (G-2) Report No. 45, 6 November 1943, USNARA RG 338.
96. Day to State, 20 December 1943, USNARA RG 59, State Dec. File 851L.01/39.
97. These messages are part of the dossier that Laigret forwarded to Pleven in support of his activities as acting governor of New Caledonia, Vergès to d'Argenlieu, 24 November 1943, ANSOM, New Caledonia c. 509, and Forest to Laigret, 14 December 1943, ANSOM, New Caledonia c.177.
98. Laigret to Pleven, 20 and 23 November 1943, ANSOM, New Caledonia c.162, and same to same, ANSOM, tel. 841.
99. Laigret, "Report on Governor's Tour through the Colony, October 18–30," 24 November 1943, ANSOM, New Caledonia c.178, and Laigret to Pleven, 28 December 1943, ANSOM, New Caledonia c.163.
100. Pleven to Laigret, 24 November 1943, ANSOM, New Caledonia c.19.
101. Charles J. Weeks, Jr., "An Hour of Temptation: American Interests in New Caledonia, 1939–1945," *Australian Journal of Politics and History* 35 (Winter, 1989): 192–93.
102. Pleven to Laigret, 17 November 1943, ANSOM, New Caledonia c.158.
103. Interview granted by Governor per-interim Laigret to American and Australian war correspondents, 16 December 1943, enclosure #1, Day to State, 20 December 1943, USNARA RG 59 State Dec. File 851L.01/39.
104. Day to State, 20 December 1943, USNARA RG 59, State Dec. File 851L.01/39.
105. Ibid.
106. Laigret to Pleven, 1 April 1944, ANSOM, New Caledonia c. 163, and Laigret to Pleven, 25 November 1943, ANSOM, Tel. 841.
107. Laigret to Pleven, 28 December 1943, ANSOM, New Caledonia c. 163.
108. HQ 1 Island Command, annex 2 (political) to Intelligence (G-2), Report No. 52, 25 December 1943, USNARA RG 338.
109. "Anti-American Attitude of M. Christian Laigret ...," 12 February 1944, Ad Hist Append, Op Arch, NHC.
110. Noel Deschamps, Australian Consul (Nouméa) to External Affairs (Canberra), 11 May 1944, AA ACT. CRS A989.
111. New Zealand's Minister in Washington to Wellington, 12 January 1944, AA ACT. CRS A989, item 43/735/310/3.

CHAPTER 7

ROOSEVELT AND DE GAULLE: CONFLICTING VISIONS OF A POSTWAR WORLD ORDER

Would the Americans ever leave New Caledonia once the war was over? The American threat to New Caledonia and to the French Empire in general was far more serious and obvious at the end of 1943 than it had been when the Americans first arrived at the beginning of 1942. Although General de Gaulle suspected a political ambition behind the American military expedition to New Caledonia, American planners had no such consideration in mind at first. The war was going badly in the Pacific, and President Roosevelt and his military advisors were concerned primarily with stopping the relentless Japanese advance. Roosevelt's thinking about American postwar security needs had not been formulated in any concrete way. Roosevelt and the State Department had on several occasions declared an American intention to restore France's territorial integrity, including the French Empire, at the end of the war. By late 1943, however, an American challenge to a restoration of the French Empire had become apparent, and events in New Caledonia had an important influence upon Roosevelt's thinking about where France and its empire would fit in the postwar world.

Anticolonialism and Yankee Imperialism

Shortly after the American entry into the war, Roosevelt asked Ambassador Leahy to inform Marshal Pétain that he wished to see France reconstituted after the war and that included the French Colonial Empire.[1] President Roosevelt assured Marshal Pétain that "as long as French sovereign control remains in reality purely French ... the government of the United States has no desire to see existing

French sovereignty over French North Africa or over any French colonies pass to the control of any other nation." At the same time he warned Pétain that any concessions to the Germans in North Africa or elsewhere "will mean the eventual relinquishment of rights within France's own Empire ... and would constitute a severe blow to the hopes of the American people that France would be preserved as a nation."[2] This was a stern warning, one that also carried a threat and rationale for intervention in French colonial territory if necessary.

The basic State Department position toward restoration of the French Empire had been established prior to the American entry into the war. During René Pleven's mission to the United States in October 1941, Ray Atherton assured Pleven that the United States intended to restore all territories that had been French in 1940.[3] In response to the formation of General de Gaulle's French National Committee in London in September 1941, the State Department set forth its policy of dealing with those authorities in the French Empire who demonstrated "manifest effectiveness" in resisting any encroachment by the Axis powers into French colonial territory.[4] Shortly after the American entry into the war the State Department's Samuel Reber reiterated this position when he wrote:

> The policy of this government as regards France is based upon the maintenance of the integrity of France and of the French Empire and of the restoration of the complete independence of all French territories. Mindful of its traditional friendship for France this Government has deeply sympathized with the desire of the French people to maintain their territories and to preserve them intact.[5]

At the time of the expedition to New Caledonia the State Department issued another statement that repeated Reber's formula, adding that the United States would support the local French authorities that effectively resisted Axis aggression.[6] This statement had reassured Admiral d'Argenlieu that the United States recognized Free-French control and administration of those territories that had rallied to General de Gaulle, particularly New Caledonia.

The Vichy Government protested that it was the only authority with legitimate sovereignty in the French Empire, including those territories that had fallen into the hands of Gaullist dissidents. The United States rejected this protest. When the United States established a consulate in the Free-French controlled city of Brazzaville in April 1942, the Vichy Government again declared that it alone was qualified to grant the exaquatur for the position. Welles replied that the United States would deal with those French citizens who were in actual control of French territory, and he added that the United States maintained unimpaired its "full respect for the sovereign rights of the people of France. They may continue to be confident that by the victory of the United Nations those rights will be restored intact to them."[7] By the time the Americans arrived in New Caledonia, the U.S. Government had assured both Vichy and the Free French of its intention to respect the sovereignty and territorial integrity of France and its imperial domain.

Roosevelt's negative views of French colonialism first became apparent to the British Government in May 1942 following the first New Caledonia crisis. Lord Halifax, the British ambassador in Washington, reported that at a meeting of the Pacific War Council on 20 May 1942, following the New Caledonia riot, Roosevelt expressed frustration over his difficulties with the Free French in the South Pacific. By this time General Patch's reports of Admiral d'Argenlieu's hostility and uncooperative attitude toward the Americans had reached the President's desk. At the meeting Roosevelt casually observed that it would not be a good idea to return all French Pacific colonies to French control after the war, nor was he sure about the status of Indochina. He concluded that no pledges should be given to France on the restoration of any French territory.[8]

French behavior in New Caledonia intensified Roosevelt's negative impression of de Gaulle, his close associates, and the political character of the Free-French movement. The conflict over the Free-French occupation of St. Pierre and Miquelon in December 1941 was more of a sore point for Secretary of State Cordell Hull than it was for Roosevelt, who dismissed that affair as a tempest in a teapot.[9] On the other hand, New Caledonia convinced Roosevelt that General de Gaulle could not be trusted since he was playing his own political game to the detriment of the U.S. war effort. Admiral d'Argenlieu had become uncooperative and, more seriously, had provoked a dangerous political crisis in New Caledonia on the eve of the crucial battle of the Coral Sea. Such events caused Roosevelt to complain to his British allies about the unreliability of the Free French. In the aftermath of the events of May 1942 he began to consider the creation of an American postwar security system at the expense of the French Empire. By late May Roosevelt's security policy began to take shape, and it was a serious threat to France's restoration as a major power.

The French defeat and collapse in 1940 convinced Roosevelt that France no longer had the capacity to serve as a guarantor of peace after the war. France no longer counted as one of the great powers.[10] In his estimation France would need at least twenty-five years to recover from the humiliation of defeat and the Nazi occupation.[11] Preservation of the postwar order would require that key points in the French Empire—Dakar, Nouméa, Indochina, Bizerte—be placed in reliable hands under a trusteeship system to assure defense of these strong points and prepare for the eventual decolonization of the French imperial domain.

In addition to his concern about American security needs, there was the president's ideological opposition to European imperialism. Roosevelt believed that French and British colonialism bore a large measure of responsibility for the social injustices that were at the heart of the world's ills, particularly during the Great Depression. From Roosevelt's perspective colonialism had been a source of conflict in the past and its continuance meant future difficulties and instability since it was a system that denied rights of self-determination to colonized peoples, and it created economic obstacles to free trade, commerce and general prosperity.[12] After the troubles in New Caledonia, Roosevelt's general reservations about imperialism and French colonial practices came together and assumed a more concrete form.

Roosevelt's comments about imposing international control over parts of the French Empire astonished officials at the British foreign office. They were well aware that in reaching agreement with the Free French over the American expedition to New Caledonia the Americans had recognized Free-French control over the island and had promised restoration of all territories that had been French in 1940. The foreign office pointed to the pledge of restoration given by Ray Atherton in 1941 and the same assurance given at the time of the American arrival in New Caledonia five months later. Roosevelt's change of position in May 1942 did not augur well for American relations with General de Gaulle and the Free French, and British officials predicted that there would be trouble.

The British foreign office objected to Roosevelt's dealing so lightly with French colonial territories, noting that "President Roosevelt seems to be adopting a rather dictatorial attitude as regards other people's property (French Pacific Islands, French Indochina)." British officials feared that after the war the United States would either retreat into isolationism or would "launch out into a Yankee imperialism under the guise of reorganizing the world."[13] Six months into the war President Roosevelt had begun to think about placing strategic points of the French Empire under some form of an international military trusteeship. At best France would have a limited role in a global peacekeeping mission, as one among a number of trustee powers who would assume responsibility for oversight of French imperial territory. By 1943 Roosevelt's intention was clear: Yankee imperialism under the guise of reorganizing the world for American security and economic interests rather than a retreat into isolationism was the likely scenario.

His opposition to colonialism led Roosevelt to seek an understanding on the problem in meetings with the Soviet head of state, Josef Stalin, at the Tehran Conference at the end of 1943 (28 November to 1 December 1943). He had already raised the issue of imperialism in his discussions with Generalissimo Chiang Kai-shek of China at the Cairo Conference directly before (23–26 November 1943) where he openly criticized the European imperial order. In these encounters FDR argued for dismantling the imperial systems after the war by placing a number of colonial territories into a trusteeship system that would eventually lead to independence. Roosevelt also raised the possibility of placing certain strategic points under international control. At Tehran Stalin readily fell in with Roosevelt's anticolonialist views, as had Chiang Kai-shek, much to Churchill's dismay.

In the initial discussion at Tehran that touched on French affairs, Stalin strongly condemned the French ruling class as "rotten to the core" and declared emphatically that France had no right to retain its empire. Even more, Stalin informed Roosevelt and Churchill that it would be "not only unjust but dangerous to leave in French hands any important strategic points after the war" since French leaders had delivered the country to the Germans.[14] Roosevelt agreed "in part" with what Stalin had to say, suggesting that no one over forty should have a role in any postwar government of France, endorsing Stalin's opinion that the French defeat of 1940 resulted from a weakness of French leadership. Roosevelt was less categorical in his view of the future control of the French Empire, arguing not so much that the empire should be taken away from France, but he wanted key French bases at Nouméa and Dakar placed under international trusteeship. In Roosevelt's view New Caledonia represented a potential threat to Australia and New Zealand, and Dakar posed a menace to the nations of the Western Hemisphere.

Admiral Halsey's condemnation of French rule in New Caledonia confirmed Roosevelt's belief, which he had earlier expressed at the time of the Casablanca Conference in January 1943, that the French were poor colonial rulers who did not deserve to have their empire completely "restored."[15] At Casablanca Churchill had been taken aback by Roosevelt's comments to the Sultan of Morocco on the inequities of colonialism, and in reaction he began to support the Free French, despite the Prime Minister's own disputes with de Gaulle over Syria and Madagascar. Officials in the British foreign and colonial offices were equally determined to block Roosevelt's plans for a system of trusteeships.

The Free French heard indirectly of Roosevelt's thoughts about American postwar security needs, and they disliked what they heard. Was New Caledonia destined to become part of an American system of security? Beyond the particular issue of New Caledonia's postwar status, a general concern for the Gaullists was how the Americans would treat France. Would France be considered an equal ally, fully entitled to regain status as a major European and global power, including sovereignty over the territories that had been French in 1940? Or would France be dismissed as a power whose weakness had enabled the expansion of Hitler's Nazi state in Europe and had provided no resistance to Japan's military advances in Southeast Asia, thereby threatening American security interests in the Atlantic and the Pacific? Would France be forced to play a secondary role to the global ambitions of the Anglo-Saxon powers? The possessive language employed by both Admiral Halsey and President Roosevelt suggested that the decision would be an American one without much regard for the interests or sensibilities of any postwar French Government. Such an attitude was anathema to General de Gaulle, who consistently argued that France could not be ignored, and he employed all means to assure that French interests would be respected.

In response to this American "menace" the Free French adopted a strategy of active resistance, and Governor Laigret's policy of anti-Americanism fit this strategy. Attacking the Americans became Laigret's method of inspiring national loyalty on this fractious island, a policy that he assumed would win approval from the French Committee of National Liberation (FCNL). The State Department meanwhile cited Laigret's action as a reason not to have confidence in de Gaulle.[16]

Anti-Americanism and the French Empire

While the 1942 New Caledonia crisis convinced Roosevelt that de Gaulle was an unreliable ally, it stiffened de Gaulle's belief that the Americans had come to the island not to defend it but to take it over "for their own account." In London General de Gaulle and his supporters became convinced that the Americans deliberately publicized the events in New Caledonia as a tactic to exploit French dissension in order to discredit the Free-French movement.[17] An American plot to take over New Caledonia became the Gaullist thesis and explanation for the events of May 1942, and it is an interpretation that persists to this day among French historians. There is no evidence in the American archives of any such plan prior to Roosevelt's 1942 statements. Nevertheless, de Gaulle decided that reconciliation with the Americans was not possible, and he intended to resist their global ascendancy.[18]

De Gaulle's fury at the Americans may be seen in a violent confrontation that he had with Étienne Boegner, an early supporter of the Free French and member of the Free-French delegation in Washington, in London shortly after the New Caledonia conflict. Boegner reported that the atmosphere at Carlton Gardens was anti-American. The Free French accused the United States "of trying to set up a world octopus; of trying to fragmentize the old French Empire in the hope of seizing it for themselves, and so forth."[19] Boegner provided a full account of his clash with de Gaulle to Alexis Léger upon his return to Washington. These notes reveal the extent of de Gaulle's bitterness toward the State Department and its refusal to recognize him as the embodiment of France.

When Boegner tried to argue that the Americans were not really as hostile to him as de Gaulle claimed and actually had shown their good will by recognizing his authority over the colonies that had rallied, de Gaulle exploded. "They detest me, these Americans," and he shouted, "I have had enough of them!" He told Boegner that Tixier, "a good and loyal Frenchman", had fully informed him of the State Department's antagonism. As a result of Tixier's report, he informed Boegner that he did not believe a word he said. Boegner tried to speak in favor of Sumner Welles, but de Gaulle lost his temper and cut Boegner off. He told Boegner to tell his friend Sumner Welles that he was "a stupid asshole (*un con*), a fool (*une ganache*), and an idiot, and from me you can tell that old moron (*ce vieil abruti*) Hull that he is a stupid asshole, a fool and an idiot. To hell with them!" He accused Boegner of being an agent of the Americans.[20] Boegner left the interview without saying good-bye or shaking hands and he became militantly anti-Gaullist.

Feelings of resentment were intense among members of the Free French in London, who were critical of Roosevelt and his attitude toward the Free-French movement. These negative views turned into a more broadly anti-American attitude for certain individuals in the movement, notably General Billotte and Admiral d'Argenlieu. Billotte had a powerful influence upon de Gaulle and was one of the more important members of his staff. He had direct and frequent access to de Gaulle, and he helped shape the General's outlook.[21] Admiral d'Argenlieu's cables from New Caledonia gave substance to the Gaullist view of American imperialism during and after the war. This profound suspicion of American intentions, and a determination to resist Yankee imperialistic tendencies set in for de Gaulle and his supporters.

Excluded from access to any inner councils or privy to high level discussions of American plans, the Free French had to guess or make assumptions about the direction of American policies.[22] The Pacific War Council, established in January 1942, was one place where a Free-French representative might have obtained information about Roosevelt's plans for the Pacific after the war, but the Free French were not invited to become members of this organization. From time to time Free-French officials requested that they be included in discussions about the future of the South Pacific, but these requests were effectively shelved.[23] An argument can be made that Roosevelt's exclusion of de Gaulle and the Free French was a shortsighted policy if he wished to have France as a postwar ally. American policy had become increasingly unilateralist under Roosevelt's guidance as the war progressed. It revealed that Roosevelt was inclined to pursue his anticolonialism even if it meant weakening his allies, France but also Great Britain.

In particular General de Gaulle believed that the American tendency to deal with local authorities, Vichy as well as Free French, was a tactic to divide and conquer. Free-French officials were concerned that the absence of formal recognition of their movement as the only representative of France's true interests and unity meant that President Roosevelt intended to liquidate the French Empire and reduce France to the level of a second-rate power.[24] For the Free French, retention of the empire was essential for France's recovery and restoration as a great power. A French general, who had been part of the antirepublican demonstrations on 6 February 1934 but had rallied to support de Gaulle, stated in January that there was a new sense of the importance of the French Empire in France. Despite the defeat of 1940 the empire showed that France was still a world power.[25]

If de Gaulle did not insist on the unity of the French Empire and French interests, he was convinced that his allies would exploit the fragmentation of the imperial domain for their own gain, whether in Syria, Madagascar, St. Pierre and Miquelon, or New Caledonia. In his instructions to Adrien Tixier, whom de Gaulle had selected to head the Free-French delegation in Washington at the beginning of 1942, he observed that the basic policy of the FCNL was to defend the rights of France throughout the world. "The unity of France and its Empire constitutes the fundamental axiom of our policy; this must constantly be made known to the State Department."[26]

At the end of 1942 General de Gaulle tried to convey the Free-French view of the harm that a division of authority caused for French interests generally and how it discouraged Free-French efforts to unite the empire in pursuit of the war effort. De Gaulle had a "frank and cordial" conversation with Admiral Harold Stark, Commander of American Naval forces in the Atlantic and one of two American military representatives to the Free-French movement in London, on the eve of Stark's return to Washington at the end of 1942. After expressing his desire to go to Washington to meet with President Roosevelt, de Gaulle asked Admiral Stark to inform the President that the United States erred in dealing separately with parts of the French Empire. He warned the Americans against mistakenly applying their own principles of federalism to a French system that was highly centralized.[27] When the Americans failed to heed this warning and insisted upon working out issues on the spot, de Gaulle became convinced that this was a deliberate tactic to weaken French authority in the empire.

A deliberate policy of confrontation became de Gaulle's method for resisting British and American pressures. In an often-quoted passage he declared that, given his limited resources, he "could not afford to bend."[28] While this attitude irritated the Americans and led to American complaints that de Gaulle was deliberately uncooperative, his intransigence won support among Free-French faithful, who considered that his refusal to yield to Allied demands was a source of strength and independence. His supporters admired him for saying "no" to defeat, to Vichy and to the Allies. Weakness could be overcome by intransigence.[29]

After the war George Boris, a socialist and in 1943 de Gaulle's head of civil affairs in London, testified that this tactic was de Gaulle's only force in light of his weakness. He was usually right to suspect British intentions in Syria and to believe that the American State Department's reaction to the St. Pierre and Miquelon affair revealed imperialistic goals.[30] René Bouscat, a military officer and resistance leader who tried to arrange a compromise between Generals de Gaulle and Giraud, said that when he went to Carlton Gardens, de Gaulle's headquarters in London, it was a "real political club where intransigence ruled."[31] René Massigli, who would soon become Free-French Commissioner for Foreign Affairs, recalled in his first meeting with de Gaulle he realized that all of France's strength resided in the General's unbending manner.[32] Resistance toward the Americans, their actions and their requests, became a form of asserting French independence and gaining unity among the Gaullist faithful.

Intransigence revealed de Gaulle's tactical approach to the conduct of interstate relations, which was deliberately confrontational and reflective of his military background. Standing one's ground or challenging the enemy can be seen as engagement on a military battlefield in which strength or even an appearance of strength to bluff an opponent can carry the day. De Gaulle believed that the exercise of military leadership required an officer to instill fear.[33] This psychology may be found in another of de Gaulle's often-quoted remarks, ironically taken from *Hamlet* in which he said: "To be great is to sustain a great quarrel."[34] And de Gaulle would both quarrel and deliberately provoke, again revealed in de Gaulle's comment at the time of the St. Pierre and Miquelon affair that he had sought a confrontation in order to stir things up, "just as one throws a rock into a pond."[35] Governor Laigret in his pursuit of a quarrel, even petty, with the Americans and his policy of provocations and pinpricks clearly followed such precepts and fell in line with the tactic of discrediting the Americans by stirring things up.

The idea of "compromise" had an unfavorable, pejorative connotation in Gaullist vocabulary, implying weakness or yielding, even to the point of an abandonment of principle. To do so would be a retreat or an abandonment of French interests, which is what had happened in 1940 when the Third Republic signed the armistice. The term "compromise" and its different usage in American English illustrated a linguistic basis for the misunderstanding that developed between the Gaullists and the Americans. For Americans the idea of "compromise" did not have the same negative implication that it had for the French. Often a "compromise" could provide the basis for mutual agreement and understanding, according to American values. The Americans could not understand why a compromise between Giraud and de Gaulle was so difficult to arrange, for example.

Gaullist hostility to compromise, particularly compromise on matters of principle became apparent during a stormy interview between President Roosevelt and André Philip, a trade unionist and resistance leader who was sent to the United States as General de Gaulle's personal representative, on 20 November 1942. The interview took place shortly after the "Darlan deal" in which General Eisenhower and President Roosevelt had accepted Admiral Darlan, a notorious Vichy collaborator with Nazi Germany, as high commissioner for North Africa in exchange for Darlan ordering French troops to cease resisting the Anglo-American landings in North Africa. Public opinion in Great Britain and the United States was outraged at any arrangement with a pro-Nazi collaborator, but General Eisenhower justified the Darlan deal on the ground that it would save American and British lives. Roosevelt backed Eisenhower against the storm of criticism. The meeting with Philip would reveal the divergence of views on the conduct of the war that was plaguing American relations with the Free French.

After missing the first scheduled meeting with Roosevelt, which was to have taken place before the Allied landings, Philip, accompanied by Tixier, arrived fifteen minutes late for the second meeting, and Philip immediately began to lecture FDR in a didactic manner on the moral improprieties of the Darlan deal.[36] Philip did most of the talking, and his lecture, delivered in an abrasive and arrogant manner, pleased neither the President nor Sumner Welles, who was present. Exasperated by Philip's manner, Roosevelt defended the deal as an unfortunate but necessary step to halt French resistance to Allied landings, save lives, and hasten the end of the war. Roosevelt informed Philip that unlike Woodrow Wilson he was a realist, and he was primarily interested in winning the war as quickly as possible. He would accept help from any source. "Today, Darlan gives me Algiers, and I cry *Vive Darlan!* If Quisling gives me Oslo, I will cry *Vive Quisling!* Let Laval give me Paris tomorrow and I will cry *Vive Laval!*"

This display of realism appalled Philip, and he echoed de Gaulle's denunciation of this action as a deal with a traitor that sullied the honor of France for cynical American interests. Philip told Roosevelt that "realism" in France was a term used to cover the defeatist policy of Pétain and Laval. "I have heard enough of that word," he admonished the President. Roosevelt's claim that he would support any Quisling, Philip observed, would be morally discouraging to the French and all other resistance movements. In the comments on the margin of the report that Tixier sent to the French National Committee, Philip compared the American president to Laval as a cynic and "realist."[37] The Free French occupied the high moral ground and looked contemptuously upon the opportunistic Americans.

Philip came away from the interview convinced that Roosevelt was an imperial dictator disguised as a "democratic" president, who wished to impose the American system on the rest of the world. A week after the interview between Philip and Roosevelt the French National Committee drew up a memorandum on Roosevelt and his policy toward France, which concluded that American and Free-French views on the future role of France were "diametrically opposed."[38] This report reflected Philip's conviction that American economic interests would insist upon compensation for the sacrifices made during the war, and these payments would be at the expense of France and its empire.

For de Gaulle, French sovereignty and interests were indivisible and not subject to any compromise, particularly when the perceived threat of "foreigners" was involved. De Gaulle condemned General Giraud's willingness to accept American conditions for rearming the French. His criticism of Jean Monnet's manner of dealing with the Americans was that Monnet, who was instrumental in securing American equipment for the French Army, was too quick to strike a bargain and was therefore "too soft" and compliant. "Monnet waffles," was how the General put it.[39] One of the Third Republic's major weaknesses in de Gaulle's eyes had been a tendency of its political leaders to yield to foreigners. Of course Governor Sautot had been too soft, too compliant in his dealings with the Americans according to Admiral d'Argenlieu.[40]

In addition to his firmness de Gaulle was strongly suspicious of all foreigners, particularly the British and the Americans. At the time of his struggle with General Giraud over who would assume leadership in liberated Algeria, de Gaulle warned his supporters in London and Algiers that "we are in the midst of strangers, for the Allies are foreigners. Tomorrow they may become enemies."[41] Such views became widespread in North Africa following the defeat of the Axis forces and the arrival of de Gaulle at the end of May 1943. Resistance leaders coming out of France were shocked at the degree of hostility toward the Anglo-Saxons among the Free French, as seen in the testimony of the labor leader, Christian Pineau.[42] Robert Murphy also reported to the State Department that the resistance people coming out of France were completely bewildered to discover that "their hero General de Gaulle, and particularly his entourage, is more bitter against the Americans than against the Germans."[43]

From Morocco the American consul reported that newsreels showing American troops in action were greeted with stony silence, whereas French forces were always cheered. He added that there was a "considerable suspicion" that the United States intended to take over Dakar. The American consul noted that anti-American feelings and anti-American propaganda had become much more open and widespread following General de Gaulle's visit to Morocco. He observed that such feelings were particularly noticeable among the Communists and Gaullists but could be found among "every class of the population."[44]

The American assistant secretary for war, John J. McCloy, who was sympathetic to the Free-French cause, complained to Colonel de Chevigné, General de Gaulle's military representative in Washington, about anti-Americanism in Algeria. He observed that the U.S. Army was uncertain of the security of its supply lines when General de Gaulle was reported to have told his colleagues, "Tomorrow America might become the enemy of France." Colonel de Chevigné denied that de Gaulle had uttered such words, which was not true. In his report to Algiers de Chevigné asked officials of de Gaulle's entourage to be more discreet and not use such "thoughtless" language around the Americans.[45]

Alarming evidence of Free-French attitudes toward the United States as "enemy" may be found in a letter sent by a Free-French air force officer to friends in the United States. The concern was the development of strong anti-American sentiments that he had discovered among twenty young Free-French pilot cadets who were completing their training in Canada under his command. The author described an incident that occurred when some of the cadets, who knew that he had been in America, asked for information about New York and the people they might encounter there. After he had explained what New York and the Americans were like, the senior cadet then exclaimed, "Isn't it a pity that these Americans, who are so nice individually, as a nation should be our enemies?" The question surprised the author. "Our enemies? Are you out of your mind? Don't you know that the Americans are our allies, our friends, that they have always been?" Yet all of the cadets spoke up and unanimously declared, "No, Sir. Henri is right. They were our friends, but now they are our enemies."[46]

Commander Kittredge, who had also become an advocate for de Gaulle and the Free French, complained to André Philip on the anti-American biases of the press in North Africa. The Free-French spokesman, Jacques Soustelle, rejected these complaints as unfounded.[47] But these attempts to disguise the extent and deliberate quality of Gaullist anti-Americanism did not deceive the Americans, who were well aware that anti-Americanism was part of the General's resistance tactic. Perception of Free-French hostility emerged during a discussion on whether or not, in light of Free-French attitudes toward the Americans and

General Giraud's marginalization, the United States should continue to arm French forces in North Africa. General Walter Bedell Smith, General Eisenhower's chief-of-staff, stated that although de Gaulle "hates our guts," the Americans should go ahead and rearm the Free French anyway.[48]

Although aware that his approach irritated the Americans, General de Gaulle realized that his tough, anti-American stance would gain him wide support across the French political spectrum in Algiers, helping to unite political parties in a common cause against an opponent that one day might become an enemy. A powerful Gaullist hostility toward the policies of the United States and an intense anti-American feeling had developed in North Africa by the time General de Gaulle had outmaneuvered General Giraud to emerge as the uncontested leader of the FCNL in Algiers.

Faced with American maneuvers to exclude him from power, de Gaulle argued that American policy toward Free, or Fighting France had been underhanded, and he called for the Fighting French to unite in face of this foreign threat. He maintained that in defending the unity of France and its empire, the governors of Free-French controlled territory did not necessarily have to adopt an "unfriendly attitude" toward the Allies, but a policy of firmness was more necessary than ever.[49] The Governor of Djibouti, who was none other than André Bayardelle the former General Secretary of New Caledonia, supported de Gaulle's position. Bayardelle, who earlier had suspected Australian designs on New Caledonia, praised the Free-French movement as an obstacle to American imperialistic ambitions and a barrier to a calculated, deliberate American intention to demean France.[50] André Philip, whose aggressive style had upset Roosevelt during their interview in November 1942, later indicated that de Gaulle fully approved his "talking tough" to the Americans.[51] Governor Laigret certainly did that.

Given the anti-American atmosphere that existed in Algiers during the summer of 1943 and clear indications that all governors of Free-French territories were to be firm in dealing with the Americans, Admiral d'Argenlieu's and Governor Laigret's actions in New Caledonia seem less surprising. The latter's dismissal or transfer of officers who seemed to be too cordial toward the Americans followed the path established by Admiral d'Argenlieu, who deliberately fostered anti-American sentiments after his troubles on New Caledonia in 1942 by forbidding the officers of his mission to receive American officers.[52] Resistance to the United States became a calculated policy for the Gaullists, and Governor Laigret, whose appointment to New Caledonia came in the summer of 1943, reflected this approach.

Relations between the Free French and the Americans were to be no more than formal, even distant, since friendships or a close relationship might cause a softening of attitudes. After the war General Billotte, who was rather stridently anti-American, complained that there were too many in London who were "soft" on dealing with the Americans.[53] Those Free French who showed any disposition to accommodate or, as Billotte had it, "grovel before" the Allies were quickly called to Gaullist order and sent to undesirable posts in the colonies. A State Department report by Bonbright observed that "friendship for the United States and a desire to help the war effort and ignore political considerations have proved fatal to the careers of French officials."[54]

Bonbright perhaps had the fate of Médecin Général Sicé in Africa in mind. Sicé had been part of the rallies of French African territories in 1940, had served as Free-French high commissioner in Brazzaville, and, like Sautot, had been a member of the Empire Defense Council. Sicé incurred de Gaulle's wrath by negotiating directly with the Americans for the establishment of a landing field at Pointe Noire in Africa without obtaining approval from Carlton Gardens or getting the compensation in the form of eight aircraft that General de Gaulle demanded as the price of the airfield. Adolph Berle, who rather liked Sicé and felt that he could work with him, reported that Sicé, who had visited him in Washington at the time of the New Caledonia crisis in 1942, had been ordered to London, "most likely to be fired."[55] Sicé in fact lost his position and was transferred to a lesser post for his transgression.

Dismissal was the fate of Maurice Dejean, de Gaulle's first commissioner for foreign affairs. In the midst of one of his tempestuous disputes with Churchill over the Mid-East, de Gaulle accused Dejean of being "insufficiently sensitive about the honor of France in his dealings with the British." When Dejean replied that he was just as French as was General de Gaulle, the Free-French leader replied that while he might be, Maurice Dejean was no longer commissioner of foreign affairs.[56] René Massigli eventually replaced Dejean.[57] Of course Admiral d'Argenlieu's accusation of compliance and softness toward the Americans also brought Sautot's career as Free-French governor of New Caledonia to an end.

American Security and the Fate of French Colonies in the Pacific

Although the American arrival in New Caledonia had been for military purposes, by early 1943 Roosevelt's thoughts about a postwar security arrangement at French expense began to take concrete form. At Roosevelt's request the joint chiefs of staff ordered the general board of the Navy to draft a report on American security needs in the Pacific "without regard to current sovereignty."[58] In three separate reports the general board, headed by Admiral Thomas A. Hart, outlined what can be described as an American system of military domination in the Pacific. By transferring control to the United States of Japanese Mandated Islands, certain British-island possessions in the Central Pacific, and all of French island territories after the war the United States would obtain a vast security zone extending from the West Coast to the shores of Asia.

The report was particularly harsh on the French and doubted the ability of the French to act as guardians of security in this part of the world. French possession of the many islands scattered over the South Pacific "constitutes a military situation incompatible with the probable responsibilities of the United States Government in these areas." France would be eliminated as a Pacific power since these islands, including the Marquesas, Society, the Tuamato Archipelago, and the New Caledonia-Loyalty Islands group, "lie in areas detached from other French interests and responsibilities" and should be shifted from French to American control.[59]

Another argument for shifting sovereignty was that France would be a weak and uncertain ally after the war. Admiral Hart observed that no one could foresee either the nature of a future government of France or how long it would take for the French State to recover and establish an effective administration over its empire. The general board assumed there would be little objection to such a transfer since most of these islands cost more to administer than any profits to be derived from their produce. Only in the case of mineral-rich New Caledonia, where the takeover would result in a net economic gain for the United States, would compensation be offered to France for the loss of colonial territory in the Pacific. Admiral Hart seemed little troubled that tidying up the imperial map of the Pacific for the benefit of American security interests would require transfers of sovereignty at the expense of America's wartime allies. The conclusion to be drawn from the general board's report is that not only President Roosevelt but also the American Navy had developed a rather dictatorial attitude toward the colonial territories of America's allies by the spring of 1943.

The issue of New Caledonia as compensation for the First World War and Lend-lease debts reappeared when President Roosevelt proposed that a group of senators undertake an around-the-world fact-finding mission to determine American postwar security needs.[60] Senator Richard B. Russell of Georgia headed a special committee that included two other Democratic senators, Albert Chandler of Kentucky and James Mead of New York, and two Republican senators, Henry Cabot Lodge of Massachusetts and Ralph Brewster of Maine. The Russell committee visited U.S. battlefields and military installations in Great Britain, North Africa, China, India, Australia, New Guinea and the Pacific, notably New Caledonia.[61]

Upon his return to the United States Senator Russell reported his findings to the Senate. He deplored what he claimed was a diplomatic unwillingness to defend American interests abroad. "Kid-glove diplomacy does not have any place in today's international dealings," he announced. Senator Russell's argument was that since American money and sweat had converted New Caledonia into an impregnable fortress and American boys were about to lose their lives in liberating France, the United States could ask for the negotiation of perpetual lease of naval bases in New Caledonia and North Africa. He called for Americans to use the leverage of their considerable investment in New Caledonia to insist upon "either title to all of New Caledonia or perpetual rights in and to the bases and facilities we have constructed".[62]

Needless to say, these remarks brought protests from Algiers and were denounced in New Caledonia. Senator Russell's report to the Senate on his fact-finding mission came at the moment when Governor Laigret had embarked upon his anti-American campaign in New Caledonia, and it added fuel to Laigret's fire. It also upset Gaullist authorities in Algiers. As a response to Senator Russell's claims, the FCNL's representative in Washington, Henri Hoppenot, suggested that "without indulging in polemics," the FCNL might remind the State Department of the American Government's promised restitution of all parts of French Empire to French sovereignty after the war. He noted that New Caledonia had been placed at the disposition of U.S. forces after Pearl Harbor, and this spontaneous act of cooperation should be used as a starting point for discussing any U.S. strategic requests.[63]

President Roosevelt's vision of a future world security order and the apparently modest role for France in this arrangement became apparent to General de Gaulle when he visited Washington and New York in July 1944. Roosevelt sketched his ideas "in broad strokes" according to de Gaulle, who sensed a "will to power" beneath the idealistic, global vision of the American president, a vision which "appeared to me to be grandiose as well as worrisome for Europe and for France."[64] In his conversations with General de Gaulle in Washington, the American president assured his French guest that such things as leased bases and a trusteeship system "could be worked out" at the end of the war. The President's breezy confidence was hardly reassuring to General de Gaulle.

The Gaullists were not alone in their anxieties over the American president's plans or in their opposition to them, and support for Free-French resistance to Roosevelt's plans appeared from unexpected sources: Australia and New Zealand. President Roosevelt's declarations to the Pacific War Council on 12 January 1944 alarmed representatives from both New Zealand and Australia. At the Pacific War Council meeting Roosevelt had stated that all islands in the Pacific south of the equator should be placed under a trusteeship with Australia and possibly New Zealand assuming responsibility for New Caledonia. Roosevelt complained to Sir Owen Dixon, the Australian minister to the United States, that "the whole French situation was a source of trouble." He thought that Nouméa, like Dakar, should be placed under a joint trusteeship for purposes of defense, with the French retaining local administrative responsibilities.[65] Like the United States and Brazil in Dakar, Australia and New Zealand would be acting on behalf of United Nations' security interests.

Roosevelt was confident that New Zealand and Australian authorities would back him up in not giving New Caledonia back to the French.[66] To the contrary, Herbert V. Evatt, the Australian minister for foreign affairs, complained bitterly of President Roosevelt's habit of deciding issues without consulting his allies. The Pacific War Council meeting confirmed his fear that the United States intended to impose its will without considering the interests of Australia and New Zealand, two states that were directly concerned with future security arrangements in the

Southwest Pacific. He became an advocate for retaining French sovereignty in New Caledonia.

Roosevelt did not bother to consult officials from Australia and New Zealand, and he kept the Free French completely and deliberately in the dark on the fate of French colonies in the Pacific, particularly New Caledonia and Indochina. In his report on the 12 January meeting of the Pacific War Council, the Australian representative in Washington, Sir Owen Dixon, observed that President Roosevelt had specifically asked that the FCNL in Algiers not be informed of these discussions. "After all," Roosevelt harrumphed, "it was not the French who were winning the war," and decisions about the colonial possessions in the Pacific would be based upon what would be best for the future security of the region, at least from an American perspective.[67] When Roosevelt discovered that his comments had reached the Free French by way of Vichy radio, he refused to call another meeting of the Pacific War Council.[68]

While the Australians had long wanted to be part of any security arrangement or postwar "police force" for the region (a memorandum from April 1943 stated that Australia should demand rights to maintain bases in Timor, New Guinea, New Britain, the Solomon Islands, New Hebrides and Nouméa), President Roosevelt's performance at the Pacific War Council produced a growing identity with the Free-French position.[69] By January 1944 the Australian position had shifted toward the idea of cooperation with the Free French rather than the Americans in any future South Pacific security arrangement. Evatt informed Johnson that Australia had a "deep obligation to the Free French" and was "publicly pledged to do its utmost to maintain the sovereignty of France in its present South Pacific possessions," pointedly adding: "Similar pledges have been given by other [members] of the United Nations."[70] Evatt continued to press the issue of Australian support for French sovereignty in its Pacific colonies in messages to Prime Minister Curtin, who was attending the Conference of Commonwealth Ministers in London. He observed that General de Gaulle's supporters had "saved the situation" in New Caledonia while French officials had yielded to the Japanese in Indochina. The Free-French defense of French colonial interests had found an ally in Australia, ironically the Dominion that at times had been suspected of having its own ambitions for New Caledonia.

In the final analysis New Caledonia, along with all of the French colonies, would be saved from the American "menace" as American attitudes toward General de Gaulle altered with the liberation of metropolitan France in the summer of 1944. More than Gaullist intransigence, American concern over the threat that the Soviet Union posed to European security played a crucial role in favoring a strong France with its empire intact. New Caledonia's fate, along with the future of the French Empire in the postwar world, was decided thousands of miles from the shores of the French colony as Allied leaders debated plans for a postwar world order. A shift in American policies toward France and General de Gaulle's government, much more than Governor Laigret's intransigence, would clear the way for an imperial restoration and overcome Roosevelt's determination that the prewar colonial arrangement had to be altered.

American policy toward de Gaulle gradually began to change during the months leading up to the Normandy landings. In late August 1943 the American and British governments provided limited recognition of the FCNL in Algiers as the organization qualified to administer liberated colonial territory and to conduct the French war effort in cooperation with the Allies. However, the American position was more restrained than the British view and explicitly omitted any recognition of the committee as a provisional government for France or the French Empire.[71] This limited acceptance was hardly reassuring to General de Gaulle concerning the prospect of forming a temporary government in France at the time of liberation.

Would the Allies, and particularly the Americans, prevent General de Gaulle from establishing his authority as France was liberated? In his opposition to General de Gaulle, President Roosevelt continued to insist that the French people should be allowed to choose their own form of government and select their own leader. He stated frequently that he would not have American armed forces impose any individual, certainly not General de Gaulle, upon the French people. This could mean the creation of an Allied Military Government of Occupied Territory (AMGOT) until such time as the French could organize elections, as had occurred in defeated Italy. Roosevelt had frequently referred to the Allied military presence in Algeria as an "occupation" in which military needs were paramount. He insisted that General Eisenhower had to have a free hand in civil as well as military matters.

Earlier the Gaullists had denounced the massive American presence in New Caledonia as an "occupation." Fears of a military rule under martial law had appeared in New Caledonia at the time of the riot and again at the time of Admiral Halsey's frustration over what he perceived to be a lack of cooperation on the part of the Free French. Throughout the American presence in New Caledonia American officers did not impose any political control of the civilian administration, which remained in the hands of the Gaullist officials and the local administrative council. Although American military rule was imposed neither in North Africa nor in New Caledonia, in light of President Roosevelt's pronouncements Gaullist anxieties about AMGOT remained very much alive on the eve of D-Day. De Gaulle dreaded the idea of AMGOT for France since it would imply that France was a defeated power to be treated as part of Allied occupation policy and not as a liberated ally.

Liberation, 1944

American military leaders opposed President Roosevelt's proposal for a military occupation of France at the time of liberation. Their opposition was based upon the impracticality of having military officers responsible for civilian government, whether in France, Algeria or New Caledonia. In Washington the Under-Secretary for War John J. McCloy warned that "it would be 'dynamite' to intervene in the internal affairs of France as we used to do in small Central American States." Any attempt to implement AMGOT would be resented by de Gaulle and would be considered "obnoxious by the French people whatever their political views."[72] After some persuading, Secretary of War Stimson supported McCloy and argued against burdening Eisenhower with responsibility for a military government in liberated France.

McCloy believed that the United States had more to gain from accepting General de Gaulle as head of the Provisional Government in France than in continuing to oppose him. There were a number of issues that would have to be resolved such as France's postwar frontiers in Europe and the status of the overseas empire. The latter issue was important for Roosevelt's security system, and McCloy rather realistically argued that the arrangement would have to be negotiated with France rather than imposed. Unless General de Gaulle was consulted on such matters, McCloy warned, "It will be extremely difficult to obtain from France the concessions in respect of her empire which I imagine we would very much like to have, such as port and air base concessions in Africa and perhaps bases or rights in New Caledonia, Indochina, etc."[73] For all practical purposes AMGOT had been abandoned before the Normandy landings.

The Allied supreme commander, General Eisenhower, was firmly opposed to AMGOT or any military occupation. He disliked the idea of having his officers absorbed in what he called "the man wasting job" of civil government. During his time as Allied commander in North Africa, Eisenhower was "plainly upset" at Roosevelt's insistence upon a military occupation and administration of French North Africa to the point of risking his military career. He told Captain Butcher that if the President insisted upon a military occupation, "he would of course carry out the order, but then [would] ask to be relieved, which would no doubt mean reversion to the rank of lieutenant colonel, and retirement."[74] To be sure, civil affairs officers were necessary, but not as military governors. Their assignment was to work with local authorities. Who would constitute these authorities? Eisenhower, unlike Roosevelt, wanted to cooperate with de Gaulle's representatives, and he secured a last-minute promise from Roosevelt on the eve of D-Day that he could do so as the Allied forces liberated French territory.[75] The trouble was that no one bothered to inform de Gaulle whose fury at the Americans, who had printed occupation currency, erupted on the eve of D-Day. De Gaulle would later claim credit in his memoirs for having blocked AMGOT, but the American military commanders in the field and the war department in Washington had no intention of introducing a military government in France, any more than they had in New Caledonia or North Africa.[76] Still the threat of imposing a military occupation was always there, and the issue of AMGOT added another dose to poison American relations with the Free French.

The liberation of Paris in August allowed General de Gaulle to establish a provisional government in the French capital. Over the next two months he sent his political commissioners throughout the country. The General's popularity convinced Roosevelt that de Gaulle was in fact the choice of the French people. After further delays, the United States and Great Britain formally recognized de Gaulle as head of the French provisional government on 23 October 1944. General Leclerc liberated Strasbourg that Fall so that by November 1944 General de Gaulle's Government controlled the entire territory of metropolitan France except for a German-held pocket around the Alsatian city of Colmar and enclaves of German resistance in some Atlantic ports. The provisional government also ruled the French Empire with the exception of Indochina, where Vichy's governor, Admiral Decoux, hung tenaciously to power under the harsh and suspicious gaze of a Japanese occupation army that eventually took over the French colony on 9 March 1945.

While the war department had resisted Roosevelt's ideas about a military government for liberated France, the American State Department began to question Roosevelt's insistence that France should not be allowed to resume its role as a colonial power. State Department officials recognized a contradiction between Roosevelt's position that would place certain French territories under an international trusteeship and promises that he had made to respect France's territorial integrity. As the liberation of metropolitan France progressed, advocates of accommodation, despite an earlier hostility toward General de Gaulle and his supporters, began to emerge. Even Cordell Hull, who had been harsh in his condemnation of French colonial practices and was a staunch advocate of opening the European empires to free trade, reminded the President of promises given. President Roosevelt ignored the reminders sent to him by Hull in January 1944 of the existing commitments that had been made to the Free French, to General Giraud on the eve of the landings in North Africa, and to the Vichy government.[77]

Under-Secretary of State Sumner Welles, Roosevelt's "global strategist," also reminded President Roosevelt of his prior promises and obligations despite his strong opposition to imperialism in general and his criticism of French colonial practices.[78] Welles mentioned the promises the president had given during Anthony Eden's trip to the United States in March 1943 on the restoration of France and its territorial integrity, including the empire, after the war. Eden had commented that Roosevelt was being "rather hard on the French" in his insistence that they should not be allowed possession of Indochina after the war, and at that time Welles reminded FDR that he was on record favoring the restoration of the French Colonial Empire. Roosevelt breezily commented that all of this could be "ironed out" later and his position would be "rectified."[79] Roosevelt remained adamant in his opposition to colonialism, despite a growing opposition to his position within the war department and, increasingly, within the State Department as well.

A more pragmatic view of an American need for a strong and allied France after the war was beginning to be heard in 1944. Welles opposed Roosevelt's ideas on disarming the French, arguing that "the loss of France as a strong, well-armed power would create a vacuum, which the Soviet Union would fill."[80] Fear of the Soviet Union's strength in Europe after the war became the argument that ultimately enabled advocates in Washington, who favored restoration of the French Empire, to prevail during the last eighteen months of the war. The shift in American attitudes and policy toward the Free French following Liberation would prove decisive, although the policy shift was not yet apparent as the war entered its final phase in 1944/45.

After the Liberation de Gaulle was in a strong position to claim France's status as one of the victorious powers upon the defeat of the Axis, but the future of the French Empire remained clouded by Roosevelt's persistent interest in obtaining military bases on French-controlled territory for his international police force. He continued to advocate a trusteeship system whereby certain British, Dutch and French colonial possessions, as well as territory conquered from the Japanese in the Pacific, might be administered by selected trustee powers on behalf of an international organization. Despite recognition of General de Gaulle as head of the provisional government and the arguments from within his own administration in favor of some accommodation with de Gaulle, Washington's challenge to French imperial sovereignty remained as the war entered what would be its final year.

President Roosevelt's concern for American security needs and his determination to reduce, if not eliminate, the French presence in the Pacific, which he had begun to consider in the aftermath of events in New Caledonia, persisted to the end of his life. He remained convinced that France would be either too weak or too unreliable to guarantee the security of certain strategic areas. In a conversation in mid-March 1945 with Charles Taussig, one of his close advisors on colonial affairs, the president repeated his view that Indochina and New Caledonia should be taken from France and placed under a trusteeship. The only concession that he would make was to allow that France might be the trustee power in these colonies if independence were guaranteed as a future goal.[81] In the meantime, the United States would insist on military rights in New Caledonia to assure a long-term security presence in the South Pacific. During a cabinet meeting after his return from the Yalta Conference, he stated that Australia's proposal to keep the United States north of the equator was unacceptable, and he called for military rights in Nouméa while leaving the "economic accruals" from New Caledonia to the French.[82] New Caledonia and Nouméa were to be part of a postwar American security system for the Pacific.

Before the battles that would bring about the liberation of metropolitan France and restore France's full independence, General de Gaulle began a counter-offensive to defend the French Empire against the "elementary sentiments" of the Americans.[83] Colonial reform was "the only way to save our empire from foreign ambitions," according to one writer.[84] De Gaulle expressed his desire for colonial reform in a speech at Constantine on 7 December 1943, and the next day Pleven read a statement that promised Indochina a new status in a more federal colonial system.[85] Whether or not de Gaulle's provisional government would actually abandon France's highly centralized system of colonial rule remained to be seen.

The Brazzaville Conference, which was held from 30 January to 8 February 1944, is often cited as evidence of General de Gaulle's determination to reform the French Empire after the war. Twenty governors-general and governors from France's sub-Saharan colonies, Madagascar and Réunion gathered at Brazzaville to propose a new French community that would strengthen ties between the empire and metropolitan France. The colonial rulers, led by Felix Eboué, who had been an early supporter of General de Gaulle and a member of the Empire Defense Council, called for greater investment in education and social reforms to improve the condition and status of indigenous peoples. On crucial political issues, such as a possibility of a more autonomous, federal system, or even eventual independence, Brazzaville was basically a reassertion of French authority. Although Brazzaville has been considered an early step toward decolonization, the reality is that autonomy and the longer-term goal of self-government were rejected. The French Empire was to remain French. From the perception of the governing elite the empire was essential to France's postwar recovery.

New Caledonia would have an important role in this imperial reconstruction, but the nature of its contribution depended upon the way in which the Caledonians responded to Gaullist plans. Would Caledonia be a source of strength or weakness? Much depended upon how politics played out in the colony as it moved from a wartime to a postwar political environment. For the Gaullists and the newly appointed Governor Tallec, the question was one of local autonomy and the ambitions of the local political class. The future place of New Caledonia in a restored French Empire turned upon their attitudes and ambitions.

In the meantime, the future status of New Caledonia and the American departure remained uncertain when Governor Jacques Tallec arrived in the French colony at the beginning of 1944 to replace the departing Interim Governor Christian Laigret.

Notes

1. Roosevelt to Leahy, 20 January 1942, Elliott Roosevelt, *F.D.R.: His Personal Letters* vol. 1 (New York, 1947–50), 1275, cited in William Roger Louis, *Imperialism at Bay: The United States and the Decolonization of the British Empire 1941–1945* (New York, 1978): 155n. 24.
2. Roosevelt to Pétain, 27 December 1941, and State to Leahy on behalf of the President, 3 November 1941, *Foreign Relations of the United States* (henceforth *FRUS*), (Washington, 1961) 1941, vol. 2, 205–6, 196–7.
3. State Department (Atherton) to Pleven, 14 October 1941, Ministère des Affaires Étrangères (MAE) Guerre 1939–45, London CNF, vol. 75.

4. Hull to Leahy, 28 October 1941, *FRUS* 1941, vol. 2, 455.
5. "Memorandum by Mr. Samuel Reber of the Division of European Affairs," 12 January 1942, *FRUS* 1942, vol. 2, 503.
6. Acting Secretary of State to the Consul at Nouméa (MacVitty), 23 February 1942, *FRUS* 1942, vol. 3, 691. Admiral d'Argenlieu published the statement in New Caledonia on 28 February 1942, and it was published as a State Department bulletin in the United States on 2 March.
7. The Acting Secretary of State to the French Ambassador (Henry-Haye), 13 April 1942, *FRUS* 1942, vol. 3, 563.
8. Halifax (Washington) to Foreign Office, 23 May 1942, United Kingdom Public Record Office (PRO) FO371/31884/Z4292.
9. Winston S. Churchill, *The Second World War*, vol. 3, *The Grand Alliance* (Boston, 1951), 667.
10. William Roger Louis, *Imperialism at Bay*, 28.
11. Minutes of President's Meeting with Joint Chiefs of Staff, 15 November 1943 aboard USS Iowa, *FRUS Conferences at Cairo and Tehran*, 195.
12. Mario Rossi, *Roosevelt and the French* (Westport, Conn., 1993), 110.
13. Marginal comments by Mr. Spaeght and Mr. Cavendish-Bentinck in Halifax (Washington) to Foreign Office, 23 May 1942, PRO FO371/31884/Z4292.
14. Rossi, *Roosevelt*, 129; Tripartite meeting of 28 November 1943 in *FRUS Conferences at Cairo and Tehran 1943*, 509–10.
15. See Louis, *Imperialism at Bay*, 226–27.
16. "Reasons Underlying this Government's Lack of Confidence in General de Gaulle," memorandum of 20 January 1944 prepared by Bonbright, U.S. National Archives and Record Administration (USNARA), Dept. of State, Mathews Hickerson File, microfilm roll 13.
17. Conversation with M. Pleven (American Policy towards the Free French) 26 May 1942, appendix 3–7, Kittredge "Present Situation ... of the Free French Movement," August 1942, Kittredge Papers, Hoover Archives, Stanford.
18. Jean-Louis Crémieux-Brilhac, *La France Libre: De l'appel du 18 juin à la Libération* (Paris, 1996), 305.
19. "Attitude of Free French in London," Memorandum of Conversation between Etienne Boegner and A.A. Berle, 1 October 1942, USNARA State Dec. File 851.01/672.
20. Eric Roussel, *Charles de Gaulle* (Paris, 2002), 298–302, has an extensive quotation from Boegner's account, which is at the Fondation Saint-John Perse, Aix-en-Provence, archives diplomatiques d'Alexis Léger, entretien de Gaulle-Étienne Boegner, 28 May 1942.
21. Interview with Jean-Louis Crémieux-Brilhac, Paris, 20 December 1993.
22. Crémieux-Brilhac, *La France Libre*, 38.
23. "Memorandum of Conversation with Henri Hoppenot, Delegate of the FCNL, 30 October 1943, *The Adolph A. Berle Diary*, Hyde Park, N.Y., Franklin D. Roosevelt Library, roll 5, frames 0158–0159. Memorandum of conversation between M. Hoppenot and M. Mathews, 13 October 1943, USNARA State Dec. File 851.01/3069.
24. Massigli, *Une comédie des erreurs, 1943–1956* (Paris, 1978), 25.
25. Memorandum on France, 29 January 1944, USNARA State, Mathews-Hickerson files M1244, roll 13.
26. Commissioner of Foreign Affairs (Dejean) to Tixier, 17 December 1941, MAE Guerre 1939–45, London CNF, vol. 310.
27. CNF London to Librance, Washington, "Report of Conversation between Admiral Stark and General de Gaulle," 19 December 1942, MAE Guerre 1939–45, Algiers CNFL-GPRF, vol. 1463, Massigli papers.
28. Charles de Gaulle, *Mémoires de Guerre:* vol. 1 *L'Appel 1940–1942* (Paris, 1954), 209. "The Gaullist Comportment" in Charles Cogan, *Charles de Gaulle: A Brief Biography with Documents* (Boston, 1996), 35–40.

29. Charles G. Cogan, *French Negotiating Behavior: Dealing with* La Grande Nation, (Washington, D.C., 2003), 87, 150.
30. Testimony of Georges Boris, 27 May and 3 June 1947, Archives Nationales, section contemporaine (ANSC) 72AJ 220.
31. René Bouscat, *De Gaulle-Giraud: Dossier d'une mission* (Paris, 1967), 61.
32. Massigli, *Comédie des erreurs*, 16.
33. See Cogan, *French Negotiating Behavior*, 135.
34. Cited in Charles Cogan, *Oldest Allies, Guarded Friends: The United States and France since 1940* (Westport, 1994), 5.
35. Charles de Gaulle, *Mémoires*, vol. 1, 184.
36. A good, brief account of this interview from an American perspective may be found in Arthur L. Funk, *De Gaulle: The Crucial Years* (Norman, 1959), 46.
37. Tixier and Philip, Libfrance to CNF, 22 November 1942, Archives Nationales, Section d'Outre-mer (ANSOM), CNF carton 8. Philip's contempt for Roosevelt has been confirmed by Jean Lacouture, *De Gaulle: Le rebelle 1890–1940*, vol. 1 (Paris, 1984), 545, and in the interview that he gave to Henri Michel in 1947, AN section contemporaine, AN72 AJ220.
38. "Le Président Roosevelt et la politique américaine à l'égard de la France," 27 November 1942, ANSOM, CNF carton 8.
39. Cited in Cogan, *Oldest Allies*, 43n. 102. See also Cogan, *French Negotiating Behavior*, 80, 131.
40. D'Argenlieu to de Gaulle, 19 May 1942, AN, Papiers d'Argenlieu 517AP.
41. Bouscat, *De Gaulle-Giraud*, 94.
42. Christian Pineau, *La simple verité 1940–1945* (Paris, 1960), 168.
43. Freeman Mathews, Memorandum for the Secretary of State of conversation with Robert Murphy in Algiers, 30 December 1943, USNARA State Department, Mathews Hickerson Files 1934–1947, subject file 1940–1947, France M1244, roll 13.
44. H. Earle Russell (American consul general) to Secretary of State, "Increasing Anti-American Propaganda in Casablanca," 1 September 1943, USNARA State Dec File 851.01/2920.
45. Colonel de Chevigné to London, 7 July 1943, MAE Guerre 1939–45, Algiers CFLN-GPRF, vol. 135.
46. Pilot Officer Raymond Alfred M_____, to Beatrice and Bruce Gould, 14 November 1943, with covering letter of Bruce Gould to Secretary of State Cordell Hull, 9 December 1943, USNARA State Dec. File 711.51/341.
47. Kittredge to Philip, 24 April 1943, AN Fla 3729.
48. Memorandum of conversation between General Bedell Smith, Ray Atherton, Freeman Mathews and Under-secretary Berle, 13 October 1943, USNARA State, Mathews-Hickerson File, roll 10.
49. De Gaulle to FF diplomatic posts, 7 April 1943, MAE Guerre 1939–45, Algiers CFLN-GPRF, vol. 1463, Massigli papers, and in Charles de Gaulle, *Lettres, notes et carnets (LNC), juillet 1941–mai 1943* (Paris, 1982), 566–67.
50. Governor Djibouti to de Gaulle, 14 April 1943, MAE Guerre 1939–45, Algiers CFLN-GPRF, vol. 1463, Massigli papers.
51. André Philip interview, 13 June 1947, ANSC 72AJ 220.
52. Report dated 1 October 1942, "The Growth of Anti-American Feeling in New Caledonia prepared by a 'local observer,'" AA CRS A981, Australian Archives, Canberra.
53. Testimony of General P. Billotte, 4 and 11 July 1950, ANSC 72AJ 220.
54. Memorandum (Bonbright), "Reasons Underlying this Government's Lack of Confidence in General de Gaulle," 20 January 1944, USNARA State, Mathews-Hickerson, roll 13.
55. "Memorandum", 2 May 1942, *The Adolph A. Berle Diary*, Hyde Park, N.Y., Franklin D. Roosevelt Library, roll 4, frames 1-3-104.
56. André Philip interview, 13 June 1947, ANSC 72AJ 220.

57. On dismissals of Sicé and Dejean, see Martin Thomas, *The French Empire at War 1940–1945* (Manchester and New York, 1998), 110, 113, 148.
58. Louis, *Imperialism at Bay*, 259.
59. Chairman of the General Board to the Secretary of the Navy, "Change in Status of Islands in the South Pacific," 6 April 1943, FDR Library, Hyde Park, N.Y., Map Room, Box 162, Naval Aide's File.
60. On prewar discussions of obtaining New Caledonia as compensation for First World War debts, see Charles J. Weeks, Jr., "An Hour of Temptation: American Interests in New Caledonia, 1939–1945," *Australian Journal of Politics and History* 35 (Winter, 1989): 188–89.
61. Gilbert C. Fite, *Richard B. Russell, Jr.: Senator from Georgia* (Chapel Hill, 1991), 188–95.
62. "Digest of Russell's Report to the Senate on His Tour of the War Areas," *New York Times*, 29 October 1943, 12:3. In the course of his trip Russell claimed that the Americans were dupes of British imperialists, comments that led to protest from the foreign office and brought a surge of anti-American sentiment in Great Britain.
63. Hoppenot (Washington) to CFLN (Algiers) 29 October 1943, MAE Guerre 1939–45, Algiers CFLN-GPRF, vol. 132.
64. De La Gorce, *De Gaulle*, 522 from de Gaulle, *Mémoires*, vol. 2: *l'unité 1942–44* (Paris, 1956), 237–38.
65. Sir Owen Dixon to John Curtin (PM), 24 June 1943, doc. 434 in *Documents on Australian Foreign Policy 1937–1945 (DAFP)*, vol. 6: *July 1942–December 1943* ed. W.J. Hudson and H.J.W. Stokes, asst. ed. Ashton Robinson & Kenneth Power, (Canberra, 1983).
66. Louis, *Imperialism at Bay*, 289–90, 299; Minister in Australia (Johnson) to Secretary of State, 25 February 1944, *FRUS* 1944, vol. 3, 187.
67. Dixon to External Affairs, 13 January 1944, doc. 13 in *DAFP*, vol. 7, *1944* (Canberra, 1988).
68. Weeks, "Hour of Temptation" 188.
69. Draft Memorandum by W.D. Forsyth (Second Secretary for Pacific Affairs, Department of External Affairs), 7 April 1943, doc. 153, *DAFP*, vol 6.
70. Evatt to Johnson, 24 February 1944, doc. 56; Evatt to Curtin, 24 March 1944, doc. 94; Evatt to Curtin, 5 May 1944, doc. 132, *DAFP*, vol. 7.
71. Robert Dallek, *Franklin D. Roosevelt and American Foreign Policy 1932–1945* (New York, 1981 ed.), 408–9.
72. McCloy, Memoranda to Secretary of War, 13 and 20 January and 29 February 1944, USNARA, RG 107 Records of the Office of the Secretary of War, ASW 370.8, France.
73. Memorandum from McCloy to Stimson, 19 June 1944, USNARA, Records of the Office of European Affairs (Mathews-Hickerson Files) 1934–1947, Reference Subject File 1940–1947: France (microfilm M1244, roll 13).
74. Alfred D. Chandler, et al. *The Papers of Dwight David Eisenhower: The War Years*, vol. 2 (Baltimore, 1970): doc. 755, p. 889 n. 2, reference to *Butcher Diary*, 4 January 1943.
75. Chandler, *Papers of Eisenhower*, vol. 3, doc. 1489, 19 January 1944, 1667–68 and n. 2.
76. Mario Rossi argues convincingly that American military leaders, particularly Eisenhower, opposed the idea of AMGOT, in "United States Military Authorities and Free France, 1942–1944," *The Journal of Military History* 61, 1 (Jan. 1997): 49–64.
77. "United State Position With Respect to French Territory After the War," 7 January 1944, *FRUS* 1944, vol. 3, 770–73.
78. In a 1942 Memorial Day speech Welles had declared that the era of imperialism was over, and his views seemed to fit with Roosevelt's anticolonialism. He presided over the committee to study postwar reconstruction, including future status of the colonial empires. See Louis, *Imperialism at Bay*, 162–3.
79. Ibid. 228. Benjamin Welles, *Sumner Welles: FDR's Global Strategist* (New York, 1997), 296–97.
80. Sumner Welles, *Seven Decisions*, 186–87, cited in B. Welles, *Sumner Welles*, 298.

81. "Memorandum of Conversation, by the Adviser on Caribbean Affairs (Tausig)," 15 March 1944, *FRUS* 1945, vol. 1, 124. Louis, *Imperialism at Bay*, 486.
82. Walter Millis, ed., *The Forrestal Diaries* (New York, 1951) entry for 9 March 1945, 33. Original cited in Weeks, "Hour of Temptation," 193.
83. André Kaspi, *La libération de la France juin 1944–janvier 1946* (Paris, 1995), 231.
84. M. Baube to René Pleven, 13 December 1943, MAE Guerre 1939–45, Algiers CFLN/GPRF 132.
85. De la Gorce, *De Gaulle*, 610.

CHAPTER 8

FROM COMBAT BASE TO REST AND REHABILITATION AREA: THE AMERICAN DEPARTURE

If President Roosevelt's musings represented an American threat to New Caledonia and the integrity of the French Empire, the Caledonians' desire for autonomy presented the Gaullists with another potential menace. From the moment of the American arrival the Gaullists feared that an American military presence offered Caledonian autonomists an opportunity to play the Americans against central Free-French authority. Laigret's anti-American policy aimed to eliminate this possibility and gain the support of the Caledonian political elite, which had been upset by Admiral d'Argenlieu's behavior in 1942. The newly appointed governor, Jacques Tallec, would confront both the American external threat and the internal, autonomist temptation. He also would face a growing restlessness among the excluded of New Caledonia, the indigenous Kanak and the indentured Asian labor populations. New Caledonia remained a challenge for any colonial governor.

Governor Tallec

Governor Tallec flew in to New Caledonia from San Francisco on 14 February 1944. Interim Governor Laigret and Brigadier General Ray Owens, General Lincoln's replacement as commanding officer of the First Island Command, met the new governor's plane. That afternoon Governor Tallec, Governor Laigret, General Owens and other ranking American and French officers reviewed American and French troops, who paraded in honor of the newly arrived governor. A welcome dinner was held that evening, and in the next few days Governor Tallec made courtesy calls on the American Army and Navy commanders.[1] The Americans hoped that the new governor would bring a less confrontational and more cooperative approach to their relations with Free-French officials on the island during the war's final months.

Governor Tallec was a graduate of the prestigious École Polytechnique. After graduation he worked for twelve years as head financial officer in Lebanon where he was at the time of the 1940 defeat. He became involved in a failed attempt to rally Lebanon to de Gaulle in 1940. Although several members of the plot were jailed, Tallec was sent back to France where he was placed under house arrest. He left France when the Germans invaded the unoccupied zone in November 1942 and made his way to London where he joined the Free French. His relationship with de Gaulle was somewhat "distant," according to his son Yves Tallec, since both were strong-willed individuals, but he had the full confidence of René Pleven.

Tallec's instructions were simple and general. He was to do what he could to assure that the war was won, and he was to keep the French flag flying in New Caledonia. Tallec was given considerable latitude to stabilize the situation in a difficult colony, which suited the new governor's administrative style. He prided himself on his independent judgment and was willing to act and then take responsibility for his decisions. Pleven assured him of his full support, and he suggested that Tallec stop in London on his way to New Caledonia for consultation with Admiral d'Argenlieu. Pleven advised Tallec to listen to d'Argenlieu, but he should not feel obliged to accept his advice and should use his own judgment in evaluating the situation in New Caledonia.

Upon reaching New Caledonia Tallec decided that he could work with the Americans, despite the negative reports of Governor Laigret. Although he recognized that they held anticolonialist views, his experience in the Middle East convinced him that the British, whose colonial practices he considered deceptive, were a greater threat to the French Empire than the Americans. At least he knew where the Americans stood. He became convinced that even if the Americans leased a base in New Caledonia after the war, they did not intend to take over the colony. In his mind Australia posed a more immediate and serious threat.[2]

One of Governor Tallec's first tasks was to reduce the anti-American sentiments that Governor Laigret had encouraged by repairing relations with American military authorities on the island. He immediately declared that he was a partisan of Franco-American cooperation. As a step in this direction, he reinstated Lieutenant de Montaudoin as American liaison officer. Governor Laigret had sent Montaudoin to the Motor Pool, ostensibly for having left open a secure safe but in reality for having been too friendly with the Yanks. He also reappointed Brocard as French censor after Laigret had removed him for allegedly being too sympathetic to the Americans.[3] Governor Tallec permitted American soldiers and sailors to use the municipal swimming pool after Laigret had placed it off-limits. Above all he established and maintained good relations with the American military leadership, including Admiral Nimitz, Admiral Calhoun and

General Rose. The only exception was Admiral Halsey with whom he occasionally clashed concerning precedence of rank. Governor Tallec wished to smooth relations with the Americans in a spirit of cooperation. Yet the postwar status of New Caledonia had still not been resolved. Governor Tallec would be sensitive to any attempt to exploit the American presence for their own purposes, whether on the part of the Caledonian autonomists, Kanak, or indentured Asian workers.

The incoming governor's arrival corresponded with the departure of his predecessor, who left New Caledonia a few days later in the company of the head of his military police, Pierre Duval. The Caledonians had hoped that Governor Laigret's tenure would be permanent and so did some of America's other allies. B.C. Ballard, the Australian consul, would have preferred for Governor Laigret to remain to counter the overwhelming American presence.[4] The New Zealand military commander, Brigadier Dove, had hosted a small party for departing Governor Laigret at which the British consul and his wife, Mr. and Mrs. Johnston, were present, but not the Americans.[5] On his way through Sydney to take up his new assignment as governor of Mauretania in the West African desert, Laigret commented that Jacques Tallec would be in New Caledonia for only a few months since the Americans intended to takeover the island.[6] Commissioner of colonies René Pleven thanked Governor Laigret for his services during "the long interim."[7]

Long interim indeed. If the arrivals and departures of governors in New Caledonia had been "the waltz of the governors" before the Second World War, the rapid wartime turnovers could be described as "fast fox-trots." Jacques Tallec would be the sixth governor for New Caledonia in the forty-four months between the fall of France in June 1940 and his arrival in February 1944, a record that eclipsed even the most lively cadence of the Third Republic's waltz of the governors. The *Bulletin du Commerce* published an editorial noting that there had been thirty governors sent to New Caledonia in the past forty-seven years and fifteen since 1925.[8]

The elimination of the office of high commissioner for the Pacific meant that conflicts between two Free-French authorities would be ending, greatly simplifying Governor Tallec's task of speaking with a single voice in asserting French interests in New Caledonia. He still would have to deal with American ambitions for a postwar security order in the Pacific, and he would confront a number of potentially divisive social and political issues at the end of the war. Governor Tallec would remain in New Caledonia for three years, leaving in 1947 after overseeing the departure of the Americans and presiding over a transformation of New Caledonia's social and political life, a transformation influenced by the legacies and memories of the wartime experience and "the time of the Americans."

For all of the grumbling about and resistance to centralized French imperial authority, it is not clear that autonomy for the Caledonians meant separation from French imperial control. The autonomists wanted a greater say about running their own affairs, mainly for the benefit of the European settler population. Given, though, the historical antagonism between local and colonial authority, Tallec understood that his handling of local politics would be important if he were to keep the French flag flying over New Caledonia at the end of the war.

In addition to the autonomist preferences of the Caledonian political elite, Governor Tallec also would have to come to terms with the growing impatience of non-European Caledonians: Kanak and Asian indentured laborers. They were determined that New Caledonia not return to a prewar system that excluded them from any political voice and condemned them to subsistence wages in the mines or isolation on Kanak reservations. Demands for Kanak political participation in the affairs of the colony began to appear on the walls of Nouméa in the later stages of the war. Asian workers wanted an end to the indentured labor system and began drafting petitions to have it abolished. As the war threat moved away from the South Pacific, New Caledonian political and social issues emerged that would test Governor Tallec's skills as an administrator.

The Americans looked on as these issues bubbled up during the last eighteen months of the war as the war's combat theatres moved to the Southwest and Western Pacific in 1944. Nevertheless, American intelligence officers continued to inform their superiors of local opinion among the diverse populations of the island. The French continued to worry about these activities, fearing that the Americans might exploit local grievances or autonomist sentiments for their own advantage. But the American interest was driven less by political ambition than a concern about the possibility that local disturbances might cause an upheaval that would threaten security for the remaining military forces on the island.

Another arrival in New Caledonia at this time was Admiral Halsey, who returned to Nouméa in February from his meetings with President Roosevelt and Admiral Ernest King in Washington and with Admiral Chester Nimitz in Hawaii. During his trip Admiral Halsey became involved in planning for the next phase of the war in the Pacific, which the Americans believed would bring the defeat of Japan. Rival views on strategy for winning the war in the Pacific pitted the Navy against the ambitions of General Douglas MacArthur with whom Admiral Halsey had cooperated in organizing the drive up the Solomons toward Rabaul. General MacArthur intended his advance along the northern coast of New Guinea to be preparation for an assault on the Philippine Islands. MacArthur wanted the Navy to support his drive north, enabling him to fulfill his promise of a return to liberate the Philippine people from the Japanese occupation.

The Navy had another strategy that called for employment of a huge fleet of aircraft carriers, battleships, cruisers, destroyers, and support craft in an advance across the Central Pacific toward the Mariannas Islands, north of the Philippines. This drive had begun in late 1943 with the American attack upon Tarawa in the Gilbert Islands. The debate over these strategies was becoming increasingly heated as Halsey departed New Caledonia on 26 December 1943, heading for Washington by way of Hawaii. In Hawaii Admiral Nimitz informed Halsey that as soon as the Solomons campaign had been completed he would be relieved of his South Pacific Command. He would then be designated as one of the two commanders of the vast Blue Fleet that would have responsibility for carrying out the advance across the Central Pacific. Halsey was delighted with the new assignment.

The assignment however depended upon whether or not there would be a Central Pacific operation. General MacArthur was determined that the Navy would not upstage his return to the Philippines. Admiral Ernest King, commander-in-chief of the U.S. Fleet, was equally determined that the Navy would not play second fiddle to General MacArthur. After several tense meetings the American commanders agreed upon a two-pronged strategy in which the ambitions of MacArthur and the Navy were accommodated. While General MacArthur's forces leapfrogged along the coast of Northern Papua and New Guinea, the Navy would continue its advance from the Gilbert Islands toward the Mariannas. Navy and Marines would bypass Japanese strongholds in the Marshall and Caroline Island groups, employing the same leapfrogging techniques that had succeeded in the Solomons, en route to a showdown with the Japanese Navy in June 1944 at the Mariannas. This divided strategy was designed to assuage the ambitions of both General MacArthur and Admiral King.

For the Central Pacific offensive, the Americans had devised two designators for the Blue Fleet in its drive toward Japan. Under Admiral Raymond Spruance, the hero of Midway, the fleet was designated the Fifth Fleet. Admiral Spruance would command the first phase of the naval offensive from the opening salvo at Tarawa to the capture of the Mariannas in June 1944. Admiral Halsey then would replace Admiral Spruance after the Mariannas campaign, and the Fifth Fleet of Spruance would become the Third Fleet under Halsey's command.

During his final months in New Caledonia Admiral Halsey oversaw the final stage of the Solomons campaign. In mid-February, American and New Zealand forces occupied the Green Islands, giving the Allies an airfield only 115 miles from the Japanese base at Rabaul whose neutralization had been the main objective of nearly two years of sea and land battles in the Solomons. American forces occupied Emirau Island west of Rabaul a month later, completely isolating the Japanese garrison, which was now bypassed and surrendered only at the end of the war. This operation, combined with MacArthur's occupation of the Admiralty Islands further west of Rabaul, brought the Solomons campaign to an end.

On 15 June 1944, Admiral Halsey turned over command of the South Pacific forces to Vice-admiral John H. Newton. After saying farewell to his staff, Halsey drove to the Nouméa dock the next morning. Soldiers, sailors and people from the town lined the way. As Halsey stepped aboard the launch that would take him to the seaplane and Hawaii, he heard the cheers of the troops. "Their cheers and the bands and the flags stung my eyes," Halsey recalled. "I never saw Nouméa again."[9]

With the shift of the American war effort to the west and north of New Caledonia, the Free-French colony became a backwater in the Pacific war. From the spring of 1944 to the end of the war the island no longer had the strategic importance of 1942/43. This new status for New Caledonia occurred one year after Admiral d'Argenlieu had proclaimed that the colony was no longer on the front line of the war in the Pacific. Soldiers were transferred from the South Pacific to MacArthur's Southwest Pacific Command while sailors and most of the warships under Halsey sailed north to further strengthen the Blue Fleet. By August 1944 Noel Deschamps, the new Australian consul, could report that "New Caledonia has completed its transition from a combat base to a supply base and hospital center."[10]

With these changes the pace of wartime life in New Caledonia became more relaxed. Nouméa's harbor was less congested. The number of American soldiers and sailors stationed on the island was reduced. Traffic eased on the streets of Nouméa and along the highways of the interior. The sky became less crowded and noisy. New Caledonia had become a place for rest and recreation by the spring of 1944. Above all, the pressure for space to house the American military declined, enabling the Americans to return some buildings and facilities to their French owners.

The American military had constructed a number of hospital buildings and wards to accommodate the wounded who were recovering from the Solomon Islands battles. One major hospital for the Navy was adjacent to the lovely bay and white beach of Anse Vata. Other hospital wards had been constructed in Dumbea Valley, not far from the estate of Michel Vergès. Hospital facilities, an American cemetery and a fine, interdenominational church at Camp Barnes became part of the Caledonian landscape.[11] A multiwinged "Pentagon" headquarters building sprawled near Anse Vata beach. Sections of land provided storage space for vehicles nearby. "Motor Pool" and "Receiving" became and remain names of districts in greater Nouméa. As the fighting moved away from New Caledonia, Americans and Caledonians in the French colony awaited the outcome of the war both in the Pacific and in Europe where the decisive battles would occur in 1944 and 1945.

Like many of his predecessors, Governor Tallec was shocked by the attitudes that he found when he arrived in New Caledonia. He observed that mentally and physically "New Caledonia is no longer in the war."[12] All the Caledonians worried about was making as much money as possible from the American military presence, he reported. This same attitude could be found among demobilized veterans of the Pacific Battalion whose first thought upon discharge from service was to set up a shop and profit from the American trade, which they were able to do thanks to preferences given to veterans for liquor licenses. The Caledonians, including the veterans, were leaving the finishing of the war to the

Allies, and no one intended to fight beside them in the Pacific.[13] Worse yet, many of the Caledonian settlers continued to harbor "a profound disaffection" toward metropolitan France. As a result, Governor Tallec realized that he would have to be careful not to provoke or offend local sensibilities, particularly in any attempt to assert a strong, central authority; otherwise he might face disturbances and a resurgence of autonomist feelings on the island. He intended to move cautiously in dealing with local politics, diplomatically calling for new elections for a governing council.

Governor Tallec's caution and the persistence of autonomist sentiments surprised Pleven. He wrote that Governor Tallec's references to disaffection among the local population puzzled him. Governor Laigret had led him to believe that the presence and unpopularity of large numbers of Americans on the island had produced a wave of nationalistic, pro-French sentiment among the independent-minded settlers.[14] Laigret apparently had been less successful in using an anti-American campaign as a way of tying Caledonians to the national, Gaullist cause than he had claimed.

Autonomist Sentiment and Social and Labor Unrest

Autonomist sentiment could be found in the administrative council, which had served as an advisory body to the governor since Governor Sautot had appointed it shortly after the rally of 1940. The council considered its role to be more than advisory. Members of the administrative council had become extremely protective of the council's rights and prerogatives, as successive Free-French officials had discovered to their dismay. The administrative council had, for example, asserted its right to control the colony's wartime economy against the demands of the central authority of General de Gaulle's governing bodies, whether the early Empire Defense Council or, more recently, the Consultative Assembly in Algiers.[15] This defiance reflected old, long-standing resentments among many European settlers in New Caledonia. If the Gaullists felt that the Americans treated them as poor relations, many of the European Caledonians felt the same about the way in which the Free French or the Third Republic had treated them. But Governor Tallec did not think that this resentment over perceived metropolitan indifference translated into a desire to become part of an American Empire in the Pacific. In any event Tallec decided to work within the context of local politics in New Caledonia to achieve certain reforms that he felt were necessary to avoid social unrest, political disturbances and unnecessarily inflammatory rhetoric.

Both Tallec's predecessors, Montchamp and Laigret, had proposed elections as a way of obtaining a more cooperative council. Eventually they backed away from calling for elections, partly from uncertainty as to the outcome. Pierre Bergès was a popular political leader, and Free-French officials hesitated to challenge him on his home turf. Admiral d'Argenlieu had tried to remove Pierre Bergès and three of his allies by abduction, but this action had produced an embarrassing riot. Tallec's caution in dealing with the touchy issue of the administrative council and its claims was understandable. Shortly after his arrival the governor postponed until later in the year the elections that Governor Laigret had promised for March 1944. In the meantime, Tallec began to prepare the ground for ending indentured labor.

Governor Tallec's arrival at the beginning of 1944 coincided with rising social unrest and the emergence of protest movements among the Asian and Kanak populations of New Caledonia. The issue was wages, which reflected the impact of the American presence upon the economy and particularly upon wage scales during the war. As we have seen, the American arrival created an immediate demand for labor: stevedores to help unload the vessels, workers to assist in the construction of facilities in Nouméa and the interior, laundry services, taxi transportation, and employees to provide refreshments in Nouméa and near the American bases scattered throughout the island.[16]

The authorized employment of the local population was initially confined to French settlers and Kanak. Employees in the shops obtained unexpectedly generous wages. During the war eighty-six bars and fifty-three shops opened in Nouméa. In 1939 service employees received average salaries of Fr1,200 per month, which by 1944 had risen to Fr4,500, the equivalent of $105 at the wartime exchange rate.[17] More modest but still significant increases occurred for the male Kanak who found employment with the American forces. Before the war approximately 20 to 25 percent of the eligible male Kanak worked outside the reservations. By 1943 a French report estimated that two-thirds of the five-thousand eligible Melanesians were working outside the reservations as volunteers in the Free-French armed forces, working for the French administration, or employed by the Americans, either legally or irregularly.[18]

The industrial labor force at Le Nickel felt the impact of the Americans soon after their arrival. American military authorities began to use space on Le Nickel's main dock, which led to a shortage of coal and the closing of one of three furnaces operating in April 1942 with the closure of a second furnace for five weeks at the end of that year. These interruptions caused a certain amount of labor discontent. A small but active communist group in Nouméa supported labor grievances. A party member toured the countryside at the end of 1942 calling for a nationalization of Le Nickel. This early flurry of worker protest subsided when the economic slowdown at Le Nickel enabled the management to dismiss those members of the union who were considered agitators.[19]

At first the indentured Asians were outside direct contact with the Americans, but they would also feel the impact of the American presence, particularly those employed legally or illegally by American military personnel. While the American market for curios provided some indentured workers with supplementary income, they had no one to look after their interests. Then the dynamic and colorful Mme Tunica y Casas, a veteran of the Spanish Civil War and a cofounder of the "Friends of the Soviet Union," took up their cause. She denounced the harsh living and working conditions that marked the existence of the seven-thousand Tonkinese who had been brought to New Caledonia before the war and whose five-year contracts had been extended arbitrarily for the duration. In 1943 she contacted the leaders of a clandestine Vietnamese union at the Société Le Nickel works at Doniambo and offered the support of the Communist Party of New Caledonia in their struggle to obtain better pay and working conditions.[20] As prices rose for many goods, the fixed pay rates for the indentured workers meant that they could no longer afford necessities. These economic grievances fed the growing discontent among the indentured Asians.

Another complication arose when the government of the Netherlands made military service compulsory for all Javanese living outside Surinam and Curaçao.[21] The Dutch ambassador in Washington informed the State Department that the Dutch consul in Nouméa would begin recruiting Javanese to participate in the liberation and economic reconstruction of the Dutch East Indies. Responding to an appeal from the management of Le Nickel, the Americans informed the Dutch Government that its recruitment of Javanese in New Caledonia would disrupt nickel production, which was considered important for the war effort.[22] Nevertheless, the Dutch Government sent a commission to Nouméa at the beginning of 1944 to discuss the drafting of Javanese for service in the Dutch armed forces.[23]

When they arrived, the Dutch delegates complained about the mistreatment of the Javanese, noting that the prewar contracts had all expired and the Javanese were being held against their wishes. They insisted that a number of Javanese be released for training in Australia.[24] The American Government, however, remained unsympathetic to the Dutch position. The Americans listened to Henry Dewez, director of Le Nickel's office in New York, who claimed that the Dutch attitude stirred up trouble for the labor situation in New Caledonia and would harm nickel production.[25] But the activities of the Dutch consul on behalf of the indentured Javanese became widely known on the island and impressed the Tonkinese, who had no other protectors than the French Immigration Service. Throughout 1944 social unrest increased in New Caledonia as the war became more distant.

Some of the indentured workers hoped for American support against their French employers. In December 1944 Tonkinese miners threatened to go out on strike at the beginning of the next year. This threat appeared in a petition that three of them sent to the commander of the American army in New Caledonia. The petition asked that the "representative from the land of Abraham Lincoln and Franklin Roosevelt" use his influence with the French authorities to obtain free status, decent wages, and improved living conditions. Although not wishing to harm the war effort, the petitioners argued that if the French refused to meet with their legal representative, the Communist lawyer Gaston Bourdinat, they would have no other recourse than to strike.[26] The American consul, Robert

Brown, expressed sympathy but took no action. He hesitated to become involved in the conflict since his main concern was to avoid any instability that might complicate or interfere with an American withdrawal from New Caledonia.[27]

If Consul Brown kept his distance from the Tonkinese and their complaints against the French administration, there were other American servicemen who did not hesitate to become involved in the struggle. The most prominent of these sympathetic American soldiers was Sergeant Lewis Feuer who was responsible for drafting the petition that appealed to the "land of Abraham Lincoln and Franklin Roosevelt." The army wanted to court-martial Feuer for his activities on behalf of the indentured Asian laborers, but Eleanor Roosevelt, who had known Feuer in New York in the 1930s, intervened and he was administratively demoted to the rank of private. He then volunteered to serve on an active front and was sent to Iwo Jima just as the fighting ended on that island.[28] Feuer and others, such as Private Forrest Crumply and an army chaplain by the name of Chapman, would meet regularly at Rabot's grocery store, which was under surveillance by army intelligence as a center for subversive activity. Another site for political discussions was a bar opened by Mme Tunica y Casas where she sold moonshine liquor to GIs for what American army intelligence described as "exorbitant prices."[29]

A confrontation occurred sooner than expected when Tonkinese workers struck Le Nickel's smelting plant at Doniambo outside Nouméa in mid-December and walked out at the Voh mine two weeks later. These strikes lasted only forty-eight hours and French internal security quickly suppressed the movement. The Tonkinese instigators of the labor unrest were brought to court where Gaston Bourdinat successfully defended them. Their acquittal brought cheers from the crowd of supporters in the courtroom. Feuer later claimed that Bourdinat's citation of *Les Droits de l'Homme* marked the beginning of the Vietnamese Revolution.[30] But the situation remained potentially explosive. The question of indentured labor became a major issue in the political debates leading up to the elections that Governor Tallec scheduled for 7 January 1945 to a governing council to replace the administrative council that Governor Sautot had formed in 1940. The composition of this council had changed only with resignations and new appointments in the interim. Tallec hoped that elections and a new council would answer critics such as Michel Vergès, who had been vocal in denouncing the unrepresentative character of Sautot's appointed council. An election offered an opportunity for public debate on such matters as the island's future status in the French Empire and the question of labor, social relations and political representation in the colony. Governor Tallec lifted wartime censorship in preparation for the electoral campaign.

The campaign opened at the end of 1944 with the publication of the Caledonian Committee's platform. The Caledonian Committee represented moderate, republican views and was headed by Pierre Bergès. Although claiming to be neither revolutionary nor autonomist, the committee's program called for wider local control over internal politics and economic life in New Caledonia.

The committee called for a modernization of industry, mainly in the mining sector, which was the backbone of the economy, a land reform to break up larger estates, and measures to improve working conditions, particularly the "postwar labor crisis that will certainly arise."[31]

A second group emerged under the leadership of the vocal critic of the established order, Mme Tunica y Casas. She formed a political alliance with the Communist landowner Florindo Paladini, who had taken a leading part in the 1940 rally and had been hostile to the leaders of the 1942 riot against Admiral d'Argenlieu. They created a Social Progress slate of candidates for election to the general council. This group demanded an end to the indentured labor system and the formation of a broadly based union to represent all laborers in New Caledonia.

The third political force in the race for the general council was the Union List that had been formed by a group of conservative landowners, mining interests, businessmen and professionals. This group advocated measures for economic development but firmly opposed nationalization of Le Nickel, land reform, or increased taxes for the purpose of social and economic reconstruction after the war. On the labor issue they advocated continued importation of indentured labor but with strict residence requirements that would prevent any unauthorized migration into the towns.

The outcome of the election for the fifteen seats on the general council showed a clear victory for the Left. Members of either the Caledonian Union or the Social Progress list, who had united to form a common front against the conservatives, held thirteen of the fifteen seats on the council. The trend was in favor of major reforms for New Caledonia. As an American intelligence report noted, "The election appears to justify the opinion that a distinct Leftish, anti-capitalist trend exists among large elements of the population, particularly among the small farmers, or Broussards, of the interior who felt that the united front would oppose the 'big interests' of Nouméa."[32] The metropolitan representatives apparently shrugged off the results as further evidence of an "impossible Caledonian mentality." The election and composition of the new governing council assured an end of the indentured labor system.

Although the Americans had kept hands off the internal, domestic politics of New Caledonia throughout their time on the island, American officials analyzed the indentured labor situation on New Caledonia in the aftermath of the election and the strikes. They were generally favorable to an end to the harsh conditions that obtained under indentured labor and sympathized with some of the complaints. The problem was not due just to agitators such as Mme Tunica y Casas. "Whatever the instigation of trouble," the State Department concluded, "it is clear that there were real grievances based upon forced retention beyond the expiration of contract combined with the existence of opportunities for far more profitable employment on the island ... ."[33] American experts noted that Le Nickel depended upon extensive use of indentured labor because of its obsolete and inefficient equipment. Indentured labor was inhumane, outmoded, and anything but a free labor market.

The management of Le Nickel agreed with this analysis. Henry Dewez informed the Americans of his desire to improve the labor situation in New Caledonia and to make Le Nickel more competitive in the postwar environment by modernizing production methods. "Reliance upon indentured laborers is … an unsound position," he observed, and he indicated a wish to improve housing and other conditions so that "the indentured laborers will remain permanently and of their own volition."[34] In a letter to his director in Nouméa, Albert Rapadzi, Dewez called for radical measures to stabilize the labor situation, including construction of new living quarters in Nouméa and in the mining villages for the workers and their families.[35] In the aftermath of the strikes the company offered an increase in wages plus bonuses for skilled workers. As for technical modernization, Dewez called for development of electrical power from construction of Yaté dam near Nouméa, which would enable the installation of labor saving equipment at the plant and relieve the company's dependency upon coal imports for power.[36]

In the meantime, labor difficulties simmered despite modest efforts to ameliorate conditions for indentured workers. An American observer noted in March 1945 that strikes had occurred in virtually all mines since the preceding November, and some were marked by bloody conflicts between strikers and French troops sent to restore order.[37] Tonkinese protesters continued to claim the right to free residency, and they plastered walls in Nouméa with their demands for freedom and equality.[38] The Dutch consul persisted in complaints about mistreatment of the Javanese indentured workers, which included penal sanctions against those who hesitated to renew their contracts. He informed Governor Tallec that the Dutch Government considered the system of Javanese indentured labor to be finished.[39] Opposition came from the small miners, who would have difficulty modernizing their operations, coffee farmers of the interior, and small shopkeepers who feared that free resident Asians would become commercial rivals.

Faced with growing pressures to end the system and fearful of additional strikes and protests, Governor Tallec announced to the people of New Caledonia on 15 June 1945 that the abolition of indentured labor would take place on 5 July 1945. He carefully prepared for this announcement by securing the cooperation and support of Pierre Bergès, whose influence with the Broussards remained a fixture of local politics. French administrators approved this measure, and the general council passed it by a vote of eleven to four. The opponents were all members of the Social Progress Group, three Broussards and a mechanic. Their opposition revealed the doubts that existed within the ranks of Pierre Bergès's party. All Asians in New Caledonia became free residents with the right to remain in New Caledonia or be repatriated at the first opportunity.

American military intelligence described Governor Tallec's declaration to be one of the most important events in New Caledonia's economic, political and social history, since it affected 50 percent of the entire labor force on the island and almost all of the non-skilled or non-supervisory labor.[40] In addition the French Government permitted the Dutch to recruit eight-hundred volunteers for military service. The French settlers were displaced but resigned in the face of this *fait accompli*. In a radio broadcast, Governor Tallec reassured his listeners that the police and military were prepared to deal with any disturbances or troubles resulting from this measure.[41]

Ending indentured labor caused the shut down of Le Nickel's smelter plant due to an inability to retain Asian labor after the abrogation decree. Tonkinese demands were for an immediate pay raise to Fr10 an hour or the equivalent of $1.80/day. Le Nickel declined to meet this demand, offering $0.90/day. When the workers refused to return after two weeks of negotiations, they were forcibly removed from their residences and relocated in a former internment camp for Japanese war prisoners.[42] Mme Tunica y Casas denounced the brutal methods that the French administration employed in breaking up the strike at Le Nickel, and noted that even the Americans were upset at the methods employed.[43]

American Materialism, Entertainment and the Issue of Withdrawal

Despite recognition given to General de Gaulle's provisional government, the issue of an American withdrawal remained in doubt at the beginning of 1945. Evidence seemed to conflict as to what the Americans intended to do as far as the French Empire was concerned. As the American war effort shifted from the South Pacific to the Philippines and the Central Pacific, a need for facilities in New Caledonia was not only less pressing, it presented an opportunity to return facilities to French control. Admiral Nimitz already had informed the commander of the New Zealand troops, General Barrowclough, that it was his intention to vacate New Caledonia as soon as possible, but that its use as a rest and rehabilitation area would probably continue until May 1945.[44] The Americans readily acceded to a request from the newly elected governing council that they give up facilities that they had taken over earlier in the war, such as the Bernheim Library in Nouméa.

Changing conditions of war in the Pacific diminished the American Navy's interest in New Caledonia as a strategic base when the main naval effort in the Pacific moved away from New Caledonia, following the conclusion of the Solomon Islands campaign in March 1944. Equipment and supplies were moved to forward bases and the size of the Navy contingent on the island dropped from nearly twenty-three thousand officers and men in September 1943 to less than ten-thousand by July 1944. Naval authorities drafted a survey of New Caledonia's potential use as a postwar base in the summer of 1945 but only at the request of the House committee on naval affairs.[45] By the end of the war the Navy had lost interest in Nouméa as a base, much to the annoyance of certain senators and congressmen, who remained determined to assert American control. At least they claimed a postwar presence in the French colony as compensation for American aid to France in two world wars.[46] The attitude that France "owed" something to the United States would persist into the future and embitter relations between the two countries.

Although local American officials insisted that they would depart New Caledonia at the end of the war, the extensive construction program on the island nevertheless suggested that the American presence might be permanent. One of the ironies of American construction in New Caledonia had been that the vast, multiwinged headquarters building at Anse Vata, the "Pentagon", was completed in December 1944 after the American Navy and Army Air Force headquarters had moved away from New Caledonia. Rumors began to circulate that this facility might become the headquarters for an American base in Nouméa after the war. The question thus arises as to the extent to which the Caledonians themselves might have been tempted by either a continuing American presence or even the prospect of an American takeover of the colony as the war drew to a close in 1945.[47]

Just two years after the war the commander of French troops in the Pacific warned that Caledonians remembered the American presence as a time of unprecedented prosperity, and they believed that a distant and weakened France lacked the resources to assist them in the harsher reality of the postwar world.[48] The colonel recommended increasing the numbers of French troops stationed on the island to avoid a crisis, although there is no evidence in New Caledonia of any movement for secession from the French Empire. Some Caledonians were greatly attracted both by the material goods that the Americans brought with them and the novelty of a new way of life. A sense of these attractions may be found in a letter from a Caledonian woman, intercepted by American censors, who wrote to a friend that everyone went out at night, spending and earning "fabulous amounts." The Americans, she wrote, liked entertainment and distractions and had introduced a number of novelties. There had been musicals, dances, choir performances, weekly band concerts on Coconut Square, variety shows, and there was even a fashion show that was "tout à fait genre parisien." She confessed that it would not be too bad if the Caledonians modernized themselves since "they have been living a half century behind in that country."[49]

Another Caledonian woman has recalled fondly the treasure troves of chocolates, enormous boxes of fruits, even GI rations, the many gifts, and "the enormous goose" consumed during the Christmas holidays. As a young girl she and her friends attended both the American movies at the two local theaters in Nouméa and the free open-air movies provided by the American services. The informal way that American soldiers and sailors would arrive to watch the outdoor movies in their jeeps at one of the first drive-in theaters in the Pacific greatly impressed her. While she and her friends admired French stars such as Jean-Pierre Aumont and Charles Boyer, Hollywood productions that featured Rita Hayworth, Joseph Cotton, Lana Turner, Clark Gable and others fascinated them. They danced to the strains of Glenn Miller, Jimmy Dorsey, and Benny Goodman. They learned the English lyrics to such wartime hits as "Sweet Sue" and "Chattanooga Choo-Choo." Only Tino Rossi held his own, it seemed, against this American tidal wave of popular culture.[50]

The local radio station of the American-operated "mosquito network" dispensed American popular music. While this network provided a variety of programming throughout the day, popular music in the form of jazz and entertainment shows prevailed over high culture. Not all observers of American popular culture in New Caledonia found the product tempting. An Australian report noted, "With the exception of symphony hours on Tuesday and Thursday evening, and an occasional Gracie Fields Show or Information Please, jive and boogie-woogie reign supreme after office hours." In impatient and racist tones, the newly appointed Australian consul, Noel Deschamps, added, "The amount of twentieth century jungle music that U.S. servicemen can absorb seems to be almost unlimited."[51] American popular music obviously did not appeal to all tastes.

The way in which American servicemen made use of government vehicles for their own private amusements also shocked the very proper Deschamps. Jeeps would be liberally used by American soldiers and sailors to take young women to and from their homes, to beach parties, to the movies and for moonlight drives. American public address systems disturbed his moments of relaxation, and he deplored the tendency of Americans "to ignore the existence of a properly constituted civilian authority responsible for the administration of the colony and to act as though it were American territory."[52] He noted that other locations, such as Brisbane, suffered from a boom town atmosphere, and, like Brisbane, many Caledonians would be pleased to see the Americans leave. While they enjoyed the prosperity that the Americans brought with them, Deschamps believed that the American presence had had a bad effect upon the morale of the population.

The American capacity to produce and transport huge amounts of both war goods and those comforts of home that were considered necessary to sustain the morale of American boys overseas was a major shock not only for the peoples of New Caledonia but wherever the American military forces appeared. A British historian has noted the astonishing and at times locally resented American material abundance that appeared in England on the eve of the D-Day landings. This materialism, he has argued, was part of General George Marshall's "deliberate strategy for dealing with morale problems of inactive but articulate troops who were far from home."[53] American warfare reflected a modern, industrialized mass society on the march, including not only large amounts of equipment and weapons, but also the PX facilities and the entertainment to make the American serviceman and servicewoman feel at home in a foreign environment. For the diverse peoples of New Caledonia, the arrival of the Americans produced a sharp encounter with modernism in its material form and in the scale of mass consumption.

The labor difficulties that arose in New Caledonia as the American departure approached resulted from the realization that there were possibilities for Kanak other than isolation on their reservations. Free resident Asians or those who escaped the harsh work in the mines discovered opportunities to work in somewhat more humane conditions, even as servants for American officers, while many Asians engaged in entrepreneurial activities selling curios and souvenirs. Three years of the American occupation in New Caledonia brought prosperity to the European settlers, but it also gave the excluded, if not the same level of benefit, at least a taste for higher wages and better treatment.[54] Some Kanak near Houaïlou would later recall that the Americans were "good to us, gave us many things and treated us better than the French did."[55]

The desire for better work and living conditions would linger after the American departure. Housing in tent facilities at Camp Joe Louis or Camp Jeanne d'Arc, combined with regular medical care, provided more comfort and a better standard of health for many Kanak than they had experienced on the reservations.[56] European Caledonians and Free-French administrators feared that generous treatment would tempt the Kanak population to prefer an American postwar control of the island. Kanak observed that African-Americans, even under segregation, received better treatment than they had under French rule.[57] Kanak were impressed that African-American servicemen could direct traffic and give orders to whites even in a military that was segregated by race. The issue of segregation, racism and racial tension within the ranks of the American armed forces was less important than the exercise of rank and authority by African-Americans in Kanak eyes.

Kanak also received the benefits of American entertainment. American public relations officers and chaplains in the U.S. Army would visit Kanak villages of the interior bringing with them more than just spiritual messages. Temporary movie theaters would be set up and play cartoons. An example illustrates the American cultural offensive among the Kanak. On 11 November 1944 an American signal corps sergeant on the island of New Caledonia photographed a group of Melanesians who were watching with evident pleasure and delight a cartoon that featured Donald Duck. The screening occurred at the French Protestant Mission at Doneva, a small village just outside the town of Hoaüilou. The caption for the photograph read: "The natives go into a joyous frenzy as Donald Duck appears on the screen. This was the first time any of them had seen a movie. The movie was part of the Army's religious and good-will work among the natives and was sponsored by Chaplain Lonnie Knight, Carrollton, Mississippi."[58]

Figure 8.1. It is Donald Duck, agent of American Imperialism.
Source. U.S. National Archives (111-SC-364406).

Not only in New Caledonia but wherever American troops appeared, public-relations officers tried to build a sympathetic image of the United States as a way of mitigating inconveniences caused by a foreign occupation force, but there was more to it. Chaplain Knight's "religious and good will work," was preaching to those who were already converted in the religious sense. His efforts were part of a propaganda campaign to present a favorable image of the American way of life that accompanied American forces rampant in all parts of the globe during the

Second World War.⁵⁹ The "good will" being spread was a taste of "the good life" as experienced in America. This activity would later be seen as first signs of an American cultural imperialism that would upset the French in the postwar world.

Some critics have seen in the language, or discourse, of Walt Disney productions a manifestation of an imperialist ideology.⁶⁰ According to this analysis, Donald Duck, like Mickey Mouse, has become an icon of postwar and wartime American cultural imperialism. Whether this was a conscious attempt to convert Kanak to the American way of life or simply an innocent gesture of good will cannot be determined from the example alone, but the French suspected ulterior motives in American contacts with Melanesians or Asians in New Caledonia. Were the Americans trying to win the affections of the Kanak for their own, ulterior purposes of annexation? For some Kanak, Asians and Caledonians American behavior and attitudes held an attraction, but there is no evidence that these acts of propaganda were part of a calculated policy to alienate the affections of the local populations. Nevertheless, French officials feared American activities were having that effect, and they suspected collusion and support for Kanak dissidents.

Reports from local French authorities confirmed the activities of other chaplains and American intelligence officers, who were in frequent contact with Kanak as well as Asian laborers. Ostensibly these officers sought information about morale problems and the possible infiltration of Japanese agents, but the French believed there was more to it. American intelligence agents often tried to recruit informants such as the Vietnamese translator, Dong Sy Hua, to work for military intelligence, an offer he quickly rejected.⁶¹ They also would go onto Kanak reservations ostensibly to check on morale and attitudes, but in the eyes of the French administration, these intelligence officers appeared to be mixing in native affairs, sometimes in an alarming way. French security claimed Americans provided arms to Kanak dissidents in the region of Ponérihouen.⁶² Indeed, these Kanak wanted to expel the French at the end of the war and seek American protection.

The instigator of this movement of Kanak volunteers for America was a Melanesian from the New Hebrides named Willy, who worked at the American airbase in Tontouta where he was relatively well paid. American practices of paying for labor contrasted with the French native labor tax, which required Melanesian males to contribute ten days of labor working on public works projects in the interior. On Saturdays Willy met with dissident Kanak from the Chamba, Goa and Goyetta tribes in the region of Ponérihouen, who began to draft lists of those Kanak who wanted to place themselves under American authority. They talked of executing the director of native affairs and other white French at the end of the war. They sought American arms and weapons from a certain Lieutenant Lee, whose unit had been stationed nearby. But when they asked Lee for American arms, he declined to supply them since there was a war going on, as he put it. When the director of native affairs arrested and removed three of the ringleaders from the Chamba tribe, the others asked Lee, by way of the local Protestant pastor, to send a detachment of American soldiers to protect them. Lee never replied to these appeals. Governor Tallec was informed of these activities, but he refused to become alarmed. He was convinced that the Americans would not intrigue with the people against the French, but he kept careful watch upon their activities.[63] Any arms that Kanak dissidents obtained was through irregular means and not the result of an American policy.

Kanak dissidence in Ponérihouen disappeared when the director of native affairs brought some of the anti-French leaders in for questioning. This intervention led to confession and repentance by one of the leaders and an apology from Great Chief Barthélemy Chouke on behalf of the Chamba and Goyetta tribes. Drawn up as the war was ending and the Americans were preparing to depart, the Great Chief's declaration to the director of native affairs stated that the Chamba and Goyetta people had been misled in asking to be placed under American authority. They wished to remain with "mother France and General de Gaulle."[64] Any temptation for Kanak who might have used the American presence or even arms to liberate themselves from French tutelage had passed by mid-1945.

Still, fears of an American takeover continued to the end as politicians in Washington persisted in seeking compensation from the French for debts owed the United States. When news reports reached New Caledonia that a group of American senators had again proposed the purchase of New Caledonia as a way of paying off wartime Lend-lease, reactions revealed ambiguities about an American takeover did arise. James Daly, normally sympathetic to the Americans, wrote an angry editorial in *France Australe* in which he declared, "New Caledonia is not for sale, nor can it be bought."[65] He claimed that Caledonians would shudder at such a sacrilegious proposal and veterans who had died defending the tricolor would roll over in their graves. A week later the governing council echoed these sentiments and passed a resolution, which it published in the press, declaring "Neither Caledonia, nor the Caledonians are for sale!"[66] They regretted that the thoughtless statements of a few senators threatened to embroil otherwise good relations between the Caledonians and the Americans. The *Bulletin du Commerce* joined the chorus on 15 August with an editorial denouncing the idea of selling the colony.

In private conversation opinion was more complex and conflicted. James Daly admitted to his American friends that he had published his editorial as honor required, but he felt that it would be to New Caledonia's economic advantage if the United States acquired the island. He feared the loss of French customs and speculated that an arrangement, perhaps like Quebec, would have to be made to accommodate French ways. Reports from the northern part of the island indicated that settlers in the Voh region were hostile to the French administration and wanted an annexation to the United States.[67] American intelligence reported that those Kanak who expressed a view seemed pleased with the prospect of an

American takeover with the exception of a few pro-Japanese tribes on the northeast coast, confirming earlier reports of strong pro-American sentiments among many Kanak.[68] But there is no evidence of an American intention to exploit these sentiments to promote dissidence or an uprising.

If there was temptation among the Caledonians, it was largely economic rather than cultural, as expressed by a French businessman who wished that the Americans would leave a garrison behind, which "would be good for Nouméa" economically.[69] While many European settlers nursed their grievances against the colonial administration, they balanced these resentments against a deep attachment to France and French culture. This feeling was particularly strong among the older settler population and among the veterans. The economic benefits from an American takeover had to be weighed against loss or diminishment of a French identity. As one person stated, "My head says 'yes' but my heart says 'no'."[70] The heart of the Caledonians would prevail. With the exception of the Communists and the anti-American Michel Vergès, opinion favored the presence of an American base in the postwar period. The Caledonians had tasted the economic benefits of an American presence during the war and would have accepted its continuance in some form.

The opposition to the American senators' proposal by the Communists and the Vergès faction was to be expected. In a series of broadsides and handbills that she distributed or had plastered on the walls of Nouméa's streets, Mme Tunica y Casas launched a thorough denunciation of American imperialistic ambitions. Another communist went to the *Bulletin du Commerce* to publicize his opinions, but he was asked to leave. Governor Tallec at one point called in Mme Tunica y Casas to ask that she tone down her anti-Americanism, as it strained relations between Allies, but she declined on the ground that she was free to express her opinions as to what was right and what was wrong. Allied censorship intercepted a letter in which she complained to a comrade in Australia that she and her husband were being punished for their views and that her husband had been prevented from going to Australia for medical treatment.[71]

The most violent objection came from the mouth and pen of Michel Vergès, who took the senators' proposal as an opportunity to denounce once more the Americans and their anti-French ambitions. For over six months Michel Vergès had been relatively quiet. He had initially presented himself as a candidate for a seat on the governing council, but this ambition abruptly ceased when Governor Tallec threatened to reveal publicly that Michel Vergès had received Fr750,000 from Admiral d'Argenlieu for his role in rallying New Caledonia to the Free-French cause.[72] This threat had been enough to silence Vergès temporarily, but in August he returned to the political fray. Vergès insisted upon an interview with the governor and then proceeded to lecture him for three hours.

What upset Vergès was Tallec's refusal to allow him to publish a bitter letter against the American politicians' proposal in the *Bulletin du Commerce*, which in the past had served as a major vehicle for airing his views. In his letter Vergès called the senators "gangsters and fascists" who had violated the ideals of Washington, Lincoln, Wilson and Roosevelt, and he placed the United States in the same category as Nazi Germany or Mussolini's Italy. The outrageous American proposal came just at the moment when the radios of the world were proclaiming final victory over the forces of fascism. The American claim to bases in the Pacific, he argued, was no more valid than if the Russians or Chinese asked for a base in San Francisco to assure their security in the Northern Pacific.

When Vergès requested and paid for front page publication of this lengthy letter, the editor of the *Bulletin du Commerce*, Fernand Legras, ordered this "monstrosity" removed from the presses and took it to Governor Tallec, who ordered him not to publish.[73] Although censorship had been lifted, Tallec justified the ban on the grounds that publication would harm French diplomatic interests on the eve of President de Gaulle's visit to Washington. Unable to publish in New Caledonia, Vergès took his letter to the British consul with the request that Mr. Johnston transmit his missive to the French colonial minister, the French foreign minister and General de Gaulle. He wanted the General to raise the issue with President Truman during his visit to the United States.[74]

Anti-Communism versus Anticolonialism

Despite the political bluster in Washington, New Caledonia and the rest of the French Empire still would be French by the end of 1945. State Department officials argued that a premature decolonization of the British and French Empires would create resentments and weaken European allies at the end of the war. Fears of a Soviet domination of the continent of Europe became the overriding concern for American policy makers during President Roosevelt's last months in office. They found an ally in the White House when Harry Truman succeeded Franklin Roosevelt as president of the United States. Truman was not committed to an anticolonial position ideologically, and he was determined to face the Soviet challenge with firmness.

The threat of an American-imposed trusteeship for parts of the French Empire was removed during the United Nations conference held in San Francisco from 25 April to 26 June 1945. Certain members of the American delegation, notably Charles Taussig, continued Roosevelt's push for a trusteeship over French colonial territory in the Pacific, such as Indochina and New Caledonia. A majority of the delegates rallied to the view that the United States could not afford to alienate either France or Great Britain over colonial issues. The State Department concluded that French management of the empire was not as disastrous as President Roosevelt believed. An internal memorandum stated that French administration had been more beneficial than harmful in Indochina and that French control would provide stability in that part of the world.[75] A lengthy State Department policy paper had earlier listed the statements made by the United

States and other governments regarding the territorial integrity of France and the need for the restoration of France as a great power.[76]

The war and navy departments also opposed any imposition of a trusteeship scheme. High-level military officials shared State's concern to have a strong France as an element of stability in the postwar world and looked favorably upon maintenance of the European empires. Although a number of New Deal liberals continued to oppose a restoration of the old imperial systems, the opposition to an ideological stand in favor of a "realistic" approach to the British and French empires prevailed in American military circles. On the eve of the San Francisco conference the French minister to China passed through Washington, where he found General Marshall and Assistant Secretary of War, John McCloy, sympathetic to the restoration of the French Empire at the end of the war.[77]

The French vigorously opposed any international oversight for their colonial domain and made their opposition to any trusteeship proposal clear at the San Francisco meeting. General de Gaulle's provisional government had declined an invitation to be one of the sponsoring nations convening the conference, mainly out of a concern that such sponsorship would obligate them to accept a trust arrangement for their colonial territories. The French feared that a trusteeship under a world organization was neither more nor less than a scheme to deprive them of their colonies.[78] They were particularly concerned about the future status of Indochina, which was still under Japanese control. The French were well aware of Roosevelt's views that Indochina should not be fully restored but placed under international supervision.

When he arrived in San Francisco, the French foreign minister, Georges Bidault, was in a truculent mood. He claimed that the French Empire had become the victim of a campaign of "ignorance and calumny" on the part of the Americans and insisted that France would be her own trustee.[79] The American delegation reported that Bidault was in a highly nervous state since his arrival in San Francisco, and his apparent frustration at the way he was treated caused him to behave in an undignified manner. The Americans attributed his peculiar behavior to a "post-liberation psychosis."[80]

Some of that psychosis may have been relieved during a conversation that Edward Stettinius, the American secretary of state, had with Bidault and the French ambassador, Henri Bonnet, on 8 May in San Francisco. Stettinius claimed somewhat disingenuously, "the record was entirely innocent of any official statement of this government questioning, even by implication, French sovereignty over Indochina" although American press and public opinion was critical of French rule in Indochina. From Washington, Acting Secretary Grew reported that Bidault seemed relieved and had no doubt forwarded these assurances to Paris.[81] The State Department reiterated that the United States was not opposed to a French restoration in Indochina and had never questioned that right even by implication.[82] These statements clearly repudiated and contradicted

Roosevelt's insistence that Indochina should be placed under a French trusteeship, but only if eventual independence was assured. By the end of the war, France's position as a colonial power in the Pacific had received support from the American State Department. Both Indochina and New Caledonia would remain French.

A strong, fully restored France had the support of President Truman as well. Despite a serious contention with France over the presence of French troops in the Val d'Aosta in Northwestern Italy at this time, Truman issued a public statement on 18 May in which he expressed his admiration for France's recovery from the war. He was pleased that France seemed prepared "to resume its rightful and eminent place among the nations which will share the largest measure of responsibility in maintaining the future peace of Europe and the world."[83] From Paris, Ambassador Caffrey reported that President Truman's statement had been very favorably received in all quarters. He added that the French were anxious and uncertain about the future, and they still suffered "from their well-known inferiority complex." Truman's statement reassured the French that France was still considered a major power, and the new American president was determined to put aside past misunderstandings.[84] Nevertheless the French continued to be described in gendered terms as flighty and unreliable.

Growing tensions and differences with the Soviet Union lay behind American support for a recovered France. De Gaulle played upon this anxiety in one of his appeals to the United States to provide assistance to French troops resisting the Japanese in Indochina following the Japanese takeover on 9 March 1945. American refusal to provide aid for France and American opposition to a French return to Indochina bewildered the French people, he claimed. He referred to his interview with Harry Hopkins at the beginning of the year in which he had stated that he did not understand American policy since it seemed to be a deliberate strategy of keeping France weak, which placed France at risk of being dominated by the Soviet Union. "We do not want to become Communist; we do not want to fall into the Russian orbit, but I hope that you do not push us into it."[85] Very effectively de Gaulle played upon American fears of Soviet domination of Western Europe as an argument for the full restoration of the French Empire.

Cold warriors within the State Department wanted to avoid alienating France and Great Britain. Assistant Secretary of State James Dunn warned his colleagues in State that in light of French fears, the United States had "no right to dictate to France nor to take away her territory."[86] Fears of the Soviet Union prevailed over the preferences of those American officials who still adhered to Roosevelt's anticolonialist views. The pattern was set: anti-Communism rather than anticolonialism would take precedence in the formation of American policy as an outline of the cold war emerged during the last months of Second World War. "Security" replaced "independence" as the watchword in colonial matters.[87]

A change in U.S. priorities became apparent during de Gaulle's visit to Washington in August 1945. In his 18 May statement Truman had proposed that de Gaulle visit the United States, an invitation that Bidault welcomed and de Gaulle accepted. On the eve of his departure for Washington, Ambassador Caffrey reported that "The Pacific in general and Indochina in particular" would be at the top of the agenda for de Gaulle's discussions with Truman. He suggested that the French would not be opposed to making certain bases available to the United States, but an agreement depended upon how the issue was presented. The French were "touchy and 'exasperated' and ... if the question of bases is put as a demand or a natural privilege it might be difficult to meet our requirements."[88]

The mood among French officials, however, seemed to be optimistic on the future of American relations with France. Bidault informed Caffrey that the French wished "to wipe the slate clean of the past, start afresh and work with the U.S. as closely as possible in the international field."[89] Although Truman and de Gaulle differed in manner and style, these two leaders reached agreement on Indochina and the Pacific. Truman assured the French leader that the United States approved of the use of French troops in the Far East, and he did not oppose a full restoration of the French Empire.[90] Whatever rumblings of an American takeover, the reality was that the Americans were preparing to leave even as the announcement of the Japanese Government's surrender on 15 August came over the mosquito network on a bright, sunny mid-winter's day in the southern hemisphere.

Notes

1. Squadron Leader McColl to Director of Intelligence, RAAF, "New Caledonia Potpourri", 9 March 1944, intelligence summary for week ending 19 February 1944, Australian Archives (AA), ACT. CRS A989, item 44/610/6.
2. Information on Jacques Tallec has been kindly provided by his son, Yves Tallec, who accompanied his father to New Caledonia and was a student in the Lycée Laperouse in Nouméa. Interview with Yves Tallec, Paris, 21 May 2001.
3. McColl to Director Intelligence, RAAF, "New Caledonia Potpourri", 9 March 1944, intelligence summary, week ending 4 March 1944, AA, ACT. CRS A989, item 44/610/6.
4. Ballard to External Affairs, n.d. but late 1943, AA, AA/975/215 3/40.
5. Colonel Salmon to Chiefs of Staff, Wellington, 21 February 1944, New Zealand National Archive (NZNA), EA ser. 1, 81/11/4, pt. 1.
6. McColl to Director Intelligence, RAAF, "New Caledonia Potpourri", 9 March 1944, intelligence summary, week ending 4 March 1944, AA, ACT. CRS A989, item 44/610/6.
7. Pleven to Laigret, 17 February 1944, Archives Nationales Section d'Outre-mer (ANSOM), telegrams 852.
8. McColl to Director Intelligence, RAAF, "New Caledonia Potpourri", 9 March 1944, intelligence summary, week ending 26 February 1944, AA, ACT. CRS A989, item 44/610/6.
9. Fleet Admiral William F. Halsey and Lieutenant Commander J. Bryan III, *Admiral Halsey's Story* (New York, 1947), 193.
10. Noel Deschamps, Nouméa Letter #2, 24 August 1944, AA ACT. CRS A989, item 44/610/17.

11. Deschamps described this New England style chapel as "an architectural gem." Deschamps, Nouméa Letter No. 3, December 1944, AA, ACT. CRS A 1066, Item P .45/99/4.
12. Tallec to Pleven, 25 April 1944, ANSOM, telegrams 870, cited in Ismet Kurtovitch, "La vie politique en Nouvelle-Calédonie (1940–1953)," 2 vols (Ph.D diss., Université française du Pacifique, 1998), vol. 1, 74.
13. Report of Colonel Benoît-Guyot (Commandant of French troops in New Caledonia), 8 April 1944, Archives of the Service Historique de l'Armée, Château de Vincennes (henceforth SHA) 12 H 4, cited in Kurtovitch, "La vie politique," 80.
14. Pleven to Tallec, April 1944, ANSOM, telegram. 852.
15. The most helpful and informed discussion of the way in which the Administrative council obtained considerable economic autonomy during the war and resisted taxation may be found in Ismet Kurtovitch, "Du Conseil d'Administration de la Nouvelle-Calédonie pendant la Seconde Guerre Mondiale," *Bulletin de la Société d'Études Historiques de la Nouvelle-Calédonie*, no. 106 (1996): 29–59; and in his thesis, "La vie politique en Nouvelle-Calédonie (1940–1953)," vol. 1, 63–75.
16. Major General Alexander M. Patch to General George C. Marshall, 17 April 1942, U.S. National Archives and Record Administration (USNARA) RG 165.
17. Kurtovitch, "La vie politique en Nouvelle-Calédonie," 63.
18. Ibid, 53–54, and Ismet Kurtovitch, "New Caledonia: The Consequences of the Second World War," in *France Abroad: Indochina, New Caledonia, Wallis and Futuna, Mayotte*, ed. Robert Aldrich and Isabelle Merle (Sydney, 1997), 36.
19. American Consulate, Nouméa, to State Department, 12 February 1943, USNARA RG 165.
20. See Dong Sy Hua, *De la Mélanésie au Vietnam: Itinéraire d'un colonisé devenu francophile* (Paris, 1993), 88–89.
21. Annex no. 2 (political) to G-2 Report no. 49, 4/12/43, USNARA 165.
22. Netherlands Embassy to State, 22 December 1943, USNARA State Dec. File 851L.f04/8; Memorandum, Société Le Nickel, 31 December 1943, annexed to Foreign Economic Administration to State, 13 January 1944, USNARA State Dec. File 851L.504/9; and Memorandum of meeting on Javanese Labor Situation, 28 February 1944, USNARA State Dec. File 851L.6176/2–2844.
23. Annex no. 2 to G-2 Report no. 55, 15 January 1944, USNARA RG 165; Royal Australian Air Force Intelligence Report, "New Caledonian Potpourri," 1 April 1944, AA ACT. CRS A989, item 44/610/6.
24. Netherlands Embassy to State, 16 May 1944, USNARA State Dec. File 851L.504/11.
25. Henry Dewez to Albert Rapadzi, Nouméa, 13 November 1944, U.S. Military Censorship Intercept, USNARA RG 338.
26. Letter addressed to Commander of Allied troops in New Caledonia, 21 November 1944, USNARA State Dec. File 851L.504/11-2244.
27. Information provided by Ismet Kurtovitch, letter from Robert Brown.
28. The account of Eleanor Roosevelt's intervention on behalf of Lewis Feuer was provided by his daughter, Robin Miller, in a telephone interview, 2 January 2003. Feuer wrote two articles, published after the war, on political, economic and social conditions in New Caledonia. Lewis S. Feuer, "Cartel Control in New Caledonia," *Far Eastern Survey* XV (19 June 1946): 184–87, and "End of Coolie Labor in New Caledonia," *Far Eastern Survey*, XV (24 August 1946): 264–67. Lewis Feuer subsequently recounted his adventures in New Caledonia: "A Narrative of Personal Events and Ideas," in *Philosophy, History and Social Action: Essays in Honor of Lewis Feuer with an autobiographical essay by Lewis Feuer*, ed. Sidney Hook, William L. O'Neill and Roger O'Toole (Dordrecht, 1988), 20–25.
29. Annex no. 2 Political to G-2 Report no. 72, 13 May 1944, USNARA, RG 165.
30. Feuer in *Philosophy, History and Social Action*, 24.
31. Annex no. 2 Political to G-2 Report no. 100, 25 November 1944, USNARA, RG 165.

32. Annex no. 2 to G-2 Report no. 109, 26 January 1945, ibid.
33. Memorandum of meeting to discuss labor conditions in New Caledonia, 23 January 1945, USNARA State Dec. File 851L.504/1-2345.
34. Memorandum concerning the affairs of the Société Le Nickel, 2 February 1945, USNARA State Dec. File 851L.24/2-245.
35. Henry Dewez to Albert Rapadzi, 7 February 1945, U.S. Military Censorship intercept, USNARA RG 338.
36. Same to same, 27 September 1944, ibid.
37. State Department memorandum, "Indentured Labor, New Caledonia and New Hebrides: Observations," 28–31 March 1945, 16 June 1945, USNARA State Dec. File 851L.504/6-1645.
38. Annex no. 2 to G-2 Report no. 119, 7 April 1945, USNARA RG 165.
39. Netherlands Ambassador to State Department, 26 March 1945, and U.S. Consul, Nouméa, to State, 28 March 1945, USNARA State Dec. File 851L.3–2845; and Annex no. 2 to G-2 Report no. 124, 12 May 1945, USNARA RG 165.
40. Annex no. 2 to G-2 Report no. 129, 16 June 1945, USNARA RG 165.
41. U.S. Consul Robert Brown, Nouméa, to State, 18 June 1945, USNARA State Dec. File, RG 165.
42. Brown to State, 16 July 1945, USNARA State Dec. File 851L.6359/7-1645.
43. Cited in Kurtovitch, "La vie politique", 265n 59.
44. Barrowclough to Army HQ, NZ, 30 October 1944, NZ National Archives (NZNA), Nimitz-Barrowclough conversation, EA ser 1, 86/1/13 pt. 1.
45. "Report on Post-War Usage of New Caledonia" prepared for House Naval Affairs Committee (n.d. but August 1945), Appendix C, folder 34(10)(F), Naval History Center, Navy Yard, Washington, D.C.
46. Charles J. Weeks, Jr. "An Hour of Temptation: American Interests in New Caledonia, 1939–1945." *Australian Journal of Politics and History* 35 (Winter 1989), 193.
47. Many years later a surge of nostalgia for the "time of the Americans" occurred when a number of European settlers, hostile to Kanak demands for independence, called for New Caledonia to become a "New California" that would assure continuing white dominance in the 1980s. See Kim Munholland, "World War II and the end of Indentured Labor in New Caledonia," in Gordon Bond, ed., *Proceedings of the Annual Meeting of the Western Society for French History*, 18 (1991): 543–553.
48. Fiche résumant le rapport du Colonel Commandant Supérieur des Troupes relatif à la situation intérieure de nos possessions du Pacifique, 13 May 1947, SHA Outre-mer, Pacifique, c. 5.
49. Gilberte X (Gilberte Hagen) ... to M. Paul Hagen, 12 June 1943, reported by the censor 2 October 1943, ANSOM, N-C, c. 177. M. Ismet Kurtovitch, a historian of New Caledonia who is also a cousin of Mme Hagen, has kindly provided the identity of the author of the letter. I. Kurtovitch letter of 3 April 1995.
50. Cited in Jacqueline Sénès, *La vie quotidienne en Nouvelle-Calédonie de 1850 à nos jours* (Paris, 1985), 280–82.
51. Deschamps to Canberra, Nouméa Letter No. 2, 24 August 1944, AA ACT. CRS A989, item 44/610/17.
52. Deschamps to Canberra, Nouméa Letter #1, 11 November 1944, AA ACT. CRS A989, item 44/610/17.
53. David Reynolds, *Rich Relations: The American Occupation of Britain, 1942–1945* (New York, 1995), xxvii.
54. David A. Chappell, "Frontier Ethnogenesis: The Case of New Caledonia," *Journal of World History* 4:2 (1993): 318.
55. Quoted in Martyn Lyons, *The Totem and the Tricolour: A Short History of New Caledonia since 1774* (Kensington NSW, 1986), 101.

56. "Three years of occupation by 200,000 American troops during Second World War gave Kanak a taste of higher wages and better treatment." Chappell, "Frontier Ethnogenesis," 318. See also Michel Naepels, *Histoire de terres kanakes: Conflits fonciers et rapports sociaux dans la région de Houaïlou (Nouvelle-Calédonie)* (Paris, 1998), 221–22.
57. HQ 1 Island Command, appendix A to annex no. 2 (political) to weekly Intelligence (G-2) Report no. 139, 25 August 1945. See also Martyn Lyons, *The Totem and the Tricolour: A Short History of New Caledonia since 1774* (Kensington, NSW, 1986), 101.
58. 161 Sig Photo Co., New Caledonia—People, 11 Nov 44, USNARA, Photography Collection, 111-SC 364406.
59. Ken Coates and W.R. Morrison, "The American Rampant: Reflections on the Impact of United States Troops in Allied Countries during Second World War," *Journal of World History*, 2:2 (1991). See also Emily S. Rosenberg, *Spreading the American Dream: American Economic and Cultural Expansion* (New York, 1982), ch. 10, on the wartime cultural offensive.
60. See Ariel Dorfman, *How to Read Donald Duck: Imperialist Ideology in the Disney Comic* (New York, 2 ed., 1991).
61. Hua, *De la Mélanésie au Vietnam*, 76.
62. "Rapport d'Adjudant Guiguen, Commandant la Brigade, sur l'état d'esprit des indigènes de la circonscription de Ponérihouen," 10 May 1943, and "Rapport d'Adjutant Guiguen, Commandant la Brigade, sur les agissements des indigènes des tribus de Goa, Goyetta et Tchamba, en 1942 et 1943," 13 August 1945, SHA, Outre-mer, Pacifique, c. 2.
63. Interview with Yves Tallec, 21 May 2001. Yves Tallec's father sent his son on a cruise with Admiral Calhoun to keep track of his contacts with natives on Maré Island, where Chief Naisseline was reported to be seeking American help in his move toward independence. Nothing came of this adventure.
64. Letter to M le Syndic des Affaires Indigènes, 5 May 1945, SHA Outre-mer c. 2.
65. Annex no. 2 to G-2 Report no. 137, 11 August 1945, USNARA RG 165.
66. Annex no. 2 to G-2 Report no. 138, 18 August 1945, ibid.
67. Annex no. 2 to G-2 Report no. 136, 4 August 1945, ibid.
68. Annex no. 2 to G-2 Report no. 139, 15 August 1945, ibid.
69. "V-J Day in Nouméa", 15 August 1945, Navy Yard, Admin. Hist Appendices, 34(10)(J) Washington D.C.
70. Annex no. 2 to G-2 Report no. 137, 11 August 1945, USNARA RG 165.
71. Ibid.
72. Le Gouverneur de la Nouvelle-Calédonie et dépendences à Maître Michel Vergès, 5 December 1944, ANSOM, Affaires Politiques, c. 509.
73. Annex no. 2 to G-2 Report no. 139, 25 August 1945, USNARA RG 165.
74. M. Vergès to M.W. Johnston, British Consul, 20 August 1945 United Kingdom Public Record Office (PRO) FO969/84 134189.
75. William Roger Louis, *Imperialism at Bay: The United States and the Decolonization of the British Empire 1941–1945* (New York, 1978), 42–43.
76. Mathews-Hickerson file, roll 13, frames 338ff.
77. Christopher Thorne, *Allies of a Kind: United States, Britain, and the War against Japan* (New York, 1978), 501.
78. Louis, *Imperialism at Bay*, 454.
79. OSS R&A report, 10/4/45, cited in Louis, *Imperialism at Bay*, 46.
80. Mathews-Hickerson file, roll 10, 0281-2.
81. Acting Secretary of State (Grew) to Ambassador in France (Caffrey), 9 May 1945, *Foreign Relations of the United States (FRUS)* 1945, vol. 6, 307.
82. Acting Secretary of State to Chargé in China (Robertson), 5 October 1945, citing cable State to New Dehli, 30 August 1945, *FRUS* 1945, vol. 6, 313. Louis, *Imperialism at Bay*, 552 and Thorne, *Allies of a Kind*, 633.

83. "Statement by President Truman of France's Role in the Settlement of Questions of World and European Interest," attached to "Memorandum of Conversation by Acting Secretary of State (Grew)", 18 May 1945, *FRUS* 1945, vol. 6, 690–91.
84. Caffrey to State, 20 May 1945, ibid. 697.
85. Same to same, 13 March 1945, ibid. 300.
86. Thorne, *Allies of a Kind*, 632.
87. Louis, *Imperialism at Bay*, 568–69.
88. Caffrey to State, 11 August and 16 August 1945, *FRUS* 1945, vol. 4, 703, 705.
89. Quoted in Irwin Wall, "Harry S. Truman and Charles de Gaulle," in *De Gaulle and the United States, a Centenary Reappraisal,* ed. Robert O. Paxton and Nicholas Wahl (Oxford and Providence, 1994), 124.
90. Thorne, *Allies of a Kind*, 633.

Conclusion

V-J Day and Postwar Assessments, Accounts and Balances

For the Americans in Nouméa the duty day had begun as another routine day on 15 August 1945. Discussions were taking place at the local headquarters on how to dispose of surplus property. The Commanding Officer, Admiral Calhoun, was in Hawaii discussing "roll-up" procedures with Admiral Nimitz. The harbor was virtually empty with no ships at anchor in the main roadstead where in 1942 at one moment eighty-six were awaiting dock space. Only a dozen or so assorted craft could be seen in what was now a sleepy port.[1]

No official celebration had been organized for V-J day, but in the streets of Nouméa impromptu parades developed. Trucks filled the streets, adorned with streamers and dragging steel garbage cans for noisy effect. All of the trucks were filled with an assortment of sailors, soldiers and Kanak according to the official history. Of all those out to celebrate, the Kanak seemed to enjoy V-J Day the most, and all vehicles soon had Kanak aboard. A mixed crowd surged through the streets, including French descendants of the deportation, Creoles, Kanak, Javanese, and Tonkinese. An indication of a postwar complexity for New Caledonia could be seen, if only briefly, in the victory celebration in Nouméa. By late afternoon the celebration intensified, and the town filled with the enthusiasm of the Kanak population. That night Melanesians danced in Coconut Square in the center of Nouméa. Ethnic divisions were momentarily put aside. Kanak, Tonkinese, Javanese, American and African-American soldiers and sailors shared a moment of celebration, and they paraded together through the streets in impromptu gaiety,. Some had to be carried away by the MPs, but there were very few fights. The war had ended, but beneath the celebration the outline of postwar colonial challenges could be seen.

Victory day brought with it an assessment of the American time in New Caledonia, now clearly coming to an end. The official historian for the navy headquarters command reflected upon how New Caledonia would regain its French character, despite the evidence everywhere of the American occupation. A bit of paint would efface the red, white and blue signs on the curio shops. The Allied bar, the California bar, the Texas bar and the Triangle bar could all be converted to their former uses. Although some of the Quonset huts were being taken down, preparations were underway for a transfer of American-built structures, such as the Pentagon or the navy hospital at Anse Vata, to French control. This transfer of surplus property would take place over the next eighteen months. There still was much to do to wrap-up the American presence in New Caledonia, but as the Australian consul had noted earlier, despite its overwhelming scale what was American was transient and what was French was permanent in New Caledonia.[2]

Still there were lasting legacies from the war and "the time of the Americans." Although difficult to measure, the American presence had an unsettling effect upon the French colonial order, seen in a growing assertiveness on the part of Kanak and Asian populations. The American-induced prosperity, however limited, opened up possibilities for better wages and living conditions. Indirect American influence contributed to the ending of indentured labor for the Asians. As for Kanak, many in American service had learned new skills such as operating tractors, machinery and other equipment, which gave them a certain amount of confidence. Under the French administration Kanak were not allowed to have vehicles. American officers occasionally presented Kanak chiefs with cars in appreciation of their assistance in recruiting Kanak workers. In his extensive study of the political evolution of New Caledonia from 1940 to 1952, Ismet Kurtovitch notes how French officials feared that friendly relations between American officers and Kanak leaders on the reservations would lead to erosion of traditional relations. Ultimately these contacts compelled the French colonial administration to reconsider its native policy.[3] Returning Kanak veterans from the Pacific Battalion expected that the suspended promise of political rights would be honored at the end of the war.

Improvements introduced by the Americans made Nouméa a brighter, cleaner and healthier place to live than the sleepy colonial town that they had found on arrival. Communications had been improved, roads were upgraded, and bridges replaced the barges crossing the many rivers along the western coast. Place names would recall the time of the Americans as the Caledonians renamed streets to honor General Patch, Admiral Halsey and other American commanders who had come to New Caledonia during the early, trying days of the war in the South Pacific. "Motor Pool" and "Receiving" became and remain names of districts in greater Nouméa. This renaming for the Americans reflected, despite the inconveniences and frictions, a favorable memory for many Caledonians.

However, a sense that something had been damaged by the American presence tempered the gratitude of the Caledonians. They thought that the amount owed under Lend-lease could be reduced. Calculations on Lend-lease led to an attempt to balance accounts on how much the Americans had invested in New Caledonia against the amount of reverse Lend-lease that the Caledonians had provided. A Communist member of the council asked that the United States pay the Fr7,875,000 ($183,000) spent on roads used by the American forces and an additional Fr7,447,387 ($173,195) spent for upkeep of installations maintained by the colony for American usage. The chief veterinarian, Dr. Jean Vergès, claimed substantial compensation for damages caused to the cattle farmers as a result of a tick infestation introduced by the mules from Australia brought by the Americans in 1942.

When Jan Bourgeau revealed that the total Lend-lease through 1944 had amounted to $48 million while reverse Lend-lease came to no more than $10 million, the council's hopes for substantial compensation were dashed. Finally the telephone system was left as compensation for the losses caused by the tick infection.[4] In addition, the Americans left behind a great deal of equipment and many buildings that were converted to postwar uses, including an oceanographic institute, an aquarium, and the headquarters for the South Pacific Commission, which was installed in the "Pentagon" headquarters at Anse Vata. There was a selloff of surplus equipment at bargain prices, which ended on orders from Paris. The French Government wanted to reserve the colonial market. Some surplus equipment, including jeeps and machinery, was dumped into the harbor, although not as much was so disposed as Caledonian legend and memory would later claim. A few American servicemen left New Caledonia with wives, who would find a different way of life awaiting them stateside.

Alongside American preparations for departure, Caledonian politics revealed the extent to which the war's experience and memory of events had become embedded in the consciousness of Caledonian residents. Old wounds and quarrels resurfaced dramatically in the campaign to elect a representative from New Caledonia to a Constituent Assembly in Paris that would draft a new constitution for a restored France and determine the future course of the French Empire in Africa, Asia and the Pacific. The electoral campaign became the occasion for Governor Tallec to uncover the maneuvers of Michel Vergès, whose activities had plagued successive Free-French governors and had contributed greatly to poisoning relations with the Americans.

The occasion was an attack upon Governor Tallec, whose "calumnies and slanders" Michel Vergès blamed for his resounding defeat in his bid to represent New Caledonia in the Constituent Assembly in Paris. As usual he published his denunciation of the governor in the local press. Governor Tallec decided to respond with a full exposé of Michel Vergès's wartime activities, including the way in which his diatribes weakened and discredited central French authority and had harmed French-American relations on the island. In so doing Governor Tallec would reveal the source of considerable misunderstanding and antagonism between the Americans and Free French in wartime New Caledonia. This public exposé was, as the American intelligence report put it, "the most sensational development for a long time in New Caledonia['s] political history."[5]

Feeling that he had to put an end to Vergès's campaign, Governor Tallec cited dozens of insulting letters that Michel Vergès had sent to Montchamp, Fourcade, Bourgeau, Laigret and himself with imagined offenses attributed to them. Vergès did so in the name of French national interests but in fact used his attacks for his own aims. Why, asked Governor Tallec in his public reply to Vergès, had he sought since 1940 to avenge his personal hatreds by invoking the name of French interests?[6] The result of these constant attacks upon representatives of General de Gaulle had discredited the authority of the Free French despite his claim to represent true Gaullism in New Caledonia. Although too late to avoid the *mésentente*, Tallec tried to set the record straight, noting that Admiral d'Argenlieu was pushed by Michel Vergès, who was acting out his personal vendetta, to commit serious psychological and political mistakes in dealing with Governor Sautot, the Caledonians and the Americans.[7]

Of all the Free-French representatives sent to New Caledonia during the war, Governor Tallec showed the most accurate understanding of the circumstances that had touched off the riots of May 1942 and had contributed so much to the wartime *mésentente* between the Free French and the Americans. He was the only governor to publicly confront Vergès and accuse him of having not advanced but actually harmed the image and prestige of Free France in the South Pacific. This did not mean that Tallec became an uncritical admirer of Sautot, whom he described as "a mediocrity."

Did the French-American *mésentente* in New Caledonia reveal a more widespread anxiety and resentment among the Gaullist Free French toward the United States? Despite Governor Tallec's report, the Gaullists would persist in their belief that the Americans had come to New Caledonia in 1942 to take it over. In Gaullist historiography events in New Caledonia are seen as part of a broader American intention to break up the Free French movement in order to more easily rearrange the postwar world at the expense of the French Empire. The Americans are held responsible for the hostile relationship that ensued. This version reappears in many French biographies of General de Gaulle and other accounts of wartime relations with the United States. A modification of this French critique of American behavior in New Caledonia is Jean-Louis Crémieux-Brilhac's *La France Libre*, which recognizes that Admiral d'Argenlieu also contributed significantly to the development of Free French hostility toward the Americans in New Caledonia and London.[8]

The Gaullists, led by Admiral d'Argenlieu, believed Michel Vergès because he expressed their own xenophobic suspicions and anxieties concerning an Anglo-Saxon threat to France and the French Empire. New Caledonia revealed the ease with which the Free French transferred the French historic colonial rivalry and suspicion of "Perfidious Albion" to the Americans during the Second World War.[9] This transfer became apparent when the American "menace" replaced the Australian threat to French interests in the South Pacific. The Gaullist legend of a threatened takeover from the moment of the American arrival in March 1942 has persisted because it fit Gaullist preconceptions about the imperialistic and domineering ambitions of the "Anglo-Saxons." Roosevelt's musings about an American enforcement of postwar security system that offered little place for France deepened the mistrust. From this point Gaullist policy toward the United States would be devoted to resisting the power, influence and ascendancy of what would later be called the American "super" or even "hyper" power, a French David challenging an American Goliath.

From an American perspective, Gaullist resistance came to be equated with a deliberately uncooperative attitude, even obstructionism, in the war effort by placing political issues ahead of military needs. In the eyes of Roosevelt or Admiral Halsey the French were uncooperative and unreliable partners in the war effort. This meant exclusion from discussions of strategy and policy, whether in New Caledonia, North Africa or in preparation for the liberation of France itself.[10] The Americans also failed to understand or appreciate General de Gaulle's concern for the unity of the empire and his anger over allied failures to accord him recognition as the embodiment of French interests. American insensitivity to Gaullist pride and French prestige was a major element of the *mésentente* between the Americans and the Free French.

The Americans at times tried to place Free-French coolness and resentment within the context of French nationalism and wounded pride. All residents of the French Empire had felt the humiliation of the 1940 defeat. The colonies that rallied legitimately claimed pride of place among the resisters of the first hour, but the shame of defeat had been erased less as a result of colonial resistance than with the victory in Europe "when Hitler [sic] finally surrendered to, among others, General de Gaulle."[11] Despite the euphoria of a common victory in Europe, American resentment at Gaullist hostility, which the Americans first encountered in New Caledonia, would persist. The result was an enduring *mésentente*, leading American historians to characterize the relationship that developed during the Second World War as one of "hostile allies" or a "cold alliance" or between "guarded friends."[12]

Governor Tallec recognized that responsibility for the *mésentente* was to be found on both sides. As the Americans prepared to leave New Caledonia, he reflected upon what had been a difficult relationship. He feared that the Americans would withdraw into isolation after the war. Concern over Soviet ambitions in Europe caused much of his anxiety. An American presence was necessary for the stability of Europe and to prevent Russian domination of France and the continent, which would occur, he claimed, if France became dependent upon the alliance with Russia that General de Gaulle had signed at the end of 1944. He stated that what the United States did was important for the whole world. "We are all Americans now," was his conclusion. He hoped that an understanding between France and the United States could be achieved, and he asked that the United States "deal a little more tactfully with French sensibilities so that minor differences do not prevent a rapprochement between people [who are] basically firm and sincere friends."[13]

Wartime New Caledonia suggested that preventing minor differences from escalating into major disputes in French-American relations would not be an easy task. It was not then, nor would it be in the next several decades. Jacques Tallec's skill in dealing with the Americans, which gained him the American medal of freedom and also insured that the French flag would fly over New Caledonia at the war's end, was not always emulated in French postwar dealings with the United States. Nor did the Americans always follow Governor Tallec's plea to deal "more tactfully" with French sensibilities after 1945.

Despite Governor Tallec's hope, the Franco-American *mésentente* would continue. Wartime New Caledonia as a "rock of contention" provides a metaphor for the difficult relationship that has marked French-American differences during and after the Second World War. The Gaullist legacy would be one of resistance to American tendencies toward domination, producing an official, Gaullist "anti-Americanism" when French interests as a global power have been at stake or when French cultural identity has confronted a perceived menace of Americanization. On the American side the contention has led to a questioning of France as an ally, often identifying French behavior and policies as hostile in opposition to American global ambitions whether in Europe, Asia, Africa or in the Middle-East. The question for the future of French-American relations then and now is: can this *mésentente* be managed without producing a permanent rift between "basically firm and sincere friends?" In the many postwar crises this basic rift has not yet occurred despite serious differences and harsh words. But the *mésentente* means that this is a relationship requiring management to assure that "guarded friends" or "hostile allies" do not become "enemies."

Notes

1. "V-J Day in Nouméa", 15 August 1945, Operational Archives, Naval History Center, Hist Appendix, 2.
2. Noel Deschamps, Nouméa Letter #1, 11 May 1944, AA ACT, CRS A989 item 44/610/17.
3. Ismet Kurtovitch, "La vie politique en Nouvelle-Calédonie (1940–1953)," 2 vols (Ph.D. diss., Université française du Pacifique, 1998), vol. 1, 44–45, 167.
4. Annex no. 2 to G-2 Report no. 113, 24 February 1945, USNARA RG 165.
5. Annex no. 2 to G-2 Report no. 149, 3 November 1945, ibid.
6. Governor of New Caledonia (Tallec) to Maître Michel Vergès, 5 December 1944, ANSOM, c. 509.
7. Gouverneur Nouméa à France Outremer 18 January 1947, reference kindly provided by Ismet Kurtovitch from Territorial Archives, New Caledonia. Governor Sautot was upset that the Gaullists would accuse him of "selling" New Caledonia to the Americans and defended himself in Henri Sautot, *Grandeur et décadence du Gaullisme dans le Pacifique* (Melbourne, 1949).

8. M. Crémieux-Brilhac's recognizes mistakes made on both sides. See Jean-Louis Crémieux-Brilhac, *La France Libre: De l'Appel du 18 juin à la Libération* (Paris, 1996), 35, 297–306, 918.
9. Charles G. Cogan, *French Negotiating Behavior: Dealing with* La Grande Nation (Washington, D.C., 2003), 41.
10. See Martin Thomas, *The French Empire at War 1940–45* (Manchester and New York), 133–39.
11. "V-J Day in Nouméa", 15 August 1945, Navy Yard, Hist Appendix, 7.
12. Milton Viorst, *Hostile Allies: FDR and Charles de Gaulle* (New York, 1965); Frank Costigliola, *France and the United States: The Cold Alliance since World War II* (New York, 1992); Charles Cogan, *Oldest Allies, Guarded Friends: The United States and France since 1940* (Westport, 1994).
13. Annex no. 2 to G-2 Report no. 133, 14 July 1945, USNARA RG 165.

BIBLIOGRAPHY

Archives and Government Documents

Australia. Australian Archives, Canberra (AA).
Australia. Department of Foreign Affairs. *Documents on Australian Foreign Policy, 1937–1949 (DAFP)* vol. 3–6. Canberra 1975–1983.
France. Archives du Ministère des Affaires Étrangères, Paris (MAE).
France. Archives Nationales, Paris (AN).
France. Archives Nationales, Section Contemporaine (ANSC).
France. Archives Nationales, Section d'Outre-Mer, Aix-en-Provence (ANSOM).
France. Archives du Service Historique de l'Armée, Château de Vincennes (SHA).
New Zealand. National Archives, Wellington (NZNA).
United Kingdom. Public Record Office, Kew (PR0).
United States. Department of State. *Foreign Relations of the United States 1940–1945.* Washington, D.C. 1957–1968 (FRUS).
United States. Franklin Delano Roosevelt Library, Hyde Park, New York (FDR Library).
United States. Hoover Institute Archives, Kittredge Papers, Stanford, California (Hoover).
United States. Library of Congress, Halsey Papers, Washington D.C., (LC),
United States. National Archives and Record Administration, Washington D.C., (USNARA).
United States. Operational Archives, Naval History Center, Washington, D.C., (Op Arch, NHC).

Books and Articles Cited

Aglion, Raoul. *L'Epopée de la France combattante.* New York, 1943.
———. *De Gaulle et Roosevelt.* Paris, 1984.
Aldrich, Robert and Isabelle Merle, eds. *France Abroad: Indochina, New Caledonia, Wallis and Futuna, Mayotte.* Sydney, 1997.

Allen, Donald Ray. *French Views of America in the 1930s*. New York, 1979.
Asselin, Giles and Ruth Mastron. *Au Contraire! Figuring out the French*. Yarmouth, Maine, 2001.
Auque, René, "Le 'Chevreuil' bâtiment FNFL." *Revue de la France Libre*, 258 (2ème trimestre 1987).
Baudoux, "Le Rapport Baudoux sur le ralliement de Georges Baudoux (fils de l'ecrivain)." *Bulletin de la société d'études historiques de la Nouvelle-Calédonie*, no. 24 (1975).
Bayardelle, André. "Le rapport Bayardelle sur le ralliement de 1940." *Bulletin de la société d'études historiques de la Nouvelle-Calédonie*, no. 20 (1974).
Bell, P.M.H. *A Certain Eventuality: Britain and the Fall of France*. London, 1974.
Béziat, André. *Franklin Roosevelt et la France (1939–1945): la diplomatie de l'entêtement*. Paris, 1997.
Bouscat, René. *De Gaulle-Giraud: Dossier d'une mission*. Paris, 1967.
Broche, François. *Le bataillon des guitaristes, l'épopée inconnue des FFL de Tahiti à Bir-Hakeim, 1940–1942*. Paris, 1970.
Brooks, Charles W. *America in France's Hopes and Fears, 1890–1920*. New York, 1987.
Cerny, Philip G. *The Politics of Grandeur: Ideological Aspects of de Gaulle's Foreign Policy*. Cambridge and New York, 1980.
Chambrun, René de. *Mission and Betrayal 1940–1945: Working with Franklin Roosevelt to Help Save Britain and Europe*. Stanford, 1993.
Chandler, Alfred D., Stephen E. Ambrose et al. *The Papers of Dwight David Eisenhower: The War Years*. 5 vols. Baltimore, 1970.
Chappel, David A. "Frontier Ethnogenesis: The Case of New Caledonia." *Journal of World History* 4, 2 (1993).
Churchill, Winston S. *The Second World War*. 6 vols. Boston, 1948–1953.
Coates, Ken and W.R. Morrison, "The American Rampant: Reflections on the Impact of United States Troops in Allied Countries during World War II." *Journal of World History*, 2, 2 (1991).
Cogan, Charles G. *Charles de Gaulle: A Brief Biography with Documents*. New York, 1996.
———. *French Negotiating Behavior: Dealing with La Grande Nation*. Washington, D.C., 2003.
———. *Oldest Allies, Guarded Friends: The United States and France since 1940*. Westport Conn., 1994.
Costigliola, Frank. *France and the United States: The Cold Alliance since World War II*. New York, 1992.
Crémieux-Brilhac, Jean-Louis. *La France Libre: De l'appel du 18 juin à la Libération*. Paris, 1996.
Cronin, Francis D. *Under the Southern Cross: The Saga of the Americal Division*. Washington D.C., 1951.

Curton, Emile de. *Tahiti 1940: Récit du ralliement à la France libre des Établissements français d'Océanie.* Paris, 1973.

Dallek, Robert. *Franklin Roosevelt and American Foreign Policy, 1932–1945.* New York, 1981 ed.

De Gaulle, Charles. *Mémoires de Guerre,* 3 vols. Paris, 1954–1959.

———. *Call to Honor 1940–1942: Documents.* tr. Jonathan Griffin. London, 1955.

———. *War Memoirs,* vol. 1. *The Call to Honor 1940–1942.* tr. Jonathan Griffin. London, 1955.

———. *The Complete Memoirs of Charles de Gaulle,* tr. Jonathan Griffin and Richard Howard. New York, 1968.

———. *Discours et messages I: Pendant la guerre.* Paris, 1970.

———. *Lettres, Notes et Carnets.* 3 vols. Paris 1981–1983.

De la Gorce, Paul-Marie. *De Gaulle.* Paris, 1999.

Dorfman, Ariel. *How to Read Donald Duck: Imperialist Ideology in the Disney Comic.* New York, 1991.

Dower, John. *War without Mercy: Race and Power in the Pacific War.* New York, 1986.

Feuer, Lewis S. "Cartel Control in New Caledonia," *Far Eastern Survey,* XV 19 June 1946.

———. "End of Coolie Labor in New Caledonia," *Far Eastern Survey,* XV 24 August 1946.

———. "A Narrative of Personal Events and Ideas," in *Philosophy, History and Social Action: Essays in Honor of Lewis Feuer with an Autobiographical Essay by Lewis Feuer,* ed. Sidney Hook, William L. O'Neill and Roger O'Toole. Dordrecht, 1988.

Fite, Gilbert C. *Richard B. Russell, Jr.: Senator from Georgia.* Chapel Hill, 1991.

Forrestal, James. *The Forrestal Diaries,* ed. Walter Millis. New York, 1951.

Fritsch-Estrangin, Guy. *New York entre de Gaulle et Pétain: Les Français aux États-Unis de 1940 à 1946.* Paris, 1969.

Fromkin, David. *In the Time of the Americans: FDR, Truman, Eisenhower, Marshall, MacArthur—The Generation that Changed America's Role in the World.* New York, 1995.

Funk, Arthur Layton. *Charles de Gaulle: The Crucial Years, 1943–1944.* Norman, 1959.

Gates, Eleanor M. *End of the Affair: The Collapse of the Anglo-French Alliance, 1939–1940.* Berkeley, 1981.

Gun, Nerin E. *Les secrets des archives américaines: Pétain, Laval, De Gaulle* (Paris, 1979).

Halsey, Fleet Commander William F. and Lt. Commander J. Bryan III. *Admiral Halsey's Story.* New York, 1947.

Harmetz, Aljean. *The Making of Casablanca: Bogart, Bergman, and World War II.* New York, 2002 ed.

Henningham, Stephen. "The French Administration, the Local Population, and the American Presence in New Caledonia, 1943–1944." *Journal de la société des océanistes*, no. 98, 1 (1994).

Hoisington, William A. *The Casablanca Connection: French Colonial Policy*. Chapel Hill, 1984.

Hua, Dong Sy. *De la Mélanésie au Vietnam: Itinéraire d'un colonisé devenu francophile*. Paris, 1993.

Hurstfield, Julian. *America and the French Nation, 1939–1945*. Chapel Hill, 1986.

Jennings, Eric T. *Vichy in the Tropics: Pétain's National Revolution in Madagascar, Guadeloupe, and Indochina, 1940–1944*. Stanford, 2001.

Judt, Tony. *Past Imperfect: French Intellectuals, 1944–1956*. Berkeley, 1992.

Kaspi, André. *Franklin D. Roosevelt*. Paris, 1988.

———. *La libération de la France juin 1944–janvier 1946*. Paris. 1995.

Koch, Howard. *Casablanca, Script and Legend: The Original Screen Plan and 25 Classic Stills*. Woodstock, NY, 1992.

Kuisel, Richard. *Seducing the French: the Dilemma of Americanization*. Berkeley, 1993.

Kurtovitch, Ismet. "Du Conseil d'administration de la Nouvelle-Calédonie pendant la Seconde Guerre Mondiale." *Bulletin de la société d'études historiques de la Nouvelle-Calédonie*, no. 106 (1996).

———. "La vie politique en Nouvelle-Calédonie (1940–1953)." Ph.D. diss., Université du Pacifique, 1998.

Lacorne, Denis, Jacques Rupnick, Marie-France Tointet, eds. *Rise and Fall of Anti-Americanism: A Century of French Perception*. New York, 1990.

Lacouture, Jean. *De Gaulle*. 3 vols. Paris, 1984–6.

Lacourrège, Gérard and Pierre Alibert, *La présence américaine en Nouvelle-Calédonie*. Nouméa, 1981.

Langer, William L. *Our Vichy Gamble*. New York, 1947.

Laveissière, Pierre. "Introduction a la lecture d'un journal et extraits d'un journal tenu a Nouméa en septembre 1940." *Neptunia*, no. 139 (1980).

Lawrey, John. "A Catch on the Boundary: Australia and the Free French Movement in 1940." *Journal of Pacific History*, 10, 3 (1975).

———. *The Cross of Lorraine in the South Pacific: Australia and the Free French Movement 1940–1942*. Canberra, 1982.

Ledwidge, Bernard. *De Gaulle*. Paris, 1984.

Legrand, Julien-Joseph. *L'Indochine à l'heure japonaise*. Cannes, 1963.

Louis, William Roger. *Imperialism at Bay: The United States and the Decolonization of the British Empire 1941–1945*. New York, 1978.

Lyons, Martyn. *The Totem and the Tricolour: A Short History of New Caledonia since 1774*. Kensington NSW, 1986.

Marder, Arthur J. *Operation Menace: The Dakar Expedition and the Dudley North Affair*. London and New York, 1976.

Massigli, René. *Une comédie des erreurs, 1943–1956.* Paris, 1978.
Mathy, Jean-Philippe. *Extrême-Occident: French Intellectuels and America.* Chicago, 1993.
Mehlman, Jeffrey. *Émigré New York: French Intellectuals in Wartime Manhattan, 1940–1944.* Baltimore and London, 2000.
Michel, Henri. *Histoire de la France Libre.* Paris, 4ed., 1980.
Morrison, Samuel Eliot. *History of United States Naval Operations in World War II.* 15 vols. Boston, 1984.
Morton, Louis. *Strategy and Command: The First Two Years.* Washington, D.C., 1962.
Munholland, Kim. "World War II and the End of Indentured Labor in New Caledonia." In *Proceedings of the Annual Meeting of the Western Society for French History* 18, ed. Gordon Bond, (1991).
Naepels, Michel. *Histoire de terres kanakes: Conflits fonciers et rapports sociaux dans la région de Houaïlou (Nouvelle-Calédonie).* Paris, 1998.
Nettlebeck, Colin. *Forever French: Exile in the United States, 1939–1945.* Oxford, 1991.
Païta, Gabriel. *Témoinage Kanak: D'Opao au pays de la Nouvelle-Calédonie 1929–1999, Récit autobiographique de Gabriel Païta*, eds, Jérôme Cazaumayou and Thomas de Dekker. Paris, 1999.
Passy, Colonel (André Dewavrin). vol 1 of 3: *Le Bureau de Londres.* Monte Carlo, 1947.
Paxton, Robert O. and Nicholas Wahl eds. *De Gaulle and the United States: A Centennial Reappraisal.* Oxford and Providence, R.I., 1994.
———. *Vichy France: Old Guard and New Order.* New York, 1972.
Pineau, Christian. *La simple verité 1940–1945.* Paris, 1960.
Pisier, Georges. "Le Ralliement de la Calédonie et l'intervention Britannique (juin–octobre 1940)." *Bulletin de la société d'études historiques de la Nouvelle-Calédonie,* no. 62 (1985).
Portes, Jacques. *Une fascination réticent, les États-Unis dans l'opinion française, 1870–1914.* Lille, 1991.
Potter, E.B. *Bull Halsey.* Annapolis, 1985.
Regnault, Jean-Marc and Ismet Kurtovitch. "Les ralliements du Pacifique en 1940. Entre légende gaulliste, enjeux stratégiques mondiaux et rivalités Londres/Vichy." *Revue d'histoire moderne et contemporaine* 49, 4 (octobre–décembre 2002).
Revel, Jean-François. *L'obsession anti-américaine: Son fonctionnement et ses causes, ses inconséquences.* Paris, 2002.
Reynolds, David. *Rich Relations: The American Occupation of Britain, 1942–1945.* New York, 1995.
Roger, Philippe. *L'Ennemi Américain: Généologie de l'antiaméricanisme français.* Paris, 2002.

Rosenberg, Emily S. *Spreading the American Dream: American Economic and Cultural Expansion.* New York, 1982.

Rossi, Mario. *Roosevelt and the French.* Westport, Conn. 1993.

———. "United States Military Authorities and Free France, 1942–1944." *The Journal of Military History* 61, 1 (January 1997).

Roussel, Eric. *Charles de Gaulle.* Paris, 2002.

Sarris, Andrew. *"You Ain't Heard Nothin' Yet": The American Talking Film, history and Memory 1927–1949.* New York and Oxford, 1998.

Sautot, Henri. *Grandeur et décadence du Gaullisme dans le Pacifique.* Melbourne, 1949.

Sénès, Jacqueline. *La Vie quotidienne en Nouvelle-Calédonie de 1850 à nos jours.* Paris, 1985.

Simington, Margot. "Australia and the New Caledonia Coup d'Etat of 1940." *Australian Outlook* 30, 1 (1976).

Strauss, David. *Menace in the West: The Rise of French Anti-Americanism in Modern Times.* Westport, Conn., 1978.

Thomas, Martin. *The French Empire at War 1940–1945.* Manchester and New York, 1998.

Thorne, Christopher. *Allies of a Kind: United States, Britain, and the War against Japan.* New York, 1978.

Viorst, Milton. *Hostile Allies: FDR and Charles de Gaulle.* New York, 1965.

Wall, Irwin M. "From Anti-Americanism to Francophobia: The Saga of French and American Intellectuals." *French Historical Studies* 18, 4 (Fall 1994): 1083–100.

———. *The United States and the Making of Postwar France.* Cambridge, 1991.

Weeks, Charles J., Jr. "An Hour of Temptation: American Interests in New Caledonia, 1939–1945." *Australian Journal of Politics and History* 35 (Winter 1989).

Welles, Benjamin. *Sumner Welles: FDR's Global Strategist.* New York, 1997.

Wyant, William K. *Sandy Patch: A Biography of Lt. Gen. Alexander M. Patch.* New York and London, 1991.

Wylie, Laurence W., *Beaux gestes: A Guide to French Body Talk.* Cambridge, Mass., 1977.

———. and Armand Bégué, *Les Français.* Englewood Cliffs, 1970.

INDEX

A

Adelaide (ship), 44, 45, 46, 47, 50, 51, 52, 55, 56, 57, 61
administrative council, 63, 101; members of, 80n. 5
Admiralty Islands, 202
Aglion, Raoul, 27
agricultural products: subsidies for, 147
Algeria: and continued resistance, 36
Allied Military Government of Occupied Territory (AMGOT), 189, 190, 196n. 75
Americal Division, 3, 89, 111, 125
Amiral Charner (ship), 45, 47, 55, 56, 59n. 54
Anglo-French Condominium, New Hebrides, 44, 46
Anse Vata: hospital, 203, 227; "Pentagon" headquarters, 203, 211, 227, 228
anti-Americanism, 4, 178–85. *See also* Laigret, Christian; Thierry d'Argenlieu, Georges; Vergès, Michel
anti-Communism, 220
Antilles, 21, 45
Archer, C.H., 82n. 51
Armed Services Command: buildings built by, 127–29, 211, 227
Armistice Commission, Wiesbaden, 16
Artigues, Major, 159
Asians
 and the American way of life, 215
 employment of, 130, 156, 163
 as indentured labor, 88, 157–58, 201, 205, 206, 207–10, 227
Atherton, Ray, 28, 112, 174, 176
Audrain, Jean, 80n. 5, 161
Australia
 and coal for New Caledonia, 37, 42
 and cooperation with the Free French, 188
 and improvement of New Caledonia defenses, 66, 67
 and Japan, 40, 85
 and fleet in Mediterranean theater, 40, 45
 as a market for New Caledonia exports, 41, 68
 and military mission to New Caledonia, 67, 68
 and representation on New Caledonia, 40, 41, 44
 and rights to bases, 188
 and Roosevelt's postwar plans, 187–88
 security problems, 40
Automatic Telephone Company of Chicago, 25
Autonomist Constitutional Reform Party, 37

B

Ballard, B.C., 45, 46, 80n. 7, 115n. 56, 151
 as Australian consul to Nouméa, 41
 and delay of de Gaulle telegram to Pognon, 47–48
 and d'Argenlieu's mission, 76
 and elections, 136
 and Laigret, 200
 and Sautot's Free French administration, 68, 81n. 41
 and an underground economy, 130, 158
Bank of Indochina, 155
Banuelos, Joseph., 105, 136
barbershops, 148
Barrowclough, Harold, 129, 210
Baudoux, Georges, 35, 38; and coup, 48–50
Bayardelle, André, 35, 37, 53, 54, 65, 71, 184
Beer, Mrs., 104–5
Belgian Congo: and Lend-lease, 26–27
Benitier, Mme, 152, 153
Bergès, Mme Pierre, 105

Bergès, Pierre
   and abduction by d'Argenlieu, 105, 115nn. 31, 60, 135, 204–5
   appointed to new administrative council, 80n. 5
   as an autonomist, 135, 136
   and d'Argenlieu, 135, 144
   as head of Caledonian Committee, 207
   and elections, 137, 142–43, 147, 207
   and a Gaullist movement, 38
   and indentured labor, 209
   and Laigret, 145, 148, 164, 166
   and Sautot recall, 98, 99
Berle, A.A., 109, 111, 185; and Montchamp, 112, 113
Bidault, Georges, 219, 221
Biddle, Anthony Drexel, 8, 25
Billotte, Pierre, 178–79, 184–85
Bir-Hakeim, 117n. 105
Bizerte: and a trusteeship, 175
black-market economy, 130, 156, 158, 159
Blandy, R.D., 46
Blue Fleet, 202, 203
Boegner, Etienne, 27, 28, 178
Boegner, Marc, 27
Boisson, Pierre, 13–14, 17
Bonbright, 185
Bonnet, Henri, 219
Bora Bora: and a United States air base, 28
Boris, George, 180
Boucher, Charles, 159–60
Bourdinat, Gaston, 206, 207
Bourgeau, Jan, 104, 131, 137–38, 142, 144–45, 228, 229
Bouscat, René, 180
Brazzaville, 1, 14, 185; and the Free French, 15
Brazzaville Conference, 193
Brewster, Ralph, 186
bridges: built to replace barges, 227
British Broadcasting Corporation: de Gaulle radio address, 10, 11
Brocard, Captain, 149, 199
Broche, Félix, 65, 66
Broussards, 64, 67, 87, 134
   as an armed civil guard, 53–54
   and the Autonomist Constitutional Reform Party, 37
   behavior of, 110
   and Bergès, 209
   and the New Caledonian coup, 48, 49, 50, 51
   call for break with Vichy, 38
   and the economy, 62, 146
   and the general council election, 208
   and Laigret, 148
   and Montchamp, 136
   number on active military duty, 90, 93
   and the Pacific Battalion, 66
   and petition to remove d'Argenlieu, 99
   and Sautot, 98, 103
Brown, Robert, 206–7
Brumelet, Clement, 80n. 5
Brunot, Richard, 13; mission of 69–73
Bugeaud, Thomas-Robert, 11
Bulletin du Commerce, 131, 151, 166, 200, 216, 217, 218
Bullitt, William, 8
Butcher, Harry, 190

C

Cabanier, Georges, 100, 101, 106, 107, 108, 143, 144
   detained by demonstrators, 105
   and Vergès, 135, 169n. 9
Caffrey, Jefferson, 220, 221
Cairo Conference, 168, 176
Caledonian Committee: and the election, 207–8
Caledonians (*Caldoches*), 3
   and American attacks upon Laigret, 167
   and the American way of life, 212, 215
   exploitation of military, 130
   loyal to own people, 104–5
   prosperity of, 91, 154, 203, 211, 223n. 47
   and service in Europe in First World War, 33
Calhoun, William L., 199, 226
Cameroon: and the Free French, 13, 14, 15, 45
Camp Barnes interdenominational church, 203
Camp Jeanne d'Arc, 213
Camp Joe Louis, 157, 213
Cap des Palmes (ship), 77
Carlton Gardens, 70, 71, 178, 180, 185
Caroline Islands, 202
Casablanca (film), 1, 2, 5nn. 1, 4
Casablanca Conference, 177
Casey, R.G., 40, 66
Cassin, René, 31n. 44, 65
Catroux, Georges, 11, 12, 23, 31n. 44, 32n. 80, 36, 65
cattle: shooting of, 149
Chad: and the Free French, 13, 14, 15
Chamba tribe: dissidents from, 215, 216
Chambrun, René de, 7
Chandler, Albert, 186
Chapman, chaplain, 207

Chardonnet, Lieutenant, 53
Châtellain, Charles, 39
Cherbourg: and d'Argenlieu, 74
Chevigné, Colonel de, 183
Chevreuil (ship), 101, 102, 115n. 68
Chiang Kai-shek: and the Cairo Conference, 168, 176
Chloe (ship), 101
Chouke, Barthélemy, 216
chrome, 3, 62
Churchill, Winston
  assured of Allied victory, 84
  and the Casablanca Conference, 177
  and Dakar, 15–19
  and de Gaulle on Syria and Madagascar, 177
  and demonstration in New Caledonia, 44
  and dispute with de Gaulle over Syria and Lebanon, 75
  and financial agreement with de Gaulle, 68
  and formal recognition of de Gaulle's leadership, 12–13
  and the Free French, 8, 13, 20
  and the French National Committee, 103
  and Tehran and Cairo Conferences, 168, 176
  and threat of German takeover of French fleet, 9
claims for property damage, 132, 147, 148, 150–51, 170n. 32
Clauzel, Bertrand, 11
coal, 37, 40, 42, 205
Coconut Square, 211, 226
coffee, 62, 147, 155
Comité des Français d'Océanie, 71
Commonwealth Ministers, Conference of, 188
Communards, 77, 87
Communist Party of New Caledonia, 35, 147, 206, 208
"compromise": usage of term, 181
Conféderation Générale du Travail, 27
Constituent Assembly, Paris, 228
Consultative Assembly, Algiers, 204
consumer goods, rationing of, 130, 156
Coral Sea, Battle of the, 103, 107, 108, 175
Courcel, Geoffrey Chodron de, 165
Cranborne, Lord, 69
Crémieux-Brilhac, Jean-Louis: *La France Libre*, 229
Creoles, 226
Cross of Lorraine, 18, 109
Crumply, Forrest, 207
Cunningham, Andrew, 17, 18

Cunningham, Harry, 25–26
Curie, Eve, 24
curios: making and selling of, 158
Curtin, John, 188
Curton, Émile de, 65, 71

D

Dakar, 14, 62
  and d'Argenlieu, 74
  failure of attempt to free, 15–19, 22, 55–56
  as Nazi bridgehead into Latin America, 9
  and a suspicion of a United States takeover, 183
  and a trusteeship, 175, 177, 187
Daly, Arnold, 91
Daly, James, 35, 216
Darlan, Jean, 56, 181
"Darlan deal," 181–82
Davio, Etienne, 72, 82n. 51
Day, Henry, 133, 136, 138, 144, 150, 163, 167
D-Day, 189, 190, 212
Decoux, Jean, 76, 85, 191
Dejean, Maurice, 108, 185
Denis, Maurice, 52
  declared a state of siege and set up roadblock, 49, 51
  interim governor to replace Pélicier, 43, 47
  orders for arrest of Gaullist leaders, 51
  and a pro-Vichy attitude, 45, 80n. 20
  supposed plan to kidnap, 47, 48
Dequen, Captain, 161
Deschamps, Noel, 203, 212
Dévillers, Leon, 80n. 5
Dewez, Henry, 206, 209
Dixon, Owen, 187
Djibouti, 12, 184
Doneva: French Protestant Mission, 213
Dong Sy Hua, 215
Doniambo, 37, 40, 206, 207
Dove, Brigadier, 200
Les Droits de l'Homme, 207
Duala, Cameroon, 15, 18
Dubois, Georges
  arrest of, 51, 52, 101, 115n. 51
  and a Broussard militia, 38, 54, 65, 90, 93, 98, 110
  and d'Argenlieu, 93–94, 99
  and Montchamp, 118
  and New Caledonian Coup, 48
  and Patch support, 110
  and Sautot administration, 68, 98

and Vergès, 66
Du Chayla (ship), 74
Dumbea Valley: and hospital wards, 203
Dumont d'Urville (ship), 39, 42, 43, 44, 46, 47, 50, 51, 53, 55, 56, 59nn. 54, 65
Dunkirk: evacuation of, 35
Dunn, James, 220
Dutch East Indies, 206; overrun by Japanese, 96
Dutch Government: and Javanese indentured workers, 206, 209, 210
Duval, Pierre, 160, 161, 200

E

Eboué, Félix, 13, 14, 17, 193
Eden, Anthony, 191
Eisenhower, Dwight D., 181, 189; opposed to AMCOT, 190, 196n. 75
Ellis, Perry, 31n. 58
Emirau Island, 202
Emmons, Carleton, 86
Empire Defense Council, 21, 23, 25, 69, 185, 193, 204
   and Brunot, 72
   formation of, 19–20
   members of, 31n. 44
Evatt, Herbert V., 187, 188
exports, 35, 40, 62

F

Fanning, R.E., 67
farms and cattle ranches: damage to, 149
Fatoux, Captain, 70
Feuer, Lewis, 207
Fifth Fleet, 202
Fighting French. *See* Free French
First Island Command, 131, 132, 146, 198
First World War, 33, 62, 165, 186
Fletcher, Frank J., 124
Florisson, Jean, 71
food, fresh: short supply of, 130, 156
Forest, Louis: and Laigret speech, 164
Fourcade, Frédéric, 111, 123, 131, 133, 134, 135, 137
   rumored as candidate for governor, 144–45, 169n. 13
   and Vergès letters, 229
France
   and an armistice with Germany, 7, 8, 9, 10, 40, 175
   liberation of, 2, 188–93
   restoration of as a great power, 218, 219

France Australe, 216, 132
La France Libre (Crémieux-Brilhac), 229
Fraser, Peter, 102
Freby, Colonel, 153, 159; and Laigret speech, 164
Free French, 111, 117n. 105
   and concern over French sovereignty, 4, 107–13
   to be called Fighting French, 117n. 105, 184
   Free, or Fighting French, 10, 20–21, 94, 95, 184
   and a policy of anti-Americanism, 177, 178–85
Freetown, 18
French Committee of National Liberation (FCNL)
   antagonistic to American military, 149, 177
   basic policy of, 179
   and the Broussards, 148
   creation of, 144
   and de Gaulle as uncontested leader, 184
   and funds from budget surplus of Caledonians, 165
   headquarters moved to Algiers, 143
   and Laigret, 162, 163, 165, 166, 167, 177
   limited recognition of, 189
   recalls made by, 159, 160
   response to Russell committee report, 187
French Congo: and the Free French, 14, 45
French Equatorial Africa: and the Free French, 13, 45
French Foreign Legion, 18, 160
French Guyana: and the Free French, 45
French Immigration Service, 206
French National Committee
   and all policies through London, 29, 86
   and American cooperation, 79, 89
   and Caledonian involvement, 143
   and censorship of news from New Caledonia, 109
   and Churchill, 103
   and d'Argenlieu 74, 86, 89, 103
   formation of in London, 174
   and Patch, 102
   and Roosevelt and Lend-lease, 28
French native labor tax, 215
French Oceania: and pro-de Gaulle feelings, 45
French Polynesia: and the Free French, 15
French settlers: and employment, 156
French West Africa: and pro-de Gaulle feelings, 45
"Friends of the Soviet Union," 205–6
Furet, François, 19

Index

G

Gabon: and the Free French, 14, 74
Garreau-Dombasle, Maurice, 22, 23
Gaulle, Charles de
  advises caution in dealing with Americans, 23
  and American plot to take over New Caledonia, 178–85
  and AMGOT, 189, 190
  and Boegner, 178
  and the Caribbean, 21, 22
  and centralized control, 29, 67, 68, 69, 86
  and Churchill, 68, 75, 177
  and colonial reform, 192–93
  and "compromise," 181
  and Dakar, 15–19
  and d'Argenlieu, 72–73, 79, 89, 90
  and declaration of war upon Japan, 84
  and defense of New Caledonia against Vichy, 66
  and Free-French authority in the South Pacific, 22, 24, 26, 76
  and French Committee of National Liberation (FCNL), 144, 184
  and a French Empire, 25, 68, 84, 179, 230
  and a French National Committee, 12, 79
  as head of Provisional Government in France, 190, 191
  and Laigret, 165
  and Menzies, 68
  as minister in Reynaud's cabinet, 8, 10
  and Monnet, 182
  and a new administrative council, 64
  and ordinance giving high commissioner powers, 78
  and a policy of confrontation, 180–81
  and "pseudo-government of Vichy," 19–20
  radio address of 18 June 1940, 10, 11
  and rallying of French territories in Africa, 13, 18, 19
  and resistance to the armistice, 9–10, 11, 20
  and Roosevelt, 2, 4, 18, 164, 178
  and Soviet domination, 220
  and Stark, 109, 180
  and Truman 218, 221
  and United Nations conference, 219
  visit to Morocco, 182–83
  visit to Washington and New York, 187
Gauss, C.E., 15
Gaveau, Charles, 33
Gerbault, Alain, 71
Germany: defeat of France and armistice, 8, 9, 10, 40, 175

Ghormley, Robert L., 106, 118, 119; contrasted with Halsey, 119–20; Gilbert Islands, 201, 202
Giraud, Henri, 144, 180, 181, 182, 184, 191
Goa tribe: dissidents from, 215
"God Save the King": singing of, 36, 44
Gould, G.A., 67
Goyetta tribe: dissidents from, 215, 216
"graveyard for governors," 137
Great Depression, 175
Greek freighter: torpedoed and asking for help, 101–2
Green Islands, 202
Greenslade, John, 22
Grew, Joseph, 219
Guadalcanal, 3, 89, 111, 119, 123–25, 129, 163
Guadeloupe: and the Free French, 21, 22

H

Halifax, Lord, 25, 175
Halsey, William S. ("Bull")
  a boost to American morale, 120
  condemnation of French rule, 168, 177
  contrasted with Ghormley, 119–20
  and demands for buildings and space, 118–19, 121–22, 125–26
  Free French as uncooperative, 189, 230
  and Laigret, 145–46, 167–68
  and Montchamp, 120–23
  not an autonomist, 137
  report to Nimitz on tonnage unloaded, 129
  residence of, 120, 121
  and Solomon Islands campaign, 201–3
  street renamed to honor, 227
  and survey of buildings constructed, 127–29
  and Tallec, 200
Hamlet, 180
Hart, Thomas A. 185, 186
Hauteclocque, Philippe de. *See* Leclerc, pseud. for de Hauteclocque, Philippe
Havana Declaration, 21
Haye, Henry, 31n. 58
Henderson Field, 119, 124, 125
Henriot, August, 80n. 5
Hettier de Boislambert, Claude, 14, 15
Hitler, Adolph, 7
  and meeting with Pétain at Montoire, 19, 22
  surrender of [sic], 230
Hopkins, Harry, 220
Hoppenot, Henri, 187
Hôtel de France, 161
Hôtel du Pacifique, 50

Houaïlou, 48, 213
Houssard, Maurice, 47
Houssin, Major, 159, 160, 161
Hull, Cordell, 111, 112, 175, 168, 191
Husson, Louis, 14, 15

I

Ile Nou, 68, 129
Indochina, 5, 12, 36
 French restoration in, 219
 and Japan, 19, 23, 26, 28, 40, 66, 76, 219, 220
 and a trusteeship, 175
 and Vichy government, 191
International Labor Office, Geneva, 27
Iwo Jima, 207

J

Janisel, Maurice, 80n. 5
Japan
 assets in United States frozen, 76
 and Indochina, 19, 23, 26, 28, 36, 40, 66–67, 76, 219, 220
 and New Caledonia mineral resources, 84, 86
 New Caledonia within sphere of influence, 23, 66, 76
 and offensive against Port Moresby, 95
 surrender of, 221
Japanese Mandated Islands: and United States control, 185
Javanese, 132, 206, 209, 210, 226
Johnson, Nelson T., 188
Johnston, W.A., 53–54, 200, 218
Journal Officiel, 78

K

Kanak (Melanesians), 3
 and benefits of employment, 130, 132, 156–57, 158, 205
 curfew imposed on troops, 152
 dissidents among, 215–16
 early revolts of, 88
 effect of American presence on, 91, 213, 215, 224n. 56, 227
 and independence, 163, 223n. 47
 number in population of New Caledonia, 87, 113n. 12
 number on active military duty, 90
 and the Pacific Battalion, 65
 pleased with an American takeover, 216–17
 and political participation, 201
 and prostitution, 153
 and service in Europe in First World War, 33
 and V-J day, 226
King, Ernest, 201, 202
Kittredge, Tracy B., 129, 183
Knight, Lonnie, 213, 214
Knox, Frank, 122, 134
Kollen, Marcel, 39
Kuroki, Takitaro, 41
Kurtovitch, Ismet, 227

L

La Foa, 49, 105, 107, 116n. 79, 136
Lagos, Nigeria: and the Free French, 14, 15
Laigret, Christian, 198
 anti-Americanism of, 138, 150, 158–65, 177, 184, 187
 and Boucher, 160
 and Caledonian interests, 150–51
 and call for reinforcement of French police, 147
 and claims for damages, 147
 and complaints against the Americans, 148–58, 163
 and d'Argenlieu policy, 145
 enthusiastically received, 145–46
 and French authority and prestige, 146, 147
 and an increase in taxes, 147
 as interim governor, 138, 145
 and meeting with Nimitz, 145
 and more French involvement in Pacific campaign, 147
 and a nationalization of Le Nickel, 147–48
 opposition to, 146
 and Pleven, 145
 and policy of provocation, 181
 praise for, 164, 172n. 97
 press conference of, 166, 167, 168
 and proposed benefits to the Broussards, 148
 and proposed elections, 204
 recall of, 163
 replaced by Tallec, 166
 request for more troops and a naval squadron, 147
 speech to administrative council, 163, 164, 167
 tour of interior with Bergès, 148
 and Vergès, 147, 169n. 27, 229
Larminat, Edgar de, 14, 17, 26, 31n. 44
Latham, John, 66

laundry services, 130, 148, 154, 205
Laval, 182
Laveissière, First Officer, 51, 56
Lavoix, M., 134
Lawrey, John, 48, 68, 115n. 56
Leahy, William, 9, 173
Leclerc, pseudonym for de Hauteclocque, Philippe 14, 15, 17, 18, 31n. 44, 191
Lee, Lieutenant, 215–16
Legentilhomme, Paul, 12
Léger, Alexis, 178
Legras, Fernand, 166, 218
Lémery, Henry, 37
Lend-lease
  and aid to the Free French, 25, 26, 27, 28, 121
  New Caledonia as possible compensation for, 165, 186, 216, 228
Le Nickel (Société Le Nickel, SLN), 80n. 5
  and absenteeism, 158
  and the American military, 158, 205
  and dependence on Australian coal, 37, 42
  and indentured labor, 208–9, 210
  as a major employer, 35, 64, 144
  and military service of Javanese workers, 206
  and nationalization, 147–48, 205, 208
  and strike of Tonkinese miners, 207, 210
Léopoldville: and the Free French, 15, 21
Ley, G.L., 35
Life, 164
Lincoln, Rush, 131–32, 144–46, 148, 151–52, 198
liquor trade, illicit, 145, 155, 160, 207
Lloyd, Lord, 14
Lodge, Henry Cabot, 186
Louis de la Trinité, Father. *See* Thierry d'Argenlieu, Georges
Loyalty Island of Maré, 65
Luke, Harry, 46, 78
  and Sautot, 75, 98
  and support of the Free French, 42, 45, 59nn. 56, 65
  visit to Nouméa, 43–44
Lyautey, Louis-Hubert-Gonzalve, 11

M

MacArthur, Douglas, 129, 201, 202, 203
MacVitty, Karl de Giers, 87
  and Brunot, 70
  and complaint to the State Department, 86
  as consul to New Caledonia, 24, 29, 31n. 58
  declined to send message to de Gaulle, 99
  and d'Argenlieu, 76, 89, 96, 97, 112
  and Kanak in the Pacific Battalion, 65
  and Sautot, 75
Madagascar, 106, 108, 116n. 83, 177, 179, 193
"maison de tolérance": for African-American servicemen, 152–53
Mangin, Charles, 54
Mariannas Islands, 201, 202
marines: and Guadalcanal, 3, 89, 111, 124–25, 163
Marquesas Islands, 186
"Marseillaise": singing of, 36, 44, 52, 53 fig.
Marshall, George, 97, 103, 219
Marshall Islands, 202
Martinique, 21–22, 47, 108
Mas, Lieutenant, 153
Massigli, René, 129, 180, 185
Massoubre, Ernest, 93–94, 116n. 74
Mayet, Just, 80n. 5
McCloy, John J., 25, 183, 190, 219
McEwen, John, 41
Mead, James, 186
Mekong River: and Thai and Vichy conflict, 23
Melanesians. *See* Kanak (Melanesians)
Menthon, François de, 159, 162
Menzies, Robert, 35, 36, 41, 45, 66, 68
Mers-el-Kebir, 9, 62
mésentente, 107–13, 112, 122, 158–65, 229, 230; definition of, 4–5
Michel, Captain, 52, 54
Midway, 202
military police: increase in, 153
Millaud, Henri, 163
minerals: export of, 35, 40, 62
Mittelhauser, Eugène, 11, 14, 36
Monnet, Jean, 182
Montaudoin, Lieutenant de, 159, 199
Montchamp, Auguste, 163, 164
  arrival in Nouméa, 111, 118
  and Berle, 112, 113
  and buildings and space, 118–19, 121–22, 125, 139n. 6
  and d'Argenlieu, 133, 134
  departure from New Caledonia, 137, 145
  and election of a new council, 135–36, 137, 142–43
  and Halsey, 120–23, 125–26
  and Lavoix, 134
  and preservation of French "way of life," 122
  and procedure for presenting claims, 150–51
  and proposed elections, 204

to replace Sautot, 106
and undermining of Fighting-French authority, 131
and Vergès, 135, 229
Montoire, 19, 22
Morlet, Georges, 80n. 5
Morocco
  Allied landings on 8 November 1942, 11
  continued resistance, 36
  and hostile fire from French troops, 2
  Sultan of, 177
"Mosquito Network" radio station, 212, 221
Moulédous, Émile, 36, 37, 43, 48, 80n. 5, 98, 99, 115n. 60, 144
Murphy, Robert, 183
Muselier, Émile, 31n. 44

N

Naisseline, Chief, 65
New Britain: Australian bases in, 188
New Caledonia
  air bases in, 26, 28, 68, 84, 87
  and the Americal Division, 89
  American cemetery, 203
  and American construction, 127–29, 203, 211
  and American forces, 5–6n. 7, 89–90, 92 fig.
  and an American takeover, 78, 216, 217
  and Australia, 37, 38, 39, 41
  and autonomists, 200–1, 204–10
  call to become "New California," 223n. 47
  and cost of the d'Argenlieu mission, 78
  coup, 48–52
  defenses, 23, 34, 56, 65, 66, 67, 85, 88, 98–99
  and delay in receipt of news, 33
  deportation of Pétain supporters, 62
  economy of, 62, 130, 146, 154, 155, 156
  facilities no longer needed as a base, 210–11
  and formation of a de Gaulle committee, 47
  as a former penal colony, 77, 87
  and the Free French, 3, 15, 18, 23, 29, 35, 36, 37, 38, 39, 41–42
  and Free French forces, 65, 90. 93
  and French identity, 217, 227
  general council elections, 207–8
  German ship appears offshore, 42
  governors of, 144–45, 200
  housing, buildings and space problems, 120
  important as line of supply in event of war with Japan, 67
  imports and exports with France or French Empire, 40
  and Japanese interests in mineral resources, 39, 41, 42, 84
  and Japanese threat, 19, 23, 39, 40, 61, 66, 76, 85, 105
  as "Le Caillou," "The Rock," 3
  and Lend-lease, 165, 186, 216, 228
  location and description of, 3, 93, 78–79
  map of, 34
  medical facilities in, 3, 133, 148, 203, 227
  and mineral exports, 39, 40, 41, 62
  most important of Free-French holdings in Pacific, 73
  and old system of central authority, 78
  "Pentagon" headquarters building, 203, 211, 227, 228
  and perpetual rights to bases and facilities, 186–87
  and the "phony war," 35
  as a place of rest and recreation, 203
  political situation on, 67
  population of, 3, 87, 88, 113n. 12
  and pro-Vichy partisans, 53–57, 62
  rationing, 130, 156
  restrictions of foreigners, 33–34, 57n. 3
  and relations with the Commonwealth, 37
  riot of 1942, 98–106, 175, 208
  and self-government, 63
  services and infrastructure improvement, 130, 133, 148, 227
  and Solomons Islands campaign, 125, 129
  strategic location of, 29, 78, 87, 93
  as a supply base and hospital center, 203, 210–15
  and surtax on exports, 33
  and taxes, 34, 35
  and United States military rights, 192
  See also Nouméa
New Caledonia-Loyalty Islands: and United States control, 186
New Guinea. See Papua New Guinea
New Hebrides, 28, 40, 41, 44, 45, 46, 47, 188
Newsweek: and attacks upon Laigret and New Caledonia, 167
Newton, John H., 202–3
New York Times: news ban broken by articles in, 109
New Zealand, 41, 102, 187–88
New Zealand Third Division, 129, 170n. 49
nickel, 3, 35, 40, 41, 42, 62, 87
Nimitz, Chester, 119, 121, 129, 145, 199, 201, 202, 210, 226

Index

Noguès, Charles-Auguste, 11
Norden (ship), 46, 50, 51, 80n. 5
Nouméa
  as American headquarters, 3, 5–6n. 7
  Australian base in, 188
  bars and shops opened in, 130, 156, 160, 205
  and Bastille Day celebration, 37
  Bernheim Library, 210
  buildings and facilities constructed in, 127–29, 139n. 6
  and a general strike, 103, 107
  harbor facilities, 133
  improvements introduced in, 227
  main assembly point for Solomons campaign, 129
  map of, 49
  and mass demonstration after abduction of Sautot, 102–8
  "Motor Pool" district, 203, 227
  planned demonstration in, 48–49
  as a possible military district, 126
  and priority of military delivery over civilian, 130
  Quonset huts, 129, 227
  "Receiving" district, 203, 227
  and a trusteeship, 175, 177, 187
  See also New Caledonia

O

Oceania: and the Free French, 28
Office of Strategic Services (OSS), 87
Oran, Algeria, 9
Orcan family: and laundry services, 154
Orion (ship), 42
Orselli, Georges, 85, 88
Overseas France: archives of, 170n. 32
Owens, Ray, 198

P

Pacific Battalion, 65, 67, 100, 117n. 105, 153, 203, 227
Pacific War Council, 175, 179, 187, 188
Païta, 49
Païta, Gabriel, 91, 92 fig., 103
Paladini, Florindo, 35, 49, 50, 147, 208
Panofsky, Erwin, 1
Papeete, 47
Papua New Guinea, 95, 129, 188, 201, 202
Parant, André, 14
Paris: liberation of, 2, 191

Patch, Alexander M., 79, 90 fig., 95, 120, 137
  and the Americal Division, 125
  and command of American defense group, 88, 89, 90, 91
  and control over all military supply and distribution, 93
  and d'Argenlieu, 93, 96–97, 112, 116n. 79, 106–7, 150–51, 175
  and a declaration of martial law, 105–6, 107
  and Dubois, 101, 110
  Gaullist condemnation of, 116n. 89
  and a neutral stand, 100 fig., 103, 104
  refused to send telegram to de Gaulle, 98–99
  and report on New Caledonia, 87
  and request for aid to Greek freighter, 101–2
  street renamed to honor, 227
Patton, George, 2
Peake, Charles, 108
Pearl Harbor, 1; Japanese attack on, 76, 84, 85
Pélicier, Georges, 33
  assassination attempt upon, 39
  and Australia, 36
  demonstrated against by Caledonians, 37
  and publication of Pétain's decrees, 37, 38, 41
  replaced by Maurice Denis, 43, 47
  and Vichy order on mineral production, 42
"Perfidious Albion," 46, 230
Perrault, Lieutenant, 52
Pétain, Philippe, 9, 21, 112
  defeatist policy of, 182
  and meeting with Hitler at Montoire, 19, 22
  and Roosevelt, 173–74
  and signing of the armistice, 8, 10, 36
Peyrouton, Marcel, 11
Philip, André, 183, and meeting with Roosevelt, 181–82, 184
Philippine Islands, 201, 202
"phony war," 35, 40
Pierre Loti (ship), 54, 55, 62
Pineau, Christian, 183
Pink House, 152–53
Pinkney, David: and detailed report on New Caledonia, 87
Plaine des Gaiacs airbase, 68, 86, 154
Pleven, René, 135, 136, 137, 143, 145, 147
  and a Free-French delegation in Washington, 27
  and Indochina, 193
  interview with Sumner Welles, 28
  and Laigret, 151, 159, 162, 164, 165, 200
  and Lend-lease aid, 25, 26

247

Index

missions to the United States, 14, 24–26, 174
and New Caledonian riot, 108
and Tallec, 199
Pognon, Raymond, 53 fig.
  acting head of Gaullist committee, 47, 48, 51, 52
  and d'Argenlieu, 99–100, 115n. 60
  and letter of support to de Gaulle, 39
  and planned coup, 47, 48
  and Sautot, 44, 98
Pointe Noire airfield, 185
Poland: defeat of, 33, 34
Polynesia: American interest in air bases in, 84
Ponérihouen, 215, 216
"Poppy Force," 79, 87, 89, 91
Port Moresby, New Guinea: and a Japanese offensive, 95
Port Vila, New Hebrides, 44, 47
Post Exchange (PX), 130, 154, 212
Potomac (ship), 7
Prinet, André
  arrested at the roadblock, 51, 52
  and d'Argenlieu mission, 97
  and issuance of manifesto and a call to gather, 48
  and petition for local autonomy, 36–37
  and resolution to recall Pélicier, 42–43
  and Sautot, 64, 103
  and Vergès, 80n. 7
prostitution, 146, 152–53
Puaux, Gabriel, 11

Q

Quièvrecourt, Toussaint de, 59n. 54
  and the coup, 50, 51, 53, 55–56
  and the *Dumont d'Urville*, 39, 42–47, 51
  loyal to Vichy and Pétain, 39, 42, 43, 46, 53
Quisling, Vidkun, 182

R

Rabaul, 96, 129, 201, 202
Rabot, Edouard, 48
race relations, 132
radio station: and Nouméa demonstrators, 104
Rapadzi, Alfred, 42, 80n. 5, 98, 209
Rapadzi, Nicholas, 64, 80n. 5
Reber, Samuel, 174
Red Cross: authorized to aid the Free French, 26
Red Cross service club, 154
Renard, Albert, 102

Réunion, 193
Reynaud, Paul, 7–8
Ricard, M., 146
Richelieu (ship), 17
riot of 1942, 98–106, 175, 208
roadblocks, 49, 50, 51, 52, 103
roads, 133, 148, 227
Robert, Georges, 22, 47, 86
Rolly, Henry, 80n. 5
Rommel, Rommel, 117n. 105
Roosevelt, Eleanor, 207; incognito visit to New Caledonia, 146
Roosevelt, Franklin Delano
  address to University of Virginia graduates, 7
  and America's rearmament, 7
  anticolonialism of, 175–77, 179
  and Cairo Conference, 168, 176–77
  and Casablanca Conference, 177
  comments aired on Vichy radio, 188
  and Dakar, 9, 15–19
  and Darlan agreement and Eisenhower, 181–82
  and de Gaulle, 2, 4, 18, 164, 178
  and direct Lend-lease aid to Free France, 28
  economic embargo on oil to Japan, 76
  and fear of a Soviet domination, 218
  and Gaullists as uncooperative and unreliable partners, 230
  and increased aid to Allies, 7–8
  lack of consultation by, 187, 188
  and meeting with André Philip, 181–82, 184
  military occupation of France opposed, 189–90
  and Pacific War Council, 168, 179
  and a peacetime draft, 84
  and postwar security needs, 173, 185–89, 192, 230
  refuses American intervention in France, 8
  and status of French Empire and fleet, 8, 9
  and Tehran Conference, 168, 176–77
  and trusteeships, 168, 176, 177, 219, 220
  and Vichy, 4
  and the "Vichy gamble," 9
  view of French defeat and armistice, 7, 9
Rose, William I., 200
Rossi, Mario, 196n. 75
Royal Australian Navy, 107
Russell, Richard B., 165; fact-finding mission, 186–87, 196n. 61
Russell Islands, 129
Rusterholtz, Hubert, 71

248

S

Saigon, 45, 47, 55, 56, 59n. 54
St. Pierre and Miquelon, 175, 179, 180, 181
Salt River, 49
Sautot, Henri, 50, 51, 53 fig., 56, 104 fig.
    abduction of, 100–101, 106
    and administrative council, 63–65, 135–36, 204, 207
    arrival of, 48, 52
    awarded the Cross of Liberation, 72
    Ballard comment on replacement of, 81n. 41
    and Brunot, 69–73
    compared with D'Argenlieu, 74–75
    and d'Argenlieu, 93–94, 95
    Empire Defense Council member, 31n. 44, 185
    Free-French administration stable, 68, 77
    given extensive powers by de Gaulle, 62–63
    and heads of administrative services, 53
    made Companion of the Liberation, 72
    and Montchamp in New York, 112
    and New Hebrides rally, 38, 44
    to New Zealand and New York, 102
    and the Pacific Battalion, 66
    and Pélicier, 44–47
    recalled by orders of de Gaulle, 97, 98, 106
    and security and welfare, 61
    and support of the American forces, 79
    as too cooperative with Americans, 95
    and Vergès, 55, 63, 66, 229
Savo Island, Battle of, 119, 124
schools and housing for teachers, 148
Second World War, 2; entry of United States into, 76
Sellier, Colonel, 153
servicemen
    assault and rape cases, 151–52
    conduct of, 131, 161–62
    with New Caledonian wives, 228
    New Zealand Third Division, 170n. 49
    number in New Caledonia, 93
    recreation centers and entertainment for, 154, 211–12
    and V-J day, 226
servicemen, African-American
    assault and rape cases, 151–52
    and houses of prostitution, 152–53
    treatment of, 213
    and V-J day, 226
75th Bomb Squadron, 154
Shafroth, Admiral, 149
Sherman, Colonel, 160
shore patrols: increase in, 153
Short, Walter C., 86
Showers, Henry A., 50, 51, 54, 55, 56, 57, 61, 62
    and plans for coup, 44–47
Sicé, Adolphe, 15, 31n. 44, 185
Sieyès, Jacques de, 27, 32n. 80
Singapore
    Japanese threat to, 66
    proposed Free-French military expedition to, 23
Smith, Walter Bedell, 184
Social Progress Group, 208, 209
Société Le Nickel. *See* Le Nickel
Society Islands: and United States control, 186
Solier, Elie, 99, 115n. 60
Solomon Islands
    Australian base in, 188
    American casualties in, 163
    campaign of, 119, 123, 125, 129, 201, 202, 210
    Japanese threat to, 96
    map of, 124
Soustelle, Jacques, 183
Soviet Union, 84, 192, 220, 230
Spruance, Raymond, 202
Stalin, Josef, 168, 176–77
Stark, Harold R., 105, 110, 119, 129, 180
    and interview with de Gaulle, 109
    letter to de Gaulle, 126, 127
Stead, Colonel, 153
Stehlin, Charles, 146, 159
Sterling, Alfred, 59n. 56
Stettinius, Edward, 219
Stimson, Henry, 190
Strang, William, 108
Strasbourg (ship), 16
Strasbourg: liberation of, 191
streets: renamed to honor American commanders, 227
street signs, 94
surplus equipment dumped in harbor, 228
Syria, 36, 45, 177, 179, 180

T

Tahiti, 47
    and Comité des Français d'Océanie, 71
    and the Free French, 15, 45, 65
    Japanese threat to, 23
Tallec, Jacques
    and abolition of indentured labor, 205

and American medal of freedom, 231
and *mésentente*, 230
and relations with American military leadership, 199–200
as replacement for Laigret, 163, 166, 193, 198–204
and scheduled elections, 207
skill in dealing with Americans, 231
and Vergès, 217–18, 228–29
Tallec, Yves, 199
Tarawa, 201
Task Force 89
Tassafaronga Island, 125
Taussig, Charles, 192, 218
taxi services, 148, 205
Tehran Conference, 168, 176–77
Templeton, John, 101, 102, 134
Thailand, 23, 66–67
Thierry d'Argenlieu, Georges, 24, 83n. 80, 90 fig., 163
  and abduction of Bergès, 204–5
  and abduction of Sautot and others, 100–101, 106
  and Admiral Stark, 127
  and anti-American attitude, 159, 175, 178, 179, 184, 198, 229
  and arrival of the Americans, 84
  bad effect on morale in the island, 77, 78, 97
  and Bergés, 143, 144, 169n. 6
  and the Broussard demonstrators, 105
  claimed held hostage, 116n. 79
  and conciliation with Caledonians, 143
  denies request to help Greek freighter, 101–2
  devotion to the Free-French cause, 73, 74, 88
  Empire Defense Council member, 31n. 44
  and the Dakar episode, 16–17, 74
  as Father Louis de la Trinité, 74
  and Laigret speech, 164
  mission of, 73–79
  and Montchamp, 118, 134, 140n. 44
  and relations with Patch, 91, 93, 103, 106–7, 150–51
  in residence in Tahiti, 111
  and roadblocks to stop Broussards, 103
  rumor of return of, 138, 142, 169n. 6
  and Sautot, 72, 74–75, 95, 96, 100–101, 106
  told de Gaulle he would leave, 108, 109, 115n. 56
  and American disregard of authority, 86, 93–94, 103
  and Vergès, 135
Third Fleet, 202

Third Republic, 181, 182, 200, 204
Time: and attacks upon Laigret and New Caledonia, 167
Timor: Australian base in, 188
Tixier, Adrien, 27, 28, 89, 111, 178, 179, 181, 182
Tonkinese, 132, 206, 207, 209, 226
Tontouta airbase, 68, 86, 215
Trade Winds bar and restaurant, 154
traffic circulation, 94
Trubert, Eduard, 80n. 5, 99, 100
Truman, Harry, 218, 220, 221
trusteeships, 168, 175, 176, 177, 187, 219, 220
Tuamato Archipelago, 186
Tulagi, 123–24
Tunica y Casas, Mme, 164, 205, 207, 208, 210, 217
Tunisia, 36

U

Ubangi: and the Free French, 14, 15
Union List: and the election, 208
United Nations conference, San Francisco, 218, 219
United States
  attitude towards de Gaulle altered by liberation, 188–89
  complaints against, 148–58
  and de Gaulle as head of provisional government, 191, 192
  entry into Second World War, 76
  equipment and facilities left in New Caledonia, 228
  and Free French, 25, 27, 110, 121, 179
  and French Empire, 18, 107–13, 174
  and French law on French territory, 158
  Gaullist representation in, 24–25
  and imperialism, 103, 109
  industrial might on side of Allies, 84
  and material resources sent to New Caledonia, 91
  materialism of, 212–13
  and Lend-lease, 26, 28, 121, 165, 186, 216, 228
  naval bases, and possible perpetual lease, 186–87, 192
  and negotiations with Vichy, 21
  and New Caledonia, 29, 40, 86, 121, 131, 165–68, 217
  and recognition of Free-French authorities, 88–89

size of American Army, 84, 86
supply routes to South Pacific, 85 fig.
and Vichy, 21, 26, 28, 112, 179
United States Navy: strategy of, 201–2
Upper Volta, 14

V

Val d'Aosta, Italy, 220
vegetable farming, 155, 156
Vergès, Jean, 228
Vergès, Michel, 47, 48, 98, 144, 145
   and anti-American feeling, 79, 131, 217–18
   and Autonomist Constitutional Reform Party, 37
   and autonomy, 147
   and d'Argenlieu, 115n. 49
   distrusted by the Broussards, 38
   estate of, 50, 203
   exposé of by Tallec, 228–29
   and Laigret speech, 164
   and letter-writing campaign, 134–35, 229
   and Montchamp, 135
   and the new administrative council, 64
   and New Caledonian coup, 48–52
   and New Caledonia's rally, 47, 53 fig., 97–98
   and Pacific Battalion, 66
   and Prinet, 80n. 7
   and a purge of Pétainists, 54
   and recall of Pélicier, 42–43
   and roadblocks, 103
   and Sautot, 55, 63, 66, 98, 207
Vergès-Prinet-Moulédous petitions, 36, 37, 48
Vichy Government
   and agreement with Japan over Indochina, 76
   and Dakar, 16, 19
   and Great Britain and the Commonwealth, 9, 37, 42
   and Japanese support to recover New Caledonia and Tahiti, 85
   and protest of U.S. recognition of Free-French, 174
   and publication of Marshal Pétain's decrees, 37, 38, 41
   and Thailand, 23
   and the Havana Declaration, 21
   assured Pélicier help was on the way, 39
   See also Pétain, Philippe
Vietnamese Revolution, 207
Vietnamese union, at Le Nickel, 206
Viti (ship), 43
V-J day: impromptu celebrations on, 226
Voh mine: and strike of Tonkinese miners, 207
Voh region, and United States annexation, 216
Vois, Paul, 80n. 5

W

Waiatapu (ship), 102
Wallis and Futuna, 102
Walpole Island, 102, 104, 105, 107, 115n. 51
"waltz of the governors," 63, 200
Wehrmacht Involvement, 7
Welles, Sumner, 25, 26, 27, 40, 174, 178, 191, 192, 196n. 77
   and interview with Pleven, 28
Weygand, Maxime, 8, 10, 11, 26
Willy, Melanesian from the New Hebrides, 215
Wilson, Woodrow, 181

Y

Yalta Conference, 192
Yaounde: and the Free French, 15
Yaté dam: construction of, 209

www.ingramcontent.com/pod-product-compliance
Lightning Source LLC
Chambersburg PA
CBHW071227080526
44587CB00013BA/1523